Introducing the History of the English Language

This essential new text provides a comprehensive, modern account of how the English language originated, developed, changed, and continues to morph into new forms in contemporary society. *Introducing the History of the English Language* first offers a rigorous, approachable introduction to the building blocks of language itself and then traces English language usage's messy development in society, beginning with its origins in the Indo-European language family and continuing chronologically through the Old, Middle, Modern, and present-day forms.

Seth Lerer deftly tells this story not as a tale of standards and authority but of differences and diversity. He draws on public and private literary sources from different regions and those in different social classes, highlighting sources from women and people of color – and introduces readers to the effects of technology on English, and the politics of dialect and racial, gender, regional, and class identity across these periods. Further, this text extensively addresses the rich diversity of English varieties, with innovative, focused chapters dedicated to American English, African American English, global English, and virtual English.

Requiring no prior knowledge of language history or linguistics, offering an array of supplemental activities as online support material, and taking a socially motivated approach to pedagogy that seeks to generate productive reflection and discussion about language difference and politics, this book enables and encourages the twenty-first-century student in the United States to see their own language use as deeply implicated in power dynamics and social relationships.

Seth Lerer is Distinguished Professor of Literature Emeritus at the University of California at San Diego, where he has also served as Dean of Arts and Humanities. His publications include *Chaucer and His Readers* (1993), *Error and the Academic Self* (2002), *Inventing English* (revised edition, 2015), *Children's Literature: A Reader's History from Aesop to Harry Potter* (2008), and *Shakespeare's Lyric Stage* (2018). He has published creative non-fiction in *The American Scholar*, *The Yale Review*, the *Los Angeles Review of Books*, and in his memoir, *Prospero's Son* (2013).

Introducing the History of the English Language

Seth Lerer

Routledge
Taylor & Francis Group

NEW YORK AND LONDON

Designed cover image: © Getty Images | cristianl

First published 2024
by Routledge
605 Third Avenue, New York, NY 10158

and by Routledge
4 Park Square, Milton Park, Abingdon, Oxon, OX14 4RN

Routledge is an imprint of the Taylor & Francis Group, an informa business

© 2024 Seth Lerer

The right of Seth Lerer to be identified as author of this work has been asserted in accordance with sections 77 and 78 of the Copyright, Designs and Patents Act 1988.

Library of Congress Cataloging-in-Publication Data
Names: Lerer, Seth, 1955– author.
Title: Introducing the history of the English language / Seth Lerer.
Description: New York, NY : Routledge, 2024. | Includes bibliographical references and index.
Identifiers: LCCN 2023035948 (print) | LCCN 2023035949 (ebook) | ISBN 9781032129716 (hardback) | ISBN 9781032129693 (paperback) | ISBN 9781003227083 (ebook)
Subjects: LCSH: English language—History.
Classification: LCC PE1075 .l85 2024 (print) | LCC PE1075 (ebook) | DDC 420.9—dc23/eng/20231106
LC record available at https://lccn.loc.gov/2023035948
LC ebook record available at https://lccn.loc.gov/2023035949

ISBN: 978-1-032-12971-6 (hbk)
ISBN: 978-1-032-12969-3 (pbk)
ISBN: 978-1-003-22708-3 (ebk)

DOI: 10.4324/9781003227083

Typeset in Times New Roman
by codeMantra

Access the Support Material: www.routledge.com/9781032129693

Contents

Figures

Tables

Preface

To the Student and the Teacher

"You know more than you think you do." Dr. Benjamin Spock's famous advice (in his best-selling book, *Baby and Child-Care*) to new parents is fitting for students and teachers opening this book. Whatever your age or background, you have experienced the English language in its variety and through some changes. Students may write and speak in the classroom differently from how they talk with friends and family. Teachers may have noticed how digital technologies have affected English composition, popular speech, and forms of written communication. The language of English has existed in various forms ever since a group of speakers in the British Isles thought of themselves as "English." The language has been changing over time, sometimes quickly, sometimes slowly. England's first printer, William Caxton, noticed in 1490 that the language differed from the one he spoke as a child decades before. He remarked on how the speech of an educated Londoner was almost incomprehensible to a farm wife in Kent. You may have similar stories to tell. You know more than you think you do.

This textbook is a history of the English language for students and teachers committed to exploring the richness and variety of speech and writing over time and across space. It presents a chronological narrative of development, from the origins of the Germanic languages in the Indo-European family, through the emergence of Old English, the changes in Middle English, the forms of Modern English, and the kaleidoscope of Englishes throughout the world. This textbook tells a story, but it also provokes response. Each chapter is designed to help students remember and integrate knowledge of historical aspects of English change and variety: sound changes over time, differences in regional dialects, patterns of syntax and grammar, and shifts in the meaning and usage of words. The sources for this information before the twentieth century are written documents. We will look at spelling as evidence for pronunciation and grammar. We will also see how, very often, that evidence appears in works of imaginative literature. Can poetry serve as a database for everyday speech? Does fictional prose tell us something about linguistic practice and social attitudes? Part of the task of this book, then, is not just to look at evidence but to explore creativity: to understand that language change goes hand in hand with the inventiveness of poets, dramatists, novelists, historians, and philosophers; to see the history of English as a history of what men and women do with and to the language.

While this book was written by a teacher of literature with four decades of teaching, it does not neglect the linguistic material required to study the history of English. It begins by examining the nature of sound production: how we describe vowels and consonants by their manner of articulation and their place in the human mouth. It introduces students to the concept of the phoneme (the smallest meaningful unit of sound in a language) and the idea that meaning in a language system is relational, rather than essential. It spends some time with the International Phonetic Alphabet and the challenges of transcribing speech and representing historical forms of pronunciation. It invites you to consider how changes in sound can be classified, but also how recent sound shifts can be described and perhaps explained. Students and teachers will find familiar things here: Grimm's and Verner's Laws, regional dialect variety, and the Great Vowel Shift. You will find treatment of sound changes in American English, as well as an introduction to the use of such resources as the *Linguistic Atlas of North America* and the *Dictionary of American Regional English*.

This book presupposes a basic knowledge of English grammar. It will build on that knowledge to illustrate grammatical changes in the systems of English morphology and syntax: that is, how individual words are used to signal relationships in a sentence and, in turn, how the arrangement of words in a sentence make up meaningful utterances. We will review the nature of grammatical categories in language (the noun, the verb, and so on), but we will also need to investigate the nature of grammatical gender in English, how word order changed and affected meaning in a sentence, and how the pronominal system of English changed and is still changing. Students will learn that "thou" and "you" were, for centuries, the singular-informal and plural-formal forms of the second person. Readers will be encouraged to explore recent changes in the grammatical and social use of pronouns: relationships among "he," "she," and "they" and the social implications of personal pronoun choice. Understanding the history of pronouns is a good example of how the study of the past can help us frame debates in the present.

This book was written in the early twenty-first century, and it addresses the developments in media, popular culture, global communication, and digital technology that have characterized this century's early decades. As a book of this time, it tries to speak to social and political relationships of language and belonging, language and power. African American English, for example, has an impact not only on groups in the United States but on social and artistic forms of expression throughout the world.

The aim of this textbook is to provide the material for an engaging classroom study and discussion of English in its historical and contemporary varieties. To this end, it presents a series of online exercises and assignments (www.routledge.com/9781032129693), keyed to each chapter, that are designed to test knowledge and inspire conversation. Some exercises, for example, are keyed to certain historical sound shifts (understanding, say, how i-mutation in the Germanic period is responsible for certain word pairs, such as "doom" and "deem" or "strong" and "strength" or "fox" and "vixen"). There will be exercises designed to get the student to try phonetic transcriptions of personal speech, to explore differences in word use over generations, and to critically and creatively use lexical resources such as the *Middle English Dictionary*, the *Oxford English Dictionary*, and the *Dictionary of American Regional English*. Using dictionaries is about more than looking up words. It is about engaging with the cultural and political presuppositions of the dictionary makers and recognizing that works such as Samuel Johnson's *Dictionary* of 1755 or Noah Webster's *American Dictionary* of 1828 are as much expressions of personal and national perspectives as they are registers of usage.

The history of English is a history of sounds and speech. But it is also a history of writing. From the earliest educators, debates about spelling were central to conceptions of the vernacular. English remains, for many students, almost inexplicable in its spelling conventions. Most of us simply rely on mnemonics ("i before e, except after c") and rote memory. The study of English spelling is, however, a fascinating story of history and identity. English is unusual among European languages in that its spelling conventions are historical rather than phonetic: we spell "knight" and "night" not because we still pronounce the initial k- or the medial velar continuant (-gh-) but because we used to. English spelling conventions were codified at a time when pronunciation was changing and when there was a new awareness of regional variations in sound. Teachers and scholars agreed that English should maintain historical spelling systems to make earlier texts comprehensible to later readers and to make texts comprehensible to anyone, irrespective of regional dialect. At times, spelling gives us evidence of change in pronunciation (especially in the personal writings of the fifteenth and sixteenth centuries). At times, it does not. This book attends to the history of writing to show how the relationship between speech and writing varies throughout the history of English. Most recently, that relationship has changed again, as texting and other forms of digital communication raise questions about how writing does not necessarily represent speech sounds and how digital culture influences public speech and writing. Writing can tell us something about language change and variation, on one hand, and language teaching, on the other. Exercises in this book provide the opportunity to explore these provocations.

All textbooks have, implicitly or explicitly, an argument. In addition to presenting information, they will press that information into a story or a claim for the importance of their subjects. These are mine. If you are reading or teaching this book, they may be yours as well.

Language variation and language change are interrelated phenomena. When we study the different forms of a language at a specific time (synchronic variation), we are aware of how those different forms respond to and contribute to change across time (diachronic change). Studying and teaching the history of

English should attend not only to earlier forms of the language but also to the ways all of us participate in making and remaking of English as we use it in different contexts and at different times.

Describing how a language works often blends into prescribing how it should work. Whenever we set out to characterize speech and writing, however objective we may try to be, we may be judging them. Dictionary makers set out to record word meanings, pronunciations, spellings, and usages. But the principles of inclusion and exclusion, the order in which definitions are given, and the ranges of possible pronunciations transcribed – all of these reflect the judgments of the dictionary maker. In teaching English at any level, we walk a line between describing and prescribing. A theme of this book is how, over time, people make decisions about what may be "good" or "standard" English. By examining earlier sets of judgments, we can see the history behind our own.

Languages are acts of social performance, grounded in the organization of communities, belief systems, and geographical and cultural landscapes to which people belong. The history of English, from this point of view, is more than a collection of data. Language exists in the minds, the mouths, and the hands of human beings. It is there to describe an inner self; it is there to describe the world in which that self lives. In this book, linguistic information contributes to a social history not just of the English language but of the human beings who use and continue to use it.

The study of the past informs our life in the present. The history of English embraces a history of attitudes toward language use and change. Debates that we may think to be unique to our own time – for example, official or standard forms, bilingualism, rapid change, colloquialism – have motivated discussions of English for centuries. In 1619, scholar and teacher Alexander Gil complained (in a study written originally in Latin) that the English language had decayed over the previous two centuries: new words had come in from French and, most recently for him, words were entering English from North American indigenous tongues (he mentions the words "moccasin," "canoe," "maize," and "raccoon"). Reading Gil centuries later, we may find it hard not to hear the voice of a high-school teacher or a cranky uncle at the dinner table. We hear our present in the past. You know more than you think you do.

Teaching and learning are pleasures. I have been a university professor for over 40 years. I have worked with community groups, parents, lifelong learners, and high-school students. At all levels, I have tried to convey the excitement and the pleasure that comes from intellectual inquiry and shared response. I have learned more from my students than they have likely learned from me. You may use this book as the primary text for a course. You may use it as the supplement or complement to other materials. However you use it, I hope you take pleasure in the interplay of conversation and the shared discovery of who you are as people who live in language.

English Phonemes and Transcribing Speech

Ever since the middle of the sixteenth century, scholars of the English language have tried to develop ways of representing speech sounds in writing. Rather than using different spellings in the standard English alphabet, scholars have developed symbols that are designed to represent, as unambiguously as possible, the sounds produced by the human mouth. In the late nineteenth century, as the study of language became more scientific and empirical, a "phonetic alphabet" emerged. This alphabet is based on Latin and Greek letters, but they are used in special ways. Each symbol represents a sound. To put it more precisely: each symbol represents the physical shape of the mouth, tongue, and vocal organs when the are producing a sound. Thus, we can look at a visual representation of the organs of speech and assign a symbol to each representation.

During the twentieth and twenty-first centuries, linguists have developed a set of phonetic symbols. This set is known as the International Phonetic Alphabet, known as IPA. There are some differences between IPA and some American linguistic practices of transcription. For the purposes of this textbook, the aim of transcription is to show the student that sounds can be represented symbolically and, furthermore, that a good transcription can tell any reader, irrespective of their regional dialect or personal habits of pronunciation, how an utterance has sounded.

To begin, Table 0.1 is the basic set of consonants in Modern English. They are arranged by the place of their articulation in the mouth (the top row), and by the manner of their articulation (the left-hand column). Here, phonemes

Table 0.1 The consonants in Modern English

	Labial	*Dental*	*Alveolar*	*Palatal*	*Velar*
Stop	pet, bet		ten, den		cut, gut
Continuant	file, vile	thin, other	sit, zit	plush, pleasure	hear
Affricate			cheer, jeer		
Glide	weird		year		
Liquid		love	red		
Nasal	mad		net		sing

are illustrated with representative words in standard spelling. When words are paired to illustrate a sound, the first is the unvoiced and the second is the voiced consonant.

Vowels in English can be single sounds. These are called **monophthongs**. The major monophthongs in Modern English are shown in Table 0.2.

In addition to these sounds, there is a low-central sound known as **schwa**, represented by the symbol /ə/. This sound usually appears in unstressed positions, as at the end of a word such as "sofa," or in the pronunciation of the word "the" in everyday speech.

Vowels that are made up of two sounds pronounced together are called **diphthongs**. To illustrate diphthongs, the sound appears in the phonetic alphabet, followed by the English word in modern spelling The major diphthongs in Modern American spoken English are:

/eɪ/ as in face
/əʊ/ as in goat
/aɪ/ as in price
/aʊ/ as in mouth
/ɔɪ/ as in choice

Here are the basics of the International Phonetic Alphabet as they will be used in this book. At times, throughout the book, additional symbols may be used to illustrate historical or regional pronunciations. Those symbols will be explained when they appear. Note that the symbols of the IPA may look like English letters, but they have special meanings. Thus, for example, the /e/ symbol does not mean that the vowel is an e; it means that it is a mid-front vowel sound.

a as in father
æ as in cat
e as in the first part of the diphthong in words such as face
ɛ as in mess
i as in machine
ɪ as in miss
ɔ as in cost
o as in most

Table 0.2 Monophthongs in Modern English

	Front	*Central*	*Back*
High	meet	big, bug	loop
Mid	get		so
	cat		put, saw
Low	swan		father

ʊ as in put
ʌ as in cut
u as in moose
ə as in the
ai as in lice
au as in mouse
ɔi as in moist
ju as in muse
b as in boy
č as in cheer
d as in dog
f as in fog
g as in gun
ǰ as in jeer
h as in hear
k as in cat
l as in long
m as in man
n as in net
ŋ as in sing
p as in pet
r as in red
s as in sit
š as in sheer
t as in tip
θ as in thin
Þ as in there
v as in vet
w as in wet
z as in zero
ž as in pleasure

Symbols between slash marks / / represent phonemes: that is, the sounds of the language that are meaningfully distinct. Phonemic transcription does not record particular features of lived pronunciation, or the changes in sound depending on word stress.

Symbols between brackets [ ] represent phonetic sound production: that is, the sounds of the language as they are pronounced. Phonetic notation can be extremely fine-grained, recording patterns of stress, or breath, or other features.

In transcriptions using the IPA, the colon /:/ is used to represent a quantitatively long vowel. Vowel quantity was meaningful (that is, phonemic) in earlier periods of English, but is no longer phonemic in Modern English. Thus, there is no difference in meaning, now, between the words pronounced [gʊd] and [gʊ:d].

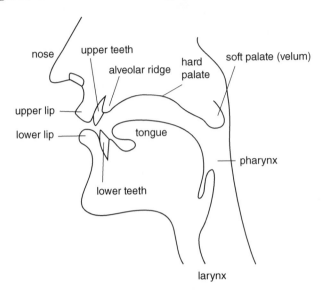

Figure 0.1 A schematic representation of the human head, with the organs of speech
production identified

Acknowledgments

I am grateful to the editors and staff of Routledge for originally soliciting this book, for their rigorous review of the proposal, and for their support during the writing of the completed text.

I have been teaching, lecturing, and writing on the history of the English Language for over 40 years. Much of my work has appeared in public lectures, in my work for the Great Courses, and in my book, *Inventing English: A Portable History of the Language* (Columbia University Press, revised edition 2015). I have returned to many examples from the history of English that I have explored earlier –to develop, qualify, and clarify my earlier engagements. Columbia University Press has generously granted permission to reproduce maps and materials that appeared in *Inventing English*. Harvard University Press has generously granted permission to reproduce maps from the *Dictionary of American Regional English*. Every effort has been made to locate the sources for other materials in this textbook, all of which appear to be in public domain or open sources.

My gratitude to professional colleagues in the field is great. I single out for thanks here: Maria Cecire, Anne Curzan, Irina Dumitrescu, Mary Hayes, Simon Horobin, Tim William Machan, Colette Moore, Lynda Mugglestone, and Robin Valenza.

I am especially grateful to Laura Poole, for her expert editing of the text of this book as it was being written, and for her suggestions and corrections throughout the process. I am also grateful to Susan Dunsmore for her exemplary copyediting of this book in production.

My greatest debt is to my students, who have always challenged my teaching and who have, most recently, provided me with insights into the changing shape of English in the twenty-first century. For insights into the changing languages of gender identity and into current forms of digital communication, I am grateful to Anadaios Box, Megan Gookin, Finn Laubscher, Aashi Patel, and Abigail Root.

Introduction

What Is Language and How Do We Study It?

Language is a system of communication that relies on sounds and symbols to describe the world as it appears to its speakers and, in turn, represent concepts or ideas that make sense of that world to societies. Although many animals communicate through sound and gesture, humans are unique in that we have developed complex systems to express what is and is not present to us. Human language can describe what is present in the world and what has happened. It can also express what is not there: imagined conditions, future experiences, hoped-for or feared outcomes. A person who knows a language can produce an infinite number of well-formed statements. Someone who knows a language can understand such statements, even if they have never been heard or read before. Whatever the origins of human language, speakers of all languages use words that have an arbitrary and conventional relationship to the things they describe. For example, there is nothing in the English word "door," the French word *porte*, or the Hebrew word *delet* that inherently or essentially means the object being described. There is nothing in particular sounds that inherently or essentially mean things (although certain sounds do have a particular emotional or aesthetic impact in certain languages).

No language is harder to learn for its native speakers than any other. By the time they are about 6 years old, children from the United States, Russia, Vietnam, India, or anywhere have the same level of command of their native language. No language is better than any other in enabling native speakers to communicate, describe, and imagine. Languages differ in structure and sound throughout the world. Some languages have sounds that other languages do not have. Some languages use case and gender to signal meaningful relationships among words in a sentence. Some languages rely primarily on word order in a sentence to create meaningful utterances.

There is no necessary direction for change in language. Over time, languages do not become simpler or more complex. As we will see, English lost grammatical gender in nouns and case endings over time. From our modern perspective, it seems to have simplified. But Modern English has a level of idiomatic expression that makes it very different, and more complex, from its earlier forms. Just

DOI: 10.4324/9781003227083-1

think of the phrases "get up," "get out," "get into," "get over," "get on," "get go," and "get down." If you did not know English, you would not understand these phrases by simply looking up "get" in a dictionary and knowing what the other words in these phrases mean.

There is no necessary timeline for language change. Languages do not change gradually or consistently over time. A modern student can read the novels of Jane Austen, for example, that were written two hundred years ago. But readers of the age of Shakespeare, at the end of the sixteenth century, would have found the language of Geoffrey Chaucer, of two hundred years earlier, almost opaque. The vernacular speech and writing of England before the Norman Conquest in 1066 seem to have been fairly stable from the seventh through the eleventh century. For many Americans born in the mid-twentieth century, however, the speech patterns and writing habits of twenty-first-century undergraduates may seem corrupt or debased. Languages do not decay. They change.

The study of language is called **linguistics**, but that word has changed over time. The discipline of linguistics in the nineteenth century centered on the historical changes in sound and on discerning particular patterns, or even laws, that governed sound change in languages over time. Nineteenth-century linguists used systematic sound changes to compare languages and reconstruct earlier forms of a common ancestor language. The idea of an Indo-European language family grew out of the recognition that groups of languages – English, Latin, Persian, Hindi, Celtic, and some others – shared common features of vocabulary and grammar. Comparing them enabled scholars to reconstruct a parent form of the language. Linguistics today means something very different. To be in a university department of linguistics is largely to see language as a feature of the mind. Studying language does not involve comparing living languages or reconstructing dead ones. It looks at structures of syntax and grammar: that is, how words and concepts are put together to make meaningful utterances. For many modern linguists, language is not something learned but acquired: this means that all humans have the innate, mental capacity to use language. We are, in some sense, hard-wired for language in this view. This position contrasts with the view that when we are born, we are blank slates with no innate ideas, concepts, or abilities. The discipline of modern linguistics has moved away from the study of sound to the study of structure. It has moved away from studying history to studying usage.

In the course of this book, we will see the implications of different views of linguistics as they bear on the study of the history of the English language. Let's introduce some key terms that will summarize and clarify these opening remarks.

To be a fluent user of a language is to be in command of two things: the conceptual, mental, or socially shaped view of a language as a whole and the ability to produce utterances that are meaningful in any situation. Swiss linguist, Ferdinand de Saussure (1857–1913) called these two features **langue** and **parole**. *Langue* is the understanding of a language as a system, the comprehensive knowledge of how a language works. *Parole* is the ability to produce statements that are grammatical and meaningful. If you have a command of *langue*, you can do *parole*. For American linguist Noam Chomsky (b. 1928), these two abilities were called **competence** and **performance**. Linguistic competence is the command of a language, but for Chomsky, it is also a feature of mind, an ability to recognize what language is and to acquire a language throughout life. Performance is, in a sense like *parole*, the ability to use that language in every possible situation. These distinctions may seem similar, but modern linguists see them as somewhat different. What Chomsky argued, and what most linguists today would hold, is that there is something about knowing a language that goes beyond the simple collection of statements of competence. As we learn and use a language, we hear and read many statements. But what is remarkable about fluency in a language is that we can produce an infinite number of statements we have never heard or read before. The relationship between performance and competence, therefore, is not a one-way street. We do not simply reproduce the things we have heard. Every parent remembers the moment when a child speaks their first sentence – not because the child has repeated a sentence from the parent, but because the child has uttered a sentence that he or she has never heard before. This phenomenon lies at the heart of a modern conception of language and its study.

Languages are made up of sounds, and what linguists recognize is that each language has a meaningful collection of sounds, where that meaning is based not on essential qualities but on difference. What does this mean? In English, there is a difference between the words "pit" and "bit." These words mean two different things. The only difference between the words is the pronunciation of the initial consonant. The sound represented by the letter p is what we would call an unvoiced, bilabial stop – a sound, in other words, made by the mouth with both lips pressed together, without the vocal cords moving, and in a single, rather than continued action. The sound represented by the letter b is what we could call a voiced, bilabial stop – a sound, in other words, just like the sound represented by the letter *p*, but with the vocal cords moving.

The sounds represented by b and p are **phonemes**. A phoneme is the smallest meaningful unit of sound in a language. The words "bit" and "pit" make up a **minimal pair**: two words that differ in only one phoneme. If we list a group of words like these, we may get the following:

bit
pit
fit
wit
sit
kit
hit
lit
zit

Such a list of words is called a **contrastive set**: a group of words that differ only in one phoneme. A **phonemic inventory** of a language is its set of meaningful different sounds. English has a phonemic inventory; every language does. In English, voicing is what we would call **phonemic**: the difference between the sounds represented by the letters p and b, s and z, and f and v is a difference of whether you move your vocal cords when you utter these sounds. There are certain languages in which some sounds are phonemic that are not so in English. In the language of the republic of Georgia, for example, there is a difference between a bilabial unvoiced stop that is aspirated and one that is unaspirated, i.e., whether there is a puff of breath involved in producing the sound. This is not a meaningful distinction in English.

How are sounds put together to make meaningful utterances? Phonemes have meaning, and when one or more phonemes come together to signify something in particular, they are called **morphemes**. A morpheme is a meaningful unit in a word that indicates a relationship to other words. For example, the English word "quick" can modify a verb (and thus become an adverb) when we add the morpheme -ly. This morpheme may be added to words to signal adverbial use. Some morphemes are thus suffixes: -ness signals making something into a noun or a concept. Some morphemes are prefixes: the difference between "come" and "become" lies in the way the morpheme be- signals a state of change or activity. Some morphemes have taken on a distinctive set of meanings in Modern English, irrespective of their original grammatical content. For example, the word "Watergate," which originally referred to a housing complex in Washington, DC, came to connote the scandal of the break-in to the offices of the Democratic National Committee there and the ensuing cover-up by the Nixon administration in the early 1970s. The morpheme -gate has come to refer to any political or social scandal: Irangate, Whitewatergate, and more. As we will see later, one of the key ways Modern American English is changing is through the creation and use of new morphemes to express particular concepts or actions. The word "explain," for example, has been broken up, with the suffix -splain created as a new morpheme. Thus, the word "mansplain" has been created to describe the condescending explanation of something by a man to a woman.

The words of a language are called its **lexis**. Every language has a collection of words that are meaningful. A lexis is constantly changing. Individual words will change meaning over time and across context. The Old English word *selig*, for example, meant holy or blessed. Over time, that word came to connote not the inner or spiritual condition of a person but their behavioral patterns: actions that were odd or out of the ordinary. Eventually, that word came to mean strange, unusual, or laughable. Our word "silly" represents a **semantic change** of a word that has remained in the language. The study of how words have meaning is called **semantics**. A language may coin, i.e., create or borrow new words to increase its lexis. By contrast, a language may create new words out of existing forms. English is distinctive among world languages in that it has, for the past five hundred years, borrowed many words from different languages. The lexis of English may be one of the largest of any language. By contrast, Icelandic is a language whose speakers have traditionally resisted borrowing words. Modern Icelandic will take concepts, such as television, and translate them, morpheme by morpheme, into native components. Thus, "television," which is made up of two parts, "tele" (across) and "vision" (sight), becomes *sjonvarp*: *sjon* meaning sight, and *varp* meaning to throw across. Historically, Germanic languages make new words in this way. Modern German has *Fernseher* (far + seer) for television. Old English took the Latin word *omnipotens*, "all powerful," and turned it into *eallmightig* (all mighty). This process of morpheme-by-morpheme translation produces what are called **calques**.

Every language has a system of expressing meaningful relationships of words in statements. This system involves what are called **grammar** and **syntax**. Grammar is the term used to describe how words are given meaning according to number, person, relationship, activity, and so on. Syntax describes the conventions of patterning that give statements in a language their meaning. In Modern English, grammar largely concerns the study of kinds of words and how they are put together. Nouns, verbs, adjectives, adverbs, prepositions, definite and indefinite articles: these are what we study when we study the grammar of Modern English. Modern English syntax is largely a matter of word order in a sentence.

English has changed in all of these ways: in phonology, in semantics, in grammar and syntax. English, like all languages, varies in these ways at a single time. Variations across regions, classes, genders, and groups of different heritages and identities all coexist at once. The distinction between change over time and variation over space is the distinction between **diachronic change** and **synchronic variation**. These are not completely separate phenomena. A central question for historians of English is how does synchronic variation become or influence diachronic change? How do differences in regional or class dialects affect an official or accepted standard, and will they change that standard over time? Can we see forms of English that are now standard in earlier dialect forms? A deeper question may be: is there really such a thing as the state of a language at any given moment? Is there such a thing as Modern American English, Middle English, African American English, Indian English, or Estuary English? The synchronic state of a language is always marked by variation. The study of historical dialects enables us to recognize just how difficult it is to define a linguistic moment.

It is important to introduce some key terms, concepts, and methods that govern the study of English over time. Scholars have developed four broad methods for the diachronic and synchronic study of English:

- **Articulatory phonetics**: the study and description of how the human mouth makes particular sounds. All sounds can be described in terms of where and how in the mouth and throat they are produced. A system of symbols, called the International Phonetic Alphabet (IPA), has been developed to represent these sounds. With the IPA, anyone should be able to recognize, describe, and represent any sound in any language. We use the IPA to represent sounds in history and in different dialects.

- **Sociolinguistics**: the study of how language operates as a form of social behavior, how it brings people into communities and cultures, and how individual and group interactions affect how a particular language is used. Sociolinguistics also embraces the social attitudes toward language variation, use, and change.
- **Comparative philology**: the method of comparing the sounds and forms of living or surviving languages to reconstruct earlier forms of those languages. Developed in the nineteenth century, comparative philology developed a set of conventions or laws that can explain relationships of sounds between languages in a family or group. It also developed these conventions or laws to explain what certain sounds became over time.
- **Corpus linguistics**: the activity of amassing large amounts of data from spoken or written evidence to chart variations over space and differences over time. For the historical study of English, corpus linguistics will take, for example, all surviving examples of the spelling of a word in surviving texts, locate those texts in time and place, and then map the differences. Digital technologies have enabled the collection and analysis of such data.

Each method has advantages and its challenges. Here is an introduction to each.

Articulatory Phonetics

Sounds can be described according to their place and manner of articulation. Humans produce sounds by moving or stopping air through the throat and mouth. It is conventional to have the face looking left in these pictures and to describe the sounds of a language moving from the front of the mouth to the back:

- **Labial sounds** are sounds that are produced with the lips. These include the sounds represented by the letters p and b. Because we use both lips to produce these sounds, they are called bilabial sounds.
- **Dental sounds** are those produced by the tongue pressing against or in between the teeth. In Modern English, the sounds represented by the spelling -th- are called interdental sounds, because the tongue moves between the upper and lower sets of teeth to produce them.
- **Labio-dental** sounds are those produced by the lips and the teeth together. The sounds represented by the letters f and v are labio-dental sounds.
- **Alveolar** sounds are produced by the tongue pressing against the alveolar ridge in the mouth. The alveolar ridge is located behind the upper teeth. In Modern English, we pronounce the sounds represented by the letters t and d in these ways. In Modern English, the sounds represented by the letters ch and j (as in "cheer" and "jeer") are alveolar sounds.

- **Palatal** sounds are those produced when the tongue arches up against the soft palate at the top of the mouth. The sound often represented by the letter *y* as a consonant, /j/, is a palatal consonant.
- **Velar** sounds are those produced further back in the mouth, with the tongue pressing against the velum (the hard palate). Sounds represented by the letters c or k and g (as in "cut" and "gut") are velar sounds.
- **Glottal** sounds are those produced in the back of the throat, by the glottis. In Modern English, we often make glottal sounds (e.g., in some pronunciations of a word such as "bottle"), but these sounds are not phonemic in English – there is no meaningful difference between saying /botl/ and /boʔl/. In some languages, glottal stops are phonemic.

These are the places of articulation of **consonants**. A consonant may be described as the interruption of the stream of breath in producing sound. Consonants have the following manner of articulation:

- **Voicing**: a voiced consonant is one produced with the vocal cords moving. If you say the word "bit," for example, and place your fingers on your throat, you can feel your vocal cords moving. If you say the word "pit," by contrast, you cannot feel your vocal cords moving. The sounds represented by the letters b and p, therefore, are sounds with the same place of articulation, but with a different manner of articulation.
- **Stops and continuants**: consonants can interrupt the flow of air by stopping it. In Modern English, we make the sounds represented by the letters p, b, t, and d as single sounds. We do not hold or continue them. Other sounds, however, can be held continuously. The sounds represented by the letters sh, zh, f, v, s, z can be held. Continued sounds can be distinguished, further, as follows:
  - **Fricatives** are produced with two parts of the mouth working together. For example, the sounds represented by the letters f and v are fricatives in that they are produced with the teeth and lips working together.
  - **Liquids** are pronounced by moving the air around both sides of the part of the mouth making the sound. The sounds represented by the letters l and r are liquids. Liquids are frequently unstable or mobile in spoken languages and in the history of languages. In English, the sound represented by the letter r often varies over time and across dialects.
  - **Glides** are produced by moving the mouth in the course of producing the sound. Glides can occur at the beginning and end of syllables, but not in the center of one. Thus, the sounds represented by the letter y in the word "yes" or the letter w in the word "water" are glides.
  - **Nasals** involve resonating the air stream through the nose. The sounds represented by the letters n and m are nasals. The sound represented by the letters ng is also a nasal.

Similarly, **vowels** are described according to where and how they are produced in the mouth. Vowels may be thought of as meaningful sounds made by the passage of air through the throat and mouth.

The place of a vowel is where it forms in the mouth. Vowels are described as high, low, and central and as front and back. In classifying the vowels of a language, linguists use a schematic representation of the mouth as a kind of grid, with the front on the left and the back on the right. The vowels are located on this grid.

Vowels also have additional manners of articulation in addition to their place in the mouth:

- **Rounded and unrounded**: vowels can be produced with the lips rounded or unrounded. The sounds represented by the letter u in English are rounded vowels. In some languages, there are rounded vowels that do not exist in Modern English: for example, the umlauted ü in German. In ancient Greek, the word *psyche* would have been produced with a high front rounded vowel represented by the letter upsilon.
- **Tense and lax**: when pronouncing a vowel, the muscles of the mouth and tongue may expend different degrees of effort or tension. Tense vowels are longer in quantitative duration than lax vowels. If you say the word "tweet," you can feel the muscles of your mouth stretch more than if you say the word "twit." "Tweet" has a tense vowel, "twit" has a lax vowel.
- **Open and close**: open vowels are pronounced with the tongue far from the roof of the mouth. Close vowels are pronounced with the tongue higher in the mouth. Open and close should not be confused with low and high. Vowels produced in the same place in the mouth may differ depending on where the tongue is. Thus, the sound in the word "thought" in Modern American English is an open, mid, back, rounded vowel.
- **Long and short**: linguists use these words to describe the quantity of a vowel, i.e., how long it is held in pronunciation. There are many languages in which vowel quantity is phonemic, i.e., where the length of time for a which a vowel is held makes a meaningful difference. In Old English, vowel length was phonemic. For example, the difference between the words spelled as *god* and *god* was that, for the former, the vowel was held for a long time (the word meant "good"), and, for the latter, it was held for a short time (the word meant "God"). In Latin and Greek, quantitative vowel length was phonemic (and was the basis for poetic meter).

The purpose of articulatory phonetics is to record the sounds of speech as unambiguously and as accurately as possible by using a conventional set of symbols. These symbols (the IPA) may look like English letters (or Greek letters or other symbols), but they should not be confused with spelling conventions in modern languages. Learning these symbols enables you to represent and understand sound changes over time.

Transcription is the practice of recording the sounds of an utterance using the symbols of the IPA. There are degrees of detail and purpose in transcription:

- A **phonemic transcription** is a record of the phonemes in an utterance. It may be thought of as an ideal representation of a set of sounds, and it may not necessarily correspond to how a living speaker actually produces those sounds. A broad phonemic transcription is written between slash marks.
- A **phonetic transcription**, by contrast, is an attempt to record as accurately as possible the actual pronunciation of an utterance by a speaker. Such an utterance may be distinguished by dialect or personal habit. A narrow phonetic transcription is written between square brackets.

A broad transcription records phonemes. A narrower transcription records what are called allophones. **Allophones** are the varied pronunciation of phonemes depending on the context of those phonemes in a given word or statement.

The following example may illustrate these concepts. Take the Modern American English word "motorboat." A broad phonemic transcription would be: /motorbot/. But most speakers do not pronounce the word in this way in everyday speech. The sound represented by the letter t in the word is often voiced. Thus, a phonetic (rather than a phonemic) transcription of the word might look like this: [modorbot].

This is a broad transcription. A narrower transcription would take account of individual pronunciations of the vowels and consonants. A narrower transcription might look like: [mo:dərbot], with the first vowel held for a longer period of time and the second vowel reduced to an unstressed schwa sound /ə/.

What do we learn from this exercise? We can see that in everyday speech, unstressed vowels are often pronounced as the mid vowel represented by the schwa /ə/. We also see that in everyday speech, it is common for the unvoiced interdental stop /t/ to be voiced as [d] when it appears between a stressed and an unstressed vowel in the middle of a word. Thus, people may say the word "metal" as if it were "medal," the word "potter" as if it were "podder." We would say that the phoneme /t/ has an allophonic variant, [d], in medial positions.

Thus, allophonic variation describes the different ways a single phoneme may be pronounced, depending on its place in a word or the dialect of the speaker. One way of defining a phoneme is the following: A phoneme represents a set of noncontrastive allophones. A phonemic transcription may be thought of as a kind of abstraction or template for pronunciation, rather than a record of actual pronunciation in everyday speech.

Sociolinguistics

Sociolinguistics is the study of language in its performed social contexts. Less concerned with aspects of mind or history than other branches of linguistics, this approach looks at language in action. It is largely driven by fieldwork: that is, collecting observed data about language use by individuals and groups. Sociolinguistics can help us understand how differences of class and wealth, for example, shape variations in English. It can help us understand how a single person can use various forms of English, depending on the social context, switching languages or dialects in different situations. Terms such as "code switching" and "register" come out of sociolinguistics, as does the idea of the speech community, a group of people who use a form of a language in a particularly distinctive, shared way. Sociolinguistics also helps us understand how issues of class and privilege and activities such as racial, ethnic, and gender passing are often matters of linguistic performance.

Sociolinguistics took shape largely as a kind of anthropological, field-based activity. Its foundational practitioners created data sets by interviewing individuals and creating questionnaires. Such fieldwork could result in the study of lexical variation. For example, do you say "pail" or "bucket," do you stand "on line" or "in line?" This kind of research could also reveal insights into phonological variation. Interviewing groups of people and inviting them to pronounce the words "marry, merry, Mary" can situate them along geographical and class lines.

In studying the history of English, a student will find examples of language use that can be productively assessed with a sociolinguistic approach. The fifteenth-century gentleman John Paston, known today for the letters he wrote to family and friends, often chose vocabulary terms for particular purposes, keyed to his addressee. In some cases, he wrote English sentences full of short, familiar words. In other cases, he used newly borrowed words from French to create a position of authority or condescension. In diaries and journals, novels and plays, we can see men and women adapting their usage to shifting contexts.

One question that emerges from a sociolinguistic approach to the history of English is: when do certain variations or idiolects become standard or accepted norms? Modern students will recognize that they speak and write differently to friends than they do to parents or teachers, and the way they speak in a job interview will be different from how they speak at home. But there may come a point when the speech of home and friendship comes to be accepted in the schoolroom or the office. Language change can be found at these junctures.

Some of the key terms from sociolinguistics that this book uses include the following:

- **Prestige language**: a particular language or a form of a language that marks social and economic status, educational attainment, or political power. During the Middle English period, French was the prestige language of the British Isles, in that it was used by the court and the aristocracy and was the language learned by those who aspired to high social status. During the fifteenth and sixteenth centuries, the so-called standard pronunciation of English changed through a process known as the Great Vowel Shift. Although there are many possible causes for this change in pronunciation, one might be the contact among different regional dialects in London during the late fifteenth century, due to migration within England. Over time, a new set of conventions for pronouncing long vowels in stressed positions emerged and came to be associated with the educated and privileged in the south of England. Other examples of prestige language or prestige dialect include the development of Received Pronunciation in twentieth-century Britain and the standardization of sound and usage by North American and British television and radio presenters. Since the eighteenth century, dictionaries have played a role in identifying "high" and "low" forms of speech and writing and marking forms as obsolete or regional. As we will see in this book, every dictionary makes judgments about language. They are social as much as linguistic documents.

- **Register**: when people speak or write to each other in particular social situations, they use a register appropriate to that situation. A register is a form of a language that uses certain words, forms, idioms, or structures to affirm a relationship between speakers. Registers can be formal or informal. For example, when speaking to a group in public or in a classroom, a speaker may be careful to use standard pronunciation and vocabulary. Among friends, however, that same person may vary the speech (saying, e.g., "wanna" instead of "want to," or "goin'" instead of "going"). Another form of register is called consultative, for example, when a patient and a physician communicate, or a lawyer and a client, the vocabulary may be technical. Intimate registers can be used among lovers or close friends and family. Terms of endearment, private names, and even nonsense words contribute to an intimate register.
- **Code switching**: this is when a person shifts between languages or forms of a language depending on the person being addressed. Children in bilingual families may speak to their mother in one language and their father in a different language. A student may speak to a teacher in one way and immediately shift to addressing a fellow student in a different way.
- **Gendered language**: some world languages have different grammatical and formal ways of signaling the gender of the speaker or of the addressee. English has no such categories, but throughout its history the ways men and women, straight and queer, speak and write have been understood to be distinctive. This does not mean that all men or all women speak in the same way; nor does it mean that one could judge whether a piece of writing or speech was by a man or a woman, a straight person or a queer person, purely on the bases of linguistic features. It does mean that in certain social situations, forms of linguistic performance will differ. What is known as **uptalk** – the habitual rising of inflection at the end of sentences, making declarative utterances sound like questions – has been understood as a gender-marking phenomenon (associated more with young women than with men). Similarly, the phenomenon popularly known as mansplaining may be assessed by analyzing distinctive features of intonation, word choice, and lexical markers of address. LGBTQ+ social groups have long developed a lexical and idiomatic use of language to create a sense of belonging, as a kind of exclusionary code, or as a way of expressing a particular view of the world.

- **Taboo**: the concept of taboo comes from anthropology. All cultures have certain forms of behavior that are so outside the norm that their practitioners are shunned or exiled from the group. Incest is a good example of a cultural taboo: a sexual activity so outside the norm that people who commit it are shunned. Cannibalism can be a taboo in the same way for certain societies, as can such things as violating the dead or blaspheming against religious beliefs. Language has its taboos, as well. These are constantly changing. Notions of obscenity have changed over time and affect the history of English. Oaths and curses often were transformed into euphemisms, forms of speech that evoked but did not explicitly state something. A word such as "zounds" became a socially acceptable form of saying what was originally "by God's wounds," an oath that was seen as transgressing the holiness of Christ's crucified body. Pun and wordplay can be subversive, evoking taboo expressions in playful ways (Hamlet's response to Ophelia, as he lies his head in her lap, "Madam, did you think I meant country matters?" is an example of wordplay used to evoke a term that could not be said on stage). Certain words in Modern English have become taboo because they signal the legacy of racist violence. The n-word has become taboo. But so have words which sound like it, even though they may have no historical or etymological relationship to it. The word "niggardly," which means stingy, came from a Middle English term, probably originally from the Scandinavian languages, and related to the word *hnøggr*. That word has increasingly become taboo. How societies regulate taboo words has been a matter of concern for as long as there have been languages.

People may also communicate in ways that do not convey specific, referential meaning but simply establish bonding or belonging. **Phatic discourse** keeps a relationship going without necessarily talking about anything outside of that relationship. Conversationalisms such as "hey," "what's up," "what's happening," "nothing much," and the like contribute to phatic discourse. Certain forms of small talk may also be phatic. Talking about the weather, for example, can be a form of phatic discourse.

People communicate in ways that go beyond words. Physical gestures, facial expressions, and body movements constitute nonverbal forms of communication that are often as meaningful – and as meaning-shaping – as words and phrases. While it is difficult for a language historian to recover these nonverbal modes of communication, there is evidence in art and literature for a history of meaningful gesture. Statues and paintings may be silent, but they have their own codes of communication. For the study of recent forms of English, it is vital to explore how we perform our language to express sincerity, irony, humor, double entendre, and so on.

Comparative Philology

Comparative philology is the method of analyzing the sounds and structures of living and recorded languages, comparing them, and seeking to reconstruct earlier sounds and words from historically distant and nonsurviving languages. The aim of comparative philology is to establish language families: groups of surviving languages that have similarities or that have differences that are systematic and regular. At the heart of comparative philology is the argument that language families have these similarities or systematic differences because they historically descend from earlier, common languages. As developed in the nineteenth century, comparative philology was based on a conviction that the study of present forms enabled the reconstruction of past forms. For biologists, the discipline of comparative anatomy or comparative morphology involved the examination of certain features of living organisms to posit earlier common ancestors of those organisms. Early comparative philology sought to establish laws that could explain these patterns of descent. The concept of an Indo-European family of languages grew out of this conviction that groups of surviving languages had common ancestors and that these linguistic common ancestors were also social and cultural common ancestors. As we will see in later chapters, the concept of an Indo-European language family necessitated a conception of a social group of "Indo-Europeans." Splits in the language family – resulting in such subfamilies as Romance languages, Celtic languages, Germanic languages, and Indic languages – were not just linguistic phenomena but cultural and geographical phenomena. The languages of the Indo-Europeans split up as different groups physically moved away from a home group or common place. It is important to understand, then, that the discipline of comparative philology has as much to do with anthropology and archeology as it does with sounds and words.

If you look at a nineteenth- or early twentieth-century textbook on language, what you will find is a great emphasis on sounds. A book such as Alastair Campbell's *Old English Grammar* (first published in 1959) devotes the first 200 of its 350 pages to sounds. The book traces Old English (OE) sounds back to their primitive Germanic forms. Most of these sounds are vowel sounds. The principle of study here, as in many earlier textbooks, is that a language is the product of a historical set of sound changes. Understanding those sound changes, furthermore, enables the student to see how the words in a language go back to earlier forms, shared by a parent or ancestor language.

A modern student may ask: how does knowing the origin of these sounds help me understand OE (or any other form of English)? The answer is that knowing these sounds helps us recognize that OE is a Germanic and ultimately Indo-European language, with a shared vocabulary and a set of sounds that can be compared with other Germanic and Indo-European languages. Thus, as we will see later, a word such as the modern English "heart" can be traced back to OE *heorte*. This word is, as linguists say, cognate with German *Herz*, Old Norse *hjarta*, and Gothic *hairto*. **Cognates** are words that languages share that can be traced back to a common ancestor. But this word also can be found in other Indo-European languages. In Latin, the word for heart is *cor*. In Greek, it is *kardia*. Scholars recognized that Indo-European words are related by sound conventions or sound laws. The sound /h/ in the Germanic languages corresponds to the sound /k/ in Greek and Latin. In Russian, the word for heart is *serdtse*. In some Indo-European languages, then, there is a relationship between words that start with the /k/ sound and words that start with the /s/ sound. Making lists of these words and the sound relationships helps us see them clearly:

Latin *centum*
English *hundred*
Avestan *satem*
Hindu *sau*

Latin *caput*
English *head*
Hindu *sira*

Latin *canis*
English *hound*
Sanskrit *śvan*

Comparative philologists take this information, and that of many similar words, and show that there are regular correspondences between the sound /h/ in Germanic languages, /k/ in the Romance and Hellenic languages, and /s/ in Indo-Iranian (and to some extent Balto-Slavic) languages. The endpoint of these comparisons is reconstructing an Indo-European form from which these all descend. Indo-European reconstructed words will be prefaced with an asterisk, and in this form they are called Proto-Indo-European terms (PIE). Thus, the PIE term for "heart" will be *kerd. The Indo-European word for "head" will be *kap.

Comparative philology is also concerned with reconstructing meaning. A head is a head and a dog is a dog. But there are certain words that are clearly related among the Indo-European languages, but which differ in meaning. Look at the following words:

Modern English *fee*
Old English *feoh*
Germanic *Vieh*
Gothic *faihu*
Latin *pecus*
Sanskrit *páśu*
Lithuanian *pekus*

These words bring together terms for cattle, property, and money. Comparative philologists reconstruct a PIE ancestor word *péku, which would have meant livestock (think of our word "pecuniary"). Such a reconstruction suggests that in the ancient culture of the Indo-Europeans, livestock was the primary marker of wealth.

Let's go back to the words for "heart." Indo-Europeanists have shown that the shared words for the bodily organ are also shared words for acts of belief. Latin *cor* means "heart." But it is also related to the verb *credo*, "I believe." The words for "host" and "guest" both go back to a PIE root, *ghos-ti, that connotes the relationship between them. In some languages, the word came to mean stranger, as in Greek *xenos* (and the Modern English word "xenophobia"). In others, it could connote an enemy, as in the Latin word *hostis*. Other forms of this root became words like Latin *hospes* (the root of "hospitality" or "hospital").

The method of comparative philology was thus concerned with reconstructing the lexical and ultimately conceptual worlds of a posited Indo-European people through the comparison of sounds in surviving or recorded languages. In addition, grammatical categories and patterns of syntax were compared among languages. At the heart of this process was the study of **phonology**, the sound systems of languages.

Comparative philology took relationships that were synchronic – that is, the forms of words in living languages – and argued that they were products of diachronic change. In the nineteenth century, this diachronic change was seen as akin to biological evolution. Although we now know that languages do not evolve from simpler to higher forms, nineteenth-century linguists often modeled relationships of language to relationships of biological organisms. Such discredited ideological notions of language development ultimately do not undermine the technique of comparative philology as a tool for showing how languages aggregate into groups or families. Used in tandem with history, archeology, anthropology, and sociology, the techniques of historical reconstruction have been used to posit a geographical site of origin for the Indo-European people, and, in turn, a set of social, religious, and literary practices that descend into modern cultures throughout Europe, Central Asia, and the Indian subcontinent. It will be the purpose of Chapter 1 to illustrate these relationships.

Corpus Linguistics

Corpus linguistics is a way of approaching language as a collection of data. A corpus is a body of texts or utterances which represents the language usage of a certain group or region. Corpus linguistics is a practice that is empirical and evidentiary. It may focus on speakers from a local group: for example, a corpus linguistics analysis of Brooklyn English would seek to record, through interviews, documentation, and recordings, the sum total of usages of speakers of English in the New York borough of Brooklyn. Such a project would take note of vocabulary choices, forms of pronunciation, syntactical and grammatical patterns, and idioms. A corpus linguistics analysis of, say, Early Middle English would survey the entire surviving manuscript evidence of English usage in Britain from 1100 to 1300. It would record variations in spelling, taking variations as evidence of variation in pronunciation. It would also record different grammatical forms of words (for example, endings for participles, forms of the third-person singular and plural). It would map this data on to the geography of the British Isles to show where and when such forms appear.

One aim of corpus linguistics, then, is what is called a linguistic atlas. A linguistic atlas is a visual map, a representation of usage marked by region. Like a weather map, a linguistic atlas has lines that demarcate certain usages. As we will see later, maps can illustrate variations in, for example, Middle English dialects as well as in Modern English and American dialects.

As with any collection of data, a corpus linguistics project is only as good as its informants. For living speakers of a language, the project relies on the honesty and directness of those who respond to interviews or fill out questionnaires. For earlier forms of a language, it relies on the conviction that scribes spelled largely as they spoke and that manuscripts could be accurately dated and located in a place of origin.

A linguistic atlas also has a concordance of usage. A concordance is a complete list of words in a corpus. A concordance to the work of an author (a concordance to Shakespeare, for example) is a list of every word used by that author, keyed to the place of its appearance. A concordance thus differs from a dictionary in that a dictionary is a collection of the words of a language with representative examples. A concordance would record every appearance of each word in a corpus. A concordance of Modern American English is almost impossible, as texts and utterances are constantly being generated. A concordance of Old English or of Middle English, however, is possible because these are limited corpora of texts.

Corpus linguistics can be pressed into the service of sociolinguistic study. Collections of data may be organized not just by place or date but by social class, level of education, or identity and background of speakers. A linguistic atlas of Brooklyn English could be organized by identity background (white, Black, Hispanic, Asian), degrees of education (high school or college completion), income level, religious affiliation, and other criteria. Corpus linguistics has been used to understand fine-grained variations in language use. Recent work in what has been called middle-class African American English sets criteria of income and geography and works through interview and questionnaire to build a corpus of usages that are distinctive to this defined group. By contrast, corpus linguistics approaches to Old English take the entire surviving body of texts produced between the eighth and the eleventh centuries and record every appearance of a word to explore the semantic range and register of that word. A dictionary of Old English, therefore, is designed to present complete data. There is no dictionary of religious Old English or a dictionary of heroic Old English. Moreover, because much surviving Old English is in the form of literary or imaginative texts, a corpus of the language will have to recognize that certain words appear only in poetry, or only in sermons, or only in historical documents. There is virtually no data for everyday spoken or written Old English. There is data for everyday spoken and written Middle English (personal letters, manuscript annotations, private writings). Thus, a corpus linguistics of a language is only as good as the corpus itself and only as reliable as the textual witnesses or living informants.

The Mechanisms of Language Change in English

These techniques of language study are all largely descriptive. They assemble data into meaningful information to distinguish different regional and historical forms of a language. The historical study of English has only recently systematically concerned itself with why language changes and the mechanisms of that change. As we begin this book, we should look at some of these mechanisms of change.

All languages change over time. Those changes include pronunciation, grammar and syntax, and words and word meanings. In the history of English, the following sets of changes occur in ways that enable us to understand how and potentially why Modern English looks and sounds the way it does.

Phonological Change

Historical linguists identify sets of sound changes that enable us to compare earlier and later states of a language. These sound changes may be systematic, meaning they affect an entire system of sounds, such as long vowels in stressed positions. They may also be local, affecting particular sounds when they occur in proximity to other sounds in a word. In the history of English, some of these major sound changes include the following:

- **OE long *a* becoming long *o***: Modern English words, such as "home," "bone," "so," "two," and the like correspond to OE words *ham*, *ban*, *swa*, and *twa*.
- **Lengthening in open syllables**: during the Early Middle English period, words from OE that had short vowels in syllables that ended with a consonant plus another vowel increased in quantitative length. Over time, these quantitative changes became qualitative. Thus, Modern English words such as "name" would have had a qualitatively short vowel in OE, *nama*. In Early Middle English, the short *a* would have become a long *a* and would have changed, later on, into a qualitatively different vowel.
- **The Great Vowel Shift**: this change occurred in the Late Middle English and Early Modern English period. It was the systematic change in the long vowels in stressed positions. The vowels a, e, i, o, and u changed their qualitative pronunciation. The vowels represented by the letters a, e, and o in Middle English were raised and fronted. The vowels represented by the letters i and u in Middle English were raised and became diphthongs. Other sound changes were at work in the history of English, many of which we explore in the course of this book.

The pronunciation of consonants also changed. Among the major consonant changes were:

- **Assimilation**: this change affected consonants that came together in a word. Linguists would say that assimilation often occurs through the ease of articulation: that is, minimizing the movement of the mouth in the course of pronouncing a word. The OE word *wifman*, over time, came to be pronounced without the /f/ sound. We would say that the /f/ was assimilated into the following /m/ sound, hence the Modern English word "woman." The OE word *husband*, by contrast, changes only in that in Modern English pronunciation, the /s/ has become voiced to a /z/, under the influence of the following voiced bilabial, /b/. This is an example of partial assimilation. In the example of OE *hlafweard*, a word meaning literally a guardian of the loaf, assimilation over time reduced the word to *hlaford*, *lavord*, and ultimately Modern English "lord."

- **Articulative intrusion**: this change involves adding a sound to a word, usually in between consonants, to enable the mouth to move smoothly between different consonants. In Modern English, many people may say the word "something" as if it had a /p/ between the m and the th. The position of the mouth in producing the bilabial nasal /m/ is ready to produce an unvoiced bilabial stop, /p/. We do not change the spelling or form of the word to correspond to this pronunciation. But, over time, certain words changed because of articulative intrusion. Thus:

  - OE *Þunor* became Modern English "thunder."
  - OE *spinel* became Modern English "spindle."
  - OE *slumere* became Modern English "slumber."

- **Loss of sound**: early forms of English had consonant clusters that have leveled out or disappeared over time. Thus:

  - OE *fnæstian* became Modern English "sneeze."
  - OE *knit* lost the pronunciation of the initial /k/ sound.
  - OE *godspel* became Modern English "gospel."
  - OE *weorðschipe* became Modern English "worship."
  - OE *lamb* lost the pronunciation of the final b.

- **Metathesis**: the transposing of two sounds. In Modern English, children may sometimes say "psghetti" for spaghetti. Here, the *s* and the *p* are transposed. In certain regional American dialects, the word "ask" may be pronounced "aks." Some people pronounce the word "nuclear" as if it were "nucular." Metathesis is a phenomenon of everyday speech and regional variation, but it also changed the pronunciation and spelling of words over time. Thus:

  - OE *brid* became Modern English "bird."
  - OE *beorht* became Modern English "bright."
  - OE *aksian* became standard Modern English "ask."

- Words also change by **analogy**: this is a process by which words become pronounced or structured to look like other words in a comparable group. A good example would be how the word "brethren" has come to be replaced by "brothers," to make the plural of the word "brother" look like the plurals for "father" and "mother" ("brethren" is now largely reserved for the specific sense of a group of men in a community, rather than genetically related men in a family). In OE, the plurals of nouns could have a final -s (*stan*, *stanas*). But, for certain nouns, the plural could have been indicated by a final -a (*hand, handa*), by a final -u (*lim, limu*), by a final -e (*cwen, cwene*), by a final -en (*eage, eagan*), or by no ending at all (*wundor, wundor*). Sometimes the plural was indicated by a meaningful qualitative change in the root vowel of the word. Many words like this survive in Modern English ("foot," "feet," "man," "men," "goose," "geese," "mouse," "mice"). We will see later how and why these plural forms originated. In OE, the plural of the word for "book" was *bec*. The form of the plural of "book" has become "books" by analogy with the regularizing of plurals in -s for most English nouns. In fact, any new noun borrowed into or coined in English will take a final -s as a plural.

- **Grammaticalization** is a process through which certain words take on new functions in sentences. In the history of English, the clearest case of grammaticalization is the change in what are often called helping or auxiliary verbs. In OE, words such as *shall* and *will, may* and *might*, were full verbs: they could function as the sole verbs with subjects and objects in a sentence. OE *sceal* (Modern English "shall") meant obliged, or has to, or ought to. In an OE poem, there is the phrase *ides sceal dyrne cræfte*. This sentence may be translated as "a woman of high or special standing (an *ides*) ought to know secret skills." The word *cunnan* in OE meant the ability to do something, or the knowledge of a skill. This sense survives into Early Modern English in the phrase, "I can skill of music." This phrase means "I have the ability" or "I know the techniques of music." In Modern English, these kinds of verbs do not function as full verbs but as markers of futurity or obligation in conjunction with other verbs. They have become grammaticalized: they function as grammatical rather than fully lexical words. A complex example of grammaticalization we shall see later is how the word "do" took on different functions in the Early Modern English period. In addition to meaning to perform or act (to do something), it came to be used as an intensifier (I do love you), as a marker of the past tense (I did love you), as a marker of the interrogative (do you love me?), and as a periphrastic replacement for a verb that is unstated in a conversation (do you love me? I do).

Semantic Change

Semantic change is the change in the meaning of words over time. Words change in meaning in many different ways, and in the history of English the following are some of the most important and familiar of those ways:

- **Homonymy**: English is full of words that sound alike but mean different things. Homonyms can cause confusion. To minimize ambiguity in language, certain homonyms drop out and are replaced by other words. An extreme example of this process can be seen in the following sets of words:

OE	Modern English
a	ever
æ	law
æg	egg
ea	water
eoh	horse
ieg	island

In these cases, words from other Germanic languages or from different dialects of OE, were brought into a standard form of English to avoid confusion as the sounds of the OE words merged together and became indistinguishable.

• **Polysemy**: words often have more than one meaning. Over the history of English, some of these meanings take precedence over others. Over time, the semantic range of the word changes. We can chart some examples of polysemy in semantic change by looking at the word "uncouth." The dates here are the recorded appearance of a particular sense according to the *Oxford English Dictionary*:

unknown	OE period–1650 Unfamiliar, strange [recorded as obsolescent by the *OED*]
strange and unpleasant	1380–present
uncomely, awkward, clumsy	1513–present
rugged, rough	1542–present
uncultured	1694–present

What we see are the ways the external or physical characteristics of individuals or objects become the primary meaning of the word, rather than the internal or social characteristic of those people or objects. Thus someone who is unknown to the group or foreign may act in ways that are crass or inappropriate (hence, "uncouth").

• **Extension in lexis**: metaphorical meanings, or figurative senses, often take over from technical or literal meanings. The word "bristle," for example, originally meant to stand up stiff; it has come to mean "to become indignant." The word "horrid" also meant bristling and sharp. It now means awful or terrifying. The word "brazen" originally meant made of brass – and, therefore, of imitation gold and cheap. Over time, it came to mean impudent or showy. The word "ardent" meant on fire. Now it means eager. The word "flagrant" also meant on fire. Now it means without care for consequences.

• **Narrowing of lexis**: certain words that once connoted general categories now mean something specific. In earlier stages of English (even up through the time of Shakespeare), the following words signaled general categories:

Meat: any form of food
Corn: any form of grain
Starve: to die
Deer: any wild animal
Wife: a woman of a certain age or status, irrespective of marital status

These words have become specialized. Meat and corn refer to specific forms of food, a deer is a specific kind of animal, a wife is a woman who is married, and starve means to die of hunger.

Social and Cultural Pressures on Semantic Change

Words and expressions often change in response to social pressures or cultural conceptions of appropriateness, register, and taboo. As we mentioned in the section on sociolinguistics, certain taboo words, and words that sound like them, may be socially forced out of usage. Other words that took on special meanings in private, coterie, or identity-based vocabularies may become widely used. Thus, words such as "gay," "queer," "camp," "drag," and "beard" are part of the everyday vocabulary of Modern American English and no longer restricted to the lexis of communities of same-sex desire. The use of the word "man" as an interjection or a marker of address (as in such phrases as, "listen, man," or "a man's got to be strong") has moved from the African American community (or, in the case of British English, Jamaican speakers) into the general community. Such uses are no longer necessarily marked as belonging to a particular register or code. Words such as "down" (as in, "I'm down with that"), "cool," "dig," and the like are no longer marked as words from African American social groups.

Generational change is a major driver of linguistic change. Children often speak more like their friends at school and play than they do like their parents. Popular cultural activities that appeal to youth carry a distinctive vocabulary, idiom, and form of speech. Forms such as "wanna," "gonna," "gotta," and so on, while still unaccepted in formal writing, are unmarked in general speech. On the other hand, words such as "thirsty," or "mood" carry a very specific register of youth culture (and would sound risible in the mouths of authoritative adults) at the time of this writing.

A **euphemism** is a form of expression in which a term that may be taboo or unacceptable in certain situations becomes translated into a phrase that is acceptable. **Dysphemism** is the opposite of euphemism: it is the deliberate reinforcement of terms of social unacceptability. The words "water closet" or "bathroom" may be euphemisms (in American English) for "toilet." The word "shitter" would be a dysphemism. Euphemism also predominates in registers of official language designed to obfuscate meaning or avoid graphic expression. Thus, the famous expression from the 1979 movie, *Apocalypse Now*, "terminate with extreme prejudice," becomes a euphemistic officialese for "assassinate." During the second half of the twentieth century, the rise of official and bureaucratic euphemisms came to be the mark of untrustworthy political governance. One person's protest is another person's insurrection. One person's flexible floor plan is another person's tear-down. The rise of this kind of language has become a hallmark of Modern American English. But so has dysphemism. Insult performance has long been a feature of African American popular talk. Rap and hip-hop often refer to acts of sexual and physical violence in explicit terms. Words such as "shit" and "fuck," which would have been unprintable throughout the twentieth century, now appear in mainstream newspapers and magazines, websites, film, and television. Obscenity has always been part of language (few discourses are as rich in curse and oath as the poetry of the ancient Roman Catullus, or the Middle English verse of Chaucer, or the writings of Jonathan Swift in the eighteenth century). How obscenity affects language over time, and how social pressures and expectations change registers of discourse, is one feature of English that this book will explore.

Sources and Further Reading

Throughout this book, I will quote and refer to material from *The Cambridge History of the English Language*, general editor Richard M. Hogg. 6 volumes (Cambridge: Cambridge University Press, 1992–2002), cited as *CHEL*, followed by volume and page number.

References to the *Oxford English Dictionary* (*OED*) will be to the online, 3rd edition, continuously updated, cited by word and definition. Available at: www. oed.com.

Students and teachers wishing to pursue the study of the history of the English language in ways that complement, and differ, from this book, may be interested in a selection of recently published histories and guides.

Algeo, J. (1972). *Problems in the Origin and Development of the English Language*. 2nd edn. New York: Harcourt Brace.
Barber, C., et al. (2012). *The English Language*. 2nd edn. Cambridge: Cambridge University Press.
Baugh, A. C. and Cable, T. (2013). *A History of the English Language*. 6th edn. London: Routledge.
Brinton, L. J. and Aronovick, L. (2016). *The English Language: A Linguistic History*. 3rd edn. Oxford: Oxford University Press.
Fennell, B. (2001). *A History of English: A Sociolinguistic Approach*. Oxford: Wiley.
Freeborn, D. (2006). *From Old English to Standard English*. London: Macmillan.
Gramley, S. (2011). *The History of English: An Introduction*. London: Routledge.

Hogg, R. and Dennison, D. (Eds.) (2012). *A History of the English Language*. Cambridge: Cambridge University Press.

Kretschmar, W. (2018). *The Emergence and Development of English*. Cambridge: Cambridge University Press.

Labov, W. (2010). *Principles of Linguistic Change*. Malden, MA: Wiley.

Milroy, L. and Gordon, M. (2008). *Sociolinguistics: Method and Interpretation*. Malden, MA: Wiley.

Pullum, G. and Ladusaw, W. (1996). *Phonetic Symbol Guide*. Chicago: University of Chicago Press.

Singh, I. (2013). *The History of English: A Student's Guide*. London: Routledge.

Smith, K. A. and Kim, S. M. (2018). *This Language, a River: A History of English*. Peterborough, ON: Broadview Press.

Approaches to the history of English geared for general readers and popular audiences include the following:

Bryson, B. (1990). *The Mother Tongue: English and How It Got That Way*. New York: Avon Books.

Crystal, D. (2003). *The Cambridge Encyclopedia of the English Language*. 2nd edn. Cambridge: Cambridge University Press.

Crystal, D. (2004). *Stories of English*. London. Allen Lane.

Horobin, S. (2018). *The English Language: A Very Short Introduction*. Oxford: Oxford University Press.

Lerer, S. (2015). *Inventing English: A Portable History of the Language*. 2nd rev. edn. New York: Columbia University Press.

McWhorter, J. (2008). *Our Magnificent Bastard Tongue: The Untold History of English*. New York: Avery Books.

Some classic, historical works, as well as contemporary works in linguistics, psychology, and cognitive science, include the following:

Bloomfield, L. (1933). *Language*. Chicago: University of Chicago Press.

Campbell, A. (1959). *Old English Grammar*. Oxford: Oxford University Press.

Chomsky, N. (1957). *Syntactic Structures*. The Hague: Mouton.

Chomsky, N. (2006). *Language and Mind*. 3rd edn. Cambridge: Cambridge University Press.

Culler, J. (1986). *Ferdinand de Saussure*. Ithaca, NY: Cornell University Press.

Curzan, A. (2011). *How English Works*. 3rd edn. London: Pearson.

Hall, C. (2011). *An Introduction to Language and Linguistics*. London: Routledge.

McWhorter, J. (2011). *What Is Language?* New York: Gotham Books.

Mencken, H. L. (1977). *The American Language*. 4th edn., with annotations and new material by Raven I. McDavid. New York: Knopf.

Pinker, S. (1994). *The Language Instinct*. New York: William Morrow.

Saussure, F. de. (2011). *Course in General Linguistics*. Trans. Wade Baskin. New York. Columbia University Press.

Smith, J. (2007). *Sound Change and the History of English*. Oxford: Oxford University Press.

1 The Indo-European Languages

With the term "Indo-European" (IE), linguists refer to a collection of related languages, ranging from those of Western and Eastern Europe through the Iranian plateau and the northern Indian subcontinent, embracing languages spoken in Asia Minor (Anatolia) and Western Asia. There are more than four hundred surviving IE languages, and nearly half of the world's population speaks one of them. Many IE languages have disappeared, some of them leaving great collections of thought and literature (Latin, ancient Greek, Sanskrit, and Avestan), some leaving records and translations (Hittite, Tocharian), and some leaving only tantalizing fragments (the ancient languages of Anatolia and the Italian peninsula).

From studying these languages, we can reconstruct several features of the linguistic and social world of peoples who probably emerged in the area north of the Black and Caspian Seas during the fourth and third millennia BCE. The study of IE became the defining practice of nineteenth-century linguistics. In the twentieth and twenty-first centuries, the study of IE has had an effect on archeology, genetics, anthropology, and sociology, and it helps us understand the nature of language relationships and the methods of the discipline.

The IE languages are genetically or genealogically related. By these terms, linguists do not mean that all the IE peoples are part of a shared gene pool. What they mean is that all IE languages historically descended from a common linguistic ancestor. They also mean that the IE languages, regardless of how different they are today, can be understood as sharing certain features of vocabulary, grammar, and phonology.

Genetic relationships in language are different from what linguists call **typological relationships**. There are many languages that organize their sentence structure and grammatical relationships by bringing together word roots with prefixes and suffixes. In these languages, words potentially become sentences. The parts of speech are said to agglutinate together, and such languages are called **agglutinative**. Turkish, Georgian, and Hungarian are some examples of agglutinative languages. They may work structurally in similar ways. But these languages are not historically related. Typological relationships are relationships

DOI: 10.4324/9781003227083-2

of structure and form irrespective of language history. The study of typological relationships may tell us something about language in the abstract. It may tell us about how humans have variously organized the making of verbal meaning in similar ways. But this does not tell us that these languages historically descended from a common ancestor. The languages of the world share various features, but they do not necessarily descend from a single language.

The idea of an original human language is the idea of **monogenesis**. Some linguists have sought to compare languages across the world to find shared vocabulary terms or certain relationships of sound and form among them. Some have posited an original human language called **Nostratic** (from the Latin, *nos*, "us"). The position of this textbook is that there is neither enough evidence nor enough rigorous methodology to reconstruct a Nostratic language. Many languages have superficial similarities. For example, the word for "mother" is some form of the bilabial nasal plus a vowel: ma, mama, and the like. Does this mean that there is an original human word for "mother"? Or does it mean that as a newborn explores the control of its mouth, bilabial sounds are the easiest or most natural to produce first? Yes, "mother" seems similar in many languages, from English to Hebrew (*ima*). But in Georgian, the word for "mother" is *deda*, and the word for "father" is *mama*.

It is also easy to think that all languages represent heard sounds in the same way. **Onomatopoeia** is the term used to describe words that are supposed to sound exactly like the sounds they represent. Thus, there is the belief that words such as "snap," or "crash" represent heard sounds. There is also the belief that animal sounds might be universal: all roosters crow, all dogs bark, all cats meow, all lions roar. Even a brief look at the words for animal and natural sounds reveals that there are no absolutely shared words across different languages: language remains (as presented in the Introduction) a system of arbitrary and conventional sounds and symbols. Even so-called **echoic words** are conventional. In English, a dog barks, but in Spanish, the sound is *guau*. In Irish (a Celtic language), the sound is *amh-amh*. In Serbo-Croatian (a Balto-Slavic language), the sound is *av-av*. In Hebrew (a non-IE, Semitic language), a cat makes the sound *yimyum* and a bell rings *tsiltsul*. In Russian, a slamming door makes the sound *bats*; in Dutch, it makes the sound *plof*. In French, a turkey goes *glouglou*. This all shows that there are no absolute and unambiguous words that every language shares, and whatever we may think we hear in the world, speakers of other languages will hear something else.

When we turn to the genetic study of language, we need to focus on structural and verbal features to establish regular relationships of sound and sense among them. The recognition that the IE languages existed in the first place was made by scholars in the seventeenth and eighteenth centuries when they saw certain similarities among the ancient languages they knew (Latin and Greek) and the languages they began to learn as colonial expansion and world trade brought them into contact with new peoples. They began to read texts in Sanskrit, the ancient language of mythic and religious texts of the Indian subcontinent. They began to read texts in Avestan, the old Iranian language of history and religion. By the end of the eighteenth century, scholars had enough data to posit a shared historical origin for a group of languages widely separated by geography.

Sir William Jones (1746–1794) was a British colonial administrator based in the state of Bengal in India. Trained as a lawyer and serving as a jurist in India, Jones became fascinated with the culture and history of his posting, and he studied Sanskrit with several local scholars. He founded the Asiatic Society of Bengal, devoted to the study of language and culture, and in 1786 he delivered a now-famous address to that society, announcing the evidence for his conviction that the Indian and European languages were related:

> The Sanscrit language, whatever be its antiquity, is of a wonderful structure; more perfect than the Greek, more copious than the Latin, and more exquisitely refined than either, yet bearing to both of them a stronger affinity, both in the roots of verbs and the forms of grammar, than could possibly have been produced by accident; so strong indeed, that no philologer could examine them all three, without believing them to have sprung from some common source, which, perhaps, no longer exists; there is a similar reason, though not quite so forcible, for supposing that both the Gothic and the Celtic, though blended with a very different idiom, had the same origin with the Sanscrit; and the old Persian might be added to the same family.
>
> (Jones 1993, vol. 3, pp. 34–5)

At the heart of Jones's observations is the idea of the comparative method: that looking at surviving forms of languages can enable us to reconstruct lost historical forms. Among the features of these languages that Jones and his contemporaries began to notice were certain vocabulary terms. For example, look at the following terms for political rule:

Latin, *rex*
Sanskrit, *raj*
Celtic, *rix*
German, *Reich*

Even a casual look at these words suggests that there is a relationship here. What Jones and his colleagues noticed was that certain grammatical categories seemed to be shared among the languages. Look at the basic forms of the verb "to bear." This is a very short comparison, but it should convey the sense of relationships among the languages. Here are the forms for "I bear," "you bear," "he/she/it bears":

Greek: *phero, phéreis, phérei*
Latin: *fero, fers, fert*

Avestan: *bara, barahi, baraiti*
Sanskrit: *bhárami, bhárasi, bhárati*
Gothic: *baira, bairis, bairith*

Again, even a cursory look at these words reveals that the first-person form ends with a vowel, the second-person form usually has an s at the end, and the third-person form usually ends with a stop. Do enough of these comparisons across languages and with many different words, and you will come up with some ways of reconstructing the IE vocabulary and grammatical system.

What you also come up with is a recognition that the IE languages have regular relationships of sound. In the example of "bear," we can see that the /b/ sound in Gothic corresponds to the /f/ sound in Latin and Greek. We can see that in Sanskrit, there was an aspirated bilabial stop, written as bh, that corresponds to these sounds.

The study of sounds therefore helps us understand the relationship among languages. It also helps us create a chronology of separation, whereby the original Proto-Indo-European (PIE) language speakers split off from one another, migrated across Europe and Asia, and settled far from one another. Sounds are thus a matter of synchronic difference and diachronic change.

One of the most basic sound changes in the IE languages may represent one of the earliest migratory movements of the IE-speaking peoples. This is the distinction between what are called **centum and satem languages**. In Latin, the word for one hundred is *centum*. In Avestan, it is *satem*. Linguists recognized that /k/ in one group of languages had a systematic relationship to /s/ in another group of languages. To rephrase this distinction in the terms of articulatory phonetics, we could say that the *centum/satem* distinction is between a velar stop /k/ and a palato-velar fricative, or continuant /s/. Thus, a word such as Latin *cordis* or Greek *kardia* ("heart") is Russian *sertse* and Lithuanian *širdis*. Another good but more complex example is a phrase that exists in ancient Greek literature: *kleos aphthiton. Kleos* is the word for "praise," or "glory," and *aphthiton* means "undying." This phrase was used to describe the ideal afterlife of a hero, earning eternal glory or praise for his accomplishments. In Sanskrit writings, there is a phrase that means the same thing: *sravas aksitam*. Scholars noticed that the initial /k/ sound in Greek corresponded to the /s/ sound in Sanskrit (they also noticed relationships of the sounds in the word for "undying").

In these sound changes is another important observation about IE languages: there are semantic as well as phonological relationships among them. There are words that connote the same thing or can be traced back to an earlier, shared meaning. In the Introduction, we saw how the discipline of comparative philology showed that in surviving IE languages, certain words, even though they may seem different, can be traced to a common shared social meaning. Thus, the words for "cattle" and "money" in surviving IE languages can be traced back to a word in PIE that represented the social idea that livestock was a form of value or commodity exchange. There is a core vocabulary among IE languages. This vocabulary includes basic words for human body parts, for natural phenomena, for family relations, and for certain activities, animals, and plants. In this basic vocabulary would be words such as "heart," "lung," "head," "foot," "night," "star," "snow," "sun," "moon," "wind," "corn," "cherry," "beech tree," "yoke," "mead," "weave," "bear" (the verb), and "sew." There would also be the words for "brother," "sister," "mother," and "father;" words for "dawn," "east," and "west;" words for "dog" and "wolf."

These shared words help us understand who the IE people were and where they originated. Because there are shared words for the beech tree and snow, for rowing a boat, and for mead (honey), archeologists theorize that the IE peoples must have lived someplace where these things were found and these activities could be performed. There is a shared word for a body of water, but there is no shared word for a very large body of water, such as an ocean. It is presumed that the IE people lived near lakes or inland seas, but not near an oceanic coastline. The IE languages share words for numbers (from one to ten and for one hundred). They also share words for some core religious figures, such as gods, and for certain domesticated animals.

What can we know about the IE people from this kind of information? The general consensus today is that they arose sometime in the fourth millennium BCE in the area north of the Black and the Caspian Seas, and that they may be associated with a group whom archeologists have called the Kurgan people. These people had copper and later bronze tools and artifacts, they buried their dead in pits, and they were most likely a pastoral agricultural group.

The origins of the IE people remains a subject of debate. What remains a subject of more vigorous debate is the question of how, why, when, and to what effect the migrations of the IE people happened. IE speakers moved east and west. The languages of Iran and north India seem to have split off about the same time. These, along with the Balto-Slavic languages, are the *satem* languages. The earliest surviving evidence for IE languages is in the area of Asia Minor known as Anatolia. Groups such as the Hittites, the Luvians, and the Luwians populated the area around modern Turkey and Syria. Their languages were recorded in cuneiform and hieroglyphic inscriptions on clay tablets as early as 1650 BCE. The earliest evidence for IE languages in the Mediterranean are the inscriptions in early forms of Greek that survive from Crete and Mycenae from about 1500 BCE. These, together with the languages of Europe, are *centum* languages.

Why did the IE people replace earlier, indigenous populations, and why did their language replace those of those earlier peoples? Broadly speaking, there are two competing hypotheses. One is agricultural and claims that the IE peoples were successful farmers who had domesticated certain grains and animals and developed techniques of farming, and that their success in these areas made them more successful or controlling in the areas to which they migrated. Another hypothesis is military. This argument claims that the IE people replaced previous groups not so much through economic achievement as through conquest. At the heart of this claim is the domestication of the horse, less than that of agricultural animals (such as goats, sheep, and cattle). Behind these claims are broader social and anthropological hypotheses: for example, that the IE people replaced a so-called Old European, egalitarian, or matriarchal society with a hierarchical paternalistic one.

For whatever reasons, the IE languages largely effaced earlier language groups over time. In Europe, Basque seems to have survived as a pre-IE language—that is, as an example of a linguistically defined people who were neither conquered or assimilated into IE hegemony, but survived in a small and restricted area of Europe. There is linguistic evidence of pre-IE people in Europe, some of whose words or expressions survived in IE. A commonly used example of this survival is the evidence of the sound cluster represented by the letters -inth. In Greek, there are words such as *plinth, labyrinth,* and *Corinth* with this sound cluster, which cannot be traced back to any IE origin. It is assumed that words like these were borrowed from an earlier, pre-IE people. There are also certain words in Greek that do not correspond to words in any other language. The ancient Greek word for king, for example, was *basileus,* a word that shows up as early as the Linear B texts in Mycenaean and that some linguists believe to be a Bronze Age borrowing from a now extinct language. The ancient Greek word for the sea (and for its feminine divine personification) was *thalassa,* another word that may have come from a pre-IE language.

Before going into IE comparative philology in detail, it is important to distinguish between words that are true cognates and words that were borrowed from another language (loan words). **Cognates** are words that survive in different IE languages, and are related according to certain principles of phonological relationships, and share a meaning or set of meanings. Cognates can be traced back to reconstructed PIE forms. There are many words in the IE languages that look like cognates but are not. For example, the word for a paved road in Modern English is "street." This word goes back to Roman Latin, *strata.* Words that look like this one appear in German (*Strasse*), Italian (*strada*), and Welsh (*stryd*). Here we have a case of word borrowing in the Roman imperial period. All roads led to Rome because the Romans built the roads. Another good example is the word for imperial ruler. Caesar gave his name to a concept. Caesar became *Kaiser* in German, *Tsar* in Russian, *Qaysar* in Urdu, *Kaysr* in Armenian, and similar sounding words in many IE and non-IE languages. Recall the Greek word *basileus.* This word, thought to be of ancient and possibly pre-IE origin, became the term of general imperial rule during the period of Alexander the Great. The term was then loaned into those languages that were spoken during Alexander's conquests and later during the period of Greek Christianity. Thus, the name Basil or Vassily (in Russian) descends from this word (as does the word "basilica," originally meaning a doorway for royal entrance). This is not a cognate, but a **loan word**.

Indo-European Comparative Philology

The IE languages comprise eight broad subfamilies, some of which have living descendants and some of which are extinct. Classifying these subfamilies used to seem straightforward, but recent scholarship suggests complex relationships among them. One way of presenting them is simply to list them:

- *Albanian*: the language of the modern Albanian people, now distinguished by three broad forms: Tosk, Geg, and Kosovar.
- *Anatolian*: the extinct languages of Asia Minor, spoken and written by the Hittites, Luwians, and Luvians (who may have been the people of ancient Troy).
- *Armenian*: the language of the Armenian people, spoken in the nation of Armenia and in the cultural diaspora.
- *Balto-Slavic*: a large group of languages that include the Slavic languages (Old Church Slavonic, Russian, Polish, Czech, Serbian, Croatian, and others) and the Baltic languages (Lithuanian and Latvian). Although there remains some debate as to whether this is a true historical subfamily or a set of languages that shared features due to contact over time, most treatments of IE consider this a historical subfamily.
- *Celtic*: the languages of modern Wales and Ireland, as well as the older languages of Old Irish, Breton, Cornish, Scottish Gaelic, and Manx.
- *Germanic*: the language family containing English, as well as historical and modern forms of German, Dutch, the Scandinavian languages, and the now-extinct Gothic.
- *Hellenic*: the languages of Greece, including Ancient and Modern Greek.
- *Indo-Iranian*: a large group of languages including those spoken historically in the Iranian plateau (Persian or Farsi) and Afghanistan (Pashto), as well as those spoken in the northern Indian subcontinent (Hindi, Urdu, Bengali, and others). Ancient texts proliferate in Old Iranian and Avestan and in Sanskrit, from which the modern Indian languages descend.
- *Italic*: the languages of the Italian peninsula, including Latin and other extinct languages (Oscan, Umbrian) and the modern Romance languages descended from Latin (Spanish, French, Italian, Portuguese, Catalan, and Romanian).
- *Tocharian*: an extinct group of languages, written and spoken in the Tarim Basin area of western China, with texts surviving from around the sixth through the ninth centuries CE. Two forms survive, known as A and B.

An alphabetical list is deceptive, however. These languages have relationships among each other (shared vocabulary, certain features of grammar and phonology). Some have unique features that may correspond to those of PIE (for example, the so-called laryngeal sounds of the Anatolian languages). For example, we can organize these languages geographically, and this geographical distinction largely corresponds to the *centum/satem* distinction discussed earlier:

centum or Western languages: Celtic, Italic, Germanic, Hellenic, Anatolian
satem or Eastern languages: Balto-Slavic, Indo-Iranian, Armenian.

This distinction is not hard and fast, however. Tocharian, which may be geographically the easternmost of the Indo-European languages, was clearly a *centum* language. Albanian has an inventory of consonant phonemes that do not seem to correspond to either the *centum* or the *satem* groups.

Another way of classifying the IE languages is historical. Based on linguistic features and their possible relationships to a PIE original, scholars have created a kind of historical tree of languages representing nodal points of difference (Figure 1.1).

Another way of classifying the IE languages would be typological: comparing the existing or recorded features of the subfamilies and creating a kind of snapshot of their relationship, irrespective of time. A wave model of these languages would look like Figure 1.2. In this pictorial representation, the languages are associated by particular phonological, lexical, and grammatical features:

- Northern and western languages share a vocabulary not found in other IE languages.
- Western languages share a common vocabulary.

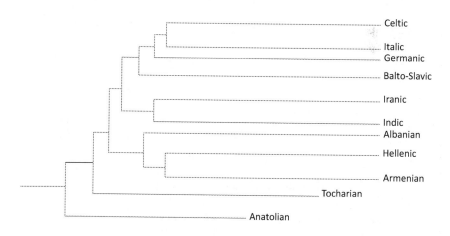

Figure 1.1 A schematic representation of the relationships among the Indo-European language groups

Note: The direction from left to right represents the passage of time, from Proto-Indo-European to the present. Branches represent relative points of separation of language groups over time.

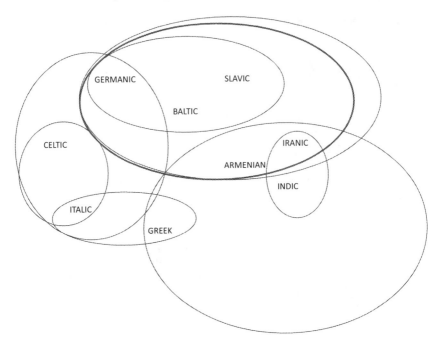

Figure 1.2 A wave model of the Indo-European languages, visually illustrating affinities (grammatical, lexical, phonological) among the major language groups

- Italo-Celtic languages have passive forms of the verb ending in -r.
- Northern languages have a dative plural case ending in -m.
- Italo-Hellenic languages share certain phonological features descending from PIE.
- Northern and Eastern languages (except Indic), share certain phonological features descending from PIE.
- Eastern languages share certain phonological features descending from PIE.
- Southeastern languages have a prefixed vowel in the past tense forms of the verb.
- Indo-Iranian languages share phonological features descending from PIE.

It is not necessary to go into great detail about the classification of the IE languages. But it is important to recognize that, based on those details, scholars have been able to reconstruct both the sounds and the meanings of words in PIE.

Let's take the example of the word for "horse" in the oldest surviving IE languages:

Sanskrit: *áśvas*
Greek: *hippos*; also in an archaic form, *ikkos*

Latin:	*equus*; also in an archaic form, *equos*
Gothic:	a plant named "horse-tooth," which looks like this: *aihwa-tundi* (as we will see, the /k/ sound in IE became the /h/ sound in Germanic)
Old English:	*eoh*
Old Irish:	*ech*
Lithuanian:	*ašva*, "mare."
Anatolian:	a surviving Luwian text with the word *ásùwa*

Thus, we know that there was a /k/ in the root form of the word in PIE. The sounds that follow in the surviving languages seem to suggest a /w/ or a palatalized /u/ sound. This sound may be represented by the letters -kw-. We know from other words that the Sanskrit phoneme /a/ came from PIE /e/ in initial vowels, but many of the other languages have a higher back vowel after palatal consonants. Thus, we can reconstruct a PIE form for "horse" as *ekwos* (throughout this book, reconstructed PIE forms come from Watkins 1985).

This method of comparative reconstruction was developed in the nineteenth century and proceeded according to certain principles:

- *Sound laws*: the phonological relationships among surviving languages that are presumed to represent historical divergences of subfamilies from the PIE parent language.
- *Antiquity of languages*: certain languages were presumed to be older than others, and therefore to represent features of PIE more accurately than more recent languages. In the nineteenth century, Greek, Latin, and Sanskrit were taken as core ancient languages.

In the early twentieth century, new language groups were discovered. Czech philologist, Bedrich Hrozny (1879–1952) deciphered the Hittite language from a collection of cuneiform tablets found in the archeological site of Boğazköy in modern Turkey. He approached that task by looking at the following phrases on tablets discovered in 1906 (Hrozny published his work on Hittite in 1917): *Nu ninda an ezzuteni water ma ekuteni.*

In Hittite cuneiform, the word transcribed as *ninda* was a pictogram for "bread." The word *ezzuteni* looks, even to modern readers, suspiciously like the word "eat." The word *watar* looks uncannily like the word "water." The word *ekuteni* seems to have, at its heart, a set of sounds that remind us of a word such as "aqua." *Nu* looks remarkably like "now." Hrozny translated this sentence as a directive for a ritual: first (or now) you will eat the bread, then you will drink the water.

Of course, not all Hittite words are so transparent. But what the discovery of Hittite did, and later in the twentieth century the discovery of other Anatolian languages did as well, was to add to the data of sounds and senses for the IE languages. The Anatolian languages, most likely the earliest recorded of the IE languages, provided new information about sound change and relationships of meaning.

In the 1980s, Calvert Watkins deciphered a set of Anatolian texts that offered striking parallels to the Homeric Greek story of the fall of Troy. In a brilliant and complex analysis, he posited that a phrase found in a cuneiform tablet, *alati wilusati*, meant "steep Wilusia." Using comparative sound relationships, Watkins suggested that the word *wilusati* corresponded to the Greek place name Ilium, or Troy. The word transcribed as *alati* corresponds to words such as *alta* (note the English word "altitude"). Based on this information, and a range of other comparisons, Watkins theorized that this phrase corresponded to the Homeric Greek formula for "high Troy," referring to the walls of Troy. The idea of a language of the Trojans emerged, tantalizingly, from this material, suggesting that there may have been a Trojan version of the story: an *Iliad* told by the losers.

Of course, IE is a language group that is made up of more than words. There were patterns of grammar and syntax that have been reconstructed from surviving languages. Here are some of those key features as they will bear on the study of the History of English.

IE was a **synthetic language**: meaning in a sentence was determined by inflectional endings on words rather than word order. Modern English has largely become an **analytic language**, in which sentence meaning is determined by word order. We will see how in the Germanic languages and earlier forms of English, inflections are important. Inflections marked cases. A noun case is a form of a noun in a particular relationship of space or action to the rest of a sentence. PIE is thought to have had eight such cases (the italic words are those in the cases described):

- Nominative: the noun as the subject of a sentence. The *ball* rolls.
- Accusative: the noun as the direct object of a verb in a sentence. I held the *ball*.
- Genitive: the noun as a possessor of another thing. The *ball's* shape was round.
- Dative: the noun as an indirect object of a verb in a sentence. I gave the *boy* the ball.
- Instrumental: the noun as an instrument of action. I hit you with the *ball*.
- Ablative: the noun in movement away from something. Rolling away, the *ball* hit me.
- Locative: the noun defined by its place in space. Dust was on the *ball*.
- Vocative: the noun as the object of address by a speaker. Oh, *ball*, where have you gone?

Not all of these noun cases survive in the IE languages, and in Modern English, much of this grammatical work is done by prepositions.

As in many modern IE languages, PIE had three noun genders: masculine, feminine, and neuter. These should not be confused with natural gender. Rather, they are the forms of nouns that govern how they are declined – that is, the system of case endings. Nouns came in groups or classes that determined how they were declined. Students of Latin may know about the five noun declensions in that language. These descend from PIE, and they correspond to declension in other languages (especially in Old English).

Verbs had tenses, but the concept of tense is not necessarily completely accurate. Many languages have past, present, and future. But many others express action in different ways (for example, action begun in the past and completed in the past; action begun in the past and completed in the present; action begun in the past and yet to be completed). The best way to think about verbs in PIE, and in many other languages, is in terms of **aspect** rather than **tense**:

- *Present or stative*: the verb describes a state of being in the present, without signaling change.
- *Imperfect*: the verb describes an action that began in the past and continues into the present. It can refer to actions that are continuous or repetitive.
- *Perfect*: the verb describes an action begun in the past and completed.

What we think of as the future tense did not exist as such in PIE. Instead, different languages developed different ways of expressing actions yet to happen. Some languages adapted the form of the **subjunctive mood**, which existed in PIE. The subjunctive is an expression of something that may happen, may be wished to happen, or should happen. It expresses a condition that does not exist. In modern English, phrases such as, "If I were a rich man," or "Oh, that Mary would be baking pies," or "let there be light," are in the subjunctive mood. Some IE languages, such as Latin, developed fully formed verbal conjugations for the future. *Amo* means "I love." *Amabo* means "I shall love." Other IE languages, such as the Germanic ones, used auxiliary verbs to express futurity. In Modern English, we say, "I go" for the present, but "I shall go" for the future.

One of the key features of PIE that survives in many languages and remains a feature of Modern English is **ablaut**. This is a word from German linguistics that means a change in sound; it refers to the meaningful, systematic variation of vowels in the same or related words. This is not a feature of sound change historically. It is a feature of sound variation that signals different meanings or aspects or features of words. The root vowel in certain words could change, depending on the changing stress of the word as inflectional endings were added. In PIE, the vowels e and o could undergo ablaut. This means that words with an e in them could sometimes appear with an o in them, depending on surrounding word stress. In other contexts, the vowel would disappear. Indo-Europeanists use the terms e-grade, o-grade, and zero grade to describe roots with these vowels. These vowels could also be lengthened.

Within PIE, ablaut could determine the different ways roots descended into later IE languages. For example, the root *ped descended into Latin through its e-grade: Latin *pes, pedes*. In Greek, the o-grade form of the word emerged: *podi*. In the Germanic languages, the lengthened o-grade survived: Old English *fot*, English "foot." These different grades also could affect what are called strong verbs in the Germanic languages:

drink, drank, drunk
sing, sang, sung

We will explore ablaut when we look at the Germanic languages and Old English. For now, it is important to recognize that the English verbal system has deep roots in IE and that languages can signal differences in meaning not only by using different words or endings to words but by systematically varying the sounds within words.

Indo-European Culture and Poetics

By reconstructing a core IE vocabulary and tracing the semantic relationships in that vocabulary in extant languages, scholars have sought to recover a cultural, religious, and imaginative world for the PIE era. Words for domesticated livestock, for the horse, for certain grains and foods, and for the yoke contribute to a sense of IE people as landed, agricultural communities. Words for deities and supernatural phenomena contribute to an understanding of IE religions as based on a paternalistic pantheon, with a strong sense of religious rite and ritual overseeing public and private devotion. Words for poets and poetry, for madness and creativity, and for the idea of weaving with words and with fiber point to a notion of poetic performance as a kind of inspired and potentially prophetic activity.

Exploring these cultural categories is not without controversy. Scholars in the 1800s tried to understand IE systems of belief as grounded in naturalistic myths around the cosmos and the seasons. In the 1900s, various anthropological approaches focused on the role of ritual and sacrifice in religious practice, for example, the practice of gift-giving, hosting, and exchange as unifying social groups; and the organization of the divine world as parallel to the human one. Some scholars posited a tripartite structure for those worlds: a priestly ruler class, a military warrior class, and an agricultural labor class. People prayed for a living, fought for a living, or worked for a living. This structure was thought to reflect a notion of the divine order of things as well. The idea of a father god, a god of war, and a god (or goddess) of harvest seemed to govern a range of polytheistic religions among the IE peoples. Greek and Latin, Norse, and Indo-Iranian mythologies all seemed to reflect these features.

Many of the IE languages have a word for a supreme god that can be reconstructed as PIE *deywós. Latin has the word *deus*. Greek has the god *Zeus*.

Sanskrit has the word *deva*, Avestan has *daeva*, Irish has *dia*, and Lithuanian has *dievas*. Words for light and day also descend from this PIE root. The name of the Roman god Jupiter comes from the compound *deus-pater*, god-father. This concept has been traced back to a PIE root meaning "sky-father," **dyeu-pəter*. As Calvert Watkins put it: "The reconstructed words *deiw-os and *dyeu-pəter tell us more about the conceptual world of the Indo-Europeans than a roomful of graven images" (Watkins 1985, p. xvii). There were deities for earth, fire, water, and wind. There were concepts of fate and social welfare, and there were deities associated with creating artifacts and smelting metals.

Many words that descend into the IE languages reflect social and religious practices. The word *credo* in Latin can be traced back to a PIE root **kerd*, meaning "heart." A PIE compound root, **kred-dhə*, added a suffix meaning "to place" (compare the Latin verb *do*, "I place," and the English word "donate"). Thus, the concept of credence or belief involved the idea of placing something in the heart.

The concept of burying the dead goes back to a root **sep*, meaning to venerate or serve. With certain suffixes, it became **sep-el-yo*, which descended into Latin as the verb *sepelire*, "to bury." This Latin term, loaned to English, becomes "sepulcher."

Words for poets and poetry also come together in a set of PIE roots. The Latin word *vates*, meaning a seer or prophet, is cognate with Old Irish *faith* (meaning "bard"), Old English *wod* (meaning "crazy"), and the Old Germanic god Woden (or Odin). These go back to a PIE root **wek*.

There are many related roots in PIE that are **wek* words. Weaving, creating, blowing air, and inspiring all seem to coalesce around this root, and words from the IE languages that can be traced back to it include *vox*, "voice," and "epic." A Greek form *ope* can mean voice. The name of the Greek god Calliope comes from *kallas* (beautiful) and *ope* (voice).

We have already seen how the Greek phrase *kleos aphthiton* corresponded to the Sanskrit phrase *sravas aksitam*, both referring to undying fame. The concept of heroism was intimately linked with the performance of story: heroes existed to have tales told about them, and the mark of true heroism was to have those stories told after their deaths. The word *kleos* stands behind the name of the hero Hercules, whose name in Greek, Herakleos, means "contributing to the fame of Hera." The initial /k/ sound in Greek corresponds to the initial /h/ sound in the Germanic languages. Thus, Greek *kleos* and Old English *hlud* are cognates. *Hlud* became our Modern English word "loud." Behind the idea of fame, then, was the idea of speech and the public broadcasting of fame. Thus, in Homer's *Iliad*, Achilles announces, "If I stay here and fight beside the city of the Trojans, my return home is gone but my glory is everlasting" (*Iliad*, 9. 412 ff.). In the Sanskrit *Rig Veda*, we can find a similar expression: "Give, Indra, wide and lofty fame, wealthy in cattle and in strength, lasting our lifetime, failing not" (*RV* 1.9.7–8). Scholars have found in the Old Irish poem known as the "Lorica of Saint Patrick" some comparable phrases: "May my fame not be pledged against death. Let there come long life, let death not come until I am old." In this text, the Old Irish word *chlú* (fame) corresponds to the Greek word *kleos*, and the Old Irish word *aes* (long life) corresponds to the Greek word *aion*, meaning "eternity" or "ever" (see Nagy 1979; Floyd 1980).

This kind of work has an almost magical quality to it, as if scholars were conjuring a cultural poetics from the shards of sounds. Indo-Europeanists, however, have progressively moved away from the older, ideological frameworks that dominated nineteenth- and early twentieth-century historical linguistics. It is important to recognize that IE studies were deeply implicated in colonial European projects and, in turn, in notions of biological evolution applied to human language. Reading the work of the early Indo-Europeanists can be challenging today. Franz Bopp, one of the founders of comparative philology, could remark on the "refined" quality of the "Indo-European race of languages." He thought of his work as a "science," and his method as a kind of "physiology" (Bopp 1845, pp. vi, xiii). August Schleicher, later in the nineteenth century, thought of language evolution along the lines of Darwinian evolution. He came up with language trees modeled on the trees of biological development. Languages worked like organisms. The term **morphology** in linguistics to describe the features of word endings and grammatical forms was taken from comparative physiology, whereby scientists would compare the physical structures of animals to trace historical progenitors. French philologist Michel Bréal, writing in 1866, noted that when reading the work of Bopp and Schleicher, "one could believe one was in fact reading a treatise on geology" (quoted in Aarsleff 1982).

Max Müller, a German-born, Oxford philologist of the mid-1800s, was hugely influential in putting forth a notion of IE religion as concerned with solar deities. But he also saw in words a kind of cultural poetics: "Our poets make poems out of words, but every word, if carefully examined, will turn out itself a petrified poem." In the early twentieth century, IE studies became the vehicle for racial discrimination. V. Gordon Childe, writing in 1926 in his book, *The Aryans*, asserted: "the fact that the first Aryans were Nordics is not without importance ... The Nordics' superiority in physique fitted them to be the vehicles of a superior language" (Childe 1926, p. 212).

This way of thinking has vanished from professional linguistics. There is nothing superior about IE languages or cultures compared with others. Nonetheless, this early work in IE revealed some distinctive, shared features of how the social and imaginative worlds came together. The work of Calvert Watkins and his students in the late twentieth and early twenty-first centuries has refined this kind of research, generating an understanding of IE poetics as a social if not ritual or even religious practice. Examining literatures from Greek, Latin, Sanskrit, Celtic, Anatolian languages, and more, Watkins and his students argue for a shared set of themes and actions for IE verbal art. The establishment of a heroic figure, the killing of a monster, the protection of life and livestock, and the journey of exile and return – these narrative features came to be expressed in a group of words and phrases shared by the IE languages. In addition, these words and phrases take on a formulaic quality. Literary formulae will be familiar to students of the Classics. "Wily Odysseus," "the wine-dark sea," "cow-eyed Penelope," and others are examples of formulaic epithets for people and things. These formulae have a regular metrical pattern, as well as a shared semantic sense and phonological relationship in the IE languages. To go back to *kleos aphthiton/sravas aksitam*, it is not just that the expression in Greek and Sanskrit correspond phonetically and semantically. They correspond metrically.

Based on this material and the research in the classics and the old Germanic languages, we can see that IE poetry was oral and formulaic. It was performed, it relied on particular formulae of action and description, and it was often organized through repetition of sounds. The idea of the oral formula and particular formulae is what makes IE poetry unique.

We will see versions of these IE features in the languages and imaginative writings of the Germanic languages and ultimately in Old English. Behind our modern literary lines lies the potential for old patterns and ideals.

Sources and Further Reading

Aarsleff, H. (1982). "Breal vs. Schleicher: Reorientation in Linguistics in the Latter Half of the Nineteenth Century." In H. Aarsleff, *From Locke to Saussure*. Minneapolis, MN: University of Minnesota Press.

Anthony, D. (2010). *The Horse, the Wheel, and Language*. Princeton, NJ: Princeton University Press.

Baldi, P. (1983). *An Introduction to the Into-European Languages*. Carbondale, IL: Southern Illinois University Press.

Benveniste, E. (1973). *Indo-European Language and Society*. Trans. Elizabeth Palmer. Miami, FL: University of Miami Press.

Bopp, F. (1845). *A Comparative Grammar*. Trans. Edward Eastwick, vol. 1. London: Madden and Malcolm.

Buck, C. D. (1920). "Hittite: An Indo-European Language?" *Classical Philology* 15: 184–92.

Campbell, C. (1985). "Line of Song Provides a Clue on Ancient Troy," *The New York Times*, January 28, p. 1. Available at: https://www.nytimes.com/1985/01/28/us/line-of-song-provides-a-clue-on-ancient-troy.html

Chang, W. and Chundra, C. (2015). "Ancestry-Constrained Phylogenetic Analysis Supports the Indo-European Steppe Hypothesis." *Language* 91: 194–244.

Childe, V. G. (1926). *The Aryans: A Study of Indo-European Origins*. London: Kegan Paul.

Floyd, E. (1980). "*Kleos Aphthiton*: An Indo-European Perspective on Early Greek Poetry." *Glotta* 58: 133–57.

Gimbutas, M. (1956). *The Prehistory of Eastern Europe*. Cambridge, MA: American School of Prehistoric Research.

Gimbutas, M. (1991). *The Civilization of the Goddess*. San Francisco: Harper and Row.

Jones, W. (1993). *The Collected Works of Sir William Jones*. New York: New York University Press.

Martin, R. P. (2018). *Mythologizing Performance*. Ithaca, NY: Cornell University Press.

Momma, H. (2013). *From Philology to English Studies: Language and Culture in the Nineteenth Century*. Cambridge: Cambridge University Press.

Nagy, G. (1979). *The Best of the Achaeans: Concepts of the Hero in Ancient Greek Poetry*. Baltimore, MD: Johns Hopkins University Press.

Renfrew, C. (1987). *Archaeology and Language: The Puzzle of Indo-European Origins*. Cambridge: Cambridge University Press.

Renfrew, C. (2008). *Prehistory: The Making of the Human Mind*. New York: Random House.

Ringe, D. (2006). *A Linguistic History of English: From Proto-Indo-European to Proto-Germanic*. Oxford: Oxford University Press.

Robins, R. H. (1987). "The Life and Work of Sir William Jones." *Transactions of the Philological Society* 85: 1–23.

Schleicher, A. (1863). *Die Darwinsche Theorie und die Sprachwissenschaft*. Weimar: Bohlau.

Watkins, C. (1985). *The American Heritage Dictionary of Indo-European Roots*. Boston: Houghton Mifflin.

Watkins, C. (1986). "The Language of the Trojans." In M. J. Mellink, *Troy and the Trojan War: A Symposium Held at Bryn Mawr College*. Bryn Mawr: Bryn Mawr College.

2   The Germanic Languages

English is a Germanic language. Even though Modern English vocabulary is drawn from many different languages, and even though the syntax and grammatical forms of Modern English look very different from German, Dutch, or Norwegian, English remains a Germanic language. Even in its Modern form, it shares a core lexis with the Germanic subfamily of Indo-European (IE). Modern English sounds can be traced directly back to Germanic (and ultimately IE) sounds, and the system of English verbs distinguishes it from other IE languages. Being aware of the relationship of the Germanic languages to IE, and of English to the other Germanic languages, helps us understand how its sounds and structures developed. Studying the Germanic languages also helps us understand how historical linguistics developed in the nineteenth and twentieth centuries. Key concepts in this discipline – regular sound laws, in particular – were discovered as German philologists explored the place of their language in the larger IE family. Finally, the study of the Germanic languages reveals how a group of migratory people developed a mythology and a literary imagination out of a shared IE inheritance and a unique geographical experience.

Just as linguists posit a reconstructed form of proto-IE based on comparing features of surviving languages, they posit a reconstructed form of what has come to be called Proto-Germanic (abbreviated as PGmc). This PGmc is believed to have split off from other IE groups sometime in the first millennium BCE. Although we have no records of this common PGmc, we have references in classical history to the Germanic peoples. Greek and Roman historians knew of them, and certain names and social practices are mentioned in their writings long before we have written evidence in a Germanic language.

Key linguistic features of the Germanic languages are the following:

- a shared, distinctive vocabulary;
- a set of systematic consonant relationships between the Germanic languages and the non-Germanic IE languages;
- a set of systematic vowel relationships between the Germanic languages and the non-Germanic IE languages;

DOI: 10.4324/9781003227083-3

- a two-tense verbal system: that is, verbs that are fully conjugated only for the present and the preterit;
- a dental suffix for a class of verbs in the preterit tense;
- a fixed stress on the root syllable of words;
- adjective endings that differ depending on whether the adjective is used with a definite article (known as strong and weak adjectives).

There are also relationships among the different Germanic languages and certain sound changes that took place after the Germanic languages split off from PIE.

Not every extant Germanic language will show these features or these changes. But they will be apparent in the earliest forms of the Germanic languages. We begin with these linguistic features and then review the migratory patterns of the Germanic peoples to show how the different languages developed. Finally, we look at the shared mythological and poetic features of the Germanic languages to anticipate our look at Old English culture and literature.

Vocabulary

The Germanic languages emerged in ways that are revealed by the common, distinctive Germanic vocabulary. For example, consider the words for a large body of water. The non-Germanic languages of IE have a variety of words, some of which may have been taken from pre-IE languages, and some of which may have developed out of PIE roots:

Greek: *thalassa*
Latin: *mare*
Irish: *muir*
Litauanian: *jura*
Hindi: *samundar*
Avestan: *drayah*

It may be argued that as each subgroup of the IE people discovered the sea, they named it differently. The Germanic words for "sea" are all obviously related:

Old English: *sæ*
Dutch: *zee*
Old High German: *seo*
Icelandic: *sær*
Danish: *sö*
Gothic: *saiws*

Most words of the Germanic vocabulary can be traced back to a PIE root. For some, their meaning in the Germanic languages is unique. In other cases, there are no clear PIE roots for certain words.

An example is the word "rune." The Germanic people developed a system of writing using phonetic symbols called runes. Each symbol had a name. No one is sure how these symbols developed, but it is clear that by the first century CE, Germanic people were inscribing names and marks of ownerships on objects using runes. In fact, the earliest written evidence we have for any Germanic language is on rune-inscribed objects.

The origin of the word *rune* is unclear. It may come from a PIE root meaning to murmur or grumble, or it may be a loan word from another language (some have suggested Celtic). Only in the Germanic languages does this word refer to a runic letter, and only in the Germanic languages does the word *rune* in its various forms connote something secret or mysterious.

Other words that appear to exist only in the Germanic languages (or whose etymologies are debated) include:

bear (the animal)
boar
bride
dream
eel
gray
hammer
leek
sheep
silver
toe
wife

Of course, many of these objects and concepts exist in other languages and in earlier forms of the IE family. But these words, in various but clearly related forms, exist in just about all of the Germanic languages. Why they are characteristic of Germanic is another matter. Some have argued that in the course of their migrations, the Germanic peoples came upon non-IE-speaking groups and borrowed words from them. Others have argued that most of these words can be traced back to PIE, but with very different meanings. A word such as "silver," for example, looks wholly Germanic (OE *seolfor*, Gothic *silubr*, Old Norse *silfr*), and may have been borrowed into the Balto-Slavic languages but by no other IE group (even though the IE languages have a word for this metal, coming from a root meaning "shining" or "bright," and giving Latin *argentum*). A word such as "bear" may ultimately go back to a PIE root meaning "brown," but only in the Germanic languages does it refer to the large forest animal. A word such as "bull" may share the PIE root **bhel*, meaning "to swell" (from which Greek *phallos* descends). But how a word for swelling or growth came to mean a male bovine is unclear. The Germanic word for "wife," OE *wif* and Old Norse *vif*, meant a grown woman, and it coexisted with a group of words coming from the PIE root *gwen*, which gave us "queen" but also OE *cwene* (which could be a derogatory term), and the Greek *gune*, which appears in the modern word "gynecology." The point is not that the Germanic languages had words for things that did not appear in other IE languages, but that they seem to have developed a special register of words alongside words from PIE.

Consonant Changes: Grimm's Law

What also distinguishes the Germanic languages as a group is a set of sound correspondences between them and the IE languages. These correspondences, or changes, are known as the First Sound Shift, more familiarly known as Grimm's Law. During the early nineteenth century, philologists recognized that the system of consonants in the Germanic languages corresponded, in a regular way, to the system of consonants in reconstructed PIE. Danish linguist Rasmus Rask noted these comparisons, but it was German scholar, Jacob Grimm, who codified their relationship. Jacob and his brother, Wilhelm were the famous Grimm brothers. We know them today largely because they collected a set of tales from Germanic folklore. The Grimms' *Fairy Tales* (which they called *Hausmärchen*, or domestic tales) were believed to represent a common story of narratives and folk beliefs of great antiquity. We now know that many of these stories were, in fact, highly literate and literary creations, shaped in the eighteenth century and reported to the Grimm brothers as if they were ancient tales. Whatever their origin, these fairy tales were as much a part of the Grimms' ethnographic and linguistic project as their study of sound laws. The aim was to recover a deep past for the German people, a kind of literary and linguistic "childhood" (in their formulation) for the Europeans. Some tales hinge on the interpretation of a name, as if philology were itself a kind of magical coding (the name "Rumpelstiltskin," for example, means "the little broken-legged one"). Wilhelm Grimm thought of these stories as the "last echoes of pagan myths," and he went on – talking as much about historical Germanic linguistics as folklore:

> A world of magic is opened up before us, one which still exists among us in secret forests, in underground caves, and in the deepest sea, and it is still visible to children. [Fairy tales] belong to our national poetic heritage, since it can be proved that they have existed among people for several centuries.
>
> (Grimm 1984, p. 240)

For a modern student of comparative philology, the etymologies and histories of words may seem like a similar world of magic, and the philologist was as much a delver into darkness as the folktale hero.

Grimm's Law was the key that opened up that world. It established a corre-spondence between consonants of the Germanic languages and the consonants of other IE languages. We can think of this correspondence in phonetic terms:

- relationships between stops and continuants;
- relationships between unvoiced and voiced stops;
- relationships between aspirated and unaspirated stops.

These correspondences have been traditionally grouped into three sets of four sounds.

IE Unvoiced Stops p, t, k

Grimm began with the IE unvoiced stops p, t, k. Words from PIE that descended into Germanic have the unvoiced continuants, f, th, and h in their place. For the non-Germanic languages, we can use examples from Latin, and for the Ger-manic languages we can use modern and historical forms of words.

p > f
Latin *pater* > English "father"
Latin *pisces* > English "fish"
Latin *pes* > English "foot"
Latin *pecunia* > English "fee"

t > th
Latin *tres* > English "three"
Latin *dens, dentis* > English "tooth"
Latin *tu* > English "thou"

Right away, we need to recognize a few things. First, when we use Latin (or any other language) for comparison, we sometimes find the sounds that changed in different cases (thus, Latin *dens*, "tooth," no longer has the sound we are looking for; but the genitive form *dentis*, does). Second, different Germanic languages will have different sounds in their modern forms. This set of differences has to do with changes in the Germanic languages. For now, these examples are meant to just introduce the sound relationships.

The third unvoiced stop that corresponds to a continuant is k.

k > h
Latin *centum* > English "hundred"
Latin *cor* > English "heart"
Latin *caput* > English "head"

This correspondence between the /k/ in IE and the /h/ in Germanic, however, largely operates in initial positions. When the /k/ sound is elsewhere in a word, it corresponds to an unvoiced fricative /x/ in the Germanic languages.

Latin, *lux, lucem* > English "light" (which, in Old English, would have been *leoht*)

In addition, the initial /k/ sound corresponds to an initial /h/ sound in forms of English that have changed. Thus, as we will see in Chapter 3, OE had a set of initial consonant clusters that were lost or simplified in Modern English. OE *hlud* became "loud," *hreaw* became "raw," and *hlahian* became "laugh." When we search for examples we find:

Latin *cruor* (bloody) > OE *hreaw*, Modern English "raw"
Greek *kleos* (fame) > OE *hlud*, Modern English "loud"

Sometimes, the word meaning has shifted so dramatically that we need to dig deeply to find correspondences:

Latin *cara* (dear one) > OE *whore* (beloved), Modern English "whore"

Finally, in this grouping, we have a fourth sound, the unvoiced stop followed by a glide. This sound would be represented by the spelling kw, which in Latin often became qu:

Latin *quod* > OE *hwæt*, Modern English "what"

Sometimes, we need to turn to other IE languages to illustrate this correspondence. In Greek, the kw sound of PIE became an initial /k/ sound:

Greek *kulkos* (wheel) > OE *hweol*, Modern English "wheel"

Voiced Stops Becoming Unvoiced Stops

The next set of sound changes that make up Grimm's Law are the voiced stops becoming unvoiced stops. But let us not be confused:

b > p
d > t
g > k
gw > kw

Based on these correspondences, Grimm realized that the first set of changes had to have happened before the second set, otherwise the sounds of the stops would merge. So it is important to remember that the p, t, k, and kw sounds in the Germanic languages do not directly correspond to the p, t, k, and kw sounds in PIE, but rather to the b, d, g, and gw sounds.

The shift from b to p rarely (if ever) seems to have occurred at the beginning of a word. Examples that we can find are, therefore, medial sounds:

b > p
Latin *cannabis* > OE *hænep*, Modern English "hemp"
Latin *labia* > Modern English "lip"
Old Bulgarian *slabu* (slack) > Modern English "sleep"
Lithuanian *dubus* > Modern English "deep"

Because there are very few examples of this shift, especially in the beginnings of words, it would be fair to say that any word in a Germanic language that begins with the letter p is a loan word from a non-Germanic language. Words such as "penny," "pepper," and "pope" are loan words from Latin. That most Germanic languages share these words indicates that the words were borrowed from Latin before the Germanic languages split up (we come back to the idea of Continental loan words soon).

Other examples in this grouping are more straightforward:

d > t
Latin *decem* > Modern English "ten"
Latin *dentis* > Modern English "tooth"
Latin *edo* (eat) > Modern English "eat"

g > k
Latin *genu* > OE *cneo*, Modern English "knee"
Latin *granum* > Modern English "corn"
Latin *ager* > Modern English "acre"

In PIE there was a reconstructed sound, gw. This sound corresponds to the k sound in Germanic, but to come up with good examples, we first need to recognize that this PIE sound became the v sound in Latin:

Latin *vivus* > OE *cwicu* (living), Modern English "quick"

Aspirated Stops Change to Unaspirated Voiced Stops

In the third set of changes in Grimm's Law, aspirated voiced stops in PIE correspond to unaspirated voiced stops in Germanic.

bh > b
dh > d

gh > g
gwh > g or w

The first three sound correspondences can be illustrated by using Sanskrit, as that is the only IE language that retained these aspirated stops:

bh > b
Sanskrit *bhratar* > Modern English "brother"

This sound became the /f/ sound in Greek and Latin. Thus, the English verb "bear" corresponds to Latin *fero* and Greek *phero*. "Brother" corresponds to Latin *frater* and Greek *phrater*.

We can use Sanskrit to illustrate the other sound correspondences:

dh > d
Sanskrit *adhara* > Modern English "under"
Sanskrit *rudhira* > Modern English "red"

gh > g
PIE *wegh*
Sanskrit *vah* ("to pull")
Latin *veho* ("I pull")
OE *weg* ("road")

PIE *ghomon*
Latin *homo* ("man")
OE *guma* ("man")

gwh > g or w
Sanskrit *gharma* ("heat")
English "warm"

The Vowels of Germanic

PGmc had a system of vowels that systematically corresponded to PIE vowels and, in turn, to the vowels of the non-Germanic IE languages. Note that these are vowels in stressed positions. In some cases, different vowels in PIE seem to have merged into a single vowel in PGmc.

Short a, o, and ə became PGmc short a
PIE *maghu* ("young person") > Gothic *magus* ("boy, servant")
PIE *owis* ("sheep") > Gothic *awister* (compare the Latinate word *ovine*)
PIE *pəter* > Gothic *fadar* ("father")

Long o and a became PGmc long o

PIE *bhlo* ("bloom") > Gothic *bloma* (compare Modern English "bloom," "blossom")

PIE *matar* > OE *modor* (compare Latin *mater* and English "mother")

Long i and ei became long i

PIE *su-ino* > OE *swin* (English "swine")

PIE *steygh* ("to walk") > OE *stigan* ("to go"; compare Modern German *steigen*, "to climb up")

PGmc Grammar and Word Stress

The nouns of PGmc and the surviving old Germanic languages were grouped into classes according to the kind of root vowel of the noun and the endings that indicated grammatical case. These declensions, or groups of nouns, corresponded to the classes of nouns in other IE languages. For example, one group of nouns in the Germanic languages was called the a-declension because, in the PGmc form, the root vowel of these nouns was the long a sound. The Old English word *stan* is a good example. This declension corresponded to Latin's second declension.

Where the Germanic languages differed from the other IE languages was in the structure of the verb and in the marking of tense. As we saw in Chapter 1, PIE had a system of marking time relationships that was more a matter of aspect than of tense. This aspect system survives in various forms in Greek, Sanskrit, and the Balto-Slavic languages. In some other IE languages (Italic, Celtic, and Germanic), this system became a pure tense system.

To review: **aspect** is a way of expressing action in terms of when it began, whether it is continuing, and if and when it was or will be completed. **Tense** is a way of expressing action in relationship to the moment of speaking. A phrase such as "I run" describes an action relative to the moment of its utterance. It tells us nothing about when I began to run, how long I have been running, and whether I will continue to run. In Modern English, we need more words to express aspect: "I am running," "I have been running," "I had been running," "I was running."

The Germanic languages have a two-tense verbal system. Only the preterit and the present tense are indicated in the forms of the verbs. These verbs were of two kinds: strong verbs and weak verbs. **Strong verbs** signal the principal parts through a meaningful change in the root vowel. In Modern English, such verbs are drink, drank, drunk; write, wrote, written; drive, drove, driven; and the like. These strong verbs reflect a system of vowel changes characteristic of the IE languages, what we have already seen as ablaut. **Weak verbs** are where the preterit tense was indicated by a suffix ending in a dental stop. In Modern English, these endings are -d or -t. Weak verbs look like these: love, loved; talk, talked; walk, walked. This feature of the weak verbs is unique to the Germanic languages.

Other unique features include fixed stress on the root syllable of a word. Regardless of whether a prefix or suffix is added, in the Germanic languages the stress remains on the root syllable. "Come," "become," and "becoming" all have stress on the root syllable. In other IE languages and in PIE, word stress was variable. Take a word such as "labyrinth," borrowed from Greek. In English, the stress would fall on the first syllable. But if you turn it into an adjective, "labyrinthine," the stress comes on the third syllable. A word such as "photograph," which was coined from Greek roots, has the stress on the first syllable. But "photographer" has its stress on the second syllable. In the IE languages, stress varied. The Greek word *lógos* ("word") had its stress on the first syllable. But the Greek word *hodós* ("road"), which should look just like *lógos*, had its stress on the second syllable. In Greek, the nominative singular of the word for "night" was *nux*, but the genitive singular was *nuktós*, with the accent on the second syllable. This phenomenon came to be known as a **floating accent**.

Knowing about Germanic word stress is important for several reasons that we explore in later chapters. For now, we need to recognize that was a feature of the Germanic languages that emerged after a series of sound changes between PIE and PGmc. How do we know?

Grimm's Law codified the correspondences between consonants in the Germanic and non-Germanic IE languages, but there were apparent exceptions. In 1875, Karl Verner suggested another law that explained how some voiceless stops in PIE became voiced fricatives or stops, rather than voiceless fricatives. The sounds p, t, and k in IE should be f, th, and h in Germanic. In some cases, these IE sounds changed as follows:

p became a voiced bilabial fricative, and then a voiced stop, /b/
t became a voiced interdental fricative, and then a voiced stop, /d/
k became a voiced velar fricative, and then a voiced velar stop, /g/

In addition, Verner illustrated that in some cases, the voiceless fricative /s/ became voiced, /z/, and then the liquid, /r/.

Verner recognized that when PGmc was emerging, word stress was not fixed but variable. These exceptions to Grimm's Law (known as Verner's Law) were a result of the changes in stress as words changed their function in a sentence or had prefixes and suffixes added. Examples of Verner's Law in the Germanic languages are best illustrated by the earliest forms of those languages. In OE, the differences between the infinitive of certain verbs and their past participle bear the traces of the sound changes marked by Verner's Law:

OE *sniðan*, "to cut"; *sniden*, "has cut"
OE *cweðan*, "to speak"; *cweden*, "has spoken"

In Modern English, some remnants of the changes described by Verner's Law survive:

was, were
lost, forlorn
seethe, sodden

Historically, there are some cases of sounds in PIE changing to Germanic sounds because of Verner's Law. The PIE root *dek* meant "a lock of hair." The /k/ sound should have become an /h/ sound in Germanic. But because of variable word stress, it became a /g/. The OE word that descends from this root is *tægel*, which means "tail." The PIE root *tekno* meant "child." By Grimm's Law, the initial t should become the unvoiced th (which it did). But the medial k did not become an h; instead, it became a g. The OE word that descends from this root is *thegn* ("thane").

The last feature of the Germanic languages that we discuss is the difference between **strong and weak adjectives**. This difference should not be confused with strong and weak verbs. In the Germanic languages, there were two ways of indicating how an adjective modified a noun. You could have just the adjective and the noun. In OE, you could have phrases such as

god man, "good man"
god wif, "good woman"

If you wanted to say, "the good man," however, the ending of the adjective would be different:

Þ*a goda man*
Þ*a gode wif*

Adjectives that precede nouns, with no other markers (such as articles or demonstratives) are known as strong adjectives. Adjectives that precede nouns with other markers are weak adjectives. The modern Germanic languages also have this distinction. In German, you say, *guter Mann* ("good man"), but *der gute Mann* ("the good man").

Germanic on the Move

These have been identified as the features shared by the Germanic languages and, therefore, the features that characterized PGmc in the first centuries after the Germanic peoples emerged as a distinct group. From their first recorded appearance in Greek and Latin histories, the Germanic peoples were defined as a migratory group. To the people of the Mediterranean, the Germanic peoples seemed to be always on the move, not colonizing in the way the Greeks and Romans did but physically moving into geographical and political spaces run by others. By the fourth century CE, Germanic-speaking people were living along the western and northern coasts of the Black Sea in what is now Ukraine. This group is known as the East Germanic people, and their language is known as Gothic. Other groups moved north and west. The North Germanic people settled in Denmark and the Scandinavian peninsula. By the first centuries CE, they were marking personal objects with runes in a form of North Germanic that became Old Norse. From Old Norse emerged Danish, Swedish, Norwegian, Icelandic, and Faroese (and the now extinct Norn language of the Shetland Islands). The West Germanic people settled largely in continental Europe, in what is now Germany but also France, the Low Countries, and the British Isles after the fifth century CE. The group known as the Franks may have ultimately given their name to France, but they were a Germanic-speaking people. The Western Germanic languages split into what are called High and Low forms (this distinction is not a value judgment but a reflection of the landscape of the speakers, highlands and lowlands). High German passed through several phases (Old, Middle, and Modern). Low German separated into Dutch, Frisian, and Old English. To be precise, Modern English descends from a Western Low Germanic language (Table 2.1).

The Germanic languages can be classed geographically and linguistically. Certain sound changes happened in the PGmc period and later that distinguishes these languages.

The first of these sound changes in the Germanic languages is known as **i/j-mutation**. Certain back vowels were raised and fronted when followed in the next syllable by an i or a j. More precisely, we could say that the phonetic environment conditioned by the high front unrounded tense vowel /i/ or the palatal glide /j/ influenced the allophonic variation of the preceding back vowels, causing phonemic change.

Table 2.1 Descendants of Proto-Germanic

Proto-Germanic			
	West Germanic	*North Germanic*	*East Germanic*
Low	High	Old Norse	Gothic
Dutch	Old Saxon	Icelandic	
Frisian	Old High German	Danish	
Flemish	Middle High German	Norwegian	
Old English	Modern German	Swedish	
Middle English		Faroese	
Modern English			

This sound change happened only in the North and West Germanic languages, not in the East Germanic ones. The only surviving example of an East Germanic language is Gothic. Our written records of the Gothic language consist almost entirely of a set of biblical translations by Bishop Ulfilas in the mid-fourth century CE. Ulfilas wrote manuscripts in an alphabet derived from Greek letters, but modern editions regularize his letter forms. Here is an example of Gothic from his translation of the story of the prodigal son (Luke 15:11–12):

Manne sums aiha twans sunus. Jah qaþ sa juhiza ize du attin: "Atta, gif mis sei undrinnai mik dail aiginis." Ah disdailida im swes sein.

[A certain man had two sons. And the younger son said to his father: "Father, give to me that portion of my possessions that runs to me [i.e., falls to my lot, is mine]." And he [the father] gave to him his own.]

We can see many features of Gothic that look Germanic. Some of the vocabulary is transparent: *manne* (man), *sums* (a certain), *twans* (two), *sunus* (sons). We can see that the word for "father" is the familiar reduplicative word, *atta*, very much like "papa" or "dada." We can see that words such as *dail* and *disdailida* recall Modern English "deal." And we can work out the meaning of the word *undrinnai* as *und* + *rinnai*, "under" and "run" – thus that which runs or falls under to me.

Scholars of Gothic recognized that there are verbs and nouns that have a set of Germanic endings that were lost in the other Germanic languages. This is where the i/j-mutation comes in.

There are five categories of words in which i/j-mutation operated in the West and North Germanic languages, but not in Gothic:

1. *Plurals of certain nouns*: foot, feet; man, men; mouse, mice; louse, lice; goose, geese. In Gothic, the plural of these nouns was signaled by a suffix beginning with j. Thus the plural of *fotus* (foot) was *fotjus*.
2. *Comparatives and superlatives*: In Modern English, we have old, elder, eldest. In Old English, the comparative of the word "young," *geong*, was *gingra*. In the text of Luke quoted here, the Old English translation (made sometime in the ninth century) calls the younger son *gingra*. In the Gothic, it is *juhiza*. Thus, there is no i-mutation here. In Modern English, as we will see in later chapters, these forms were reworked by analogy, so we say "young, younger," or "old, older." In Gothic, "old, older," was *alþeis, alþiza*.
3. *Feminines of nouns*: In Modern English, the only surviving example is the female form of "fox," which is "vixen."
4. *Verbs formed from nouns*: doom, deem; whole, heal; gold, gild; moot, meet; full, fill. For some of these examples, we need to use the Old English forms to see the vowel mutations more clearly. Thus, the word "whole" was *hal* in OE. The verb "heal" was *hælan*. In Gothic, "doom, deem," were *dom, domjan*. "Full, fill," were *full, fulljan*.

5. *Nouns formed from adjectives*: long, length; strong, strength; foul, filth; hale, health. In Gothic, "foul, filth" were *fuls, fuliþ*.

What can we do with our knowledge of i/j-mutation? First, we can recognize that this change must have happened after Gothic split off from the common group of PGmc languages. Gothic maintains sounds that existed in PGmc, and the North and the West Germanic languages underwent sound changes of their own. Therefore, we can assume that this sound change happened sometime after the fourth century CE.

Second, we can date the appearance of some loan words in the Germanic languages based on how they went through i/j-mutation. The Germanic people had been in contact with the Latin-speaking Romans for centuries. Roman historian Tacitus describes their culture and society in his work *Germania* (written in the first century CE). Germanic-speaking people were increasingly part of Roman society during the centuries of imperial rule in Europe, long before the Germanic groups of Vandals and Goths participated in the conquest of Rome in the 400s. Many words for luxury goods, foods, domestic life, building skills, and early Christian concepts were borrowed from Latin into the Germanic languages. We know this because all surviving Germanic languages have these words.

i/j-mutation helps us date the borrowing of these words. Here are some examples. Latin *moniterium* meant a place where money (*moneta*) was made. The word had to be borrowed in the older period of the Germanic languages before i-mutation happened. The -i in the syllable after the -o affected that o in the same way the i or j affected the preceding vowel in the North and West Germanic languages. By i-mutation, then, this word became what is recognizably our word "mint." The word for "money" was borrowed later, after the i-mutation had run its course. Similarly, the Latin word *monasterium* became the word "minster." The word was borrowed again later to give us "monastery." The Latin word *unicium* ("one twelfth") became "inch." The Greek word *kuriakos* was borrowed in the Germanic languages and became OE *cirice*, German *Kirke*, and Danish *Kierke*. Our Modern English spelling "church" is not etymological; rather, it is a later spelling convention to represent this mutated sound.

This information tells us that i/j-mutation happened only once in history. It was a sound change that completed its course at a certain time. When we see Modern English words borrowed from Latin, we often look at words that were borrowed and reborrowed at different times. "Monastery" and "minster" come from the same word but represent acts of reborrowing. So, too, for "money" and "mint." By contrast, several words that underwent i/j-mutation in the Germanic period were reformed or changed by analogy later. Thus, we do not say "house, hice," but "house, houses." We do not say "book, beech," but "book, books." In Old English, however, you really did say *boc, bec*.

The Second or High German Sound Shift

A later sound change affected the High German languages., the set of languages spoken in the highlands of continental Europe. The Low German languages were spoken by people who had migrated to the coastline, or lowland areas, of Europe. We can date the High German sound shift to sometime between the sixth and the eighth centuries. This shift can be codified as follows:

PGmc	p	t	k	d
High German (after vowels)	ff	tz	ch	t
High German (elsewhere)	pf	z	—	t

This sound shift explains phonetic relationships between English and Modern German, and it is useful to know for recognizing Germanic cognates in both languages.

pan	Pfanne
grip	Griffe
to	zu
foot	Fuss
make	machen
reckon	rechnen
alike	gleich
token	Zeichen
time	Zeit
bite	beissen
heart	Herz
ship	Schiff

Germanic Poetics

Germanic literature took many forms. There were epics about heroes, histories of migrants, stories of battle, tales of gods, spells, and charms. Among the earliest mentions of the Germanic peoples are their social rituals for literary and religious performance. Tacitus remarked on their heroic battle songs, their praise of certain gods, and their divination practices. Among the earliest surviving works of literature in the Germanic languages are heroic tales set during the time of the continental migrations. Stories of kings such as Ermanaric the Goth (died 376) and invaders such as Attila the Hun (died 453) place this material as early as the fourth century (although no sustained texts survive before the ninth). Having inherited a concept of prophetic verse from IE, the Germanic languages developed a notion of poetry as something inspired, mad, and magical. The IE root *wet, as we saw in Chapter 1, descended into a variety of languages: in Latin *vates* and in Old Irish *faith*. In the Germanic languages, this root can be found in the name of the god Odin (or Woden). He is the master of what in Old Norse would have been *oðr*, a word meaning mind, spirit, or poetic craft. Odin supposedly invented runes and gave one of his eyes for wisdom. In OE, the comparable word would have been *woð* or *wod*. To be *wod* was to be mad. To be a *woðbora* was to be a bearer of wisdom and experience.

This cultural emphasis on wisdom and inspired poetic prowess led to several developments in the literatures of the Germanic languages. All developed what could be called a **gnomic literature**: that is, a literature of folk wisdom, parables, and advisory maxims. Often these kinds of poems take on the form of a father–son dialogue. They rhetorically rely on imperatives, that is, how things ought to be or should be. The content of such wisdom literature centered on the importance of speech used wisely, the value of traditional learning, the need to conform to the order of things, and the need to have one's self-control mirror the order of the outside world.

Some examples from surviving Germanic literatures can help us see the maximal strain in this verse. In the Old English *Beowulf* (whose single surviving manuscript dates from about the year 1000), the hero of the poem defeats the monsters and says farewell to King Hrothgar. He invites the king's son to visit him, and he caps off his invitation with the statement:

> feorcyþðe beod
> Selran gesohte þam þe him self deah.

> *(Beowulf,* lines 1838–9)

[Far countries are well sought by him who is himself strong – i.e., a man who is good already will be improved by foreign travel.]

In the Old Norse epic *Hávamál* (probably from the ninth century, but surviving in a manuscript from the thirteenth), we find a more developed sense of this sentiment:

> Vitz er þörf, þeim er víða ratar,
>   dælt er heima hvat;
> at augabragði verðr sa er ekki kann
>   ok með notrom sitr.

> (Crawford 2019, p. 5)

[A man who travels widely needs brains, everything is easy at home. A man who knows nothing and goes to sit with the wise will become a laughing stock.]

The point is made again in the *Hávamál:*

> Sa einn veit, er viða ratar,
>   ok hefir fjold um farið

hverio gedi styrir gumna hverr,
  sa er vitandi er vitz.

(ibid., p. 10)

[Only the man who travels widely and has made many journeys, only he knows what kind of character each man possesses – if he himself is a man of good sense.]

These moments reflect a social world of travel and hospitality. What they reflect, as well, is a world of social judgment. Praise and blame are central to many literary traditions, but they take on a special force in the Germanic literatures. The literary form known as the **flyting** is a drama of insult. Characters fight with each other through words, and words become weapons, often full of accusations of sexual deviance, mindless behavior, and drunkenness. The dramatic setting of the flyting is either inside the hall, at drinking parties or political counsels; or outside, meeting by chance or design on a field of battle or a road. There is a repertory of insults: appearance, acts of cowardice, heroic failure, irresponsible behavior, failings of honor, alimentary taboos (e.g., eating corpses, drinking urine), sexual irregularities (promiscuity, castration, bestiality, etc.). Beowulf's argument with the upstart courtier Unferþ is a classic example of a flyting, as they challenge each other's boasts. Unferþ taunts Beowulf with stories of his youthful exploits, but Beowulf shoots back, calling him *beore drunken* ("drunk on beer," *Beowulf*, 531), and asserting that the monster Grendel would never have ravaged the Danish hall had Unferþ been as brave as he claimed.

In Old Norse, this technique was developed to a very high order, as gods and men curse each other back and forth. "Drunk you are, Loki, out of your mind [*orviti*]; why do you not cease? For overdrinking causes every man to be reckless with his tongue" (Heimdall's curse to Loki in *Lokasenna*, 47). In the Old Norse poem *Harbarðslioð*, Thor and an old ferryman (Odin in disguise), trade insults with a vigor worthy of a modern rap battle. Harbarð accuses Thor of being so afraid in one of his adventures that he wouldn't even fart or sneeze (*hnjose ne fisa*), to which Thor calls Harbarð *ragi* (cowardly, even womanish) (see Clover 1980).

At the heart of the poetics of the Germanic languages was the structural feature of **alliterative metrics**. In many poetic traditions, the poetic line (or metrical unit) is determined by the number of syllables, the relationship of stressed to unstressed syllables, and (occasionally) rhyme and repetition. In the Germanic languages, the structure of the metrical unit was keyed to the repetition of initial consonants or vowels of words in stressed positions. As we will see in Chapter 3 on Old English, this alliterative poetics shaped a poetry that was most likely oral in composition and performative in how it spread. Of course, all our evidence for old Germanic poetry is textual, but it is clear that these surviving texts record and reflect traditions of social performance. Old English and Old Norse verse speak of recitations at social gatherings and feasts, accompaniment by the harp or lyre, and the privileged position of the performing poet in the community.

This figure was known in Old English as the *scop*. In Old Norse, he was known as the *skald*. *Scop* comes from a PGmc (and ultimately PIE root) word meaning to shape or create. The *scop* was the shaper of words. The Old Norse *skald* etymologically comes from root words meaning to speak aloud, to judge verbally, or to shout. Our Modern English word "scold" comes from the same root.

Scops and *skalds* developed a highly complex system of alliterative metrics, with repeated sounds giving the poetic line and the poetic passage a level of power and coherence. Often, such metrical patterning worked with a personal narrative voice, an "I" that spoke of exile or in elegy. The OE poem known as "The Seafarer" opens brilliantly with these patterns and motifs:

Mæg ic be me sylfum soðgied wrecan,
Siþas secgan, hu ic geswincdagum
Earfoðwhile oft prowade,
Bitre breostceare gebiden hæbbe,
Gecunnad in ceole cearselda fela,
Atol yþa gewealc.

[Permit me by myself to deliver my true song,
To speak of journeys, how I often suffered
Days of affliction, a time of hardship,
Abided bitter breast cares,
Experienced at the keel many seats of care
The terrible tossing of the waves.]

The alliterative repetitions ring here: the opening s-alliterations in the first two lines, the b- stops of line four, the hard /k/ sounds of line five. The seafaring traveler of this poem is kin to the many Germanic travelers of the advisory maxims we saw earlier, and the alliterative structure of this poem may recall the advice of the Old Norse poem *Hávamal* (literally, the sayings of the High One):

Vitz er þörf þeim er víða ratar
[Wits he needs who would travel widely.]

What is also striking about Germanic verse is its highly metaphorical language. In the passages quoted here, we can see how the Germanic languages build new words by compounding smaller ones. In the opening lines of "The Seafarer," *breostceare* may literally be translated as breast + care, but it connotes something deeper: a sorrow deep in the heart. The word *cearselda* may be made up of the words for "care" and "seat" or "place," but it goes beyond that physical condition to evoke an ongoing experience, or situation, or pain. The word *ceole*, "keel," is an example of metonymy: the use of a part for a whole. We can still say keel or sail when we mean ship (just as we may say wheels for a car or wings for an airplane).

Germanic poetry developed these metaphors into a complex system of what were called **kennings**. Kennings are noun metaphors (the root of the word is *ken*, knowledge). Each kenning is a kind of puzzle in miniature. "The road of the whale" is a kenning for the sea. "The cauldron of tears" is a kenning for the eye. Kennings became such a highly developed system of figurative language that in the twelfth century, Icelandic scholar Snorri Sturlusson wrote a whole book about them, an Old Norse *ars poetica*, known as the *Skáldskaparamal* (literally, "talk about skald making"). Here is a good example of his poetry, from the final section of that work, known as the *Háttatal* ("talk about meters"):

Drífr handar hlekker
þar er hilmir drekkr.
Mjök er brögnum bekkr
Blíþskálar þekkr.

(Faulkes 2007, p. 35)

[The link of the hand snows
where the king drinks.
The bench of the blithe bowl
is comfortable for men.]

The subject of the first sentence is *handar hlekkr*, "link of the hand." This is a kenning for "gold": that is, gold is worn in links on the hand in the form of rings or bracelets. The verb *drífr* means "to snow in drifts" (the word is cognate with "drift"). *Hilmir* is a poetic word for "king," and *drekkr* means "drink." So the first sentence means: "Where the king drinks, it snows gold": or more to the point, wherever a king is happy or well taken care of, then he will be generous. The subject of the second sentence is *bekkr*, "bench," followed by the genitive compound *blíþskálar*. *Blíþ* is obviously our word "blithe." The word *skál* means "bowl," but it is cognate with our word "scale" – that is, a scale consisted of two bowls, or containers, for weighing. But it also survives in the injunction "Skoal!," a toast raised when the drinking bowls were raised. The verb is the verb "to be," *er* (is), and the predicate phrase is *mjök þekkr brögnum:* "very comfortable for men." *Mjök* is cognate with "much"; *þekkr* is cognate with "thank," and thus thankful, worthy of thanks, hence comfortable; *brögnum* is the dative plural of *bragnar*, a poetic word for "heroes" or "men."

Old English and Old Norse are just two of the languages in which the earliest Germanic literature appears. On the European continent, there were heroic poems in Old High German, biblical epics in Old Saxon, and scriptural translations in Gothic. The Old High German *Hildebrandslied* (surviving in a manuscript from the early ninth century) begins with a powerful first-person, alliterative voice:

Ik gehorta ðat seggen
Ðat sih urhettun ænon muotin
Hiltibrant enti Haðubrant untar heitun tuem
Sunufatarungo iro saro rihtun
Garutun se iro guðhamun gurtun sih iro suert ana
Helidos ubar hringa do sie to dero hiltiu ritun.

(Klaeber 2008, p. 339)

[I heard it said
That warriors met in single combat
Hildebrant and Hadubrant among two armies
Son and father prepared their armor
Readied their battle gear, girded on their swords
The warriors, over the ring mail when they rode into battle.]

This is an ancient story, a battle with father and son, set during the dynastic conflicts of the Germanic fifth century. The tensions of that time generated the great literary legends for a millennium of Germanic poetry: *Beowulf*, the Old Norse Eddic poems, the Middle High German *Niebelungenlied*, and many others all look back to this formative period of heroes and kings.

Germanic groups who settled in the British Isles in the fifth and sixth centuries, after the end of Roman hegemony, brought these literary traditions. with them. The earliest surviving Old English poetry – Cædmon's Hymn, from the late seventh century – bears the inheritance of shared Germanic technique: alliterative verse, complex noun metaphors, and a tradition of oral, public performance. Old English may be described as a Low West Germanic language. But it may also be described as the inheritor of a way of imagining the world and the history of its speakers.

Sources and Further Reading

Aarsleff, H. (1967). *The Study of Language in England, 1780–1860*. Princeton, NJ: Princeton University Press.

Alter, S. G. (2003). *Darwinism and the Linguistic Image*. Baltimore, MD: Johns Hopkins University Press.

Bammesberger, A. (1992). "The Place of English in Germanic and Indo-European." In *CHEL*, vol. 1. Cambridge: Cambridge University Press, pp. 26–66.

Clover, C. (1980). "The Germanic Context of the Unferth Episode." *Speculum* 55: 444–68.

Crawford, J. (2019). *The Wanderer's Havamal*. Indianapolis, IN: Hackett.

Dronke, U. (1969). *The Poetic Edda*, vol. 1: *Heroic Poems*. Oxford: Oxford University Press.

Faulkes, A. (2007). *Snorri Surlusson, Edda: Háttatal*. 2nd edn. London: Viking Society for Northern Research.

Frank, R. (1978). *Old Norse Court Poetry*. Ithaca, NY: Cornell University Press.

Gordon, E. V. (1957). *An Introduction to Old Norse*. 2nd edn., rev. A. R. Taylor. Oxford: Clarendon Press.

Gordon, I. L. (1969). *The Seafarer*. London: Methuen.

Grimm, J. K. L. (1984). *On the Origin of Language*. Trans. Raymond A. Wiley. Leiden: Brill.

Hoad, T. (2006). "Preliminaries: Before English." In Lynda Mugglestone (Ed.), *The Oxford History of English*. Oxford: Oxford University Press, pp. 7–31.

Klaeber, F. (2008). *Beowulf*. 4th edn, (Eds.) R. D. Fulk, Robert E. Bjork, and John D. Niles. Toronto: University of Toronto Press.

Lieberman, A. (1998). "Germanic and Scandinavian Poetry." *Scandinavian Studies* 70: 87–108.

Page, R. I. (1977). *An Introduction to English Runes*. London: Methuen.

Page, R. I. (1987). *Runes*. Berkeley, CA: University of California Press.

Pedersen, H. (1962). *The Discovery of Language: Linguistic Science in the Nineteenth Century*. Trans. John W. Spargo. Bloomington, IN: Indiana University Press.

Prokosch, E. (1939). *A Comparative Germanic Grammar*. Philadelphia, PA: Linguistic Society of America.

Robinson, O. (1992). *Old English and Its Closest Relatives: A Survey of the Earliest Germanic Languages*. Stanford, CA: Stanford University Press.

Verner, K. (1877). "Eine Ausnahme der ersten Lautverschiebung." *Zeitschrift für vergleichende Sprachforschung* 23: 97–130.

Wright, J. (1892). *A Primer of the Gothic Language*. Oxford: Clarendon Press.

Zipes, J. (1988). *The Brothers Grimm: From Enchanted Forests to the Modern World*. New York: Routledge.

3   The Old English Period

Old English (OE) describes the Germanic vernacular spoken and written in the British Isles from roughly the middle of the fifth century until the early twelfth century. OE shared features of grammar, sounds, and vocabulary with other early Germanic languages and many modern ones. It was highly inflected, using word endings to determine the relationships among words in a sentence. Nouns had grammatical gender (masculine, feminine, and neuter); they belonged to certain groups or classes (depending on their sound histories of their roots); they were declined in a variety of cases, depending on their grammatical function; and there had to be agreement with adjectives that modified them (that is, similar endings depending on the number, case, and gender of the noun). Verbs were conjugated according to tense and number; verbs were also grouped into classes depending on their sounds and sound histories; and certain verbs formed their tenses by changing the root vowel (strong verbs, such as drink, drank, drunk) and others formed their tenses by adding a suffix (weak verbs, such as live, lived). OE had a distinctive sound (one that has been reconstructed, with reasonable accuracy, by scholars over the past three hundred years) and a distinctive way of forming letters in writing (adapting old runic letters for sounds not found in the Latin alphabet). It was the medium of prayer, scholarship, history, poetry, and philosophy for more than four hundred years.

This chapter illustrates the distinctive features of OE and gives students basic reading knowledge of the language so that they may understand its place in English linguistic history and the literary imagination. We will also see how studying OE gives us access to a political and social world, to myth and religion, and to creativity and culture. OE was not a single, static language, however. Over the seven centuries of its use, it changed: new words came in from Latin and Scandinavian languages; word endings appear to have been leveled out or even lost; patterns of word order and particulars of literary style evolved. In addition, OE varied in sound and sense across the British Isles. Scholars have identified four major regional dialects by examining the spelling of words in surviving manuscripts. Old English was the language of kings and agricultural workers, poets

DOI: 10.4324/9781003227083-4

and monks. It was a vernacular marked by nuance and variety, depending on the who, when, and where of its use.

The evidence we have for OE lies wholly in surviving written documents. The scribes of the pre-Conquest period, however, had been largely trained in writing Latin, and OE had sounds that did not appear in the Latin language. Thus, scribes had to develop certain spelling conventions for OE sounds, and one of the ways they did that was to adapt the old runic letters for some of these sounds.

- Æ, æ: The so-called æsch, representing a short, unrounded, mid-vowel.
- Ð, ð: The edth, representing an interdental continuant, now written as *th*. (Note: in the international phonetic alphabet, this symbol is used for the voiced interdental; it was not used in this way in OE manuscripts.)
- Þ, þ: The thorn, representing an interdental continuant, now written as *th*. (Note: this letter and the edth were used almost interchangeably in OE manuscripts.)
- There was also a letter adapted from the runic *wynn* symbol, ᚹ, and representing the glide, now written as w. Almost all modern editions of OE texts replace this letter with a w.

Long before there was writing, there was speech and song, poetry and prayer. A famous poem known today as Cædmon's Hymn was purportedly composed in the late seventh century. We know about it because the scholar and churchman, the Venerable Bede, told the story of its composition in his *History of the English Church and People* (completed in 731). Bede wrote in Latin, and he gave a version of Cædmon's Hymn in Latin prose. The earliest surviving OE text of the poem is written in the Northumbrian dialect and is datable to the mid-eighth century. *Beowulf*, perhaps the best-known piece of OE literature, may have been circulating as oral tales for hundreds of years before it was written down around 1000. At the very end of the ninth century, King Alfred inaugurated a program of translation and textual production designed to bring his literate subjects into the knowledge of the worlds of classical philosophy and history and Christian scriptures.

This is all to say that OE survives in a written form and in a set of institutional contexts that were designed for Latin learning, religious devotion, and political rule. There are no personal letters in OE. There are no diaries or journals. Much of the poetry of the period – from *Beowulf* through biblical epics on Daniel, Genesis, and Exodus, to lives of the saints – is so concerned with mythic and religious material that it does not necessarily give an accurate contemporary portrait of life in the British Isles.

Throughout this book, I avoid the phrase "Anglo-Saxon." It is a term that has long been used to describe the society and the language of pre-Conquest England. In the twentieth and twenty-first centuries, however, the term has been appropriated by political movements and people who wish to privilege an imagined white, northern European racial identity. It has become so marked by this usage that professional scholars have vigorously debated changing the name of the field. For the purposes of this book, I consistently refer to the Germanic vernacular of the British Isles as OE and to the historical period as pre-Conquest England.

The Old English Vocabulary

Broadly speaking, the OE words that survive in Modern English are short, often monosyllabic terms for basic natural and human features. Such nouns include parts of the body, basic minerals and elements, features of the landscape, and core principles of belief. The verbs include basic activities of everyday life. Adjectives, adverbs, pronouns, and articles also survive, but with different meanings and different spellings.

The core vocabulary of the English language remains old and Germanic. About 80 percent of the most commonly used words today are descended from OE. When we approach an OE text, we should not be put off by the apparently alien look of the language. For example, here are the opening lines of *Beowulf:*

> Hwæt we gar-dena in geardagum
> Þeodcyninga þrym gefrunon
> Hu ða æþelingas ellen fremedon
> [Hey, we of the Spear-Danes, in days of yore,
> Of those kings of a people, have heard of their power,
> How those nobles performed great deeds.]

Many of the words here can be shown to be ultimately transparent to Modern English speakers:

Hwæt:	Modern English "what," here used as an interjection, a call for people to listen.
We:	Modern English "we," the first-person plural.
In:	Modern English "in," the preposition.
Geardagum:	*Gear* means past times; it becomes the word "yore" in Modern English.
Dagum:	Modern English "day." *In geardagum* is in the dative case, a grammatical form signaled by the preposition "in."
Þeodcyninga:	*Þeod* is a word that has dropped out of modern usage. It means "people."
Cyninga:	Modern English "kings."
Þrym:	Another word that has disappeared; "multitude" or "great power."

Gefrunon:	the verb means "to ask about" or "to hear about." It is related to the OE verb *frinan*, which is cognate with modern German *Fragen* (question).
Hu:	Modern English "how."
Đa:	Modern English "those."
Æþelingas:	OE word for members of a ruling aristocracy, specifically the sons of a king or nobleman.
Ellen:	a noun meaning "valor" or "deeds of strength."
Fremedon:	a verb meaning "made," "did," or "performed."

This exercise with *Beowulf* shows how a basic vocabulary of English remains after over a thousand years. It also shows that those words that have dropped out of the language were words for particular social or political groups and for people of prestige. All of what we might call the high value words – for power, for members of the ruling class, for ethical ideals and values – were ultimately replaced with words of French and Latin origin after the Norman Conquest. As we shall soon see, our words for valor, nobility, a people, and power came in with the Normans (or soon after). They are from a Romance-language vocabulary. In these, as in many cases, the words for institutions and individuals of power come from the language of those who control those institutions or wield that power.

OE was not simply a language of monosyllables. Like the other Germanic languages, ancient and modern, OE (or more precisely, the linguistic culture of OE speakers) resisted borrowing words from other languages and, instead, coined words for concepts and beliefs, new things and new ideas, from the existing lexicon. Broadly speaking, there were four ways that OE built new words out of existing ones:

1. *Determinative compounding*: noun + noun. *meadheall*, "mead hall"; *dægeseag*, "day's eye," thus, daisy; *hwælrad*, "road of the whale," thus, the sea; *banlocan*, "bone-locker," hence, the body. Sometimes, new words could be made of two nouns with similar meanings: *holtwudu*, "woods woods," hence, a forest.
2. *Modification compounding*: adjective or adverb + noun, or a noun + participle. Sometimes these compounds produced new nouns: *idelhende*, "empty-handed"; *eftcyme*, literally "after coming," thus, return; *ofermod*, literally "over or great mood," thus pride. Sometimes they produced new adjectives: *isceald*, "ice cold"; *lindhæbbende*, "shield bearing."
3. *Prefix formations*: determinative prefix + noun. Some familiar prefixes that changed the meaning and use of words to make new words include:

    a. *Be:* around; also connoting an action with another word. *Betimber*, to make out of timber, thus "to build"; *betynan*, "to make enclosed"; *begretan*, "to lament over."

    b. *Ge:* with or in shared activity; *gefrinan*, "to ask about"; *gewreon*, "to clothe or cover up."

    c. *For:* totally or completely; *forberstan*, "to completely blow up"; *formyltan*, "to completely melt away."

    d. *Un:* the negative prefix; *unhalig*, "unholy"; *unbrad*, "unbroad," that is narrow; *unsceamfulness*, "unshamefulness," that is, immodesty.

    e. *Wiþ:* against; *wiþstand*, "to stand against," and hence withstand; *wiþcwedan*, "to speak against," thus contradict.

4. *Verbal formations:* noun + verb to make a new verb. *Rodfæstnian*, literally "to make fast to the rood (i.e., cross)," thus crucify.

By reading OE verse and prose, we can see how the resources of the language could be used to create vivid verbal expressions of moral conditions. Such texts may be difficult for us to crack, but if we think of them as puzzles to be solved, we can read them with fluency and appreciation.

    For example, consider the *Sermo Lupi ad Anglos*, the Sermon of the Wolf (i.e., Wulfstan) to the English, delivered by Bishop Wulfstan in 1014. The speech survives in several manuscripts, with some variations, but even on the page we can almost hear the bishop lamenting the decline of society, the terrors of everyday criminality, and the fears of the retribution to come.

> Hēr syndan þurh synlēawa, swā hit þincan mæg, sāre ġelēwede tō maneġe on earde. Hēr syndan mannslagan and mæġslagan and mæsserbanan and mynsterhatan:and hēr syndan mānsworan and morþorwyrhtan; and hēr syndan myltestran and bearnmyðran and fūle forleġene hōringas maneġe; and hēr syndan wiċċan and wælcyrian; and hēr syndan rȳperas and rēaferas and woroldstrūderas and, hrædest is tō cweþenne, māna and misdǣda unġerīm ealra.
>
> (Whitelock 1967, p. 91)

[Here are through the injury of sin, as it may seem, too many sorely wounded in the country. Here are man slayers and kinsman slayers and priest slayers and persecutors of monasteries, and here are perjurers and murderers, and here are harlots and child killers and foul lying whorers, and here are witches and valkyries, and here are plunderers and robbers and despoilers, and to speak most quickly, a countless number of all crimes and misdeeds.]

This is an essay in the art of making words in Old English. Wulfstan takes a noun and adds it to a verb, over and over, as if he is pounding together the different parts of language, making them stick. He uses words for very specific, ecclesiastical crimes (some of these he may have coined): *mynsterhatan*, the persecution of monasteries. He then juxtaposes them with old words for base desire (*horingas*, harlots, whores). There are witches here (*wiccan*), but there are also choosers of the dead, *wælcyrian*, a word cognate with the Old Norse *valkyrie* (in Old Norse, the *val* were the honored dead; Valhalla was the hall of the honored dead). Wulfstan takes a prefix and gives it power. There are deeds and there are misdeeds (*misdæda*). All of this (his last word here is transparent, *ealra*, "all") makes up so many sins and terrors that they are uncountable. OE *rim* meant "a number of things." *Gerim* meant "computation of numbers." *Ungerim* meant "an uncountable number."

Three and a half centuries before Wulfstan, the poet Cædmon came to express what was then a new, Christian set of beliefs in an idiom drawn from an older tradition of Germanic verse. Bede told his story (in Latin) in *History of the English Church and People*. Sometime between 657 and 680, Cædmon, a Yorkshire cowherd, was inspired to compose verse in the English vernacular. In those times, laborers and herders would often gather in the evenings; a harp would be passed around; each would take turns singing. When the harp came to Cædmon, we are told, he declined. He could not sing; ashamed, he left the group. One evening, an angel appeared to him. "Cædmon," the angel addressed him by name, "Sing me something." Cædmon said he could not sing, but the angel said he could. When he asked what he should sing about, the angel said, "Sing to me about the creation of the world." So Cædmon raised his voice and in the dialect of his native Northumbria, sang:

> Nu scylun hergan hefaenrīcaes Uard,
> metudæs maecti end his modgidanc,
> uerc Uuldurfadur, sue he uundra gihwaes,
> eci dryctin or astelidæ
> he ærist scop aelda barnum
> heben til hrofe, haleg scepen.
> Tha middungeard moncynnæs Uard,
> eci Dryctin, æfter tiadæ
> firum foldu, Frea allmectig.

(Whitelock 1967, pp. 181–2)

> [Now we shall praise heaven-kingdom's Guardian,
> The Creator's might, and his mind thought,
> The works of the Glory-father: how he, each of his wonders,
> The eternal Lord, established at the beginning.
> He first shaped for Earth's children
> Heaven as a roof, the holy Creator.
> Then a middle-yard, mankind's Guardian,
> The eternal Lord, established afterwards,
> The Earth for the people, the Lord almighty.]

Even though Bede told his story in Latin and went out of his way to say that he was translating Cædmon's poem into Latin prose, the OE version of the hymn survives in several different versions. The one quoted here is the earliest of them, appearing as a marginal annotation, written out as continuous prose, at the bottom of the page of the Latin text of Bede's *History*. This is a written text of the late eighth century (recording a poem supposedly composed a hundred years before). There were later copies of the poem, in the dialect of the court of King Alfred at the end of the ninth century and later in the tenth and eleventh centuries. You don't need to know anything about OE dialects to recognize that this text looks different from that of Wulfstan, preserved in manuscripts from the eleventh century. We explore dialect differences later in this chapter.

We can see how the basic words of Cædmon's Hymn take Christian concepts that had been at work in England for only a century and effectively translate them into a familiar, Germanic vernacular. *Uard* (pronounced "ward") means a guardian or warden, a temporal lord of a people. *Metud* comes from the verb *metan*, to mete out. Lordship is an act of gift-giving in Germanic cultures, and the figure of God as a kind of gift-giver translates a new religious figure into an older social idiom. *Uuldurfadur* is made up of two words: *uuldur*, meaning "glory," and *fadur*, meaning "father." *Dryctin* (a word cognate with modern Scandinavian words for king and queen, *drott* and *drottnin*) is a political ruler. *Scepen* means shaper; creation is an act of shaping. *Frea* is another old Germanic word for a ruler. There are other, older Germanic resonances here. The image of God creating Heaven as a roof resonates with stories of hall building in myth and epic. *Middungeard*, the middle yard of human habitation, reminds the mythologist of the Old Norse *Midgard*, the middle space between the underworld and the upper world of the gods.

Between the time of Cædmon and Wulfstan, OE changed. Among those changes was the adoption of certain loan words from Latin and Scandinavian languages. The Catholic Church had become a major force in the lives of people in England. Schools, monasteries, churches, and cathedrals became the focal points for community life. But the OE-speaking peoples also lived, off and on for centuries, with Scandinavian-speaking groups. From the early ninth century on, Old Norse speakers raided the English coast. The second half of the ninth century saw the establishment of Danish rule over much of the northeastern British Isles. Although the Danes were effectively thrown out in the mid-tenth century, the Norse still wanted England. From 1016 to 1035, England was ruled by a Dane, Cnut, and his heirs oversaw the nation until 1066, when Edward the Confessor became king. But Edward's reign was short-lived, and in the ensuing dynastic conflict, William the Conqueror (who, although coming from Normandy, was of Scandinavian descent) succeeded.

The British Isles had long been a multilingual place with Celtic and Latin, OE and Old Norse, and soon OE and Norman French. Even though OE resisted accepting large numbers of loan words, such words did come into the language, and they came in waves. Words of Latin origin had been borrowed during the earlier, continental period of Germanic migration (the first through fifth centuries CE); new words were coming in during the so-called insular period of settlement (the fifth through eleventh centuries). The earliest words from Latin entering the Germanic languages were mostly words for foodstuffs and luxury items. During the period of Christianization, after the mid-sixth century, Latin words from the church, schooling, and philosophy entered the language. Table 3.1 separates these groups of words by period of borrowing: during the Continental period, before OE split off (before the fourth century CE); during the period of Roman colonization of Britain (when Germanic peoples were moving to the British Isles, *c.* third to fifth centuries CE); during the period after the Christianization of the British Isles (after the sixth century CE); and, finally, words from Latin that were translated as calques into OE.

Table 3.1 Some words of Latin origin in Old English

Words borrowed from Latin	Old English form
Into the German languages	
caseus	cese (cheese)
vallum	weall (wall)
caupo	ceap (goods or value)
campus	camp (a military encampment)
monasterium	mynster (a monastery)
mille	mile (a measure of distance)
piper	pipor (pepper)
vinum	win (wine)
scola	scol (school)
During the Roman colonial period in Britain	
portus	port (harbor, gate)
montus	munt (mountain)
turris	tor (tower, outcrop)
After Christianization	
credo	creda (creed)
missa	mæsse (mass)
sanctus	sanct (holy)
prestus	preost (priest)
templum	tempel (temple)
organum	organe (organ)
Latin words translated into OE	*OE calque forms*
omnipotens	eallwealdend (all ruling)
omnipotens	eallmihtig (all mighty)
proscribere	forscrifian (proscribe)
discipulus	leorningcniht (knight of learning)

In addition to borrowing directly, like many modern Germanic languages, Old English created calques: words made up of part-by-part (or morpheme by morpheme) translations of Latin or learned words. OE calques often took words from Latin learning and similarly translated them. Sometimes OE would put Latin and older Germanic words and word parts together. *Bishop* is a word borrowed from the Latin, *episcopus*. In OE, a bishop's seat in a church was the *biscopsetl*. A word like *cristendom* takes a Latin term and adds an OE suffix to it. A word like *sealmscop* takes a word ultimately from Latin (*psalm*) and appends it to a distinctively OE poetic term for a poet (*scop*, coming from the verb "to shape"). In such a compound, we can see how OE writers expressed new concepts in old ways, in essence, granting to the psalmist David the status of something like a native singer of tales.

Few words from the Celtic languages survive in OE. They tend to be words for places or particular kinds of geographical formation: Kent, Thames, Avon (the general term for a river), *cumb* (a valley), and *dun* (dark or gray).

Because the Scandinavian languages shared with OE a common Germanic heritage, it may be difficult to distinguish true loan words from cognates that were simply pronounced differently. There are many pairs of words that descend into Modern English with an OE and a Scandinavian origin. Some of these words survive in regional dialects and are characteristic of northern and northeastern British speech (where the influence of Scandinavian people had been longest):

OE / Scandinavian
shirt / skirt
from / fro
ship / skipper
church / kirk
milch / milk

Certain words that were already in OE and were cognate with Scandinavian words took on meanings from the Scandinavian languages. For example, the word *wiþ*, which, as we have seen, meant "against" in OE, came to be used increasingly as the Old Norse word *við* had been used (meaning "with"). The OE word *dream*, which meant joy, came to be used to express an imagined or fancied experience of that joy, often projected or felt in sleep. The Old Norse word *dream* meant precisely that, and this meaning has replaced the older, OE one in later English.

The study of the OE vocabulary thus reveals many things. It shows us how the traditional, Germanic language habits of word formation operated for centuries in the British Isles. It shows us how a newly Christianized people could translate and transform concepts into familiar forms. It shows us how languages in contact do not simply provoke borrowings but stimulate translations, compoundings, calques, and appropriations. Table 3.2 shows how words from Old English

Table 3.2 Some Old English words in Modern English

Old English word	Modern English form
	Little change in meaning
eorðe	earth
mann	man
God	God
god	good
woruld	world
word	word
heofon	heaven
fæst	fast
nu	now
tin	tin
hlaf	loaf
lord	lord
sittan	sit
beran	bear
cnawan	know
	Slight change in meaning
dom (judgment)	doom
bread (bit)	bread
sellan (give)	sell
sweltan (die)	swelter
uncuð (unknown)	uncouth
sceppan (create)	shape
sælic (odd, wondrous, holy)	silly
wiþ	with
smæl (thin, tender)	small

are often short words for everyday things, parts of the body, basic objects or aspects of the world, and common adjectives and adverbs.

OE Sounds

Even though there are no ways of knowing precisely how people spoke OE, scholars have been able to reconstruct the OE sound system in various ways. First, they have relied on systematic sound laws that enable us to trace the changes in the phonetic values of vowels and consonants over time. Knowing the history behind a sound (from Indo-European through Germanic) can give us a sense of its value in OE. Second, early scribes spelled pretty much as they spoke. There were few (if any) spelling conventions in OE that transcended regional dialect differences or changes over time. Unlike in Modern English, where spelling conventions have long been codified irrespective of pronunciation ("knight," "ghost," "through," and so on), earlier forms of the language reproduced sounds in letters. Thus, certain scribes may have spelled the same words differently depending on their regional pronunciation or their historical period. Third, because the Latin alphabet had been adapted to record OE, most of the sounds represented by those letters were those of Latin. The pronunciation of Latin, especially ecclesiastical and school Latin, has been remarkably stable over time. Thus, if we know how a letter represented a sound in Latin, we can reasonably assume that it represented that sound in OE.

In OE texts there are no so-called silent letters. Every letter represents a sound. There were also some distinctive sounds in OE, unlike any other Germanic language or any other form of English. The most obvious of these sounds are consonant clusters. Such clusters may be linguistically described as having an aspirant before a liquid or a glide. Thus, the clusters hr-, hl-, and hw- were the initial sounds in such words as:

hring:	Modern English "ring"
hlaf:	Modern English "loaf"
hlahian:	Modern English "laugh"
hwæt:	Modern English "what"
hwile:	Modern English "while"

The glide represented by the letter w could be followed by an r or an l in the beginning of a word:

wlitan:	"to look"
writhan:	"to writhe"
wrixlan:	"to turn"

The digraph -gh- and, occasionally, the -h-, appearing in the middle or the end of a word would have been pronounced as a velar fricative/x/. Thus:

Þurgh
cniht
burgh

The sound of a consonant could vary depending on where it appeared in the word. The fricatives represented by the letters f, thorn, and s, would have been unvoiced at the end of a word and voiced in the middle of a word. Thus:

stæf / stafas
smiþ / smiþas
hus / husian

The word *ofer* would have been pronounced as if it were "over." The word *feþer* would have had a voiced -th- sound.

The sounds represented by the letter -g- could also vary depending on their place in the word. Thus, the word for day, *dæg*, would have been pronounced /*dæj*/. But in the nominative plural, *dagas*, it would have been pronounced as a velar stop: /daɣas/. In the prefix ge-, the letter would have been pronounced as a glide, /j/. As the first letter before a back vowel, it would have been the palatal stop /g/, as in the word *gar* ("spear"). But before a front vowel or diphthong, it would have been a glide, as in the words *giedd* ("song") and *gear* ("year").

The OE vowel system varied according to regional dialect, but for modern students who read literature largely written in the West Saxon dialect, the vowels may be described as follows. Long vowels in stressed syllabus (a, e, i, o, u) largely would have been pronounced as they are in modern European languages. OE also had distinctive diphthongs:

beon
deor
deaþ
neah
seofon

In OE, vowel length was phonemic. The quantitative length of the vowel mattered. This feature of the language no longer exists in Modern English. There is no meaningful difference between saying "good" and "gooooood," stretching out the time it takes to speak the vowel sound. But in OE, two words could mean different things depending on the length of time you took to speak the vowel.

God: short o, "God"
god: long o, "good"
sunne: short u, "sun"
sunu: long u, "son"
stellan: short e, "place"
stelan: long g, "steal"

OE Grammar and Morphology

The Verb

There were two major kinds of verbs in OE (we will explore others shortly): strong and weak. Strong verbs signaled tenses with a meaningful change in the root vowel. Weak verbs signaled the difference between present and preterit by adding a dental suffix.

Strong verb classes are marked by the series of changes in the principal parts of the verb. These are: infinitive, preterit third-person singular, preterit plural, and past participle. When scholars describe a class of strong verbs, they list a sequence of four vowels. In Class I of strong verbs, the OE vowels of the principal parts are long i, long a, short i, and short i (it is conventional to write a line over the vowel to indicate quantitative length in OE words):

bītan, bāt, biton, biten
rīsan, rās, rison, risen
wrītan, wrāt, writon, writen

In Modern English, the full distinctions of principal parts tend not to be preserved. Thus, the modern forms of these verbs would be:

bite, bit, bit, bitten
rise, rose, rose, risen
write, wrote, written, written

There are seven classes of strong verbs in OE. It is important to know these classes if you wish to translate a piece of OE writing. If you find a word such as *druncen*, you will recognize that it is the past participial form of a verb. You will see that the vowel -u- in the verb stem corresponds to the vowel -i- in the infinitive. Thus, you can go to a dictionary and look up the verb *drincan* and find that it means "to drink."

Knowing about strong verbs is important for understanding the history of verbs and verb formation in Modern English. If you see a verb that has different forms according to a regular change in the root vowel, you know it comes from OE. There are no new strong verbs in English. Whenever a new word comes into the language, or whenever a word came into the language in the post-OE period, it came in as a weak verb.

Table 3.3 lists the strong verbs in order, classes I through VII, with the four principal parts: infinitive, preterit singular, preterit plural, and past participle. Each class had many words. The words presented here are representative of the verbs in a class. All have Modern English equivalents, and you can compare these forms to their modern descendants.

Note that certain strong verbs have become weak verbs over time. Thus the verb "help" (which remains a strong verb through the time of Chaucer) has

Table 3.3 OE strong verb classes

Class	Infinitive	Preterit singular	Preterit plural	Past participle	Modern English word
I	rīsan	rās	rison	gerisen	rise
II	dūfan	dēaf	dufon	gedofen	dive
III	helpan	healp	hulpon	geholpen	help
IV	beran	bær	bǣron	geboren	bear
V	wrecan	wrǣc	wrǣcon	gewrecen	wreck, avenge, as in "wreak havoc"
VI	standan	stōd	stōdon	gestanden	stand
VIII	cnāwan	cnēow	cnēowon	gecnāwen	know

become a weak verb: help, helped. The idiom "wreak havoc" comes from this OE verb (not from the verb *wreck*, meaning "destroy"). It, too, has become a weak verb ("wreaked havoc").

Weak verbs form their past tense by adding a dental suffix (usually *-ed*). Their infinitive forms usually end in *-ian*. Weak verbs were often formed from other words, and the relationship between the source and the verb was often shaped by sound changes in the earlier Germanic period, such as i/j-mutation. Thus, OE *dom*, meaning "judgment," took on a verbal form that eventually became *deman*, to judge). The adjective *cuð*, meaning "known," took on a verbal form that eventually became *cyðan*, "to make known." The adjective *hal*, "whole," eventually took on a verbal form, *hælan*, "to heal." Some verbs were transformed into different verbs. The verb *sittan* ("to sit"), a strong verb, could be the source of a new, weak verb, *settan*, "to set down." The verb *drincan* ("to drink"), which was a strong verb, could be the source of a new, weak verb, *drencan*, "to drench."

As in Modern English, a verb in OE had to give four pieces of information:

- the person of the verb's subject: first, second, and third;
- the number of subjects for the verb: singular or plural;
- the tense of the verb: in OE, the tenses were present and preterit (as in all the Germanic languages, there was no conjugated future tense; expressions of futurity were expressed with modal verbs such as "shall" or "will");
- the mood of the verb: that is, the way a verb is used to convey a condition:

  - indicative (basic statement of fact or experience)
  - subjunctive (a statement of something that might or could be, a counterfactual)
  - imperative (a command).

We can see how this information was conveyed through suffixes appended to the verb and at times to changes in the root vowel of that verb. A good general guideline is to say that:

- verbs in the first person tend to have no vowel ending, or end in *-e*;
- verbs in the second person end in *-st*;
- verbs in the third person end in *-th* (written as ð or þ);
- infinitives of verbs end in a vowel or vowels + *n*.

There were other groups of verbs in OE. Most obvious to modern readers would have been irregular verbs such as those meaning "to be." That verb, *beon*, had two forms in the present tense:

Ic eom, Ic beo
Þu eart, þu bist
he is, he bið

In the past tense, the forms are:

Ic wæs
Þu wære
he wæs

The plural forms in the present tense would have been *sindon* and *beoð*. In the past, it was *wæron*.

Finally, there was a small group of words known as preterit-present verbs: *witan, cunnan, magan,* and a few others. These tended to be what we now call helping verbs or modal verbs.

Here is the full conjugation of the verb *singan*, "to sing" (strong verb, class III), presented so that you can see the endings at work in marking grammatical relationships.

singan "to sing"

Infinitive:	*singan*
Present participle:	*singende*
Past participle:	*sungen*

Present indicative

Singular first person:	*singe*
Singular second person:	*singest*
Singular third person:	*singeð*
Plural all persons:	*singað*

Present subjunctive

Singular all persons:	*singe*
Plural all persons:	*singen*

Imperative (second person commands)

Singular:	*sing*
Plural:	*singað*

Preterit indicative

Singular first person:	*song*
Singular second person:	*sunge*
Singular third person:	*song*
Plural all persons:	*sungon*

Preterit subjunctive

Singular all persons:	*sunge*
Plural all persons:	*sungen*

The Noun

Nouns appear in different cases, depending on how they are used in a sentence. Modern students of English will be familiar with the genitive case: the form of a noun signaling possession. Today we mark that case with a spelling of an apostrophe followed by an -s (John's book, the girl's toy, our nation's strength). In OE, the genitive was also usually marked with a final -s (but not always). The most challenging part of OE grammar is the use of the dative case. The dative case marks a noun as the indirect object of a sentence, as an object moving from one place to another, as an instrument of action, and sometimes as the direct object of certain verbs. These relationships, in Modern English, are signaled by prepositions (to, in, with, etc.). In *Beowulf*, for example, the line, "*Him se yldesta onswarode*" means "To him the eldest answered." *Se yldesta* is in the nominative case; *him* is in the dative case.

Like verbs, nouns were classified in OE according to their vowel roots, and many of these classifications (known as declensions) were specific to the grammatical gender of the noun. The vowel of the root goes back to an older Germanic vowel form. It may not appear in OE. Thus, it is important to recognize that noun classifications, unlike verb classifications, may be a bit opaque to the beginner. Although a word like *stan*, "stone," may be obviously in the a-declension, words such as *heofon*, "heaven," *scip*, "ship," and *heofod*, "head," were also a-declension nouns.

Here is the declension for the noun *stan*, "stone."

Singular

Nominative and accusative:	*stan*
Genitive:	*stanes*
Dative and instrumental:	*stane*

Plural

Nominative and accusative:	*stanas*
Genitive:	*stana*
Dative and instrumental:	*stanum*

Other classes of nouns were the o-declension, the i-declension, and the n-declension. There were other declensions, represented by fewer nouns (these are called minor declensions).

There was also a group of nouns that signaled their grammatical categories through a change in the root vowel. These changes go back to i-mutation in the Germanic period. Nouns like the following descend into English with their vowel changes intact (this is a list of nominative singular and plural forms; in OE, the mutated form would have also occurred in the genitive and dative/instrumental singular).

mann / menn
fot / fet
toþ / teþ
gos / ges
lus / lys
mus / mys

In a few cases, nouns that changed their vowel through historical i-mutation have been reformed into regular-looking nouns. In OE, the plural of the word *boc*, "book," was *bec*. The plural of the word *burgh* (a town) was *byrig*.

OE Pronouns, Adjectives, and Adverbs

Like Modern English, Old English had singular and plural forms of pronouns. But it also had what is known as a dual form. This form descends from an older Germanic (and ultimately IE) form connoting action among two people. Thus, a phrase in Modern English such as "we two went out," would take the dual form (*wit*). If we wanted to talk about "the two of us," we would say (depending on the case of the pronoun) *uncer*, *unc*, or *uncit*. If we wanted to address two people ("you two over there"), we would say *git*, *incer*, *inc*, or *incit* (depending on the case).

As in all earlier forms of English and the Germanic languages, there were two forms of the second person (in addition to the dual): þu-forms, which were singular, and ge-/eo-forms (the origin of our modern "you"), which were plural. Although the masculine, feminine, and neuter were clearly signaled, they were not done so through forms completely recognizable today. The third person in all genders and cases was a word that began with an *h-*. Words that begin with th- (they, them, their) entered English in the later Middle English period and were adaptations of northern dialectical (and ultimately Scandinavian) forms. The form of the feminine, "she," is also a later Middle English dialectical form that became part of standard English by the end of the fifteenth century. If we look at the third person in OE, it might be confusing to see the word *him* as a form of the plural (what would now be "them"), or *heo* as a form of the feminine (what would now be "she").

Here are the personal pronouns of OE (note that these are West Saxon forms and thus the forms that the student will most often encounter in modern editions).

First Person

	Singular	Dual	Plural
Nominative	Ic	wit	we
Genitive	Min	uncer	user, ure
Dative	Me	unc	us
Accusative	Mec, me	uncit, unc	usic, us

Second Person

	Singular	Dual	Plural
Nominative	þu	git	ge
Genitive	þin	incer	eower
Dative	þe	inc	eow
Accusative	þec, þe	incit, ine	eowic, eow

Third Person Singular

	Masculine	Feminine	Neuter
Nominative	he	heo, hie	hit
Genitive	his	hiere, hire, hyre	his
Dative	him	hiere, hire, hyre	him
Accusative	hine	hie, hi, hy	hit

Third Person Plurals, All Genders

NB: the different spellings reflect various forms as they appear in manuscripts.

Nominative:	*hie, hi, hy, heo, hio*
Genitive:	*hiera, hira, hyra; heora, hiora*
Dative:	*him, heom*
Accusative:	*hie, hi, hy; heo, hio*

As in the other Germanic languages, OE had strong and weak adjectives (not to be confused with strong and weak verbs). Adjectives had to be declined like nouns. If you were going to modify a noun, the noun and the modifier had to agree in number, case, and gender. Thus, *sum mann* meant a certain man, in the nominative singular. *Sumum mannum* meant to or with a certain man, in the dative singular. *God mann* meant a good man. *Godum mannum* meant to or with a good man in the dative singular. If you wanted to specify that particular man, you had to use an adjectival form that was different. By placing the definite or demonstrative article before the adjective, you changed the ending of the adjective. The good man would be *se goda mann*. Notice that the word for "good" has changed here. The weak form would be used, too, when the adjective follows a possessive pronoun (e.g., in a phrase such as "my good man").

OE Syntax and Word Order

Because the meaningful relationships among words in an OE sentence were determined by the case endings of those words, rather than by their order, OE syntax may seem very different from that of Modern English. In highly inflected languages, such as Latin, word order does not determine meaning: "puer amat puellam" means the same as "puellam amat puer": "the boy loves the girl." In Latin, the nominative case of the noun for boy tells us that he is the subject of the sentence; the accusative case of the noun for girl tells us that she is the direct object of his love. In Modern English, "the girl loves the boy" means something potentially completely different from "the boy loves the girl." But in OE, this sentence would be: "*Se cniht lufiaþ þam mægden.*" Here, the grammatical categories are signaled by the definite articles. *Cniht* and *mægden* were nouns whose nominative and accusative forms were the same. The form of the neuter accusative definite article, *þam*, tells us that the boy here loves the girl (or perhaps more etymologically and poetically, that the knight loves the maiden).

It may seem that word order is irrelevant. But it was really not. Patterns of word order became codified in OE prose and poetry. To ask a question, you inverted the order of the noun and the verb. For example, the sentence *Þu hæfst gefera* means "You have a friend." The sentence *hæfst þu gefera* means "Do you have a friend?" The sentence *Þu wære todæg on huntnoþe* meant, "You were hunting today." The sentence *Wære þu todæg on huntnoþe* means, "Were you hunting today?" Word order could change in imperative commands, negative statements, or subordinate clauses.

The most notable feature of OE word order was the marking of when/then clauses. The words *Þa* and *Þæt* (also written *ða* and *ðæt*) could mean both "when" and "then." How can we tell the difference? OE developed a word order pattern that made this distinction.

Þa + subject + verb = when
Þa + verb + subject = then

Here is an example from OE prose. King Alfred's Preface to his translation of Gregory's *Pastoral Care* is one of the great works of early English prose writing. Composed at the end of the ninth century, it reflects on the state of learning in England, on the need to rebuild literacy in the vernacular, and how Norse raids on English monasteries and settlements undermined the teaching of language and literature. Alfred reflects on this recent history and he writes: *Ða ic ða ðis eall gemunde, ða gemunde ic* [When I remembered all of this, then I remembered ...]. Alfred uses the same words to signal two different experiences, a when/then relationship. He does it again a few sentences later: *Ða ic ða ðis ealle gemunde, ða wundrade ic* [When I remembered all of this, then I marveled at ...]. What we could say, therefore, is that temporal and causal relationships now signaled by vocabulary were signaled by word order.

The Dialects of OE

OE had four major regional dialects, distinguished mainly by the pronunciation of vowels in stressed position, but also marked by differences in consonant clusters and occasional differences of idiom and grammar. The origin of these dialects can be traced to original settlement patterns by different Germanic groups in the fifth and sixth centuries. Texts survive in these dialects from different periods, and scholars rely on the spelling of their scribes to reconstruct the sounds of these dialects. The four dialects are:

1. *Northumbrian*: the form of OE written and spoken north of the Humber River and south of the Firth of Forth. The earliest texts in OE appear in this dialect.
2. *Mercian*: the form of OE written and spoken north of the River Thames and south of the Humber. It survives largely in a collection of interlinear glosses, written in the ninth century, to a manuscript of Latin psalms and hymns (this text is known as the Mercian Hymns).
3. *Kentish*: the form of OE written and spoken in the southeast of England, roughly corresponding to the modern county of Kent, south of the River Thames. Sustained texts in this dialect are a set of charters written in the early ninth century.
4. *West Saxon*: the form of OE written and spoken in the southwest of England. West Saxon became associated with the standard form of OE largely because it was the dialect of King Alfred the Great, under whose aegis many vernacular texts were prepared; and because it was the dialect in which the major manuscripts of OE poetry were written. There are texts in West Saxon running from the ninth through the eleventh centuries, and in the course of this time aspects of the written language changed. In the nineteenth century, scholars considered Early West Saxon to be the language of King Alfred, and many OE texts were re-edited to conform to the reconstructed form of this dialect.

It is worth looking at some representative examples of these dialects to note their primary features. The Lord's Prayer survives in many forms throughout the OE period. Here is the opening of the prayer in three different dialects: West Saxon, Northumbrian, and Mercian (there is no Kentish version of the text). These texts come from interlinear glosses in Latin manuscripts (Toon 1992, pp. 432–3):

West Saxon:	Fæder ure þu þe eart on heofonum
	si þin nama gehalgod
Northumbrian:	Fader urer ðu bist in heofnum
	sie ðin noma gehalgad
Mercian:	Feder ure þu eart in heofenum
	se þin noma is gehalgad

Describing the differences among the dialects requires some technical language and a knowledge of the older, Germanic origin of the vowel sounds, but a useful way of putting it would be the following.

The older low back vowel /a/ from the West Germanic languages was fronted in West Saxon. That means that the vowel was pronounced further forward in the mouth into an *aesh* sound. In Mercian, that vowel was moved even further into the front of the mouth. In Northumbrian, the sound remained the older sound. Hence, *Fæder, Fader, Feder*. Vowels before the letter -r in West Saxon and Mercian "broke" – an older, monophthong became a diphthong. Hence, *eart* and *eart*. The word for "name" is differently spelled here because in West Saxon the older Germanic /a/ sound did not change before a nasal consonant. In Mercian and Northumbrian, it was rounded into an /o/ sound. Hence, *nama, noma, noma*.

There are other differences to note throughout the body of OE texts. For example, later in the Lord's Prayer, the word for the first-person plural (Modern English "us") varies. In the phrase, "give us this day our daily bread," the word "our" appears as follows:

West Saxon: urne
Northumbrian: userne
Mercian: ur

Later on, in the phrase, "forgive us our sins," the word "our" appears:

West Saxon: ure
Northumbrian: usra
Mercian: ussa

In Modern English, one word, "our," covers the genitive singular and plural. But in OE, the different genders of the noun governed by the possessive would give different case endings.

What we can learn, even from this brief account, is that OE scribes were clearly trying to represent the sounds and forms of their language in writing, and those sounds and forms varied from region to region in pre-Conquest England. What we can also learn is that even though West Saxon was, in effect, the "standard" form of OE for literary and cultural documents, many of our modern pronunciations actually come from non-West Saxon forms. Most obvious would be the Modern English word "old," which comes from the non-West Saxon form *ald*. OE long a became long o (*ban*, "bone," *ham*, "home"). So our modern form must come from *ald*. In West Saxon, this low back vowel broke before -l, and so it would have appeared *eald*. Why certain forms became part of standard Modern English has to do with patterns of migration and the location of later sources of power in different dialect areas, for example, London was not part of the West Saxon-speaking area of southern England.

OE Poetry

Like all old Germanic verse, OE verse was structured according to patterns of accent and alliteration. The metrical line was built on a pattern of repeated, initial consonant or vowel sounds in stressed positions. The unity of the poetic line was determined by the alliterative patterning that bound together two half-lines, each one a metrical unit. For example, consider this wonderful moment from *Beowulf* when Grendel appears for the last time, just before his fight with Beowulf:

Ða com of more	under mist-hleoþum
Grendel gongan,	Godes yrre bær;
Mynte se man-scaða	manna cynnes
Sumne besyrwan	in sele þam hean.

(lines 710–13)

[Then came from the moorland, under the misty slopes,
Grendel going, he bore God's ire;
The evil foe intended to entrap
Some of the men there in that high hall.]

The alliterative patterning is particularly powerful here, the repeated m-sounds followed by the hard g's, and then the m's again and the initial s's. This is a good example of metrical form being used for dramatic effect.

These metrical forms, however, were not loose and indiscriminate. Each half-line of OE verse had to fit a pattern, and scholars have classified these patterns into five metrical groups. OE meter is a complex and contested subject. For the student of the history of English, it is worth being aware that there are differences – that is, not all OE poetic lines were exactly alike. Compare these half-lines:

Stiðum wordum
Þurh Meotudes meaht
On flot feran
Frea ælmihtig
Hrimcealde sæ

Alternating weak and strong syllables, along with the number of these syllables, make up a pattern for each half-line. What mattered was less the actual number of syllables than the number of stressed (and alliterating) syllables. In the few lines of *Beowulf* quoted above, we can see how each half line is a little different in syllabic number and pattern. We can also see how sometimes there are two alliterating syllables across the half-lines and sometimes three.

Modern editions of OE poetry (since the early nineteenth century), arrange the verse line into two half-lines, separated by a large space. To read OE poetry today, then, is to read writing that is editorially presented to us as poetry, but that in its manuscript context, would almost always have been written out as continuous prose.

Much of OE literature is therefore a literature of the scriptorium, a literature written by and for those trained in the arts of letter-making. Sometimes we can get a glimpse into this lettered world in poems that take literacy as a theme. Here is a riddle from the Exeter Book, a manuscript of OE poetry composed around the year 1000. Many of the riddles take an ordinary object or phenomenon and make it weird and wonderful. This riddle looks at a bookworm – not a nerdy scholar, in our modern sense, but a literal larval pest that eats the pages of the text.

Moððe word fræt.	Mē þæt þuhte
wrǣtlicu wyrd,	þā ic þæt wundor gefrægn,
þæt se wyrm forswealg	wera gied sumes,
þēof in þȳstro,	þrymfæstne cwide
ond þæs strangan staþol.	Stælgiest ne wæs
wihte þȳ glēawra,	þe hē þām wordum swealg.

(Whitelock 1967, p. 173)

[A moth ate words. It seemed to me
A remarkable occurrence, that I should speak about this wonder,
That the worm, a thief in the night, should swallow
His glorious song, and their strong place. That thieving guest
Was no whit the wiser, when he had swallowed the word.]

The worm is eating the pages and the words written on them. As strange as this may seem, the worm gets nothing from its food. The words it eats do not make it wiser. An obvious statement, but in the world of the monastery, where ingestion and rumination were the key metaphors for reading and understanding, this little beast represents a kind of spiritual illiteracy. Double meanings are everywhere here, as they are throughout the OE riddles. The "thief in the night" is not just a buggy eater but the devil himself, something almost apocalyptic. The monks in this monastery would remember the words of St. Paul that the day of the Lord will come as a thief in the night (1 Thessalonians 5:2).

In this poem about words, we can see the OE poet building a vocabulary of aesthetic response. Terms such as *wrætlic* and *wundor* show us that the world is full of strange but often remarkably crafted things (*wrætlic* appears throughout OE literature to evoke something carefully made or sometimes magically imbued with power). Notice, too, how the poet makes new words out of familiar parts. *Stælgiest* means the stealing guest or the stealing stranger; in this single word we can see a whole history of cultural transgression: the guest who breaks the rules of hospitality, the outsider who comes in and takes a treasure. Our bookworm appears as a miniature Grendel, breaking in and swallowing not the bodies of the warriors but the words of the monks.

OE poetry deliberately invites such word play and associative thought. In addition to alliteration and rhythm, an organizing principle of its poetics is the use of figurative or metaphorical expressions built from word compounds. These are the kennings of the Gmc tradition. In OE we see kennings such as the following:

swan-rad:	road of the swan = sea
hwæl-rad:	road of the whale = sea
Godes condel:	God's candle = sun
ban-hus:	bone house = human body
hilde-leoma:	battle light = the gleaming metal sword in battle
word-hord:	the hoard of words = the speaker's mental command of a language; the phrase *word-hoard onleac*, unlocked the word-hoard, means "spoke."

Some of our Modern English words descend from such metaphorical compounds. Our word "window" comes from an old Scandinavian kenning that literally meant "the eye for the wind." In OE, the word for such a hole in the wall was *eagduru*, "eye-door," or *eagþyrel*, "eye hole." The Scandinavian words replaced these terms, so that by early Middle English we get a recognizable word. But look at that OE word: *eagþyrel*. OE (and Middle English) had a verb, *þyrlan*, which meant to drill or poke a hole in something. Our homely eye hole may have disappeared, but our familiar "nostril" still echoes back to *nosþyrl*, a hole in the nose.

This is the poetics of OE: a driving alliteration and rhythmical stress that scaffolds a highly metaphorical way of looking at the world. It is this verbal system that would change dramatically with the Norman Conquest and the introduction of French linguistic and literary models into English life. Alliterative verse would survive in regions outside London (*Sir Gawain and the Green Knight* is perhaps the most famous example of provincial alliterative poetry). But for the Geoffrey Chaucer – Londoner, courtier, Member of Parliament, and master of rhyme and iambic pentameter – this old poetics would be so much "rim, ram, ruff" (as the character of the Parson puts it in *The Canterbury Tales*). But, as we shall see, even the most Francophile of writers could not escape the echoes of the pre-Conquest past.

Sources and Further Reading

Baker, P. S. (2003). *Introduction to Old English*. Oxford: Blackwell.

Bosworth, J. and Toller, T. N. (1971). *An Anglo-Saxon Dictionary*, rev. Alastair Campbell. Oxford: Oxford University Press, 1971). Available at: https://bosworthtoller.com

Campbell, A. (1957). *Old English Grammar*. Oxford: Oxford University Press.

Dumitrescu, I. (2018). *The Experience of Education in Anglo-Saxon Literature*. Cambridge: Cambridge University Press.

Getz, R. and Pelle, S. (in progress). *The Dictionary of Old English*. Toronto: University of Toronto Press. Available at: https://doe.artsci.utoronto.ca

Keynes, S. and Lapidge, P. (1983). *Alfred the Great: Asser's Life of King Alfred and Other Contemporary Sources*. Harmondsworth: Penguin.

Klaeber, F. (2008). *Beowulf*, 4th edn., (Eds.) R. D. Fulk, Robert E. Bjork, and John D. Niles. Toronto: University of Toronto Press.

Lass, R. (1994). *Old English: A Historical Linguistic Companion*. Cambridge: Cambridge University Press.

Mitchell, B. (1995). *An Invitation to Old English and Anglo-Saxon England*. Oxford: Blackwell.

Mitchell, B. and Robinson, F. C. (2007). *A Guide to Old English*. 7th edn. Oxford: Blackwell.

O'Keeffe, K. O. (1991). *Visible Song: Transitional Literacy in Old English Verse*. Cambridge: Cambridge University Press.

Pulsiano, P. and Treharne, E. (Eds.) (2001). *A Companion to Anglo-Saxon Literature*. Oxford: Blackwell.

Shippey, T. A. (1972). *Old English Verse*. London: Hutchinson.

Smith, J. (2009). *Old English: A Linguistic Introduction*. Cambridge: Cambridge University Press.

Stenton, F. (1971). *Anglo-Saxon England*. 3rd edn. Oxford: Clarendon Press.

Thornbury, E. (2014). *Becoming a Poet in Anglo-Saxon England*. Cambridge: Cambridge University Press.

Toon, T. (1992). "Old English Dialects." In *CHEL*, vol. 1. Cambridge: Cambridge University Press, pp. 409–51.

Trilling, R. (2009). *The Aesthetics of Nostalgia: Historical Representation in Old English Verse*. Toronto: University of Toronto Press.

Whitelock, D. (1967). *Sweet's Anglo-Saxon Reader in Prose and Verse*. 15th edn. Oxford: Clarendon Press.

4   Middle English

The term "Middle English" (ME) is used to characterize the period in the English language between the Norman Conquest of 1066 and the end of the fifteenth century. Simply asserting these endpoints raises problems, however. Are the beginning and end of this period determined by external events: political change; the imposition of a new, prestige language in the British Isles; and the eventual reassertion of English by royal rulers and leaders? Or are these endpoints determined by internal linguistic changes: the loss of the Old English (OE) inflectional system, the increase in French and Latinate vocabulary, and the systematic changes in the pronunciation of consonant clusters and of long vowels?

Of course, both internal and external factors shape the broad features of ME. But unlike OE, written ME varied greatly from region to region and from time to time. Certain works of literature, such as *Sir Gawain and the Green Knight* (probably composed in the mid-fourteenth century under aristocratic patronage in the West Midlands) appear in a dialect and a prosody that may have made it incomprehensible to, say, a Londoner of Chaucer's time and class. It is not as if, with the imposition of Norman rule by William the Conqueror, OE suddenly disappeared. Scribes and scholars were writing in recognizable forms of OE well into the mid-twelfth century. OE texts from the time of Wulfstan were intelligible to readers over a century later. By contrast, famous works such as *Beowulf* and the poems of the Exeter Book lay unread for centuries, with virtually no effect on English life and literature until their rediscovery in the late 1700s.

ME is a complex and multilayered period in English linguistic history, and the aim of this chapter is to illustrate the varieties of its forms and the imaginative, personal, and social uses to which it was put. There is no single, accepted editorial form of ME (in the way that many OE texts have been editorially normalized into West Saxon). There is no single representative literary voice for ME. Geoffrey Chaucer and William Langland were contemporaries in late fourteenth-century England (and may have lived in London at the same time). Compare the

DOI: 10.4324/9781003227083-5

iambic pentameter, rhymed lines, and Romance lexicon of *The Canterbury Tales*
with the alliterative patterns of *Piers Plowman*:

> Whan that Aprill with his shoures soote
> The droghte of March hath perced to the roote,
> And bathed every veyne in swich licour,
> Of which vertu engendred is the flour.
>
> (Chaucer, *The Canterbury Tales*, lines 1–4)

> In a somer seson, whan softe was the sonne,
> I shoop me into shroudes as I a sheep were,
> In habite as an heremite unholy of werkes,
> Wente wide in this world wondres to here.
> Ac on a May morwenynge on Malverne hilles
> Me bifel a ferly, of Fairye me thoghte.
>
> (Langland, *Piers Plowman*, lines 1–6)

Chaucer and Langland begin their poems with scenes of seasonal change, specific references to time and place, and the development of a clear narrative per-
sona. Whereas Chaucer writes in rhymed, iambic pentameter couplets, and his
vocabulary juxtaposes words of OE origin (*shoures, soote, droghte, roote*) with
words of French inheritance (*veyne, licour, vertu, engendred, flour*), Langland's
lines are based on alliterative repetitions in stressed syllables, with a vocabulary
that juxtaposes OE words with those of religious Latin. *Somer, softe,* and *sonne*
are all OE words. So are *went, wide, world,* and *wondres*. While the word *unholy*
(OE *unhalig*) is English, *habit* and *heremite* are newer, Latin terms from the
world of the Church. Langland's *shoop* is a form of the old strong verb *sceapan*,
to shape, or in this case, dress oneself in something (that verb has now been re-
formed, by analogy, as a weak verb).

Now look at a story of seasonal change from *Sir Gawain and the Green
Knight*:

> After þe sesoun of somer wyth þe soft wyndez
> Quen Zeferus syflez hymself on sedez and erbez,
> Wela wynne is þe wort þat waxes þeroute,
> When þe donkande dewe dropez of þe leuez,
> To bide a blysful blusch of þe bryȝt sunne.
>
> (*Gawain*, lines 516–20)

The season of summer is recognizably there, as is the west wind, Zephyr, and the
imagery of fertile fields and liquid life. But the spelling is noticeably different
(the use of the final -z to signal plurals; the Qu- for the more familiar Wh-, the

thorns still there for th-). The lexical world of this poem differs markedly from that of Chaucer and Langland. Notice the juxtaposition of words from OE and from Latin and French. *Zeferus* is from Latin, and what he does here is *syflez himself*: gently blows or whistles through, from French verb *sifler*. *Sedez* is our word "seeds," and it goes back to an OE (and ultimately Indo-European) root. But *erbez*, herbs, comes from Latin by way of French. Words such as *wynne* (joy), *wort* (root), and *waxes* (increases) are pure OE. But look at the alliterating words *donkande dewe dropez*. *Dew* and *dropez* are OE, but *donkande* is most likely from Old Norse and related to our word "dank" (notice that in the dialect of this poem, the gerund form that southern and London ME would have signaled with -ing is -*ande*). Look at the words in the last line of this quotation:

- *Bide*: to abide or remain in expectation of something; OE.
- *Blysful*: blissful; OE.
- *Blusch*: blush; not OE, but borrowed from other Germanic languages; its appearance in *Gawain* may be the first recorded use in English, and its etymology baffles even the editors of the *OED*.

ME, then, was not just a period of complex linguistic change and regional variation. It was a time when writers and speakers of English were aware of its changing nature and exploited those changes for imaginative and social purposes.

During the ME period, the British Isles were functionally a trilingual culture. This statement does not mean that every person could read and write English, French, and Latin. Nor does it mean that any single person or group would have encountered all of these languages in the course of their lives. What it means is that these three languages were the media for intellectual, literary, religious, and administrative organization for more than four centuries. It means that the idea of an English vernacular was constantly being negotiated among different groups. It means that in certain cases, people were literate and expressive in all three languages and expected certain groups of readers to be as well. Chaucer's contemporary John Gower wrote long poems in English, French, and Latin; he would not have done so if he was not assured that each would have a knowledgeable readership.

Finally, during the ME period we have the first sustained examples of personal expression in the vernacular. People began writing letters to each other in the late 1300s, and by the 1450s the practice of written personal communication became so widespread that we now have great caches of family and institutional correspondence in clear and fluid English prose. People wrote prayers and personal reflections in their books. Assemblies of texts copied out or remembered fill common books. As you read more and more ME, you come to realize that you are not only reading texts prepared by professional scribes (there are plenty of those) but are also reading the accounts of personal voices.

This chapter begins by delineating the changes that were going on in OE in the eleventh and twelfth centuries. It reviews the major linguistic features of ME and illustrates how various writers used the resources of their local or personal form of ME to give expression to religious faith, social conflict, and literary fiction. Finally, it delineates the key features of the dialects of ME, and it explores some of the personal voices that we can recover from the written page.

From OE to ME: Changes in Sound and Structure

Over the six centuries that OE was the dominant vernacular in England, the language changed in pronunciation, grammatical form, and expressive organization. To read texts in late OE is to see the distinctions in word endings progressively leveling out. Various noun endings (-um, -an, -en, and so on) come to be written increasingly as simply a vowel and nasal. It has been argued that because OE (like the old Germanic languages) had such a powerful stress on the root syllable of a word, the word endings became increasingly unstressed and, in turn, indiscriminate. The vernacular texts of the eleventh and twelfth centuries look different from those of earlier periods. Because scribes wrote largely as they spoke, and because texts continued to be copied or composed throughout the eleventh and twelfth centuries, we can chart some of the major changes from OE with reasonable assurance.

One of the most important documents for studying the political and linguistic history of late pre- and early post-Conquest England is the *Peterborough Chronicle*. The monks of the abbey of Peterborough (in Cambridgeshire) participated in making what we now call the *Anglo-Saxon Chronicle*. This text, which appears in a variety of versions written at different times and places in England, offers a prose history of England, organized by year. Some of these yearly entries (or annals) are clearly imagined, copied from previous texts, or are more cases of lore and legend than history.

Whatever their relationship to lived experience, the texts of the *Peterborough Chronicle* illustrate how scribes were coping with the changing grammar and sound of their language. A good example is the changing form of the introductory formula for each entry. Each entry begins with a phrase that translates as "in this year." The entry for 1083 in the *Peterborough Chronicle* uses this formula in a way that to us looks like textbook OE: *On þissum geare.* The preposition "on," meaning "in" or "during," took the dative case, and the endings -um and -e of the next words mark the dative, masculine, singular forms of their words.

In the 1000s and 1100s, case endings started to level out, and prepositions became more important than case. The entry for 1117 opens: *On þison geare.* Here, the adjectival ending has leveled out to a back vowel plus an indiscriminate nasal. Perhaps the scribe is recording the sound of his language. Perhaps he is recording what he thinks a grammatical ending should be, even though it no longer corresponds to his speech. For whatever reasons, the scribal spellings of the opening formula continue to change, and by 1135 it reads: *On þis geare*. The adjectival ending has been completely lost, even though the final -e in the noun may still signal the dative case. All sense of that signaling has been lost in the final entry of the *Peterborough Chronicle* from 1154: *On þis gear*.

These examples are revealing but not absolutely accurate. Modern scholars have shown that the *Chronicle* entries from 1122 to 1131 were all written at the same time and back-dated. The entries for 1132 to 1154 were also composed at one time. We do not get real-time, year-by-year representations of speech. What we do get is the scribal attempt to represent changes in language: that is, evidence that writers and readers recognized that their language was changing and that it was their responsibility to record that change.

Based on this material, and a host of other examples, we can systematically delineate a set of changes in the leveling of inflectional endings through what has been called vowel reduction. Endings that were made up of a vowel and a consonant gradually reduce to a single vowel (or an indiscriminate, unstressed vowel and a consonant). Endings that originally had different vowels gradually reduce to a final -e. Endings that consisted solely of a final -e tended to disappear entirely.

These changes and many others seem to have been going on almost irrespective of the effect of Norman French on OE. Peterborough, for example, was far from the site of the initial conquest and further still from the administrative center of Anglo-Norman rule. Yet the OE of this *Chronicle* is changing in the century after 1066, looking (from our perspective) more "modern" as the years go by.

The *Peterborough Chronicle* offers valuable evidence for the development of early ME prose as a medium of personal expression. The entry for 1137 surveys the entire period of the tumultuous reign of King Stephen (1135–1154). This is a piece of writing with a real voice: a work of historical prose that carries literary weight and reveals the resources of mid-twelfth-century English used to their full effect.

Ðis gær for þe king Stephne ofer sæ to Normandi, and ther wes underfangen forþi ðat hi wenden ðat he sculde ben alswic alse the eom wes and for he hadde get his tresor – ac he todeld it and scattered sotlice. Micel hadde Henri king gadered gold and sylver, and na god ne dide me for his saule tharof.

(Clark 1970, p. 55)

[In this year the King Stephen traveled over the sea to Normandy, and there he was received because of the fact that they believed that he should be [treated] just as the uncle [King Henry I] was, and because he [Stephen] had received [inherited] his [Henry's] wealth – but he [Henry] had dispersed and scattered it foolishly. King Henry had gathered a great deal of gold and silver, but it was not used for the benefit of his soul.]

At the linguistic level, this passage bears all the marks of late OE. Even though most of the grammatical endings have dropped out (there is no ending for *Đis*, the final -e in *gære* probably represents the remnant of the dative case), there remain identifiable OE verb forms. The verb *faren*, "to travel," was a strong verb; its past tense is, as here, *for*. The infinitive in verbs still ends in -en. A word such as *underfangen*, literally "taken in under," represents OE word formation at its most traditional. The word for Stephen's uncle, Henry I, is *eom*, corresponding to the West Saxon OE word *eam* (the word in various forms survives well into the later ME and regional early Modern English periods). The verb *wenden*, "they believed," shares the root of the word *wene*, still found in certain English dialects.

But there is much here that is new. All traces of grammatical gender have disappeared. The thorns and edths of OE spelling remain, but they share space with new scribal forms of th-. There are also new words. What Stephen has inherited here is his uncle's *tresor*, his wealth or treasure. The word comes from the Latin, *thesaurus*. Here, it appears in an Old French form, and it is the first recorded use of this word in written English. But what Henry had done with that *tresor* is pure OE: *todeled* (with the root of the modern "deal" recognizable). Henry also *scatered* it, a word of remarkably complex and unsure etymology (maybe it is a dialect form; maybe it is related to an older Germanic word), that appears for the first time in English writing here.

What we see in this passage is verbal innovation and grammatical and phonological change, but also some traditional forms. Syntactically, the passage preserves how OE distinguished between "when" and "then" clauses:

> Þa þe king Stephne to Englaland com, þa macod he his gadering æt Oxenford.
> When the King Stephen arrived in England,
>   Subject   Verb
> Then made he his assembly at Oxford
>   Verb   Subject

As we read on in this passaage, we see more and more something new juxtaposed against the old. For example, when King Stephen arrests two of his bishops, he puts them in *prisun*, a word that appears first in the 1123 *Peterborough Chronicle* entry and then in this one. When the chronicler tells us that in spite of everything, Stephen really was an ineffective ruler, that's when the real atrocities start to happen.

> Þa the swikes undergæton ðat he milde man was and softe and god and na justise ne did, þa diden hi alle wunder.

(ibid., p. 55)

[When the traitors understood that he was a mild man and was gentle and good and did not inflict punishment, then they all performed atrocities.]

Once again, we have the traditional þa/þa clauses to distinguish "when" and "then." The terms for Stephen's character are taken from the OE heroic vocabulary: mild, soft, good. The word *wunder* here means not so much "wonder" but terror. In OE, it had an umarked plural: like one sheep, two sheep, there was one *wundor*, two *wundor*. But then we find the word *justise* – a very special word in the Norman French legal vocabulary. The *OED* defines it as "the exercise of authority or power in maintenance of right." This entry from the *Chronicle* is the word's first appearance in written English.

The new words entering the chronicler's lexicon are words for legal and administrative control. As Norman French came with the new kingship under William the Conqueror, these were the words that gave voice to new structures of power. A word such as *castle* came in with the Normans. Pre-Conquest English people did not build monumentally in dressed stone. Churches and large buildings would have been built of wood or flint cobble, mortared together. But when William landed, the first thing he did was build large stone buildings. In the words of the *Peterborough Chronicle* for 1086 (writing on the conqueror's death), "Castelas he let wyrcean" (He had castles built), and the word "castle" comes from the Latin, *castrum* (a fortified settlement) into the Norman French of the Conqueror. So when King Stephen's renegade noblemen seek control, they build castles: "Aevric rice man his castles makede, . . . and fylden þe land ful of castles." Every rich man: *rice* is certainly an OE word (it goes back to Germanic and Indo-European words for forms of rule: *Reich* in German, *rix* in Celtic, *raj* in Sanskrit, *rex* in Latin). But it is also a word in Norman French, and in that language it carried a different connotation, specifically noble and mighty.

Reading the *Peterborough Chronicle* shows us the ways writers tried to sustain a tradition of OE prose while responding to and recording linguistic and cultural change. A century after its completion in 1154, King Henry III, in the year 1258, in his Provisions of Oxford, announced that he would continue to respect the strictures of the Magna Carta, that great document of 1215 in which King John gave up his absolute authority to a newly emerging confederation of barons and a nascent Parliament. Henry thought himself more a Continental than an English monarch. He appointed many non-English-born men to positions of power, favored his French relatives, and seemed to ignore what the barons of a previous generation had won. By October 1258, things had come to a head, and the nobles forced Henry to pull back: to reaffirm a commitment to the Magna Carta and a commitment to a Parliament that would meet three times a year.

Henry's proclamation was issued in Latin, French, and English. That English form is the first official royal document in the language since the Conquest, and even though it is clearly a translation from the French text, it offers a remarkable example of how Middle English was becoming a fluent medium for political expression.

Henry, þur3 Godes fultume King on Engleneloande, Lhoaverd on Yrloande, Duk on Normandi, on Aquitaine, and Eorle on Anjow, send i-greting to all

hise holde, i-lærde and i-leawed on Hundendoneschire. Þæt witen 3e wel alle
þæt we willen and unnen þæt þæt ure rædesmen, alle oþer þe moare dæl of
heom þæt beoþ i-chosen þur3 us and þur3 þæt loandes folk on ure kuneriche,
habbeþ i-don and schullen don in þe worþness of Gode and on ure treowþe,
for þe freme of þe loande, þur3 þe besi3te of þan toforen i-seide rædesmen,
beo stedefæst and i-lestinde in alle þinge abouten ende.

Henry, par le grace Deu, Rey de Engleterre, sire de Irlande, duc de Nor-
mandie, de Aquitien, et cunte de Angou, a tuz sez feaus clers et lays sauz.
Sachez ke nus volons et otrions ke se ke nostre conseil, u la greignure partie,
de eus ki est esluz par nus et par le commun de nostre reaume, a fet, u fera, al
honour de Deu et nostre fei, et pur le profit ne notre reaume sicum il ordenera
seit ferm et estable en tuttes choses a tuz jurz.

(Mossé 1968, pp. 187–9)

[Henry, by the grace of God, King of England, Lord of Ireland, Duke of
Normandy and of Aquitaine, and Earl of Anjou, sends greeting to all of his
subjects, the learned and the unlearned, in Huntingtonshire. You all know
well that we want and desire that our counselors, the greater portion of whom
that have been chosen by us and by the people of our kingdom, have acted
and should act according to the honor of God and fidelity to us, and for the
good of the realm, according to the provisions of those aforesaid counselors,
that they be steadfast and firm in all things forever.]

The English version takes a set of French terms, already emerging in the mid-
thirteenth century as the common words for power and social value, and translates them back into earlier OE forms.

Le grace Deu	Godes fultume
Clers et lays	i-lærde and i-leawed
Sachez ke	Ðæt wite 3e wel alle þæt
Conseil	rædesmen
Le commun de	loandes folk on ure kuneriche
nostre reaume	

In OE, *fultume* meant "aid" or "help." Etymologically, it is related to the modern word "full," and it connotes completion or a kind of making whole. By the
mid-thirteenth century, this was already an archaic word (it may be its last datable appearance in writing here). The phrase *i-lærde and i-leawed* translates as
"the learned and the lewd," an old alliterative pairing (*lewed* in OE meant not
obscene but common or untutored). The French phrase *Saches ke* means "you
know that." Here, it becomes an OE correlative clause, which might be rendered
today as: "That fact, let all of you know, namely that ..." A counselor is now a
rædesmen, an adviser, a giver of *rad*, which in OE meant advice. Such a word

would be familiar to readers of OE verse such as *Beowulf* (where Hrothgar has men who give him *rad*), and to us today, who know the infamous pre-Conquest King Æthelred as "The Unready" (Æthelred unræd, Æthelred, the ill-advised). The common of our realm becomes the folk of the land in our kingdom, a phrase of powerful, local connotation (OE *kuneriche* defined the country as under a specific ruler, a king, while the French word *reaume* connoted a core abstract or general sense of political control).

Looking at the different versions of the proclamation, we see how French was translated into English and how an official kind of English was developed: an English that was deliberately archaic and formal, one that would have reminded its readers of old phrases and old times, one that in effect makes the Francophone Henry III into a more familiar English king. Later in the text, we can see this process continue, as French words become OE ones:

honour	treoþe
profit	freme
reaume	loande
form et estable	stedfæst and i-lestinde
commandons	hoaten
enemi mortel	deadlice i-foan
tresor	hord

By writing in an already old-fashioned-looking English, the proclamation sends a message. In the words of the scholar Thorlac Turville-Petre, the translator of the text

> recognized the value in the propaganda of patriotism of reaching beyond the constituency of royal officials and appropriating (however speciously) the language of the 'loandes folk' in order to involve a wider section of the population in the political program of reform.
>
> (1996, p. 9)

The Sounds and Forms of Early Middle English

We can learn much about language and power from these texts. What can we learn linguistically? Final vowels and endings become increasingly unstressed. Prepositions become increasingly important. The words *þe* and *þæt* become the usual form of the definite and demonstrative article. The OE prefix ge- that signaled the participial form of verbs has been reduced to an unstressed i- prefix. OE long *a* became a long *o* sound in ME. The proclamation's -oa- spellings record this process in a scribal attempt to represent a new pronunciation.

One of the most important sound changes in early ME is known as lengthening in open syllables. Put simply, certain short vowels in OE words were quantitatively lengthened if those vowels appeared in syllables that were open, that is, in which there was a consonant followed by another vowel. The best example of this change is the pronunciation of the OE word *nama*. In OE, the first *a* would have been quantitatively short. In ME, this word would have had a quantitatively lengthened *a*. Other vowels were similarly lengthened. The word *abidan* in OE had a quantitatively short *i* sound. By the early fourteenth century, that vowel had lengthened, and the ME word would have been pronounced /abi:də/.

Not every change worked in the same way. The OE word *stæf* became the ME word *staf* (OE short æ became ME short a). But the plural of this word was *stafas*: the root vowel of the word was now in an open syllable. In ME, this would have been pronounced /stɑ:vəs/. This new long *a* sound ultimately became the diphthong /ei:/ in Modern English, due to the changes wrought by the Great Vowel Shift. Similarly, words such as "name" and "blame" took on this sound. For this reason, we say "staff" with a short *a*, but "staves" with the diphthong coming from a long *a*.

Of course, there were exceptions. ME *path/pathes* did not become, in Modern English, /pæþ/, /pei:þz/. Several words that had lengthening of this kind in ME wound up with modern pronunciations shaped by analogy: that is, forms of pronunciation that made certain words look like other words. Modern English staff/staves may be an exception now, but it is a telling exception that reveals a sound change in ME.

Like many sound changes, lengthening open syllables did not happen in all dialects of ME, nor did it happen at the same time. Modern scholars have debated whether it is a systematic sound change at all or a set of compensatory processes prompted by other changes in syllabic context. Nonetheless, we study and teach these changes to explain how Modern English sounds emerge from earlier environments.

Other changes that were going on during this period, and that help explain modern pronunciations, include the metathesis of certain OE sound groups. Metathesis is the transposing of sounds, for example, in the pronunciation of "spaghetti" as "psghetti," or the regional American pronunciation of "ask" as "aks." During the early ME period, new pronunciations of the following OE words emerged:

beorht > bright
hutte > bird
thunnor > thunder
thurgh > through
axian > ask

For the modern student encountering ME, most of what you will find will look like the following.

Vowels

The basic system of long vowels:

- /aː/ a low back vowel, in words such as *save* and *caas*; pronounced as in Modern British English "father."
- /ɛː/ a mid-front vowel, in words such as *lene, heeth, breath*; pronounced as in Modern English "they're."
- /eː/ a mid-front vowel, in words such as *need, sweete*; pronounced as in Modern English "hey."
- /iː/ a high front vowel, in words such as *bite* and *fine*; pronounced as in Modern English "beet."
- /ɔː/ a mid-back vowel, as in *holy*; pronounced as in Modern English "broad."
- /oː/ a mid-back vowel, as in *do, so*, or *mone*; pronounced as in Modern English "dough."
- /uː/ a high front vowel, as in *mus*, and *hous*; pronounced as in Modern English "shoe."

ME also developed a set of diphthongs:

- eIi, ey: the spelling for the diphthong pronounced as /ei/ or /ai/, and found in words such as *daie, weye, may*.
- oi, oy: the spelling for the diphthong pronounced as /oi/ or sometimes /ui/, and found in words such as *boy, annoy*.
- ou, ow: the spelling for the diphthong pronounced as /ou/ in words such as *fought* (sometimes these spellings appear in words that were probably still pronounced with a /uː/, such as in *howse*).

ME short vowels, by and large, may be pronounced as in Modern English. But readers should note that the sounds represented in the words "put" and "cut" (which no longer rhyme) were the same in ME (the sound /ʊ/).

Finally, many ME words end with an unstressed *e*. This sound may at times be a remnant of an old grammatical ending, or it may mark that the vowel in the previous syllable has been lengthened. Thus, the word *toune* in the phrase, "out of toune" is a remnant of an old dative ending, whereas the word *name* is spelled to indicate that the older, OE short vowel /a/ has been lengthened quantitatively as /aː/. In both cases, the final e should be pronounced as the unstressed schwa sound /ə/.

Consonants

Although the system of OE consonant clusters was simplifying during the ME period, some remain. OE *hring, hlahian, hwaet*, and the like came to be pronounced without the initial aspirated *h*. But the word *knight* in ME remained pronounced /knixt/, with the initial *k* still sounded and the digraph -gh- representing a velar continuant. So a word such as *gnawen* (to gnaw) would have been pronounced with the initial *g*.

In reading ME texts, you will see some spelling conventions that descend from OE, some that are borrowed from French, and some that developed on their own by particular groups of scribes. The interdental continuant (voiced or unvoiced) that in OE was represented by the thorn and the edth was gradually replaced by the spelling th. The OE thorn, in certain scribal contexts, came to look more and more like the letter y (in many manuscripts, a dot over the y signals a thorn). Early printers maintained this convention. Thus, it is not uncommon to see the definite article appear as if it were "ye." A phrase such as "ye olde tea shoppe" is thus a matter of misreading early orthography and not a matter of historical pronunciation.

In ME, scribes developed the letter *yogh*, *3*, out of the OE *g*. This letter could represent several sounds, depending on its place in the word:

the glide /j/: *3eothe, 3eare, 3onge*
the velar continuant /x/: *thought, through, knight*
the unvoiced alveolar stop /ɣ/ as in the name La3amon.

Stress and Syllables

ME words from OE maintained their stress on the root syllable of the word. This was usually the first syllable, except when there was a prefix. This habit largely remains in Modern English.

Polysyllabic words from Latin or French tended to be pronounced with all syllables, with the stress on final one. Thus, *marriage* would have had four syllables in ME. *Governance, steadfastnesse*, and similar words would have had their stress on the final syllable before the unstressed (but still pronounced) final *e*.

Nouns

Grammatical gender had largely disappeared in written ME by the fourteenth century. OE case endings had leveled out, often to final -e. While prepositions were increasingly used to mark relationships among words in a sentence (as opposed to case endings), in many cases, ME did preserve word endings that marked grammatical relationships. Many nouns were still written with a final -e when they were in the dative case (that is, as the indirect object of a verb or as part of a prepositional phrase). The final -s and -es came to represent the possessive (except in certain cases) and (except in certain other cases) the plurals of nouns.

Exceptions to these general rules came from OE words with different ways of marking or not marking plurals. Thus, OE (like other Germanic languages) had nouns with so-called mutated plurals: that is, the plural was signaled by a change in the root vowel, the product of i-mutation during the Germanic period. ME preserved many of these:

foot / feet
goose /geese
mouse / mice

But several older mutated plurals came to be re-formed by analogy with -s plurals. Thus, the OE plural of *boc, bec,* came to appear largely as *bokes* by the time of Chaucer. The OE word *broþer* had the plural form *breþer*. In certain regional dialects (especially southern ME), an older *en* plural was added on, giving the Modern English word "brethren." Plural endings in -en also survive in words such as "children," and "oxen."

Some words in OE did not have an inflected plural. Thus, the plural of the words for "sheep," "fish," "wonder," "word," and "thing" was unmarked (as it still is, in Modern English, for "sheep" and "fish").

Verbs

The ME system of verbs largely descends from OE. There are only two conjugated tenses (present and past). Futurity is marked by additional, so-called modal or helping verbs ("shall," "will," and the like).

One of the features that distinguishes ME dialects is the ending of verbs, and in some dialects the endings of the second- and third-person singular would have been -s or -es, rather than -st and -th, respectively.

Most strong verbs from OE survive in ME as strong verbs. By the later ME period, the distinctions between the vowels among the four principal parts of the verb may have leveled out. For example, the verb "to shoot" survives in four distinct forms in the thirteenth-century text of the *Ancrene Wisse: Scheoten, scheat huttenen, ishoten.* By Chaucer's time and place, however, the forms have been reduced to *shoot, shot, i-shot(en)*. Verbs such as "ride," "drive," and "write" wind up with only three forms:

ride, rode, ridden
drive, drove, driven
write, wrote, written

Some OE strong verbs came to be re-formed as weak verbs in the course of ME. Thus the verb *weax*, meaning "to wax" or "grow," became a weak verb: wax, waxed.

Some verbs took on different meanings or grammatical functions, depending on whether they appeared in the strong or the weak form. Thus,

hang, hung, hanged
shine, shone, shined

Here the distinction is between transitive and intransitive: "I shined my shoes," but "the sun shone."

OE weak verbs remained weak verbs in ME. Any verb that entered English (then or now) from another language entered as a weak verb.

Personal Pronouns

ME is the period in which a great variety of personal pronouns appear, depending on the time and place of the written text. OE personal pronouns were words that began with *h*. Thus *he* was the masculine; *heo* was the feminine; *hir* was the plural possessive "their," and so on. Three things happen in the course of ME that change the system of pronouns:

- H-forms are regularized in the South and East Midlands.
- Sh- and sch- forms for the feminine third person come to appear in the West Midlands and are eventually absorbed into the metropolitan, literate standard.
- Th- forms, which descend from Scandinavian forms and predominated in northern dialects, become part of the metropolitan, literate standard.

Although there are many possible reasons for these changes, one likely cause is the migration of people from the north and Midlands to London during the late 1300s and early 1400s. Plague, famine, and the lure of the city led many to leave their rural homes. Many of the scribes in the official scriptorium of government (known as the Chancery) came from the north and the Midlands, and their dialects may have helped standardize the th- forms for the plural pronouns.

The study of pronoun forms in ME has characterized a great deal of work in dialectology and historical change. It remains a complex subject. Often, different manuscripts of the same text may have different forms of the pronouns. Pronominal forms were far from standard in the ME period and far from standard during the first centuries of Modern English.

In addition to these regional and temporal variations, ME preserved the OE forms of the second person, thou-forms and you-forms. In OE, this distinction was largely a matter of number: thou-forms were singular, and you-forms were plural. During the ME period, perhaps under the influence of French, these forms also came to distinguish informal and formal terms of address and relationship, perhaps modeled on the French *vous* and *tu*. Generally speaking, the informal thou-forms were used when a superior spoke to an inferior, when a parent spoke to a child, or when a lover spoke to someone intimate. God was always addressed in the informal/intimate (as in other European languages). You-forms were used when addressing more than one person, when speaking up to a superior or a stranger, or when seeking to distance oneself, formally or socially, from another. In Chaucer's *Clerk's Tale*, for example, patient Griselda will address her husband, the Duke Walter, in you-forms:

Remembre yow, myn owene lord so deere,
I was youre wyf, though I unworthy were.

(CLT, lines 881–2)

Walter responds, dismissing her and telling her to take only the clothes she had on when he took her in:

'The smok", 'quod he, "that thou hast on thy bak,
Let it be stille, and bere it forth with thee."

(ibid., lines 890–1)

When Walter finishes testing Griselda and drops the pretense of his anger, he turns to her and uses the thou form of intimacy:

Thou art my wyf, ne noon oother I have.

(ibid., line 1063)

Idioms and Verb Phrases

ME adopted many phrases from French, using English words but keeping the French idiom. Most of these constructions rely on a verb together with an object. Thus, phrases such as the following were based on French models: "Do battle; give offence; have mercy; make peace, take care." In Chaucer's ME, the nouns are French nouns, illustrating that Chaucer is adapting French idioms into his language. He will take the verb "do," for example, and use the following noun objects in new ways: correction, diligence, execution, offense, oppression, service.

The Scandinavian Element in ME

Studies of ME vocabulary stress the role of French in augmenting the lexical resources of the vernacular. French became the prestige language of the court, and most of our words for government, administration, cuisine, high culture, fashion, and the built environment enter into English between the thirteenth and the fifteenth centuries. But ME is more than an OE substrate with a Francophone veneer. English speakers were in contact with speakers of Old Norse (ON) from the ninth century onward. In fact, England was ruled by Scandianvian kings in the early eleventh century (Cnut was king of England from 1018 until his death in 1035, and simultaneously king of Denmark and Norway). During the ME period, many Scandinavian words and pronunciations entered the northern dialect. Many of these words and sounds became part of educated or official English in the London courts and bureaucracy by the end of the fifteenth century.

There are several ways we can trace this Scandinavian impact. First, there are words that were cognate in OE and Scandinavian languages but with somewhat different meanings. OE *dream* meant "joy"; ON *dream* meant "dream." The ON meaning replaced that of the OE. Similarly, OE *deor* meant "wild animal"; ON *deor* meant "deer." Although OE had a kenning for "window," our word comes not from that metaphor but from an ON one: *vindauga*, "eye for the wind."

Second, there were many words that OE and ME shared with Scandinavian languages, but these had different pronunciations. Some of them became distinctions of ME dialect, and some were distinctions of vocabulary. Words with sh in English were sk words in Scandinavian; words with ch in English were k in Scandinavian. Thus, the following words meant the same things:

church   kirk
milch   milk
ship   skip
shirt   skirt

In the course of the ME and early Modern English period, however, these variants took on different connotations. Thus, while "shirt" and "skirt" were both items of clothing, they came to refer to different kinds of clothing. A ship came to be commanded by a "skipper," a very different occupation than that of a "shipper." A "milch" cow came to mean a particular and regionally distinctive animal; "milk" became the common term for the liquid. While just about everyone went to "church," the word *kirk* became a familiar but distinctive regional variant.

Third, words that were unique to the Scandinavian languages entered regional English and, later, metropolitan speech and writing. Often, these words had distinctive sounds: *ill, ugly, muggy*, and the like. Chaucer marks these words as northernisms in his *Reeve's Tale*. By the end of the fifteenth century, they were acceptable words in London English.

Finally, and most noticeably, ME appropriated the Scandinavian forms of the third person. OE forms, and Midland and southern ME forms, were h-forms: *he, hem, hir, hire*. Northern forms were th-forms: *they, them, their, theirs*. Charting the change from h- to th-forms has preoccupied historians of English for decades, and the regional and temporal variations among them have been mapped with a great degree of detail.

Although the data is complex, it would be fair to say that by the fifteenth century "they" was the form that had become standard for the third-person plural nominative, whereas "their" and "them" do not appear to be the norm until the last third of the fifteenth century.

Different Forms of French in ME

Words from French entered ME at different times and in different ways. During the first centuries of Norman rule, words came into use from Norman French. These were largely words for particular religious, social, political, and architectural concepts. Among the earliest were words such as (in their Modern English equivalents):

castle
honor
justice
martyr
miracle
prison
privilege
rent
treasure
virtue

A second wave of French loan words came in from Central French. When Henry II became king in 1154, he began a three-century rule from the House of Plantagenet, a dynasty originally from Anjou in France. Their French was different from that of the Normans. Because the Normans descended from Germanic-speaking peoples, the phonology of Norman French bears the influence of Germanic sounds. By contrast, Central French preserves sounds more directly descended from Latin. Here are groups of words that may be distinguished by Norman and Central pronunciation. In effect, what we are looking at here are patterns of reborrowing of words into English over time.

- Norman French had a /w/ sound and spelling for Central French words with a /g/ sound and a *gu* spelling.

  - wiles   guile
  - William   Guillaume
  - war   guerre
  - warden   guardian
  - warrantee guarantee

- Norman French had a /k/ sound, spelled with a *c* for Central French words with a /č/ sound, spelled *ch.*

  - castle   château
  - cap   chapeau
  - cattle   chattel
  - carriage   chariot

In addition to these differences in pronunciation, the French court established firmer relationships with continental French culture and literature. In fact, many works in Old French, such as the *Lais and Fables* of Marie de France and the *Chanson de Roland*, may have been composed in England (or at the very least copied by French scribes in England). New words were entering English for complex social structures and philosophical concepts. The following words are recorded from the early 1300s on (though they may well have been in use before then), and are grouped by spellings that enable a modern student to find French words in English:

ei, ey: obey, air, fair, quaint
oi, oy: boy, joy, toy, royal, exploit
ioun, ion: explanation, relation
ment: amendment, commandment
ence or aunce: eminence, reference
our, or or: color, favor

A third wave of Francophone borrowings began in the late fourteenth century, with the sustained literary activities around the court of Richard II (r. 1377–1399) and with the influence of Chaucer's poetry on later fifteenth-century writers. While Chaucer's role in expanding the vocabulary of English may be exaggerated (he coined very few words, and many words attributed to his first usage were in fact in circulation before he wrote), he took on the rhetorical pose of a linguistic innovator. His readers and later imitators described him as the "purifier" of English: that is, they attributed to him a language that was richer with French and Latin terms and purged of what they called the "rudeness" of the older OE vocabulary. No matter whether Chaucer used the following words for the first time, they have long been taken to be characteristic of a new, Chaucerian literary vocabulary:

assent
engender
expression
inspire
intention
judgment
laureate
predication
protestation
remembrance
steadfastness
verdict

ME in the Fourteenth Century

The period from about 1330 to 1420 offered an efflorescence of prose and verse writing in English. At the beginning of this period, the manuscript containing the so-caled Harley Lyrics and the Auchinleck Manuscript (containing, among other works, the romance known as *Sir Orfeo*) represent how European literary forms were adapted to a vivid vernacular (both manuscripts also contain works in French and Latin). At the end of the period, Chaucer, Langland, Gower, mystical writer Julian of Norwich, and religious autobiographer Margery Kempe were composing long, sustained works of fiction, devotion, and instruction.

This is also the time when sustained texts in ME regional dialects came to be written down: The *Ayenbite of Inwit* in the south, the *Cursor Mundi* in the north, *Gawain and the Green Knight* in the West Midlands, and Chaucer's poetry in a largely East Midland-derived London form. Calling these"dialect" works, however, may be misleading. There was not any recognized "standard" form of English until the late fifteeenth century at the earliest. London and Westminster were centers of official and commercial power, but so were cities such as York and Lincoln. Great aristocratic courts flourished from Chester to Northumberland. Religious sees and houses were active from Canterbury to Cambridgeshire and beyond.

Fourteenth-century Chaucerian English (which is really the language of early fifteenth-century manuscripts written in London by scribes trained in royal and commercial scriptoria) is generally taken as a benchmark for students of ME. Perhaps the most famous of Chaucerian passages is the opening of *The Canterbury Tales*, an 18-line sentence that revels in new vocabulary, old forms, and the transformation of literary conventions into an original authorial voice:

> Whan that Aprill with his shoures soote
> The droghte of March hath perced to the roote,
> And bathed every veyne in swich licour
> Of which vertu engendred is the flour;
> Whan Zephirus eek with his sweete breeth
> Inspired hath in every holt and heeth
> The tendre croppes, and the yonge sonne
> Hath in the Ram his half cours yronne,
> And smale foweles maken melodye,
> That slepen al the nyght with open ye
> (So priketh hem nature in hir corages),
> Thanne longen folk to goon on pilgrimages,
> And palmeres for to seken straunge strondes,
> To ferne halwes, kowthe in sondry londes;
> And specially from every shires ende
> Of Engelond to Caunterbery they wende,
> The hooly blisful martir for to seke,
> That hem hath holpen whan that they were seeke.

(lines 1–18)

Chaucer's status as a linguistic innovator stems, in many ways, from passages such as this one. Words like *engendered* and *inspired* were new words at the end of the fourteenth century, coming from Latin and French. Words such as *vertu* and *melodye*, although also Romance-derived, had long been in the ME lexicon. But there is more than lexicography here. Chaucer, like many of his contemporaries, was acutely aware of etymologies and contexs. The word *vertu* comes from the Latin *vir*. It signals masculine prowess. In this scene of meteorological power, with the showers of April piercing the drought of March and engendering things, gender is everywhere. So a word such as *melodye* means not "song" but the sounds of bliss or mirth, heavenly or earthly (in *The Miller's Tale*, after Nicholas has sex with Alisoun, he takes up his harp and vigorously "maketh melodye"). For all the Englishness of this landscape – signaled by words of OE origin such as *holt, heethe, croppes, halwes, londes,* and *shires* – there is a highly Francophone world here. These birds "That slepen al the nyght with open ye" (every word here from OE) do not have hearts but *corages* – the French word (by Chaucer's time, a word that could mean the bodily organ as well as the emotional condition shaped by a strong one: that is, courage).

The rites of pilgrimage are Latin and Romance ones. The words for this practice – *palmeres, pilgrimages, martir* – contrast with the word for the people performing them: *folk*. Finally, although Chaucer is writing in iambic pentameter rhymed couplets, a metrical form carefully developed from Continental verse, he concludes this great opening sentence with a single rhyme and an evocation of the older, alliterative prosody of pre-Conquest England. *Seke* and *seeke* rhyme here (our words "seek" and "sick") closing off this final couplet securely. Although the pilgrims are in search of the martyred Thomas Becket, he comes off as a very English saint: holy and blissful. In the final line, the repeated emphases of the initial sounds – *hem hath holpen* – slow down the pace of reading (this poetry, as all ME poetry, would have been read aloud). Chaucer is using the older h-form for the third person, juxtaposed against a newer th- form. He uses the older, strong form of the verb "help," *holpen*.

At the level of syntax, Chaucer's ME still sustains the older OE word patterns signaling "when"/"then" clauses, even as there are now two words to distinguish them. Over the centuries of ME use, interrogative words came to be used as relatives. In OE, relative pronouns were demonstrative pronouns. A phrase such as, "the man who" would be, in OE, "Se mann se." Words such as *who, what, which,* and *when* came to be used as relative pronouns and temporal markers. The OE patterns we saw in King Alfred's Preface to the *Pastoral Care*: "Ða ic ða ðis eall gemunde, ða gemunde ic" were long gone by Chaucer.

Yet Chaucer still used old syntactic patterns. A distillation of the first sentence of *The Canterbury Tales* would be:

When April pierces...
Then long folk

When= Subject + Verb
Then = Verb + Subject

Syntax, vocabulary, sound, and sense all come together in this passage to show us how Chaucer carefully uses the resources of his vernacular to shape a vivid sense of seasonal change and local identity.

Of course, there is much more to ME than Chaucer and *The Canterbury Tales*. Medieval lyricists appropriated Continental forms of verse (the pastourelle, the rondeau, and others) to offer supple, vernacular expressions of love and nature. Religious writers recorded prayers and penance, lives of the saints, and mystical moments. While Latin remained the medium of intellectual and devotional expression in the university and the Church, English was increasingly the vehicle for personal expression. The fourteenth-century anchoress Julian of Norwich (*ca.* 1342–*ca.* 1416) wrote her *Revelations of Divine Love* in the 1380s, recording a series of visions that she had in 1373 during a grave illness. Julian knew French and Latin. Her writings circulated in her native East Anglia and possibly in metropolitan London. She crafted a way of being devout in English. Here is a brief moment of self-reflection.

> Botte God forbede that ye schulde saye or take it so that I am a techere, for I meene nought soo, no I mente nevere so. For I am a womann, leued, febille, and freylle. Botte I wate wele this that I saye. I hafe it of the schewynge of hym that es soverayne techare. Botte sothelye, charyte styrres me to telle yowe it, for I wolde God ware knawenn and my eveynn-Crystenne spede, as I wolde be myselfe, to the mare hatynge of synne and lovynge of God.
>
> (Wogan-Browne et al. 1999, p. 81)

Julian develops what her most recent editors call a "language of equality" here – one that addresses all possible English Christians. She writes consistently in the *yow* forms, the plural; she often transforms Latin religious terms into vernacular ones. Her word *schewynge*, for example, translates the Latinate "revelation," and it does so in a way that is powerfully conscious of the etymology of that word. *Revelation* is from *re-velare*, literally a pulling away of the curtain (the Latin word is a calque on the Greek, *apocalyptein*, apocalpyse, which literally means a pulling away of a covering). While there are some words from Latin and French here, they fit into patterns that would be familiar from older English rhythm and structure. *Febille* and *freylle* ("feeble and frail") are French, but they work in an alliterative pairing that evokes the OE formulae. God is a *techare* (OE), but he is a *soverayne* one. That word had powerful resonances in the late 1300s: political rule, individual power, unique authority. So, while Julian talks about *hate* and *love* (OE words), she makes clear that she is guided by *charyte*, a word that recalls the *caritas* of St. Paul and a whole tradition of the Church Fathers.

Julian of Norwich is one of many personal voices in ME, and what is clear about the English language in her lifetime is that it increasingly became the medium for a personal voice. For the first time in the history of the vernacular, we can actually hear what people sounded like: in idiom, in dialect, and in the flow of speech. ME is the moment when "speech-like" utterances appear as speech, and we can explore the voices of ME as human voices much like our own.

The Voices of Middle English

During the fifteenth century, several English families began to write letters to friends and relatives. This practice grew out of the needs for aspiring gentry and aristocrats to manage lands and monies. Many of these letters are little more than itemized accounts. This practice also responded to the social fact that during that time, family members often moved away from home. Some sought adventure or success in London. Some married outside of expectations. Some tried service at various courts. By the 1450s, writing letters in English became a recognized way of sustaining relationships and, furthermore, developing a personal vernacular that is often as unique as the person speaking and writing.

Among the many pieces of evidence for these uses of English, the letters of the Paston family of Norfolk have been treasured for their range and vividness. Agnes Paston (*ca.* 1405–1479) was the long-lived and brilliantly opinionated matriarch of this family. Many of her letters survive, most of them probably dictated, and several of them rich with personal and local detail.

In a letter dated November 8, 1451, she remarks on the local responses to a wall that she was building around her property. In several other letters, we can see how this work sat ill with her neighbors: it restricted movement across the landscape, and it signaled an assertion of privacy and property at odds with community standards. Here we may actually hear something of the men and women of her time. She writes to her husband, John:

> I gret ȝou well, and lete ȝou wete þat Warne Harman, on þe Sonday after Hallumes Day after ensong, seyd oponly in þe cherch-ȝerde þat he wyst wyll þat and þe wall were puddoun, þou he were an hondryd myle fro Paston, he wyste well þat I wolde sey he ded yt and he xuld bere þe blame, seying, 'Telle yte here ho so wyll, þou it xuld coste me xx nobyllys it xall be puddoun aȝen.' And þe seyd Warnys wyfe wyth a lovde vosse seyd, 'All þe deuyllys of hell drawe here sowle to hell for þe weye þat she hat mad!'
>
> (Davis 1971, pp. 43–4)

[I greet you well, and I want you to know that Warren Harman, on the Sunday after All Hallows Day after evensong, said openly in the churchyard that he knew well that, if the wall were pulled down, even if he were a hundred miles away from Paston, he knew well that I would say that he did it and he should bear the blame, saying, "Tell whomsoever you will, even if it cost me twenty nobles, it would be pulled down again." And his same Warren's wife said with a loud voice, "May all the devils of hell draw her soul to hell on a account of this pathway that she has made!"]

This letter is an essay in vernacular quotation. It centers on recording what people said and how they said it. Agnes (or her scribe) conveys the sound and sense of local speech. For example, the word written as "puddon" is a colloquialized combination of the idiom "put down," recorded in the mid-fifteenth century as meaning pull down or dismantle. The double *d* represents what linguists would call the flapping of the medial unvoiced *t*, and it gives us a little window into the sonic features of the local English. The syntax of these speeches seems to contrast with that of the surrounding representation of indirect speech. Notice the complex patterning of the subordinate clauses and subjunctives: he said openly in the church yard that he knew well that, if the wall had been pulled down, even though he were a hundred miles from Paston, he knew well that Agnes would say that he did it and should bear the blame for it. Compare this with: "Tell it to her, whoever would, that even though it would cost me twenty nobles it shall be pulled down again." And when Warne's wife speaks, in a loud voice, we get a line of direct, idiomatic English talk: "May all the devils of hell drag her soul to hell on account of that path she has made!"

What makes these statements colloquial speech? Scholars have identified a range of locutions in ME that may offer a window to the sound and sense of everyday talk. Insults and curses have long drawn on the talk of the townsfolk. They are real, however, often because they are so formulaic. As Colette Moore puts it, "Maligning and belittling one another is apparently a long-standing pragmatic use for language" – something we could apply to Warne's wife and to characters in Shakespeare and the "dissing" of modern putdowns.

Colloquial obscenity, in fact, emerges in the ME period (people no doubt cursed and swore in Old English, but it was not written down). Chaucer is famous for his vulgar characters: the Host of his *Canterbury Tales*, declaiming that the Chaucerian pilgrim's *Tale of Sir Thopas* "is nat worth a tord"; the Shipman, whose tale is full of fart jokes; and the Merchant, who protests that he is a "rude" (unlearned) man and describes a wild scene of sex in a pear tree, with the old January unknowingly lifting up his young wife, May.

ME literature is full of such vulgarity. The cycle plays from the north of England are famous for their vivid portrayals of biblical characters as if they were local men and women. The *Townley Play of Noah* features the great ark builder and his wife as a bickering couple:

Noah: We! Hold thy tong, ram-skyt, or I shall the still.
Wife: By my thrift, if thou smite, I shal turne the untill.

Noah: We shall assay as tyte! Have at thee, Gill!
          Apon the bone shal it bite.

(Bevington 1975, p. 297)

Noah: Whoa! Hold your tongue, ram-shit, or I shall still it for you.
Wife: By my life, if you hit me I shall hit you back.
Noah: Let's give it a try, then! Have at you, Jill!
          You'll feel it bite down to the bone.

Domestic tension increasingly becomes the topic of popular drama and verse in the fifteenth century. It also became the focus of personal prose. For Margery Kempe, the domestic and the spiritual go hand in hand. Now famous for her autobiography, Margery traveled the world at the end of the fourteenth and the beginning of the fifteenth centuries, going on pilgrimages to Rome and Jerusalem, writing of her many pains of childbirth (she gave birth 14 times) and her conflicts with her husband, and giving expression to a deeply felt devotion to religious life. She is one of English literature's great originals. *The Book of Margery Kempe*, which she dictated to a male scribe in the late 1430s, tells of her adventures both lived and imagined. Here is a remarkable passage, in which Margery recounts an argument with her husband on Friday, Midsummer's Eve, 1413. They are traveling together, when her husband turns to her and says:

> Margery, if her come a man wyth a swerd and wold smyte of myn hed les than I schulde comown kendly wyth yow as I have do befor, seyth me trewth of yowr consciens – for ye sey ye wyl not lye – whether wold ye suffyr myn hed to be smet of er ellys suffyr me to medele wyth yow agen as I dede sumtyme?

(Staley 1996, p. 37)

> [Margery, if a man came by with a sword and wanted to cut off my head unless I should commune kindly with you [that is, have sex with you], as I have done before, tell me truthfully from your conscience – for you say you will not lie – whether you would stand to have my head cut off or stand for me to meddle [have sex] with you again, as we once did?]

Margery wonders why he brings this up now, as they have not had sex for eight weeks. He replies that he wants to know, and she answers:

> Forsothe I had levar se yow be slayn than we schuld turne agen to owyr unclennesse.
> [Truthfully, I would prefer you to be killed than that we should return to our unclean acts.]

To which the husband bluntly answers: "Ye arn no good wife."

In the course of their conversation, it emerges that they have not had sex for eight weeks because he was just too afraid to touch her, implying that she would not let him go any further. A long discussion follows, in which they try to reach an agreement: He wants to have sex with her, but he also wants her to pay off his debts and dine with him on Fridays as they used to do. Fridays were fasting days in the medieval Catholic Church, and the deeply devotional Margery will have none of this. In the end, after much debate, they reach an agreement: Margery will pay his debts, she will eat with him, but she will not have sex with him.

For all the craftedness of the narrative, this extended piece of domestic drama has all the feel of colloquial speech. With few exceptions, just about every word in this dialogue descends from Old English. Those exceptions are the ones that matter. The ME verb *communen* came from French and, by the early fifteenth century, took on the sense of doing something together. To "comown kindly" here is to engage in common activity in a natural way. Elsewhere, Margery tells us that she had no desire to "comown fleschly" with her husband. It is a relatively new expression, and Margery puts it in her husband's mouth, as if he were ventriloquizing her own idiom. Speaking for himself, the husband uses another term, rich with connotation. To "meddle" came from French as well, meaning blending or bringing together. Again, it is a relatively new word in the early fifteenth century, and what we see in this dialogue is an emerging way of talking about sex, a new development of idioms that, if we do the lexicography, we see almost exclusively in prose rather than in verse. In the end, it is the plainest of plain talk that hits us still, six hundred years after this conversation: "Ye arn no good wife."

Middle English, then, is a world of learning and lore, of great poets and everyday people. To get a greater sense of the voices of Middle English, we can turn to the study of its dialects.

Middle English Dialects and Dialectology

The historical study of English has been reshaped by the great projects of corpus linguistics such as the *Linguistic Atlas of Late Middle English*. Scholars have sought to document all recorded forms of spelling, sounds, and forms and map them on to particular regions of the British Isles. What emerges is a kind of weather map of language – with lines indicating borders of spelling and sound. Such maps give us a strong sense, now that the standard maps of ME geographical regions need to be more fine-grained than before in order to grasp the variation in the language (Figures 4.1 and 4.2).

In the twenty-first century, these data-driven projects have come under new scrutiny. Scholars now recognize that individual manuscripts many not be fully accurate representations of regional speech. Specific scribes have been identified who produced texts that sometimes reflected their own particular habits of

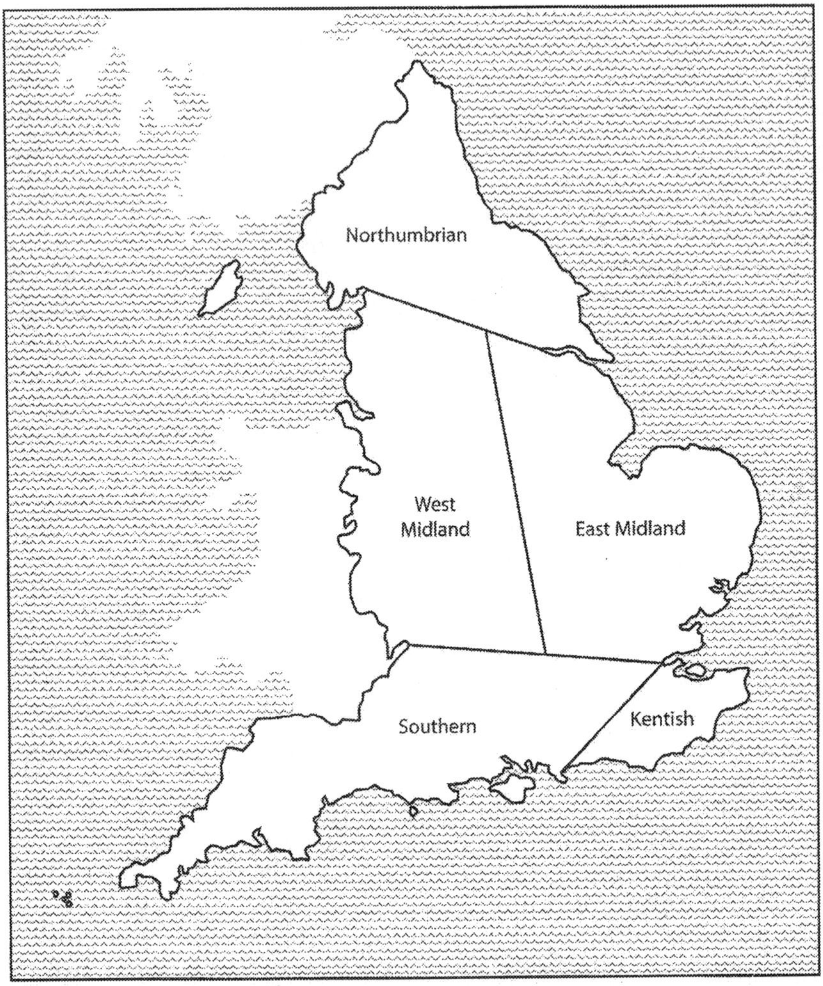

Figure 4.1 The major Middle English dialects. A basic, coarse-grained map, dividing England into the five major dialect regions, *ca.* 1200–1350

Source: Lerer (2015)

spelling or the spelling conventions of the authors or exemplars from which they copied. What was once thought of as a regional dialect, for example, may really be what has been called a "single scribal idiolect" (Horobin 2015, p. 151).

It has also become clear that region was not the only variable in ME dialect variety. Certain features may be determined by social and class variation, by professional training, and by the personal choice of writers. A small example of this complexity may illustrate how difficult it is to use written texts as evidence of

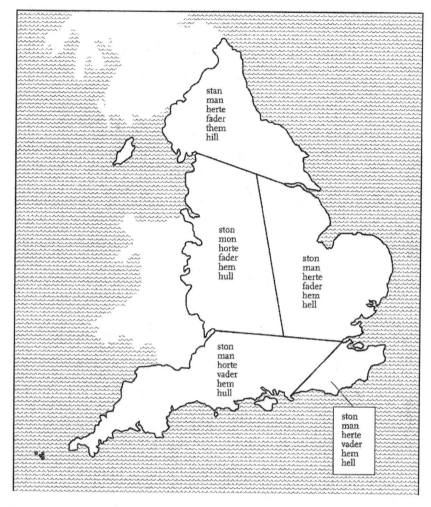

Figure 4.2 Middle English dialect variation according to key words and sounds. A finer-grained map, dividing England into linguistic regions based on the Middle English pronunciation of earlier Old English sounds and forms of the third-person plural pronoun

Source: Lerer (2015)

regional variation and temporal change. In the letters of the Paston family from the mid-fifteenth century, many of the texts were actually written by professional scribes, taking dictation or perhaps copying from the author of a letter (many of the men of the Paston family wrote their own letters, but none of the women did). The scribe James Gloys wrote letters for Margaret Paston and her husband, John Paston I. In a letter from 1446, signed by John, Gloys varied the forms for the plural possessive pronoun. Our modern form "their" appears once, while the form "her" or "here" appears nine times. In 1469, in a letter for Margaret Paston, Gloys uses the form "their" nine times; "her" or "here" never appear. One scholar who has examined these letters (and many others) in great detail concludes: "This shows that the scribe may have been less a factor than the text type, or the addressee, or even temporal factors in language change" (Bergs 2005, p. 180). Were the old h-forms of the possessive dropping out in favor of th-forms? Is there a difference between the habits of men and women of the family? Is the scribe changing his habits? We cannot know. What we can know is that regional variation and temporal change are far more complex processes than traditional textbooks present and, furthermore, this complexity is as rich and challenging as the language variation we find in our own time and place.

In addition to this empirical work, historical readings of fourteenth- and fifteenth-century writers reveal a deep awareness of regional variation in the vernacular. Writing in 1385, Englishman John of Trevisa commented on the variations in English of his time. He translates the Latin work of Ranulf Higden, the *Polychronicon* (a history of the British Isles), but he adds this material to argue for a political and social context to the dialects of his time:

> Also Englischmen, þey3 hy hadde fram þe bygynnyng þre maner speche, Souþeron, Norþeron, and Myddel speche (in þe myddel of þe lond), as hy come of þre maner people of Germania, noþeles, by commyxstion and mellyng furst wiþ Danes and afterward wiþ Normans, in menye the countray longage is apeyred, and some useþ strange wlaffyng, chyteryng, harryng and garryng, grisbittyng. Þis apeyring of þe burþ-tonge ys bycause of twey þynges. On ys, for chyldern in scole, a3enes þe usage and manere of al oþer nacions, buþ compelled for to leve here oune longage, and for to construe here lessons and here þinges a Freynsch, and habbeþ, suþthe þe Normans come furst into Engelond. Also, gentilmen children buþ y-tau3t for to speke Freynsch fram tyme þat a buþ y-rokked in here cradel, and conneþ speke and play wiþ a child his brouch; and oplondysch men wol lykne hamsylf to gentilmen, and fondeþ wiþ gret bysynes for to speke Freynsch for to me more y-told of . . .
>
> Al the longage of the Norþhumbres, and specialych at 3ork, ys so scharp, slyttyng and frotyng, and unschape, þat we Southeron men may þat longage unneþe undurstonde. Y trowe þat þat ys bycause þat a buþ ny3 to strange men and aliens þat spekeþ strangelych, and also bycause þat þe kynges of Engelond woneþ alwey fer from þat contray.
>
> (Mossé 1968, pp. 286–89)

[Now the English, even though they originally had from the beginning three kinds of speech, Southern, Northern, and Middle (in the middle of the country), as they came from three groups of people from Germania, nonetheless, by mixing together and meddling first with the Danes and then with the Normans, in many people the native language has been corrupted, and some use strange *wlaffyng, chyteryng, harryng* and *garryng, grisbittyng*. This corruption of the native language is due to two causes. One is because children in school, contrary to the habit and manner of all other nations, are compelled to forsake their own language and construe their lessons and [name their] things in French, and they have done so since the Normans came first into England. The second is because the children of gentlemen are taught to speak French from the time they are rocked in their cradle, and the child can speak it and play with his toys in it. In addition, socially ambitious men want to present themselves as if they were gentlemen, and they try with great effort therefore to speak French in order to be thought better of.

The whole language of the Northumbrians, and especially that of York, is so sharp, cutting and scratching, and unshapely, that we Southern men may scarcely understand it. I believe that this is because they live near strange people and aliens that speak strangely, and also because the kings of England always stay far away from that part of the country.]

Trevisa makes three points that have long governed the study of ME dialects. First, he argues that original dialect boundaries were based on patterns of settlement by the Germanic peoples. Second, he recognizes that language is a socially stratified pattern of behavior. There will always be a prestige language (in this case, French), and some regional forms will become prestige forms (in his case, writing as a Londoner, he disparages the northern dialects). Third, the northern dialect is unique, and that uniqueness comes from a particular mix of geographical and social factors.

A century later, William Caxton raised the question of what the proper form of English should be in his printing of canonical literature. In the preface to his prose translation of a French version of the *Aeneid* (the *Eneydos*, printed in 1490), he tells a story of some Londoners who set sail for the Low Countries and are blown back across the English Channel to the Kentish shore. One of the shipmates goes in search of food and finds a farmhouse. He speaks to the woman there, but she says that she cannot understand him because she does not speak French. The man is offended, because he was not speaking French to her. Clearly his London accent and vocabulary were opaque to her. When he asks if she has any food, in particular any eggs, she remains baffled. As Caxton explains, the word for "eggs" in London English is precisely that. But in Kentish English, the word is *eyren*. We can say now that "eggs" is a form brought to London by northern English speakers and *eyren* is a descendant of the OE word from southern dialects.

These stories make clear that English men and women lived in a world of regional variation and linguistic challenge. The study of ME dialects can help us understand the sociolinguistic condition of vernacular life in medieval England. It can show us how dialect could be represented in texts to make political arguments. Furthermore, it can show us how modern historical linguists develop a methodology of evidence collection and assessment and, in turn, its representation in visual form.

Let's look at a systematic account of the major features of the regional dialects of ME. Not all regional texts will have these features, but they are useful to distinguish the broad outlines of variation and help us see how literary writers of the ME period evoke dialect difference.

Northern

- OE /a:/ remains /a:/: ham, ban, stan.
- sh is written as sk; ch is written as k: skirt, kirk, skip, benk.
- Present participles end in -ande: lovande, havande.
- Final -ish adjectives appear as -is: Inglis, frekis.
- Forms of the verb "to be" appear as es, er, are.
- Third-person pronouns are Scandinavian loan forms, beginning with th-.
- Third-person singular ends in -es: "he loves."
- Scandinavian loan words such as ill, ilk, ugly, muggy.

East Midland

- Present participle ends in -end(e): havend.
- Third-person singular ends in -eth: "he loveth."
- Present plural and infinitive forms end in -en: to given, to loven.
- Third-person pronouns begin with h-.
- Forms of the verb "to be" appear as ben-forms.

West Midland

- OE /a/ followed by a nasal is written as o: hond, lond, mon.
- Feminine third-person singular pronouns are ha, heo, rather than "she."
- Final -ed endings are unvoiced and spelled -et: i-curet, i-fostret.
- Plural present indicatives end in -eth: giveth, vs. East Midland given.

Southern

- Voicing of initial f and s to v and z: vox, vor, vinde, zen.
- Infinitives and past participles formed without final -n: "to springe."
- OE /y/ remains a rounded vowel, spelled as u: cumeth, sunne.
- Third-person pronouns appear variously as hi, hore, hom.

Kentish

- OE /y/ becomes unrounded, written as e: ken (from OE *cynne*, "kin").
- Voicing of initial f and s to v and z: vox, vor, vinde, zen.

- Third-person plural forms are ham, hare.
- The present participle ends in -inde: havinde.

During the late fourteenth and early fifteenth centuries, literary texts from London offer a mix of forms. Although there is no absolute consistency, the standard editions of Chaucer's poetry, for example, will have the following features:

- OE /æ/ became /a/, thus OE *fæder* became ME father.
- OE /y/ was unrounded and spelled i: thus, OE *kynning* became ME king.
- OE /eo/ became a monophthong, spelled e: thus, OE *deop* became ME depe.
- Third-personal feminine nominative pronoun appears as "she."
- Third-person plurals can be th-forms as well as h-forms, often depending on grammatical case. Note Chaucer's line: "That *hem* hath holpen, whan that *they* were seke."

For students of English literature, this information helps explain episodes of humor and social criticism. Chaucer's *Reeve's Tale*, for example, has long been seen as an extended satire on the rustic northernisms of its two university student characters. Here are some examples of how these two students, John and Aleyn, speak:

> "Symond," quod John, "by God nede has na peer.
> Hym boes serve himself that has na swayn."

> "Our manicple, I hope he wil be deed,
> Swa werkes ay the wanges in his head."

> "... se howgates the corn gas in.
> Yet saugh I nevere, by my fader kyn,
> How that the hopur wagges til and fra."

> "I is as ille a millere as ar ye."

> "I have herd seyd, 'man sal taa of twa thynges
> Slyk as he fyndes, or taa slyk as he bringes.'"

These examples show what Londoners would have heard as characteristic features of northern English. Words such as "no," "fro," "so," and "two" (which came from OE /a:/ words) are spelled with the -a-. The third-person singular of the verb ends in -es, rather than -eth (*werkes, wagges*). The ch sound in a word such as *swiche* (Modern English "such") is pronounced with as a -k. Forms of the verb "to be" and of the first-person pronoun are northern forms: thus, "I is" rather than the Midland or southern forms, "I am," or "Ich be," which would have been familiar to a London readership. Finally, the Scandinavian vocabulary appears here: *boes* (for the word "behooves"), *til* (for "to"), *taa* ("for take"), and *ille*.

Of course, the *Reeve's Tale* is literature. Its themes include the decay of language, the challenges of using everyday speech to represent the world of experience, and the ways sex and money become forms of exchange. The world of the *Reeve's Tale* has long been seen as fitting for a tale-teller described, in the general prologue, as a "sclendre, choleric man" (a skinny, angry man). The dialect humor contributes to these thematic concerns, and the coarse foolishness of these students distills itself into a poetic line whose echoic form and liquid assonances sum up the whole *Tale*: "I is as ill a millere as ar ye."

By contrast, speakers of northern English could mock the south for its pretentions. In the *Second Shepherd's Play*, one of the cycle dramas from the town of Wakefield in Yorkshire, the comic character of Mak appears. He is a thief and a con man, but here he pretends to be a southern English gentleman. His lines resonate with forms drawn from southern, Kentish, and Midland dialects. Again, this is not a philological transcription but a work of literature. If Chaucer's students speak a storyteller's northern, Mak offers up a kind of stage southern, full of sounds and words that the Wakefield audience would associate with the courtly vocabulary of a Gallicized London.

2nd Shepherd:	Mak, where has thou gone? Tell us tithing.
3rd Shepherd:	Is he commen Then ilkon take hede to this thing.
Mak:	What? Ich be a yoman, I tell you, of the king;
	The self and the some, sond from a great lording,
	And sich.
	Fie on you! Goith hence
	Out of my presence!
	I must have reverence:
	Why, who be ich?
1st Shepherd:	Why make ye it so qwaint? Mak, ye do wrang.
2nd Shepherd:	But, Mak, list ye saint? I know that ye lang.
3rd Shepherd:	*I* trow the shrew can paint, the dewill might him hang!
Mak:	Ich shall make complaint, and make you all to thwang
	At a word,
	And tell evyn how ye doth.
1st Sheperd:	Bot, Mak, is that soothe?
	Now take outt that Southren tothe
	And sett in torde!

(Bevington 1975, pp. 390–1)

Mak pretends to be more than he is. He uses "Ich" for the northern "I" (though not consistently), and says "Ich be" rather than the "I is" of the Reeve's students. He tries to sound southern when he says "sich" for what would have been northern "swilk." When he says "goith" and "doth" he is putting the -th ending on verbs that would have had an -s ending in the north. When the play's scribe spells "goith" in this strange way, it is clear that he is overstressing the pronunciation of the vowel: instead of the long *a* sound in the *Reeve's Tale*, "gas," we have the long *o*, overdone here. When Mak uses words such as "presence," "reverence," and "complaint," he is speaking like a caricatured courtier, full of polysyllables and Gallic terms.

Of course, the locals find this ridiculous. Their northernisms shine brightly against the backdrop of Mak's faux Southern: *ilkon*, *wrang*, and *lang*. In the end, they tell him to take his southern tooth and stick it in a turd – a curse as literary as it is laughable (in Chaucer's *Pardoner's Tale*, the angry Host tells the Pardoner to take his relics and stick them in a "hogges turd").

What can the study of ME dialects teach us? At the linguistic level, such research shows us the great diversity of the English language, with levels of variation even in single texts. At the methodological level, such work challenges what we consider to be evidence of linguistic use: are we looking at authorial manipulations, scribal conventions, or the true voices of ME speakers? At the literary level, such a study can show us how questions of social identity and personal character lie in language: just what does speech represent, the world or the self?

The study of ME dialects raises important questions about the relationship between regional variation and historical change. One of the challenges that runs through the history of the English language is the reason for language change. What we can see here is that forms and sounds that became "standard" often come from different regions. As northerners moved to the south (to be educated, to try to make their way in the bureaucracy, to aspire to courtly patronage, or to find work in the city), they brought their language with them. From our modern point of view, ME dialects have a place in the vector of language change. Northern dialects, for example, seem phonologically conservative but morphologically advanced. In other words, from our perspective, the standard forms for the th- pronouns and certain verb endings look modern, whereas the pronunciations of certain vowels seem old-fashioned.

But other regional variations also tempt us to find them on the timeline of development. Here is Dan Michel of Northgate's version of the Lord's Prayer, written in his own hand, in a manuscript dated 1340, from Canterbury, in Kent:

Vader oure þet art ine hevens, y-hal3ed by þi name, cominde þi riche, y-worþe þi wil ase in hevene: and in erþe.bread our eche-dayes: yef ous to day. and vorlet ous our yeldings: as we vorleteþ our yelderes. and ne ous led na3t: into vondinge. and vri ous fram queade. zuo by hit.

As an autograph manuscript by a known writer with a place and a date, this work, known as the *Ayenbite of Inwit*, offers valuable information about how a writer represented his speech. There are the Kentish voicings of initial f and s: *vader*, *vorlet, vonding, vri, zuo.* The present participle ends in -inde (*cominde*). There are features that look back to Old English, too. Earlier in the text, Dan Michel states that he wrote his work in the library of St. Augustine's church at Canterbury, except he does not say library but says "bochouse." That word (literally a book-house) takes us back to the kennings of Old English, to the bone-lockers and whale roads of *Beowulf.* His opening "Vader oure" is classic OE word order, with the postponed possessive (father our, instead of our father). Finally, there is the title itself. Dan Michel's book is a translation of an earlier, French collection of moral tales, and this new title offers a brilliant example of retro-translation. *Ayenbite* means "again-bite," and it translates, morpheme-by-morpheme, the Romance word we now know as "remorse." *Inwit* means "inner knowledge" and also translates, as a calque, the Romance word "conscience." Even Dan Michel's phrase, "zuo by it," vernacularizes the more familiar "Amen" ending to the prayer. Here, we see a regional writer transforming Continental Christian learning into local English. He reminds us that ME is not just the language of high culture and great poetry but, also, of individual feeling and simple prose.

Sources and Further Reading

Bennet, J. A. W, and Smithers, G. V. (1968). *Early Middle-English Verse and Prose*. 2nd edn. Oxford: Clarendon Press.

Benson, L. D. (Gen. Ed.) (1987). *The Riverside Chaucer*. 3rd edn. Boston: Houghton Mifflin.

Bergs, A. (2005). *Scribal Networks and Historical Sociolinguistics: Studies in Morphosyntactic Variation in the Paston Letters (1421–1503)*. Berlin: Mouton de Gruyter.

Bevington, D. (1975). *Medieval Drama*. Boston: Houghton Mifflin.

Burrow, J. A. and Turville-Petre, T. (2005). *A Book of Middle English*. 3rd edn. Oxford: Blackwell.

Cannon, C. (1999). *The Making of Chaucer's English*. Cambridge: Cambridge University Press.

Clark, C. (Ed.) (1970). *The Peterborough Chronicle*. 2nd edn. Oxford: Clarendon Press.

Davis, N. (1971). *The Paston Letters and Papers of the Fifteenth Century*. 3 vols. Oxford: Oxford University Press. Vol. 1 available at: https://quod.lib.umich.edu/c/cme/Paston

Horobin, S. (2015). "The Nature of Material Evidence." In T. W. Machan (Ed.), *Imagining Medieval English*. Cambridge: Cambridge University Press, pp. 147–65.

Lerer, S. (2015). *Inventing English*. Rev. edn. New York: Columbia University Press.

Linguistic Atlas of Late Middle English (LALME). Available at: http://www.lel.ed.ac.uk/ihd/elalme/elalme.html

Machan, T. W. (2005). *English in the Middle Ages*. Oxford: Oxford University Press.

Machan, T. W. (2012). "Chaucer and the History of English." *Speculum* 87: 147–75.

Middle English Dictionary. Available at: https://quod.lib.umich.edu/m/middle-english-dictionary/dictionary

Milroy, J. (2008). "Middle English Dialectology." In *CHEL*, vol. 2. Cambridge: Cambridge University Press, pp. 156–206.

Mossé, F. (1968). *A Handbook of Middle English*. Trans. James A. Walker. Baltimore, MD: Johns Hopkins University Press.

Samuels, M. L. (1972). *Linguistic Evolution*. Cambridge: Cambridge University Press.

Schmidt, A. V. C. (Ed.) (1995). *The Vision of Piers Plowman: A Critical Edition of the B-text*. London: Dent.

Staley, L. (1996). *The Book of Margery Kempe*. Kalamazoo, MI: The Medieval Institute.

Tolkien, J. R. R. and Gordon, E. V. (Eds.) (1967). *Sir Gawain and the Green Knight*. 2nd edn. Oxford: Oxford University Press.

Turville-Petre, T. (1996). *England the Nation*. Oxford: Clarendon Press.

Wogan-Browne, J., et al. (1999). *The Idea of the Vernacular*. University Park, PA: Penn State University.

5   From Middle English to Modern English

From today's standpoint, it is tempting to see the rise of an official, standard English as inevitable. In the year of Geoffrey Chaucer's death, 1400, French was the language of the court and high culture. Parliament had been addressed for the first time in English in 1362, but the records of that speech were kept in French. The Church reform movement associated with John Wycliffe, known as Lollardy, sought to make English the language of the Bible and church devotion. But the movement was ruthlessly put down, and by the early fifteenth century, English versions of the Scriptures were deemed heretical. University and school instruction remained in Latin. Far more manuscripts survive today in French and Latin than in English.

By the time of the death of William Caxton, England's first printer, in 1491, everything had changed. King Henry V had his will prepared in English in 1422 (the first English king since the Conquest to do so). London guilds had been preparing statutes in English since the 1420s. The institution of official textual production, known as the Chancery, was making English the language of law and diplomacy. Chancery-trained scribes began copying the literary works of Chaucer, Gower, and their imitators into a form of language and a written hand befitting the vernacular bureaucracy. Personal prayer books and spiritual manuals in English proliferated. English literary prose – virtually nonexistent before Chaucer – emerged as a supple medium of narrative. As the English monarchs and nobles increasingly began to see themselves as "British," cultural ties to the European Continent (even though the Crown still held possessions in France) began to shift. When Henry VII named his first son Arthur, it signaled a new claim to history and power. Although young Arthur died before becoming king, his younger brother, Henry, fostered a court culture of vernacular lyric, epic, history, and oratory. English printers from Caxton onward contributed to the style and spelling of English. By the time Henry VIII broke with the Roman Catholic Church in the mid-1530s, English seemed to be everywhere – from the Bible to the bookshop, from the schoolroom to the sermon.

For earlier historians of the English language, this trajectory seemed as natural (if not as fundamentally good) as the move from Catholicism to Protestantism,

DOI: 10.4324/9781003227083-6

or from the manuscript to the printed book. What one influential textbook called "the triumph of English" is now known to be a highly contested and contingent event, shaped by social and political changes during a century marked by popular uprisings, dynastic wars, religious strife, economic changes, and popular migrations driven by climate change.

During this century, the sound of spoken English and the spelling of written texts changed dramatically. Writing in the Preface to his *Eneydos* of 1490, Caxton noted that the English of that year differed markedly from the language of his childhood (he was probably close to 60 at the time). A century later, Thomas Speght needed to add an extensive glossary to his edition of Chaucer's *Works* (1598), as the Middle English was no longer transparent to his readers.

Historians of English have attributed these changes to the following factors:

- *The Great Vowel Shift*: the systemic change in the pronunciation of long vowels in stressed positions, whereby Middle English low back vowels were raised and fronted and Middle English high vowels became diphthongs.
- *The impact of the Chancery* on spelling and grammatical conventions, particularly the regularization of th-forms for the third-person pronouns, the changes to verb endings in the second and third person, and growing recognition that English spelling and pronunciation were diverging quite a bit.
- *The loss of grammatical gender and complex case endings in nouns*, the rise in prepositions for marking relationships, and the regularization of word order for primarily determining meaning in a sentence.
- *The increasing social appetite for loan words* from Romance languages and other languages contacted through trade, exploration, and colonization.

This chapter takes readers through these four broad areas of language change – phonology, morphology, syntax, and lexis – to show how the English language of 1600 was very different from that of 1400. Because many of these changes have become the subject of scholarly reassessment in the twenty-first century, this chapter also explores some of the reasons historians of English see such changes as systemic and, in turn, what the evidence may be not just for language change itself but for the popular awareness that the language was changing and how to cope with it.

The Changing Sounds of English

From about the mid-1400s until the end of the 1500s, the system of English pronunciation changed dramatically. Writers of the time recognized these changes, and they began to notice how the spelling of English words increasingly deviated from their pronunciation. English spelling remained (and largely remains to this day) historical: that is, it preserves old conventions of using letters to represent sounds, even if those sounds have changed. At one point, as we have seen, the word "knight" would have been pronounced /knɪxt/. Even with the loss of the kn-consonant cluster, the changing quality and quantity of the vowel, and the loss of the medial velar fricative /x/, we still spell this word this way, even if we say /naɪt/.

What happened was not just a complete change in pronunciation but a changing relationship between the spoken and written forms of English. The twentieth-century scholar John Hurt Fisher put it this way: "the most important development of the fifteenth century was the emergence of writing as a system coordinate with, but independent from, speech" (Fisher et al. 1984, p. 26). Yet because many people still spelled as they spoke, spelling conventions were adapted to changes in pronunciation. We can trace the shifting vowel sounds in the handwriting of people of the fifteenth and sixteenth centuries, even though we can see the codification of spelling as conventions in the printers and official document-makers of that period.

What we call the Great Vowel Shift (GVS) was the systematic shift in the pronunciation of qualitatively long English vowels in stressed positions. Low back monophthongs were raised and fronted. High monophthongs became diphthongs. We owe the codification of these changes to the great Danish linguist Otto Jespersen, who concisely put it in *Modern English Grammar:* "The great vowel-shift consists in a general raising of all long vowels" (Jespersen 1909, p. 231). Jespersen saw this sound change as a kind of chain, with the vowels arranged along the chain like links. Any pressure on the chain affected the links and, in a sense, pulled the vowels along. Figure 5.1 presents how Jespersen illustrated the GVS. The changes at the top of Figure 5.1 leave spaces or pull sounds from the lower forms of the chart. Thus, the Great Vowel Shift, in this representation, begins with the high vowels becoming diphthongs.

According to this account, the first thing that happened to the English vowel system was that the high front vowels /i/ and /u/ became diphthongs. Their pronunciation changed from that of a single vowel to a double one. This change did not happen all at once. Over time, these monophthongs came to be pronounced as if there were a semivowel or glide. What Jespersen's diagram represents is the beginning and the end of a sequence:

/iː/ > /ai/
/uː/ > /ou/

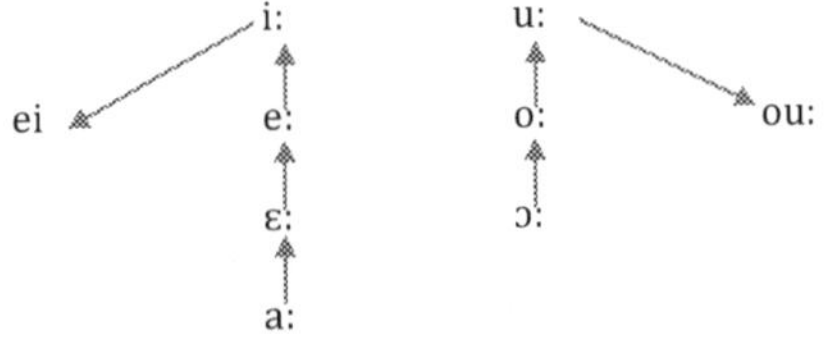

Figure 5.1 The "pull chain" representation of the Great Vowel Shift

Source: Based on Jespersen (1909)

ME words such as *bite, mite, I,* and *my* would have been pronounced as if they had the /i:/ sound: that is, as if (in Modern English) they were written "beet," "meet," "Ee," and "me." Our Modern English pronunciations give this vowel a sound as if it were written more like ahh-eee. Similarly, ME words such as *hus, mus, lus,* and *ure* (the ME spellings) became "house," "mouse," "louse," and "our." Here the sound shift was from a /u:/ sounding like ooo and becoming a sound more like aah-ooo.

In the traditional version of the GVS, this was the first pull on the chain. The move of the high front vowels created a kind of phonetic vacuum in this space, filled by the mid-front and mid-back vowels. Thus, /e:/ became /i:/. Words like ME *meet, beet,* and *feet* (which would have sounded like Modern English "mate," "bate," and "fate") changed into their modern pronunciation. Among the back vowels, /o:/ became /u:/. Words such as *do* and *to* (which would have sounded like "doe" and "toe") became pronounced with the oo sounds. The back vowel represented by the symbol /ɔ:/ was an open mid-back vowel. It appeared in Middle English in words such as *so* and *go* (sounding something like "saw" and "gaw"). This vowel was raised to the /o:/ sound. The low vowel /a:/ was similarly raised. Jespersen's chart shows this sound becoming the open mid-vowel /ɛ:/ and then the higher, close vowel /e:/. This /ɛ:/ sound was like the sound in the word "egg," if you held it for a bit longer than usual.

Teachers have developed tricks to help students remember the GVS. One of them is the mnemonic "My feet ache, so do ours." These six vowels in Middle English would have been /mi: fe:t a:k, sɔ: do: u:rz/. In Modern English, they appear as /mai: fi:t e:k, so: du: ou:rz/. Scholars now know that this set of changes was not immediate or as simple as Jespersen's model might suggest. A more finely grained version of the GVS is given in Figure 5.2. This is a more detailed model than Jespersen's. Here, the Great Vowel Shift is marked as a series of movements of the vowels over time, with steps listed in chronological order. Here, too, the Great Vowel Shift begins with the diphthongization of the high vowels, but later changes in those diphthongs are also recorded.

What Figure 5.2 shows us is, first, that the high front vowels changed over time into different diphthongs before settling into their modern pronunciation. Words such as "my" and "out" were probably pronounced something like "muhy" and "uhoot": /məi/ and /əut/ by the end of the 1500s. This chart shows that the low vowel /a:/ changed pronunciation over time before settling into the /e:/ sound. It also shows that the older, ME sounds /ɛ:/ and /e:/ had merged. Thus, words from ME /ɛ:/, such as "meat," "feat," and "beat," came to be pronounced the same as words from ME /e:/: "meet," "feet," and "beet." These sets of words would not have rhymed in ME poetry. They do rhyme by the time of Shakespeare.

What neither figure shows us is exactly when, where, and why these changes were happening. Fortunately, from the mid-1400s, we have a variety of written evidence to help us see not only how the sound of English was changing but how writers and speakers were adapting to that change. In addition, beginning in the mid-1500s, we have the evidence of a growing group of scholars, known

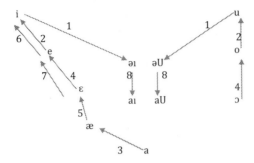

Step 1: i and u drop and become the diphthongs əɪ and əU, respectively

Step 2: e and o move up, becoming i and u

Step 3: a moves forward to become æ

Step 4: ɛ becomes e, and ɔ becomes o

Step 5: æ moves up to become ɛ

Step 6: e moves up to become i
     A new sound e was created in Step 4; now that e moves up to i

Step 7: ɛ moves up to become e
     The new ɛ created in Step 5 now moves up to merge with e

Step 8: The diphthongs əɪ and əU (which were the sounds in such words as "mice" and "mouse") drop further down to become new diphthongs aɪ and aU

Figure 5.2 Changes in pronunciation during the Great Vowel Shift

as **orthoepists**, who were fascinated by the shifts in English pronunciation and sought ways to represent temporal change and regional variation as precisely as they could. Not all of this evidence is clear; some of it is contradictory. But what is important is that for the first time in the history of the English language, people actually tried to record that history as it happened.

Some of the earliest evidence for changes in pronunciation appears in the personal letters of the mid-fifteenth century. In the letters of the Paston family, we can see people trying to adapt the conventional spellings of their time to new sounds. What we are reading here is really late ME, so we need to recognize that the letters in their words have the values of ME sounds.

In words spelled *myte* and *hyre* (Modern English "meet" and "here"), these writers are using the letter y to represent the high front vowel /i:/. This spelling shows us that the ME open and closed e (the phonemes /ɛ:/ and /e:/) would have been raised and fronted. Rather than saying, as one did in Chaucer's time, /me:t/ and /hɛ:rə/, these writers in mid-1400s Norfolk were saying /mi:t/ and /hi:rə/.

The high front vowels of ME were clearly beginning to become diphthongs at this time and place, too. A spelling such as *abeyd* (Modern English "abide") indicates that the ME /i:/ sound had become a diphthong, probably pronounced something like /ei/. Similarly, the word "our" is often spelled *aur*, "out" appears as *owt*, and "house" appears as *hows*. These words in ME would have been pronounced with the /u:/ sound. Now, they are clearly diphthongs (whether those diphthongs were /əu/ or /au/ has been the subject of vigorous debate among historical linguists).

Finally, spellings such as *mayd* for the word "made" have been understood as trying to represent a raised and fronted version of the ME sound /a:/. Instead of saying, as Chaucer would have, /ma:də/, the Pastons would have been saying something closer to /mɛ:d/ or /me:d/, or maybe a diphthong like /ɛi/ (the question of when people stopped pronouncing the final -e in these kinds of words is also a matter of great debate).

This evidence is not clear and concrete. It does not tell us what was going on, say, in London or in the West Midlands at this time, nor does it tell us that these letter writers were consistently changing their pronunciation. What it does tell us is that people were clearly trying to cope with their language changing in their own lifetimes.

We can see another kind of evidence in the work of the orthoepists (a coinage based on Greek roots: *ortho* means "right," and *epos* means "diction"). This was a group of men, active from about the mid-1500s until the early 1700s, who set out to record the sounds of spoken English and, in the process, judge what the best kind of pronunciation should be. The orthoepists' project was both descriptive and prescriptive: it set out to describe how people spoke to promote a form of English that was seen as "good." What was good about it was that it was the speech of the educated, the upper classes, those of southern England, London, and the universities of Oxford and Cambridge. Again, what counts as evidence here is highly mediated by social judgments.

Nonetheless, we can take descriptions like those of John Hart, writing in his *Orthographie* of 1569, as attempting to be phonetically and physically accurate. In describing the vowels, Hart states where the tongue should be relative to the mouth, how the lips should be rounded, and how forceful the breath should be. He makes clear that the high vowels of ME were diphthongs by his time (Hart even uses the word "diphthong" to characterize these sounds). He is equally precise about the consonants.

For the pronunciation of the letters t and d, Hart advises to lay "your tongue full in the palate of your mouth, and touching the hardest of your fore-teeth." This describes a dental stop. A century later, a certain W. Holder wrote (in *Elements of Speech*, 1669) that these sounds are made "by the end of the Tongue to the Goums." These are clearly alveolar or alveolar-dental sounds.

From early spellings and from later writings of the orthoepists, historians of English have sought to chart the changes in pronunciation during the time of the

GVS. Other vowels were changing in pronunciation, too. The short vowel /a/ was changing to /æ/, giving what became our modern pronunciation of words such as "cat" and "bat." The short /u/ sound was also undergoing changes. In some words, it became the lowered, rounded vowel /ʊ/. This is the sound in the modern pronunciation of "put." In other words, the vowel was centralized and unrounded. This is the sound /ʌ/ as in the modern pronunciation "cut." These sounds also began to merge with sounds coming from ME /o:/. Thus, the standard modern pronunciation of "put" and "good" have the same vowel. The pronunciation of "cut" and "blood" have the same vowel. But certain words, such as "food" have the /u:/ sound.

Consonants were also changing. The old initial clusters kn- and gn- (in words such as "knight" and "gnat") were becoming, uniformly, pronounced as [n]. By 1640, writer Simon Daines (in *Orthoepia Anglicana*) records that these were "inclin[ing] to the force of N." So, too, the old velar fricatives in such words as "knight," "might," and "night" were disappearing. By the end of the sixteenth century, poet Edmund Spenser could rhyme the words "night" and "knight" with words such as "quite" and "delight." Clearly, by this time (his *Faerie Queene* first appeared in 1596), the old medial fricatives were gone. Sometimes, these fricatives wound up being pronounced as the continuant /h/. There is evidence from the mid-sixteenth century that the word "laugh" may have sounded something like "lauh." By the time of Shakespeare, it was being pronounced as /laf/.

As with all changes in language, there can be many causes. Here are some of the possible reasons for these changes in pronunciation.

Dialects in Contact

During the fifteenth and early sixteenth centuries, the northern counties of England faced economic decline. Periods of bad harvests and bad weather overlapped with changes in the wool trade between the northern and East Midland parts of England and the Low Countries. The great "wool towns" of the 1300s and 1400s – towns that grew rich on sheep production and wool export – began to lose economic vitality. These changing conditions led many young men to leave rural England and seek economic and social security in the great cities, London in particular. The movement of people from different regional dialects into London may have had an impact on the pronunciation and ideals of standard English. Regional standards came into conflict. Over time, a new system of pronunciation developed that could be promulgated as a standard.

The Loss of French as a Prestige Language

In the course of the fifteenth century, French gradually lost ground to English as the language of the court and commerce. Legal records, parliamentary debate, and commercial transactions came to be written in a form of English that eventually became what some see as a "London standard." In addition to these social and commercial changes, literary tastes became increasingly monolingual. Chaucer's poetry was copied in manuscripts that were often the product of royal, aristocratic, and gentry patronage. Chaucer himself came to be seen as the "father of English poetry" and as the source of a "pure" and "refined" English. When William Caxton established his printing press in Westminster in the 1470s, Chaucer's works were some of the first books he printed. Over time, the need for a prestige language or form of language remained. But instead of having that prestige language as French, it became a form of English. By the end of the 1400s, a written and printed form of English emerged that increasingly came to be associated with the centers of power and prestige.

The Rise of Linguistic Authorities

In the Middle English period, scribes were trained to write in particular local styles, often reflecting regional pronunciations and grammatical forms. By the mid-1400s, a scribal community in London had developed that stressed training in a particular standard, irrespective of the idiolect of an individual scribe. The cultivation of Chaucer's poetry as a linguistic and literary ideal contributed to this increasing sense of English as having standards. Once English poetry began to be copied by scribes trained in producing official documents – with the letter forms and spellings based on those official documents – the literary and political authority of the vernacular came together. Printers not only reproduced English texts, they also prefaced their editions with assessments of the linguistic value of the texts they printed, and they brought earlier English writings into line with current trends in spelling. Along with the establishment of schooling in English and the impact of humanist theories of rhetorical education, printing and pedagogy came together to reinforce the idea that there should be an educated standard of language.

In the end, then, a phenomenon such as the GVS may have been a matter of not just sounds but society. Matthew Giancarlo has suggested that "the social fixation upon one variant among several dialectical options available" was what crystallized new pronunciations (2001, p. 35). With changes in spelling and grammar and the rise of a class of scholars focused on creating new standards, the social changes of the fifteenth and early sixteenth centuries initiated a larger set of changes that made English something very different from what it had been before.

The Changing Look of English

The English of the early 1500s not only sounded different from the English of Chaucer, it looked different, too. Spelling conventions began to develop as conventions, and the gap between individual pronunciation and public writing grew wider. The ways grammatical relationships were signaled by word endings (morphology) was also changing, as English completely lost any vestiges of grammatical gender and many cases of the noun (except for the genitive). So, too, the many different endings for person and number in verbs, and the old principal parts of verbs, were leveling out. The famous King James version of the Bible, printed in 1611, may give us the impression that early seventeenth-century English was still inflected: that people said "hath" and "doth," that old grammatical gender still survived (in a phrase such as "the salt hath lost his savor"), and that the distinctions between the formal and the informal second person ("you" and "thou") were still rigorously in place. But the King James version was a product of deliberate archaizing. It came from the hands of men who were highly educated, who were in middle age and thus learned their language decades before, who were deeply influenced by earlier sixteenth-century Bible translations, and who were seeking to give their great work the patina of old authority. It is quite clear that by this time, "you" was the default form of address in everyday speech, words such as "hath" and "doth," even if spelled in this way, were pronounced "has" and "does." Evidence from the mid-sixteenth century onward points to "has" and "does" as everyday pronunciations, and the distinction between "you" and "thou" – originally, one of number and intimacy – starts to blur (with "you" as the everyday form and "thou" as the marked form).

Once again, we are looking at the differences between speech and writing. Among the many influences on the look of English writing was the development of what has been called a Chancery standard in the fifteenth and early sixteenth centuries. The Chancery was the institution charged with producing official documents in the English court from about 1380 to 1460. It taught a house style of writing: letter forms, spelling, and particular morphological and grammatical features of vernacular English. Several features of this Chancery standard came to be accepted into what we think of today as modern standard English.

In words such as "night," the -gh- spelling signaled the length of the previous vowel, rather than the pronunciation of the consonant as a velar fricative. This spelling convention influenced the appearance of many words whose pronunciation was changing but whose spelling was not. Thus, words such as *high, ought, slaughter, right, though,* and *nought* continued to be spelled with the -gh- even though the old ME /x/ had disappeared.

The plurals of nouns are almost always indicated with an -s, sometimes written with the letter 3, which adapted a French convention for -es.

Some northern English forms become part of Chancery standard. Perhaps due to the influx of young men from the north of England in the 1400s, northernisms of spelling and morphology predominate. The standard southern and Midlands adjective ending, for example, was -lich (this was Chaucer's usage). In the north, the -lich ending was reduced to -ly. A word such as *fulliche* came to be written as *fully*. So, too, certain -ich spellings became standardized as northern ones. Chaucerian *liche* became *lyke* (for our word "like").

Third-person forms become standardized from northern forms. In Midlands and southern English, as in Chaucer, the words for "they," "them," "their," and so on were h-words: *he, hem, hir*. The word for the feminine third-person singular was *heo*. The th-forms descend from Scandinavian words, and the word "she" (spelled in various ways in the fifteenth century) probably grew out of changes in pronouncing the initial aspirant in the English Midlands and, by the end of the fifteenth century, emerged as a new standard. The Middle English letters thorn and edth (þ, ð) begin to be replaced by -th- spellings.

When Caxton set up his press in Westminster, he did so to associate his work with the center of royal power and the production of sanctioned documents (Westminster was the seat of the royal court and the Chancery and was a separate town from London). His edition of Chaucer's *The Canterbury Tales* from 1483 reveals the impress of Chancery English on his editing. He prints the third line of the *General Prologue:* "And bathyd euery veyne in suche lycour." Earlier manuscripts had the ME form *swiche licour*. Caxton is using the Chancery form of *suche* (our Modern English "such"). Later on, Caxton printed the line: "And smale foulis make melody." Chaucer's ME would have had the plural of the verb signaled by an -n suffix: *maken* melody. In the last line of the first sentence, Caxton changed the pronominal form and the whole sonic feel of the line: "That them hath holpyn when they were seke." The most authoritative manuscripts, and the standard modern editions of *The Canterbury Tales*, have the line as: "That hem hath holpen, what that they were seke." Caxton takes the old *hem* and replaces it with the newer, northern-derived and Chancery-sanctioned *them*. Even though he preserves the ME form of the participle for the verb "help" (*holpyn*), he gets rid of the word *that* in the line, making the syntax more direct and in keeping with the fluidity of Chancery prose.

What these and many other changes reveal is that English was becoming what linguists call a language of "zero marked categories." The first person of verbs loses a suffix. The second person retains the -st ending. The third person ends in -s or -th. The past ends, generally, in -ed. By the 1600s, some of these markers were disappearing, so that in Modern English we have only the -s to signal the third-person singular and the -d to signal the past tense.

One of the major changes in word use that affected early Modern English syntax was the changing uses of the word "do." In Old and Middle English, you asked a question by inverting the word order: you know the way; know you the way? By the middle of the sixteenth century, "do" was becoming the marker of the interrogative: do you know the way? Similarly, when older English forms used word order to signal emphasis, early Modern English speakers began to use forms of "do": I went to the store; I did go to the store. The forms of the verb "do" could become replacements for verbs: did you go to the store? I did. The verb "will" came to function in what linguists would call these periphrastic ways. Thus, in the *Book of Common Prayer* of 1549 (the first English-language collection of prayers and rituals for the Anglican Church), the priest turns to the bridegroom and says: "Wilt thou have this woman to thy wedded wife?" The man should answer, "I will."

Given these changes in the look and sound of English, scholars of the sixteenth and seventeenth centuries vigorously debated what English spelling should be. John Hart, in his *Orthographie* of 1569, argued that we should spell as we speak. There should be "as many letters in our writing, as we doe voices or breathes in speaking and no more." To this end, Hart developed a remarkably inventive system of phonetic writing (which did not catch on). But his attempt has given us valuable evidence for how English was (or should have been) pronounced in the early modern period. His attempt was as much social and political as it was linguistic. For him, the best English was that of the "learned":

> that speech which euery reasonable English man, will the nearest he can, frame his tongue thereunto; but such as haue no conference by the liuely voice, nor experience of reading, nor in reading no certaintie how euery letter should be sounded, can neuer come to the knowledge and use of that best and most perfite English.

(Hart 1969, 21r)

Reason and literacy go together here. English can be perfect. He notes later on that this better English will be the language of London and the university towns, not from places such as "Newcastell upon Tine" or "Cornewale."

Hart's younger contemporary, Richard Mulcaster, thought somewhat differently. Mulcaster was the director of the Merchant Taylors' School in London. He was Edmund Spenser's teacher. In his *Elementarie* of 1582, he favors "custom" in English spelling. English, he writes, must "rest content with the number of our letters." Spelling reformers like Hart will only "cumber our tong, both with strange caracts & with nedeless dipthongs, enforcing vs from that, which generall rule hath won, and rested content with" (Mulcaster 1970 [1582], pp. 88–9). Mulcaster is one of the first teachers to enforce the idea of spelling rules as rules. He affirms that we should spell words beginning with h (*honest, humble, honor, hostage*, and so on) even though, in everyday speech, they are pronounced "upon the o, not aspirate."

By the early 1600s, a notion of "good" English emerges – not just according to education or class but according to naturalness. Milton's teacher, Alexander Gil (1564–1635), the headmaster of St. Paul's School, published a book about the English language in 1619. His *Logonomia Anglica*, written in Latin, offered a guide to proper grammar and pronunciation. Gil was one of the orthoepists, and his attempts at phonetic transcription have helped scholars recover the speech sounds of the age of Shakespeare. But his uncompromising judgments are what strike readers today. He wants English "to conform not the pronunciation of plowmen, working-girls, and river-men (*bubulci, muhercule, potiores*), but to that used by learned and refined men (*docti* and *culte eruditi viri*)" (Gil 1972, p. 87). Once again, acts of linguistic description become acts of linguistic prescription. Speech marks social class. Gil's concern is to record how a particularly culti- vated and erudite group of men talk and then make those ways a standard for others. He differentiates affected pronunciations of the socially aspirant from the sounds of the cultivated. In these cases, he is also contrasting regional variation (his affectations are from "the Eastern Dialect;" Dobson 1968, p. 149) with a metropolitan standard. Here are some of his examples, using his spelling system to attempt to reproduce sounds.

Affected	*Acceptable*
len	laun (linen)
kembric	kambric (cambric)
kepn	kapon (capon)
meds	maidz (maids)
ple	play (play)
gi	giv (give)

The history of English pronunciation at this time, then, is not just a matter of sound changes and regional variations. It is a matter of institutional authorities judging and advising ways of speaking based on class and learning.

The Changing Words of English

From the death of Chaucer to the birth of Shakespeare, English dramatically increased its lexical stock. Words were borrowed from other languages, and they were coined anew. Intellectual and professional disciplines developed their own, rarefied vocabularies. Travel, commerce, and colonial expansion brought words from other European languages and from Africa, Asia, and North America. Rhe- torical education in the schools encouraged a linguistic inventiveness. Before looking at these new words, we should recognize that the increase in the vocabu- lary was not just a matter of external forces. Words were borrowed from other languages, but there had to be a reason for doing so. One of those reasons was a new attitude toward the vernacular at the beginning of the sixteenth century. Writing in 1533, Sir Thomas Elyot, gave voice to a cultural moment: a desire to "augment" English. This desire was not just linguistic; it was aesthetic and political. The idea of English political expansion during the reign of Henry VIII affected the English language, too. The rhetorical trope of amplification – the verbal means of expanding or developing an argument or description – came to be the centerpiece of Renaissance literary education and performance. The desire to simply make English bigger took hold. These are some of the ways the English vocabulary was augmented.

Word Formation and Word Coinages

Making new words was, and remains, relatively easy. Take a base word or a root and add a prefix or a suffix. Prefixes could be negative (un-, dis-, mal-); they could be locative (mid-, sub-, super-, trans-); they could be temporal (pre-, post-); they could be quantitative (bi-, tri-, mono-, pan-, multi-). Suffixes could turn words into new nouns (-ness, -ity, -hood). They could make new adjectives (-ly, -ish, -worthy, -some). They could make new adverbs (-ly, -wise). They could make nouns into verbs (-ate, -er).

Words could also be compounded. We saw how in OE and the Germanic languages, the primary means of creating new words (or translating Latin terms into the vernacular) was by compounding. As in OE, compounding could be of the noun+noun type ("bookseller," "bullfrog"). It could be of the modifier + noun type, creating noun phrases ("drawing room," "walking stick," "dancing girl").

Nouns could become verbs and verbs could become nouns, sometimes without any modification ("bargain," "bottle," "trumpet"). Sometimes these differences came to be indicated by change in word stress: óbject, objéct; tórment, tormént; récord, recórd.

Aureation and Inkhorn Terms

Poets in the fifteenth century developed a rarefied vocabulary of polysyllabic words of Romance origin, designed to gild or make "aureate" the diction of their verse ("aureate," from the Latin word for "gold"). They argued that this kind of vocabulary would be more stable and lasting than English, that English was constantly varying over time and space, but Latin would remain stable. Words that had a Latinate feel to them, even though they seem strange and affected to us today, were perceived to be somehow less subject to the corrosion of time (and hence, golden not just because they were ornamental but because they would not tarnish). In the early 1500s, the coining and borrowing of words that existed only on the page, rather than in everyday speech, made these words only out of the inkhorn: that is, words of such rarefied origin and polysyllabic strangeness that they could only exist in formal writing. Some writers favored these words; others dismissed them. Thomas Wilson, in *The Arte of Rhetorique* (1909 [1553]), found them excessive. Some of them have disappeared: *accersited, adepted, condisciple, fatigate*. Others have survived: *celebrate, frivolous, sublimity*.

What this kind of vocabulary did functionally was not just increase the word stock but foster a sense of different registers of diction. **Register** is a key feature in the sociolinguistic study of a population. We can say the same thing in many ways, but with many different effects: the difference between "kill" and "annihilate," "love" and "cherish," "drink" and "imbibe," "speak" and "orate," "orate" and "bloviate" are all differences of register. This practice of having multiple words for the same concepts, some native, and some based on loans, emerged in the early 1500s as a social practice.

Sustained Borrowing from French and Latin

French words entered English through the Norman Conquest, the educational and social institutions of the later Middle Ages, the royal court, and literary and legal discourses. Even though French was disappearing as the official or prestige language by the middle of the fifteenth century, the penchant for borrowing words from French remained a matter of social aspiration and fashion. Such loans were not just single words. Phrasal expressions based on French models came to be marks of class or hierarchy: "at your service," "pay a visit," "do a favor." Latin words came into English through learning and religion. But Latin had an effect on early Modern English in the structure of words. Such Latin prefixes as ex- and con- made possible a whole system of new words. Suffixes such as -ence (from Latin -entia), though used for French loans, came to be deployed to make new words out of old ones.

This borrowing was not uniform. We can see over time how the kinds of words borrowed from Latin in particular changed. Using the *Oxford English Dictionary*, we can date the period for the following kinds of loan words. There are many words in each category; this is just a sampling.

- For the late 1400s, the *OED* records these words first recorded in English: instruct, hostile, popular, victim.
- For the first half of the 1500s, these words appear: integer, genius, junior, acumen, folio, circus, axis.
- For the second half of the 1500s, we see: vacuum, genus, species, corona, innuendo, decorum, compendium, militia, sinus, virus.

This is a highly selective list, but it represents a trend. Words from Latin increasingly come to be words for technical, scientific, and physical phenomena. We can see registers develop: tiers of language use.

We can see these changes in some representative samples of English prose. Here are three writers on the English language:

> Certaynly it is harde to playse euery man / bycause of dyuersite & chaũge of langage. For in these dayes euery man that is in ony reputacyon in his coũtre. wyll vtter his cõmynycacyon and maters in suche maners & termes / that fewe men shall vnderstonde theym / And som honest and grete clerkes haue ben wyth me and desired me to wryte the moste curyous termes that I coude fynde / And thus bytwene playn rude / & curyous I stande abasshed. but in my Iudgemente / the comyn termes that be dayli vsed ben lyghter to be vnderstonde than the olde and aũcyent englysshe.
> (William Caxton, Preface to the *Eneydos*, 1490; Caxton 1928, pp. 108–9)

> His highnesse benignely receyuynge my booke, which I named the Gouernour, in the redyng therof soon perceyued, that I intended to augment our

Englyshe tongue, whereby men shoulde as well expresse more aboundantly the thyng that they conceiued in their hertes (wherfore language was ordained) hauing wordes apte for the purpose; as also interprete out of greke, latine, or any other tonge into Englysshe, as sufficiently, as out of any one of the said tonges into an other.

> (Thomas Elyot, *Of the knowledge which Maketh a Wise Man*,
> 1533; Elyot 1946, p. xii)

Rhetorique is an art to set furthe by vtteraunce of wordes, matter at large, or (as Cicero doeth saie) it is a learned, or rather an artificiall declaracion of the mynde, in the handelyng of any cause, called in contencion, that maie through reason largely be discussed …. First therefore an Orator muste labour to tell his tale, that the hearers maie well knowe what he meaneth, and vnderstande him wholy, the whiche he shall with ease do, if he vtter his mind in plain wordes, suche as are vsually receiued, and tell it orderly, without goyng aboute the busshe. That if he doe not this, he shall neuer do the other. For what manne can be delited or yet be perswaded, with the onely hearyng of those thynges, whiche he knoweth not what thei meane. The tongue is ordeined to expresse the mynde, that one mighte vnder|stande anothers meaning.

> (Thomas Wilson, *The Arte of Rhetorique*, 1553; Wilson 1909 [1553], p. 2)

All three writers use Francophone and Latinate words to discuss language change. Caxton's vocabulary remains Chaucerian: "diversity," "reputation," "abashed," "communication," and "curious" are all attested from the last decades of the 1300s (almost all appear in Chaucer's own writings). Elyot's vocabulary is similarly familiar, but he uses particular loan words in new ways. "Augment," a coinage of the fifteenth century, becomes part of a rhetorical vocabulary for copiousness, and Elyot's usage is contemporary with a new sense of the verb as (in the words of the *OED*) enabling a "raise in status or rank." His sense, too, of "apt" words is a new usage ("apt," coming from Latin *aptus*, shows up only in the last decades of the 1400s). In fact, Elyot's use of "apt" as (in the words of the *OED*) "of language: suitable or appropriate to express ideas," paraphrases Cicero's views of rhetoric, and what we have here is not so much a new English coinage as the use of a Latin word in an English setting.

For Thomas Wilson, the words of rhetorical performance are similarly new and newly applied. "Artificial" is a post-Chaucerian coinage, but it does not connote falsity. It means something learned through art. The word "persuade" enters English in the late fifteenth century in the contexts of rhetorical education: that this is the job of public speech. The word "utter" originally meant to sell or give out, and only in the late 1400s and early 1500s did it come to mean "to speak." Wilson's most colloquial and plain moment, "tell it orderly, without goying aboute the busshe," is, in fact, relatively new. The *OED* cites this text as the first appearance of the phrase in this form (the phrase, "beat about the bush" appears a few decades earlier).

What we also see in these writers is a changing sense of what is natural or appropriate in language. Caxton's concerns are largely external. He wants to please his readers and communicate as clearly as possible to the largest audience: "comyn terms that be dayli vsed ben lighter to be vnderstonde." For Elyot and Wilson, what matters is an inner, almost philosophical relationship of word and thing. Notice how they both use the word "ordained" to define language. It is as if, now, the job of words is to express something that has been set from above (the word "ordained" still carries with it that sense of a religious approval or decree). Plainness, then, for Elyot and Wilson, is different from plainness in Caxton. It carries with it, now, a sense of clarity, of naturalness. Rhetoric is about order: about the ranging of words in sequence to make an argument. "To tell it orderly" resonates with the word "ordained" – the idea is that the use of speech is something as well shaped as Creation itself. "The tongue is ordained to expresse the mynd, that one mighte vnderstande anothers meaning."

What these examples show are three writers who are very self-conscious about their vocabulary choices. They juxtapose words of French and Latin origin with phrases that have, if not the origin, then the feel of "native" English. They make the case for a plain or direct style, while at the same time using words that were part of a polysyllabic lexis of rhetorical writing. Even though most of their words were not new at the time of writing, these writers use them to develop a professional, disciplinary vocabulary. This feature is also what is new in English. Scholarship, law, medicine, and various trades and crafts developed their own professional vocabularies. What we are witnessing is the development of a discipline of rhetoric in English.

New Worlds of Words

The period of early Modern English was a time of great physical and intellectual movement. Trade, colonization, war, and exploration brought English speakers into contact with Spanish, Portuguese, and Dutch peoples. A maritime vocabulary developed from these languages. Words such as "dock" and "yacht" came from Dutch in the sixteenth century; "keelhaul," "cruise," "jib," "knapsack," and "smack" (meaning a single-masted sailing ship) came in the first half of the seventeenth century.

Many words from Spanish and Portuguese were not only loan words from colonial expansion but were the media through which words from non-European languages came into English. Words such as "maize" and "potato" were New World, Native American words that passed through Spanish. A word such as "fetish," originally meaning a small idol or carved object of veneration, came from Portuguese but began to mean a distinctively African object.

A good example of word borrowing and semantic transformation is "hub-bub." It appears in English in the 1500s as a kind of echo word or onomato-poeia, referring to the incomprehensible sounds of Irish and Welsh Gaelic. Soon it was transferred to the sound of Native Americans. Edmund Spenser, in *Faerie Queene* (1596), can associate it with the sound of the bagpipes. Early New England colonists used the word to characterize a game played by the Massachusetts Indians. Half a century later, John Milton characterized the noisy debate of the newly fallen angels in Hell as "a universal hubbub wild" (*Paradise Lost*, 2.951). His Hell, then, is a place of non-European noise, a place as alien and wild as any imagined North American or Irish coast.

Not everyone was happy with these linguistic developments. Alexander Gil saw good English as a matter of word choice and pronunciation. He condemned Chaucer as "notorious by the use of Latin and French words." He saw this influx as appealing to the "uneducated masses," who "admire most what they least comprehend." English had become a wilderness in which "daily wild beasts of words are tamed, and horrid evil-sounding magpies and owls of unpropitious birth are taught to hazard our words." For Gil, English is now a bastard tongue, and anyone who reads him cannot help but recall his famous student's later vi-sion of a Hell of bad sounds. Milton again:

> At length a universal hubbub wild
> Of stunning sounds and voices all confus'd
> Born through the hollow dark assaults his ear
> With loudest vehemence.

> (*Paradise Lost*, 2.951–4)

Read Gil in his original Latin and you get an eerily similar scene: *ita quotidie fera vocum monstra cicuriat* (literally, "everyday, the feral monsters of words are tamed" Gil 1972).

To tame these words, scholars began to produce dictionaries. At first, these were compilations of what were called "hard words," loans and new coinages. Joseph Bullokar's *Expositor* (1616), Henry Cockeram's *Dictionairre* (1634), and Edward Phillips's *New World of English Words* (1658) responded to the need for guidance. Phillips's title, one could argue, makes the English vocabulary into a new land to explore and colonize. Each dictionary offers a collection of words from the arts and sciences of the time. Cockeram organized his *Dictionairre* into three parts, moving from the familiar to the *outré*: first, the hard words new to English; then what he called "vulgar" or familiar terms, together with synonyms; and third, terms for mythological and newly found creatures. These are what he calls "the choisest words ... now in vse, wherewith our language is inriched and become so copious." His aim is to enable readers to develop "a more refined and elegant speech." In that last section, he offers nothing less than a kind of wild creation: "Gods and goddesses, Giants and Deuils, Monsters and Serpents, Birds and Beasts, Riuers, Fishes, Herbs, Stones, Trees, and the like" (Cockeram 1968, title page).

Cockeram and his contemporaries sustain the concerns of Caxton, Elyot, and Wilson: to judge and select, to prescribe and teach good English. What is truly new here is not just discrimination or opinion; it is the idea that the English language could be assessed *aesthetically:* that is, that concepts of beauty, purity, style, and form were becoming the criteria for language use – in admitting new words, in shaping the syntax of sentences, in coming up with rules for grammar and spelling.

Looking up words in these early dictionaries may not tell us much at first glance. Familiar words get brief definitions:

augment:	to increase
augmentation:	an increasing
artificial:	cunning, well-contrived, skillful

Bullokar's definitions appear also verbatim in Cockeram. To get to the real heart of these books is to see how they augment the language by coming up with new Latinate terms for common experience. A page from Cockeram lists words that we still use today (though some spellings have changed): *proximitie* (defined as "to approach or draw neere"), *pulchritude* (defined as "fairenessse, beautie"), *punctuall* ("not missing haires breadth, to the purpose"), and *purgative* ("which hath virtue to purge"). But there are other words that have dropped out of usage, or that Cockerham himself may have coined. He offers words such as *puellaritie* and *puerilitie*. These seem to exist simply because they can (from the Latin, *puella*, "girl," and *puer*, "boy"). Cockeram augmented the material in Bullokar here, for the earlier *Expositor* had *puerility* as "childishness." Bullokar also had *pudicity* as "chastity." Phillips's *New World of Words* has Bullokar's *pudicity* as "chastity, modesty." He has *puerile*, "belonging to a child, childish, boyish," and *puerility*, "boyishness, childishness, a childish trick." There are also some bizarre words and definitions. *Pupillate* means "to cry like a Peacocke." *Pullation* means "the hatching of Chickens" (a word found nowhere else, and that Cockeram probably made up). And the word *publican*, which might look transparent to us (the keeper of a pub or tavern), gets this strangely angry definition: "An odious name among the Jewes, for commonly they were wicked livers, hiring the common Prophets of the Citie at a certaine rent."

The history of words like these tells us as much as the history of words for any of Cockeram's imaginary creatures. It shows us how early modern English scholars were trying to find learned terms for everything, even a hatching of chickens. These are not guides to usage but displays of erudition.

In such a world, not only were there new words, but old words were changing meaning. Semantic shifts in English happened with greater frequency during the early modern period, and the result was what we call **polysemy**. Polysemy is the condition of words having more than one meaning. Such multiplicity of meaning may be synchronic – that is, it may reflect how words were used to describe different things. But it also may be diachronic – that is, how older meanings survive along with newer meanings, creating ambiguity and the possibility of wordplay.

The Introduction to this book illustrated polysemy with the examples of "silly" and "uncouth," words of OE origin that originally connoted inner conditions or states of being and later came to refer to the outer appearances of such beings. If you were "silly," you may have been blessed or touched by the spirit. Over time, if you were "silly," you were acting in a strange and foolish way. Similarly, something that was "uncouth" was simply unknown. An uncouth person, however, came to be someone who is rude, strange, or behaving in an unacceptable way. Cockeram defines *uncoth* as "unknown, strange." A generation later, Phillips can define it with its full range of new connotations:

> **Uncouth**, odd, rough harsh, unpolished, foreign, barbarous; from the *Saxon* Word *Uncuth*, which signifies unknown, and is us'd in the old *Saxon* Laws, for a Stranger that comes to an Inn Guest-wise and lies there but one Night.

This example gives us far more of a sense of semantic change in motion than the chart of dates in the introduction. It shows us how the meaning of a word has changed and behind that change lies a narrative of action. Phillips makes his definition of "uncouth" about the ancient "Saxon" world of laws and language, a world of rough, unpolished English (what Caxton would have called "rude" and what poet John Skelton, writing in the 1480s, would have called his own "unpullysht" words, "naked and plain").

As we will see in later chapters, polysemy made possible the rise of pun and wordplay. Words from technical vocabularies were becoming common. Older words were coming to mean appearances rather than essentials. On one hand, we have the teaching of the schoolmasters: a desire for plain speech, a correspondence between word and thing, and a belief that language or the tongue was somehow "ordained" to be and do something. On the other hand, we have the increasing playfulness of rhetorical performance, the sense that words were elusive and that word play was something socially destabilizing. The bantering thugs that open Shakespeare's *Romeo and Juliet* spend much time punning on the words "coals" and "collier" – a game that hinges on a knowledge of the French word *collions*, for testicles (a good example of what the early dictionary makers would have called puerility). The foolish rustics in *A Midsummer Night's Dream* can have their silly character of Thisbe, in their puerile play, say to the character of Wall, "My cherry lips have often kissed thy stones," another pun that goes back not to learned French but to the oldest of OE metaphors. Shakespeare can write a sonnet to a loved one, stating that his "bonds in thee are all determinate" – a complex image bringing together a new, commercial sense of investment bonds coming to term with an older sense of the bonds of love having been determined.

More and more, the history of English becomes a contest between the learned and the lewd, between the arbiters of language standards and the playfulness of clowns and poets. In Shakespeare and his contemporaries, we see English becoming a medium of literary wit and power in ways that still influence our language today.

Sources and Further Reading

Caxton, W. (1928). *The Prologues and Epilogues of William Caxton*. (Ed.) W. J. B. Crotch, Early English Text Society, Original Series 176. London: Oxford University Press.

Cockeram, H. (1930). *The Dictionaire of 1623, by Henry Cockeram*, with a prefatory note by Chauncy Brewster Timber. New York: Huntington Press.

Cohen, M. (1977). *Sensible Words: Linguistic Practice in England, 1640–1785*. Baltimore, MD: Johns Hopkins University Press.

Davis, N. (1971) *The Paston Letters and Papers of the Fifteenth Century*. 3 vols. Oxford: Oxford University Press.

Dobson, E. J. (1968). *English Pronunciation: 1500–1700*. 2nd edn. Oxford: Oxford University Press.

Elyot, T. (1946 [1533]). *The Knowledge Which Maketh a Wise Man* (London, 1533), (Ed.) Edwin Johnston Howard. Oxford, OH: Anchor Press.

Fisher, J. H. (1996). *The Emergence of Standard English*. Lexington, KY: University of Kentucky Press.

Fisher, J. H., Richardson, M., and Fisher, J. L. (1984). *An Anthology of London English*. Knoxville, TN. University of Tennessee Press.

Giancarlo, M. (2001). "The Rise and Fall of the Great Vowel Shift? The Changing Ideological Intersections of Philology, Historical Linguistics, and Literary History." *Representations* 76: 27–60.

Gil, A. (1968 [1619]). *Logonomia Anglica* (London, 1619). Facsimile Reprint, English Linguistics 1500–1800, No. 68. Menston: Scolar Press.

Gil, A. (1972). *Logonomia Anglica*. (Eds.) Bror Danielsson and A. Gabrielson. Trans. R. C. Alston. Stockholm: Almqvist and Wiksell.

Hart, J. (1969). *An Orthographie* (London, 1569). Facsimile Reprint, English Linguistics 1500–1800, No. 209. Menston: Scolar Press.

Jespersen, O. (1909). *A Modern English Grammar on Historical Principles*. vol. 1, *Sounds and Spellings*. Heidelberg: Carl Winter.

Lass, R. (2008). "Phonology and Morphology." In R. Lass (Ed.), *CHEL*, vol. 3. Cambridge: Cambridge University Press, pp. 56–186.

Lerer, S. (1993). *Chaucer and His Readers: Imagining the Author in Late-Medieval England*. Princeton, NJ: Princeton University Press.

Mack, P. (2002). *Elizabethan Rhetoric*. Cambridge: Cambridge University Press.

Mulcaster, R. (1970 [1582]). *The First Part of the Elementarie* (London, 1582). Facsimile Reprint, English Linguistics 1500–1800, No. 219. Menston: Scolar Press.

Nevalainen, T. (2008)."Early Modern English Lexis and Semantics." In R. Lass (Ed.), *CHEL*, vol. 3. Cambridge: Cambridge University Press, pp. 332–458.

Phillips, E. (1658). *A New World of English Words* (London, 1658). Facsimile edition available at: https://quod.lib.umich.edu/e/eebo/A54746.0001.001?view=toc

Price, O. (1970 [1665]). *The Vocal Organ* (London, 1665). Facsimile Reprint, English Linguistics 1500–1800, No. 227. Menston: Scolar Press.

Wallis, J. (1972). *Grammar of the English Language with an Introductory Grammatico-physical Treatise on Speech*. Translated with a commentary by J. A. Kemp. London: Longman.

Wilkins, J. (1968 [1668]). *An Essay Towards a Real Character, and a Philosophical Language* (London, 1668). Facsimile Reprint, English Linguistics 1500–1800, No. 119. Menston: Scolar Press.

Wilson, T. (1909 [1553]). *The Arte of Rhetorique* (London, 1553), edition of 1585. (Ed.) G. Mair. Oxford: Clarendon Press.

6 English in the Age of William Shakespeare and the King James Bible

Literary writers have always had an effect on language development. Dante's use of the Florentine dialect in the *Divine Comedy* (1325) helped standardize the Italian vernacular. Martin Luther's German translation of the Bible (the New Testament in 1522, the Old Testament in 1534) provided a new model for German. For Italy, France, and several other European nations, establishing national academies of language, often with literary figures in leadership, codified accepted usage and vocabulary in the seventeenth and eighteenth centuries. England always resisted establishing a national linguistic academy, and matters of literary and everyday judgment were left to writers like Jonathan Swift, dictionary makers like Samuel Johnson, and teachers such as William Lowth and Joseph Priestley.

Behind much of this sense of an emerging English standard in the seventeenth and eighteenth centuries was the example of William Shakespeare (1564–1616) and the King James Version (KJV) of the Bible (1611). Like Geoffrey Chaucer, Shakespeare was valued as a linguistic innovator. He is credited with coining new words, appropriating new loan words, and creatively transforming everyday speech. How much of this Shakespeare actually did has long been debated. He did not coin the upwards of six thousand words attributed to him (though in many cases, he took existing words and added modifying prefixes such as un-). Although he did bequeath a host of indelibly memorable phrases into English, many of them were modeled on earlier rhetorical examples, popular proverbs, and classical adages.

Nonetheless, Shakespeare affected the development of English in a way unlike any other writer, and one aim of this chapter is to explore the nature of his vernacular usage and its impact. Much research has been conducted on recovering the pronunciation of the English of his time, and this chapter explores the sounds of speech around 1600. Much research has also been done on Shakespeare's relationship to the traditions of vernacular schooling and rhetorical education of the Renaissance, and this chapter looks at how relationships between grammar and style developed. Shakespeare used certain words and phrases that remain unmistakably unique in modern usage, and we also consider some of those.

DOI: 10.4324/9781003227083-7

The KJV did not really change the English language as much as it codified a register of formal English. Public speech, religious discourse, sermons, parables, and historical narratives all found themselves seasoned with the flavor of this book. The men who created its translation were the leading scholars of their time. Their aims were to fashion a linguistic sensibility that would be seen as authoritative and resistant to change. To these ends, their language was archaic in its own time, often drawing on English translations from earlier in the 1500s and drawing on their educational experience from decades before.

Shakespeare and the KJV are two pressure points in the history of English: one innovative, the other conservative. Together, they help us see how the English language of the early 1600s influenced the following centuries of usage. More broadly, they help us understand how the history of English is not only a story of people speaking and writing but also of authorities modeling that speech and writing for the future.

The Sounds of Shakespeare

Shakespeare was writing for the stage and for print from the 1580s until his death in 1616. His poetry and plays were printed in various forms throughout his life, and in 1623 the *First Folio* of his works appeared – a collection of 36 plays, organized as comedies, histories, and tragedies, along with a preface by the editors and commendatory verses in memory of the author. Even in its printed form, Shakespeare's work was designed to be spoken: performed on the stage, or read aloud. In fact, silent reading as a social habit, although not unknown in earlier historical periods, did not become the social norm until the nineteenth century. Pronunciation, though, is not just a matter of historical interest. The literature of early Modern English plays with sound and sense. It has, deliberately, an aural effect. Words rhyme, lines scan, and even passages of prose have rhythm. We need to hear this language as much as see it.

During the late sixteenth and early seventeenth centuries, the sound changes associated with the Great Vowel Shift (GVS) were still in process. Some words that do not rhyme today rhymed in Shakespeare's time. By contrast, some words that rhyme today did not back then. There was taste for pun and wordplay in Renaissance English school room and the stage. Did different pronunciations enable puns that we can no longer appreciate? Did spelling influence pronunciation and, in turn, our ability to recover certain bits of verbal sport?

How much we can rely on printed texts as evidence is also up for debate. We know that Shakespeare's works and the poetry, prose, and drama of his time were often printed without an author's oversight or approval. Printers made mistakes. Sometimes, they recast passages they did not understand. Sometimes, they added words and letters that were not in the original. Sometimes they misheard (if they were taking dictation) sounds. Different printers had different conventions for spelling, punctuation, and capitalization. Much could go astray between the pen of the author, the hand of the copyist, the mouth of the narrator, and the printing press. Early English bookmaking was a mess by modern standards.

If you believe that all rhymes are perfect, that writers pun and play whenever they get the chance, and that metrical lines scan with regularity, then you are going to come up with an approach to historical pronunciation that will reflect that belief. Perhaps instead you believe that metrical regularity was something imposed on early modern writers by later editors; that the spellings of early printed books do not fully reflect pronunciation; and you believe that the orthoepists, for all their knowledge and dedication to establishing standard English pronunciations, were concerned more with telling people how to speak than describing actually how they did speak. If you hold these latter positions, then you will have a very different notion of historical pronunciation.

The aim of this book is to give the broad outlines of the range of acceptable, historical pronunciations in the age of Shakespeare. To do so, we identify a few key features of that pronunciation: what linguist David Crystal has called "signature sounds." In what follows, symbols in square brackets [ ] are attempts at phonetic transcription. They represent how certain words may have been pronounced or may be pronounced. Symbols between slash marks // are phonemic transcriptions, representing the meaningful phonemes of a time and place, whether or not they were actually pronounced in that way.

Diphthongs

The most notable difference between early Modern English pronunciation and our own is that of the diphthongs that developed from the high front vowels of Middle English. Modern standard pronunciation gives /ai/ and /au/, as in the words "mice" and "house." During the GVS, there was a period of time and a certain set of places where the pronunciation of these diphthongs began with a lower and more central sound, represented by the schwa symbol, /ə/. Words such as "mice" and "house" would have been /məis/ and /həus/. We may still hear these sounds in some regional British and North American dialects. The general consensus is that these were the pronunciations of these diphthongs in Shakespeare's time.

By contrast, certain sounds that we pronounce today as diphthongs were probably closer to monophthongs in Shakespeare's English. The GVS raised and fronted the long monophthongs in stressed positions. Later sound changes made some of them diphthongs. A word such as "goat" is pronounced today as [gəot]. A word such as "face" is pronounced today as [fæis]. A word such as "pure" is, in American English, usually pronounced [piur] or even [pjur]. Some have argued that in modern standard English, there are no true monophthongs, but that all long vowel sounds are pronounced with the mouth moving from one position to another. As we will see in other chapters, certain global forms of English (notably Australian) tend to exaggerate these sounds, making them even into triphthongs, for example, [faiəs]. The general consensus is that in Shakespeare's time, sounds such as these were probably long monophthongs: "goat" /goːt/; "face" /fɛːs/; "pure" /puːr/.

The Status of r

The pronunciation of the /r/ sound is one of the defining features of a dialect and of a historical state of the language. Forms of the language with a pronunciation of the r in the environment of surrounding vowels are called **rhotic**. Adding the r pronunciation is called **rhotocization**. An /r/ that follows a vowel is called a **postvocalic r**. Rhotocization is a feature that often distinguishes modern American from modern British English. Pronunciations of the words "car," "far," "partial," "very," "lard," "lord," and the like often distinguish a British from a North American speaker. They also distinguish, as we shall see, certain regional dialects of North American English. The famous caricature of the Boston Brahmin accent, "park your car in Harvard Yard" as [paːk yɔː kaː ɪn haːvaːd jaːd], is a good example of a nonrhotic American dialect.

In early modern England, the postvocalic r was extremely variable. It was probably more commonly pronounced than in modern British English. Words such as "nurse," "curse," "north," "flower," and names like "Orlando" and "Ferdinand" had a stronger and more obviously pronounced r than they do today. The orthoepists are not uniform in their descriptions. Playwright Ben Jonson (1572–1637) wrote an English grammar, and his remarks may reflect early seventeenth-century habits. The sound /r/, he wrote, "is sounded firme in the beginning of the words, and more liquid in the middle, and ends." A century later, a certain M. Flint, writing in French about English pronunciation noted that r is often "greatly softened, almost mute, and slightly lengthens the preceding vowel" (*CHEL*, vol. 3, p. 115). By the end of the eighteenth century, writers on English pronunciation agree that the /r/ sound has largely been lost after a vowel. For the student seeking to evoke the sound of Shakespeare's English, pronouncing the /r/ is a good rule of thumb.

The sound /r/ influenced other vowels. Words with -er- spellings, such as "clerk," "servant," and "mercy" had an /ɛ/ sound in Middle English, but by the later 1500s, they were pronounced with an /a/ sound. Queen Elizabeth I wrote *clark, saruant*, and *marcy*. Some of these words reverted to /ɛ/ sounds, especially in American English, but some kept both. The words "university" and "varsity" are essentially the same but with different pronunciations. The university at Berkeley is pronounced with an /ɛ/, but the eighteenth-century Bishop Berkeley is pronounced with an /a/. The words "vermin" and "varmint" are also the same, but are pronounced differently because of historical and regional variation.

Rounding and Retracting after /w/

The pronunciation of the glide /w/ influenced the following back vowel /a/. This new sound is represented by the symbol /ɒ/. This change was happening in the seventeenth century. Thus, the following words no longer rhyme: war/car, wart/ cart, wad/cad, and so on. This sound change, however, did not occur if the vowel was followed by a velar consonant. Thus, "wax" rhymes with "lax," "wag" rhymes with "lag," and so on. Shakespeare seems to rhyme the words "granting" and "wanting" in Sonnet 87. If we accept these as true rhymes, the influence of /w/ on the following vowel happened later than the composition of this poem (the sonnets were printed in 1609 but were most likely composed in the 1590s during the vogue for sonnet sequences in England).

Short u Sounds

Words such as "put" and "cut" apparently rhymed in Shakespeare's time. Ben Jonson's prefatory poem to the *First Folio* of Shakespeare's plays (published in 1623) begins by characterizing the portrait of Shakespeare on the frontispiece.

> This Figure that thou here seest put,
> It was for gentle Shakespeare cut;

In the phonetic alphabet, the symbol /ʊ/ represents a low back rounded vowel, and the symbol /ʌ/ represents a low back unrounded vowel. In Modern English, "cut" would be /cʌt/ and "put" would be /pʊt/. Early modern pronunciations were probably closer to /ʊ/ (see Lass 2008, p. 90).

Elision

There is evidence from the orthoepists and the metrical patterns of Renaissance poetry that certain sounds were not pronounced. The initial h was almost always dropped. The name of Hamlet's friend, Horatio, would have been pronounced as "Oratio," providing us with punning wordplay on the relationship of virtue and speech. There is also evidence that the final -g in gerunds and participles was dropped ("posessin'," instead of "possessing"). In multisyllable words, medial sounds would often be elided. Thus, a word such as "everybody" would have sounded something like [ɛvribdi], "delivery" would have been [dəlivrəi], and "venomous" would have been [vɛnməs]. In poetry and everyday speech, people often reduced unstressed words to the schwa sound. In a phrase such as "one and two," the word "and" would have been reduced to [ən].

From information like this, some have argued that Hamlet's advice to his actors, to speak his speech "trippingly on the tongue," means to speak quickly and with much elision.

Words and Forms

Shakespeare wrote when the lexis of English was growing dramatically. Loan words from European and non-European languages, coinages for scientific and technical terms based on Latin and Greek roots, and the rhetorical concept of *copia* (the "aug-menting" of the language as we saw in Chapter 5) all contributed to what we see now as a statistical spike in size of the English vocabulary. The *OED* records 2,200 words that are first attested in Shakespeare (he is the most frequently cited author in the *OED*). Of course, this does not mean that Shakespeare invented these words. Nor does it mean that for his readers and his audiences, these words would have been seen and heard as his alone. It means that Shakespeare, in an authoritative and influential way, contributed to the changing English vocabulary of his time, and lexi-cal authorities such as the *OED* rely on his works more than others. (As an aside, the author who has the second largest number of citations after Shakespeare in the *OED* is nineteenth-century novelist Sir Walter Scott, probably because he recorded many regional and colloquial terms from Scotland and the north of England.)

Some of these words may be genuinely new. Shakespeare coined them out of pre-existing loans from Latin and other languages. Sometimes (in the case of a word such as "bandit"), he borrowed directly from another language. A sample includes: accommodation, assassination, barefaced, bandit, countless, courtship, dwindle, majestic, premeditated, submerged. A sample also includes those words that were already current in English but to which Shakespeare added a prefix: dishearten, dislocate, impartial, inauspicious, indistinguishable, invulnerable. It includes those words to which he added a suffix: amazement, dexterously, lonely, palmy (meaning triumphant), obsequiously. Of course, it includes those words he made his own by adding a negative prefix: unhappy, unhand, unmask, unlock, untie, unveil, unbend, unmake, unprovoked, unsex. A list of Shakespeare's words also includes compounds he concocted from every-day speech: fat-witted, fly-bitten, fortune-teller, green-eyed, honey-tongued, ill-tempered, lily-livered, pale-faced, puppy-dog.

Shakespeare's lexical inventiveness was at the level of the morpheme. He built new words out of old parts. In the process, he revealed something of the linguistic experimentation of his time – a sense that new words did not come out of thin air but grew from the creative play of the writer or the speaker.

Lists of words, however, do not tell the whole story. Shakespeare often used familiar words in new ways. One of his strategies was to take words from a technical vocabulary and deploy them metaphorically. Here is a transcription of Sonnet 87 as it first appeared in the 1609 edition of the Sonnets.

> FArewell thou art too deare for my possessing,
> And like enough thou knowst thy estimate,
> The Cha ter of thy worth giues thee releasing:
> My bonds in thee are all determinate.
> For how do I hold thee but by thy granting,
> And for that ritches where is my deseruing?
> The cause of this faire guift in me is wanting,
> And so my pattent back againe is sweruing.

Thy selfe thou gau'st, thy owne worth then not knowing,
Or mee to whom thou gau'st it, else mistaking,
So thy great guift vpon misprision growing,
Comes home againe, on better iudgement making.
Thus haue I had thee as a dreame doth flatter,
In sleepe a King, but waking no such matter.

Here, Shakespeare takes words from investment and trade and turns them into a vocabulary of love. The word "deare" goes back to Old English and means both cherished and expensive. Here it functions as a kind of pun on which the language of the sonnet balances. The word "estimate" as a noun meaning valuation or price was not recorded until the 1560s. "Bond" connotes a tie to a person but also a legal and financial agreement (again, a sense not recorded until the late sixteenth century). That these bonds are "determinate" means that they are coming to term. The speaker's "patent," in this sense, is a kind of legal right, a formally decided agreement or license. The double sense of the sonnet raises questions about how changing structures in law and commerce change human relationships. There is a back and forth here: releasing, granting, swerving, giving, and coming home again. Like those who sent out ships in exploration, we await a return on the investment in a literal and figurative sense.

Looking at this sonnet in its first printing tells us something about spelling and pronunciation in the early 1600s. The word for "charter" appears as "Cha ter," as if the r was mistakenly dropped in the print shop. The spelling "ritches" implies that the printer wanted to convey the articulative intrusion of the t-sound in a word that many may have still heard as the French-derived *riche*. The gu-spelling in "guift" represents a convention designed to show the /g/ sound as a velar stop rather than palato-velar fricative (what we would informally call a hard as opposed to a soft g). If we hold that Shakespeare writes true rhymes here, the pairs "possessing"/"releasing," and "granting"/"wanting" had vowel sounds that are now different. In the case of the former, the rhyme was probably on /ɛ/; in the latter, the rhyme was probably on /a/.

The verbal strategy of this sonnet is polysemy – the knowledge that the same words can mean different things. As we have seen, the age of Shakespeare was the great age of polysemy, as words overlap in referents and connotations. It is the age when the social concept of linguistic register clearly takes shape: the idea that there is a form of language appropriate for certain social classes or professions. Register can be professional, casual, learned, courtly, and so on. But register sometimes requires translation. Take this example from *Macbeth*, where Macbeth juxtaposes words of high and common diction, trying to find the range and register appropriate for this moment:

Will all great Neptune's ocean wash this blood
Clean from my hand? No; this my hand will rather

> The multitudinous seas incarnadine,
> Making the green one red.
>
> (*Macbeth*, Act 2, scene 2, lines 61–4)

Macbeth panics. There is so much blood. How can he wash it off? The vocabulary here dovetails with the emotional content of the scene, as if the blood and the words are all too great to wash away. The episode builds to the line full of polysyllables: "The multitudinous seas incarnadine," and then – as if Macbeth has to translate for himself and us – back to simple, monosyllabic familiar words, "Making the green one red." The *OED* records no use of "multitudinous" before 1603. Shakespeare is one of the earliest citations (even though the *OED* gives a date of 1616 for *Macbeth*, scholars know it was written and performed closer to 1606). This passage is the first quotation offered by the *OED* for "incarnadine" as a verb, "to redden" (and all subsequent uses may be influenced by Shakespeare's usage).

What matters here is not simply then a record of which word is new. What matters is how Shakespeare foregrounded his linguistic inventiveness and made the question of language use central to a moment in a play.

Shakespeare's later plays are far more linguistically inventive than his earlier ones. *Macbeth*, *Hamlet*, *King Lear*, and *The Winter's Tale* – plays of the first decade or so of the sixteenth century – use language in ways that almost no one else had done before. The theme of these plays is the question of whether language is even capable of representing the world. In *The Winter's Tale*, Leontes has speeches that seem to make no syntactic sense. His language resists paraphrase or, in the words of Shakespearean scholar Stephen Orgel, represents a "poetics of incomprehensibility" (Orgel 1991). The moment early in the play, when Leontes imagines that his wife has cheated on him with his best friend and that his son may not be his own, comes off as opaque to us as it did to the play's earliest critics:

> Can thy dam? – may't be? –
> Affection! thy intention stabs the centre:
> Thou dost make possible things not so held,
> Communicatest with dreams; – how can this be? –
> With what's unreal thou coactive art,
> And fellow'st nothing: then 'tis very credent
> Thou mayst co-join with something; and thou dost,
> And that beyond commission, and I find it.
>
> (*The Winter's Tale*, Act 1, scene 2, lines 137–44)

A modern editor's punctuation here is a desperate attempt to make some sense of this flow of words. Orgel's point is as much literary as it is linguistic: "We need to remember that the Renaissance tolerated, and indeed courted, a much higher degree of ambiguity and opacity than we do; we tend to forget that the age often found in incomprehensibility a positive virtue" (Orgel 1991, p. 434).

It becomes very hard simply to use Shakespeare (or any literary work of the time) as evidence for everyday language usage. But it becomes easy to recognize that this was an age when a new attitude toward the English vernacular was emerging. The growth of vocabulary made possible sharp shifts in register, changing pronunciation enabled pun and wordplay, and the work of the orthoepists raised questions about whether any form of writing could represent language at the moment.

Can words suffice? King Lear may ramble on with big words, but at moments of high drama, he is left simply to scream.

Never, never, never, never, never!
Howl, howl, howl, howl!

In *King Lear*, we witness verbal *copia* at a high level of dramatic **dysphemism** (the sustained use of deliberately offensive vocabulary; the opposite of euphemism). Registers of language include praise and blame. The tradition of the flyting in Germanic literature and the obscenities of Chaucer and the Middle English drama have shown us a great tradition of bad talk. When Kent in *King Lear* confronts the arrogant servant Oswald, he takes these traditions to a new level. He calls the servant:

A knave; a rascal; an eater of broken meats; a base, proud, shallow, beggarly, three-suited, hundred-pound, filthy, worsted-stocking knave; a lily-livered, action-taking knave, a whoreson, glass-gazing, super-serviceable finical rogue; one-trunk-inheriting slave; one that wouldst be a bawd, in way of good service, and art nothing but the composition of a knave, beggar, coward, pandar, and the son and heir of a mongrel bitch: one whom I will beat into clamorous whining, if thou deniest the least syllable of thy addition.

(*King Lear*, Act 2, scene 2, lines 11–17)

This is a linguistic essay on the compound word. Notice the hyphenated terms here, each one a moment of Shakespearean coinage ("lily-livered," which we may think of as the parlance of the Hollywood western, is Shakespeare's invention). As much as for Lear or Leontes, ordinary words do not suffice at moments of great anger or emotion.

We can look up all these terms in the *OED*. But will it give us a true history of meaning? Shakespeare's influence on the English language is as much a function of his place in dictionaries as it is in culture. Take a small example from *Hamlet*. In Hamlet's famous "To be or not to be" soliloquy, he meditates on where we go after death, and he imagines the afterlife as "The undiscovered country from whose bourn / No traveler returns." Look up "bourn" in the *OED* and it will tell you that it means a boundary or terminal point on a journey. But find the section in the definition that begins with *Hamlet*, and you see something else.

The quotations that the entry offers are quotations that *specifically allude to Hamlet's line*. This section does not tell us about the currency of the word "bourn." It tells us about the impact of Hamlet's phrase on later literary writers. It is a history of influence, rather than a story of language.

Grammar and Morphology

Shakespeare comes off as a linguistic innovator. But he used certain grammatical forms that seem archaic to our eyes and ears. Take multiple negatives. Modern grammar teaches us that double negatives should be avoided. Two negatives make a positive. This view, however, is an imposition by eighteenth-century teachers who wanted English to look more logical or rational than it seemed. Multiple negatives were perfectly acceptable for centuries. Chaucer's description of the Knight in *The Canterbury Tales* has a staggering quadruple negative: "He *never* yet *no* villainy *ne* said, unto *no* manner wight." Shakespeare did the same thing. Look at the double negative from *Julius Caesar*: "I sawe Marke Antony offer him a Crowne, yet 'twas *not* a Crowne *neyther*, 'twas one of these Coronets" (*Julius Caesar*, Act 1, scene 2, line 234). Or this one from *Twelfth Night*: "And that *no* woman has; *nor never none* shall be mistress of it" (*Twelfth Night*, Act 3, scene 1, lines 159–60).

Shakespeare also piled on comparatives and superlatives. Perhaps the most famous example is the line from *Julius Caesar*: "This was the most unkindest cut of all" (*Julius Caesar*, Act 3, scene 2, line 184). The following phrase from *A Midsummer Night's Dream* may seem just wrong to modern readers, but it was perfectly acceptable at the end of the sixteenth century: "For the more better assurance" (*A Midsummer Night's Dream*, Act 3, scene 1, line 18). These examples tell us something about English that has changed. But Shakespeare wrote during a period of change, and old and new forms jostle in his texts. We have seen, for example, that the -th ending of the third-person singular verb was already perceived as old fashioned by the early 1600s. Shakespeare's printers show us this form at a precise moment in transition. *Hamlet* survives in several printed texts: an early quarto (that is, a small, inexpensive edition of a single play) from 1603, a later quarto from 1604, and the *First Folio* of 1623. They differ, often wildly, in words and lines and scenes. Here is a line from Polonius early in the play. The 1604 quarto prints: "And borrowing dulleth edge of Husbandry" (*Hamlet*, Act 1, scene 3, line 563). The *First Folio* prints: "And borrowing duls the edge of Husbandry." Notice that once the -eth has been replaced by -s, a syllable is lost. To make the line scan, the *Folio* editors added the word "the."

We can see language change. Another example would be in a single text, where old and new forms appear. Here are stage directions in *Henry IV, Part 1* (Act 5, scene 4, line 76), from the *First Folio* of 1623:

Enter Dowglas, he fights with Falstaffe, who fals down as if he were dead.
The Prince killeth Percie.

Here is the same text from the 1598 quarto edition of the play:

> Enter Douglas, he fighteth with Falstaffe, he fals down as if he were dead, the
> Prince killeth Percy.

What these printings reveal is how unstable certain forms of English were at the time. Another way of putting it would be to say: we see the difference between the two endings of the verb as a matter of diachronic change; these printers clearly saw the difference as a matter of synchronic variation.

The second-person pronoun also was changing in the early seventeenth century. Even though the you-forms were becoming the unmarked usage, Shakespeare and his contemporaries often staged a drama of the pronoun to signal social and emotional relationships.

To review, thou-forms were singular and informal. They could be used to address an intimate friend or lover, or they could be used to talk down to an inferior. God is always addressed in the thou-form (as He is addressed in the singular informal in other European languages, such as French and German). You-forms were plural and formal. They could be used to speak up to a superior or to address a stranger or an audience. By the early sixteenth century, you-forms were becoming the default mode of address. Thou-forms remained, but they were increasingly used as what linguists call the marked form: that is, something unusual or distinctive and, therefore, something that calls attention to the moment.

Shakespeare distinguished between thou and you forms for dramatic effect. Nowhere is this clearer than in the exchange in *Richard III* between Richard and Lady Anne. Here is a transcription from the *First Folio* edition of 1623 of the passage in Act 1, scene 2, lines 129–45, when they meet:

An.   Thou was't the cause, and most accurst effect.
Rich.   Your beauty was the cause of that effect:
        Your beauty, that did haunt me in my sleepe,
        To vndertake the death of all the world,
        So I might liue one houre in your sweet bosome.
An.   If I thought that, I tell thee Homicide,
        These Nailes should rent that beauty from my Cheekes.
Rich.   These eyes could not endure y^t beauties wrack,
        You should not blemish it, if I stood by;
        As all the world is cheared by the Sunne,
        So I by that: It is my day, my life.
An.   Blacke night ore-shade thy day, & death thy life.
Rich.   Curse not thy selfe faire Creature,
        Thou art both.
An.   I would I were, to be reueng'd on thee.
Rich.   It is a quarrell most vnnaturall,
        To be reueng'd on him that loueth thee.

Richard seeks to woo Anne. She rejects him. She opens with a contemptuous "thou," as if she were speaking to a servant. Richard responds with a formal "you," addressing a superior. They exchange thou- and you-forms, and in the final line he addresses her with "thee." Here, it is the "thee" of intimacy. The subtleties of this passage would not have been lost on Shakespeare's readers or audience. We can well imagine actors stressing the pronouns in performance – in fact, the whole episode begins and ends with the second-person singular, and many of the lines begin with the pronoun.

For dramatic and literary effect, Shakespeare can draw on a feature of English grammar. He can also draw on features of pronunciation for sonic resonance. "Thou" and "my," as we have seen, would have had versions of the diphthongs as /əu/ and /əi/. The words "cause" and "haunt" would have the diphthongs /au/. If David Crystal is right, the unstressed words in the passage would have been reduced to schwas. "One hour" would have sounded like /ən ur/. Finally, there is the printer's mark abbreviating the word "that": y^t. The letter that appears as y descends from the Old English thorn, þ, and came to be used as an abbreviation for the spelling th. *Ye* was never "ye" by these conventions. It was "the."

Did people in the early 1600s actually speak like this? Compare this highly wrought scene with a transcript of the trial of Sir Walter Raleigh, made in 1603. Raleigh, a former favorite of Elizabeth I, fell out of favor with her successor, James I, and he was put on trial for treason. The publication of the trial records claims to have been "exactly and faithfully taken," and we can almost hear the contempt in the language of the Attorney General, Sir Edward Coke. Raleigh says, "Your words cannot condemn me," and Coke replies: "Nay, I will prove all. Thou art a monster; thou hast an English face, but a Spanish heart." Later on, Coke and Raleigh go back and forth, Raleigh addressing Coke with you-forms (respect, however ironic here), and Coke speaking to Raleigh in thou-forms (undisguised contempt).

Coke: Thou art the most vile and execrable traytor that ever lived.
Raleigh: You speak indiscreetly, barbarously and uncivilly.
Coke: I want words sufficient to express thy viperous treasons.
Raleigh: I think you want words indeed, for you have spoken one thing half a
            dozen times.
Coke: Thou art an odious fellow, thy name is hateful to all the realm of England for thy pride.

(Sutherland 1953, pp. 86–7)

This is a moment worthy of Shakespeare. Like Anne and Richard, or Kent and Oswald, these men search for words that match the moment. Coke offers up a lexicon of condemnation: "vile," "execrable," "traitor," "viperous," "odious." The *OED* guides us: "viperous" connotes treachery and venom, "very common," the dictionary states, "in the seventeenth century; now rare or archaic." "Execrable" means cursed, and the *OED*'s examples hover around the late sixteenth and seventeenth centuries. "Odious" comes from the Latin, *odium*, meaning hatred, again a word that jumps out of Renaissance texts. Raleigh responds as if he is a literary critic, judging the language of his accuser: "indiscreetly," "barbarously," "uncivilly." These are words that were not brand new in the early seventeenth century, but they were new enough, and all connoted the quality of language.

All of them appear in Shakespeare in some form. Coke's accusation of "an English face but a Spanish heart" has all the feel of the plays, where the face and heart would frequently be juxtaposed, as in *Romeo and Juliet*: "O serpent heart, hid with a flowering face" (Act 3, scene 2, line 73). The playgoer would also hear Coke's "viperous treasons" in the accusations of Coriolanus as a "viperous traitor" (*Coriolanus*, Act 3, scene 1, line 286). *Romeo and Juliet* is a play of the mid-1590s, *Coriolanus* of the very early 1600s. Raleigh and Coke may have actually said these words, but they did so in consciousness of their literary resonance.

This is how we should understand Shakespeare's impact on English. More than just offering particular words or phrases, he gave voice to a way of using language that we retain: a sense of public drama, of curse and anger, and of love and loss.

The King James Bible and its Impact on English

Like Shakespeare, the King James Version (KJV) of the Bible lies at the intersection of the innovative and the archaic. Even though its translators were the leading scholars of Latin and Hebrew of their time, much of its vernacular was cobbled together out of earlier translations, especially those of John Tyndale (whose New Testament appeared in 1526) and Miles Coverdale (whose Bible appeared in 1534). In the decades after its publication in 1611, the KJV was already perceived as old-fashioned. Certain grammatical uses, in particular the -th suffix for the third-person singular verb and the grammatical gendering of particular nouns (for example, in the phrase, "if the salt have lost his savor," Matthew 5:13) were perceived as unrepresentative of everyday spoken usage. By the middle of the eighteenth century, scholars, clergy, and theologians had come to find the language of the Authorized Version old and "low." Anthony Purver's "Quaker's Bible" of 1764 concluded with a list of obsolete terms from the KJV. Yet a century or so later, many of these words were brought back into use by literary and political writers seeking the patina of biblical authority. For example, among the words listed by Purver as archaic in the mid-eighteenth century, the following were brought back into currency in the mid-nineteenth: *avenge, eschewed, laden, ponder, unwittingly,* and *warfare*.

These perceptions were only part of the early reaction to the KJV. John Selden (one of the most accomplished scholars of Hebrew of the early seventeenth century) considered its translation excellent at the literal level but objected to the unidiomatic quality of its style. He said it rendered the Bible's language "into English words rather than into English phrases" (McGrath 2001, p. 265). It is also true that the KJV did not immediately supersede other English Bibles. The Geneva Bible (originally printed in 1560), remained popular, especially among the Puritans, and was reprinted until 1644. It was not until the restoration of the English monarchy with Charles II in 1660 that the KJV was effectively asserted as "the" Bible. Although the KJV informed the texture of John Milton's poetry and John Bunyan's prose by the end of the seventeenth century (and the phrasing of their contemporary US poet Anne Bradstreet), it is not until the nineteenth century that the English-speaking world's worship of this text really took hold.

The men charged with translating the Bible for the KJV were not self-conscious innovators in vernacular expression, nor did they see their task as fundamentally concerned with augmenting or enhancing the English lexicon. By age and temperament, they were conservative in usage. They included Lancelot Andrewes, Dean of Westminster Cathedral; Edward Lively, the Regius Professor of Hebrew at Trinity College, Cambridge; John Harding, the President of Magdalen College, Oxford; and John Rainolds, a scholar of rhetoric and Greek and President of Corpus Christi College, Oxford. Along with many other participants, they created an unmistakable biblical voice. Here is the opening of Genesis, from the first printed edition of the KJV.

> In the beginning God created the heaven and the Earth. And the earth was without forme, and voyd, and darknesse was vpon the face of the deepe: and the Spirit of God mooued vpon the face of the waters. And God said, Let there be light: and there was light. And God saw the light, that was good; and God diuided the light from the darknesse. And God called the light, Day, and the darknesse he called Night: and the Euening and the Morning were the first day.

Some of the spellings will seem odd to us: the printer's conventions of u for v, the final e's in words such as *forme* and *dakrnesse*, and capitalization of major nouns. But this is recognizably the Bible as we know it.

Compare this opening with another royally sanctioned translation. In 1537, Thomas Cranmer, Archbishop of Canterbury, approved a version of the Bible for King Henry VIII. Printed by John Rogers under the pseudonym Thomas Matthew, this text begins:

> In the beginning God created heauen and erth. The erth was voyde and emptye and darcknesse was vpon the depe & the spirite of God moued upon the water. Than God sayde: let there be light: & there was light. And God sawe the light that it was good: & deuyded ye light from the darcknesse & called the light the daye & the darcknesse the nyght: and so of the euenyng & morning was made the first daye.

What is different here? The KJV adds words to give a rhythmic flow to the sentences. The additions of the definite article "the" and the conjunction "and" create what we think of today as the sound of biblical English. Finally, in their fidelity to the Hebrew original, the KJV translators give us an unforgettable image: "the face of the deep."

Where the KJV has had an impact, and where it participates most fully in the linguistic changes of its own time, is therefore not in the rise of vocabulary but in the codification of idiom. Famous phrases such as the following mutated Hebrew expressions into vernacular English for the first time:

Beat their swords into plowshares
To everything there is a season
Be horribly afraid
Suffer the little children
A thorn in the flesh
Be fruitful and multiply
Let us now praise famous men

We might think of the KJV as innovative in these ways, but in fact, many of its most famous expressions can be traced back to earlier English translations. Phrases like these, new to the translation, are relatively few. David Crystal (2010) counts no fewer than 257 expressions unique to the KJV. Many of its most familiar phrases came from earlier English translations:

Apple of his eye
Salt of the earth
Pride goes before a fall
The twinkling of an eye
Ye of little faith

The KJV sanctioned these phrases and, in the process, participated in an early Modern English habit of creating a language full of memorable expressions. Renaissance education was rhetorical. It taught that language should be organized in clear ways and should rely on figurative expressions. Metaphor, simile, analogy, and other tropes filled public and private speech. The word "trope" comes from the Greek word meaning "turn," and what we see here are turns of phrase. Those turns had to be memorable, short, and vivid. To argue was to offer aphorisms or maxims. Classical writers had developed aphorisms as short, distilled ways of talking about life: *festine lente* (make haste slowly), *caveat emptor* (let the buyer beware), *carpe diem* (seize the day). Examples of this kind influenced English life, as well. Shakespeare's characters talk in memorable ways because, in essence, they were taught to do so. Phrases such as the following have become so much a part of English that we barely recognize them as Shakespeare's:

Frailty, thy name is woman.
All that glitters is not gold.
What's in a name?

The better part of valor is discretion.
The Lady doth protest too much.
All the world's a stage.

What makes these phrases memorable is not just their content but their rhythm. Even in prose, Shakespeare gives us maxims that scan as verse. "The better part of valor is discretion" is a perfect iambic pentameter line, even though Falstaff speaks in prose. Even when Shakespeare's characters are giving voice to common ideas, they do so in pithy and memorable ways. The equation of the world and the theater, for example, is as old as the theater itself. The Renaissance humanist Erasmus, in *Praise of Folly* (1511) wrote, "For what else is the life of a man but a kind of play?" (mid-sixteenth-century English translation of his Latin). The difference between that phrase and "All the world's a stage" is the difference between a long sentence with conditional phrases (for ... but) and a simple short equation: x is y, the world's a stage.

Of course, one could go too far. Polonius in *Hamlet* gives advice to his son, Laertes, that is little more than a list of familiar adages:

Give thy thoughts no tongue.
Give every man thy ear, but few thy voice.
Neither a borrower nor a lender be.
To thine own self be true.

In this scene of the play, Polonius comes off as an unoriginal, trite gasbag. Everything he says would have been well known to an audience in the early 1600s.

And this is the whole point. English has become a language full of maximal statements, and the idea of the cliché really comes from the ways these Renaissance phrases came to do the work of everyday speech. This feature of the language, as much as changes in pronunciation or grammar, distinguishes our modern English from that of the past. Shakespeare and the KJV made an indelible impression on our language because they provide authoritative collections of such phrases. They provide models for later writers to write memorably, and this is where the true impact lies. We remember Samuel Johnson for his pronouncements ("When a man is tired of London, he is tired of life"). We remember Oscar Wilde for his witticisms ("True friends stab you in the face"). We remember Abraham Lincoln for his biblical tone ("Four score and seven years ago"). We remember Martin Luther King Jr. for his assertions ("I have a dream"). We remember John F. Kennedy for his soaring exhortations ("Ask not what your country can do for you; ask what you can do for your country"). When we hear a new maxim, we think that it must be old, even though it has been coined by our contemporaries. What Shakespeare and the KJV bequeath to the history of English, then, is not just words or phrases but the template for a memorable way of speaking. They become repositories for such phrases, and we will see how later dictionary makers, teachers, grammarians, and literary writers shaped the English language by their example.

Sources and Further Reading

All quotations from early printings of the Shakespeare's plays and the poems, and from the *First Folio* of 1623, are from the facsimiles online at Internet Shakespeare Editions, available at: https://internetshakespeare.uvic.ca.

Alexander, C. (2004). *Shakespeare and Language*. Cambridge: Cambridge University Press.

Blake, N. F. (2002). *A Grammar of Shakespeare's Language*. New York: Palgrave.

Bloom, H. (2011). *The Shadow of a Great Rock: A Literary Appreciation of the King James Bible*. New Haven, CT: Yale University Press.

Burke, D. G., et al. (Eds.) (2013). *The King James Version at 400*. Atlanta, GA: Society of Biblical Literature.

Campbell, G. (2011). *Bible: The Story of the King James Version, 1611–2011*. Oxford: Oxford University Press.

Crystal, D. (2008). *Think on My Words: Exploring Shakespeare's Language*. Cambridge: Cambridge University Press.

Crystal, D. (2010). *Begat: The King James Bible and the English Language*. Oxford: Oxford University Press.

Crystal, D. (ongoing), Original Pronunciation. Available at: http://originalpronunciation. com/GBR/Home.

Görlach, M. (1992). *Early Modern English*. Cambridge: Cambridge University Press.

Hamlin, H., and Jones, N. W. (Eds.) (2011). *The King James Bible after 400 Years*. Cambridge: Cambridge University Press.

Kermode, F. (2000). *Shakespeare's Language*. London: Allen Lane.

Lass, R. (2008). "Phonology and Morphology." In R. Lass (Ed.), *CHEL*, vol. 3. Cambridge: Cambridge University Press, pp. 56–186.

McGrath, A. (2001). *In the Beginning: The Story of the King James Bible*. New York: Doubleday.

Meier, P. (ongoing). "The Original Pronunciation (OP) of Shakespeare's English." Available at: http://www.paulmeier.com/OP.pdf.

Nicholson, A. (2003). *God's Secretaries: The Making of the King James Bible*. New York: HarperCollins.

Norton, D. (1985). "The Bible as a Reviver of Words: The Evidence of Anthony Purver, a Mid-Eighteenth-century Critic of the English of the King James Bible." *Neuphilologische Mitteilungen* 86: 515–33.

Norton, D. (2011). *The King James Bible: A Short History from Tyndale to Today*. Cambridge: Cambridge University Press.

Orgel, S. (1991). "The Poetics of Incomprehensibility." *Shakespeare Quarterly* 42: 431–7.

Orgel, S., and Braunmiller, A. R. (2004). *The Pelican Shakespeare*. Harmondsworth: Penguin.

Sutherland, J. (1953). *The Oxford Book of English Talk*. Oxford: Clarendon Press.

7   The Age of Regulation

British English, 1650–1800

It may seem as if the changes to the English language after the death of Shakespeare were minor. The sounds of English did not go through the major alterations of the Great Vowel Shift (GVS). Except for a few apparent idiosyncrasies, grammar remained stable. The lexicon, though growing consistently, remains largely comprehensible, whether we are reading Milton, Samuel Johnson, or Jane Austen. But spoken and written English did change in this period. Teachers and scholars regularized spelling and grammar. Lexicographers sorted out those words that were appropriate and inappropriate. The seventeenth and eighteenth centuries are the great age of prescriptivism in the history of English: a period of regulating, reining in, and recording.

Reading English of this period comes with its own challenges. Many of us think that the letters f and s were interchangeable, but if we look closely at the handwriting and the printing of the time, we see an important difference. The letter s had two forms. The short s, looking like our modern letter, appeared primarily at the ends of words. The long s, looking suspiciously like an f, was used in any position in a word except the end. This long s did not have the cross-bar of an f, and so it is important to look closely at texts to see the difference. What we also notice are differences in the use of other letters. U and v and i and j were largely interchangeable. Their usage was often dictated by the letters around them. Thus, if a word had many letters with individual short strokes (known as minims), a j or a v would be used to make things look clearer. The difference between *uice* and *vice* does not indicate pronunciation or word history. It indicates an attempt to avoid many minims in sequence. In British English, words such as logic, music, and ethic ended with a ck rather than a c. Spelling is still variable in the mid-seventeenth century, but was becoming more fixed by the middle of the eighteenth.

This was also the time when literary English came to be a model for everyday speakers and writers. Notions of the "best authors" and the "best English" merged. Although not everyone was expected to be an imaginative writer, those who aspired to social acceptance were expected to know the canon of English literature and its linguistic models.

This chapter begins by outlining phonological and grammatical changes in British English in this time period. It moves to the work of Samuel Johnson

DOI: 10.4324/9781003227083-8

in codifying the vocabulary and yoking it to literary sources. By looking once again at the orthoepists (whose work extended into the eighteenth century), by exploring the grammatical work of Robert Lowth and Joseph Priestley, and by interrogating Johnson's lexicography, this chapter illustrates how much we still owe to this era. English of an earlier time may still be legible to us, but we would not speak or write the way we do without the work of seventeenth- and eighteenth-century writers and teachers.

Sound, Sense, and Spelling

From our modern perspective, the sound changes of the GVS were complete by the middle of the seventeenth century. The evidence for English pronunciation at the time comes from several sources. The orthoepists of the mid-1600s, like their sixteenth-century counterparts, were concerned with the physical production of sounds in the mouth. John Wallis's *Grammatica Linguae Anglicana* of 1653 (written in Latin) sought to chart these sounds, classifying them and arranging them according to the place and manner of articulation. Wallis (1616–1703) was a brilliant polymath; he contributed to the development of calculus, worked as a cryptographer, and wrote treatises on philosophy and religion. His grammatical work is as rigorous as anything else he did, and he contributed to the concept that the study of language should be as precise and organized as mathematics.

Figure 7.1 is his summary chart, or what he called his "synopsis" of all the sounds in English.

We can see the beginnings of the systematic organization of sounds. Even though his descriptive terms are different from ours, Wallis recognized that each sound has a unique place in the mouth.

John Wilkins's *An Essay Towards a Real Character and a Philosophical Language* (1668) presented a systematic set of pictures with the parts of the mouth identified and the shape of the mouth for the production of each sound (Figure 7.2). These pictures are not merely descriptive, they were designed for English and non-English speakers to be able to pronounce words correctly. Wilkins supplements his detailed description of vowel sounds with a visual model.

Among the aspects of that correct pronunciation was the completion of the raising and fronting of the old long vowels of Middle English. Mid-seventeenth-century pronunciation of those vowels would be the following:

bite /ɛi/
meet /i:/
meat /e/
mate /ɛ:/
out /ɔu/
boot /u:/
boat /o:/

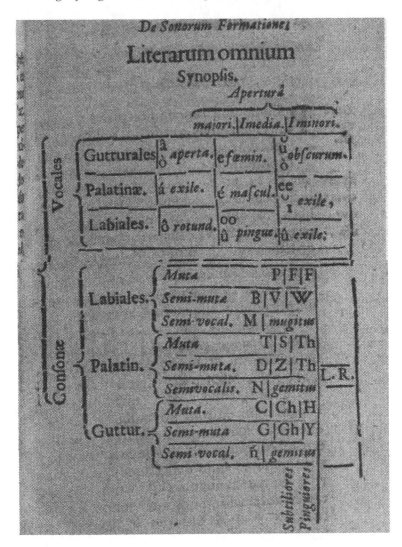

Figure 7.1 John Wallis's chart of English sounds

Source: Wallis (1688)

These are not yet our contemporary pronunciations. For example, "meet" and "meat" do not rhyme, and the diphthongs in "bite" and "out" are still a bit higher in the mouth than what modern standard English would claim: /bait/, /aut/.

Information from the seventeenth- and early eighteenth-century writers also points to words such as "can" and "wan," and "scar" and "war" still rhyming. The rounding of the back vowel after the glide /w/ most likely did not happen

Figure 7.2 John Wilkins's illustration of the shapes of the mouth and English sounds
Source: Wilkins (1668)

(or was not accepted as a standard) until the second decade or so of the 1900s. So, too, the initial glide in the word "one," which we pronounce as /wun/, did not become standard until the mid-eighteenth century or so. Thus, Shakespeare and Milton rhyme "one" with "shone" and "soon" (probably on /o/).

A new sound entering British English during this time was a long, low, back vowel, represented by the phonetic symbol /ɑː/. This is the sound that one may hear in certain British and American accents in the word "father." It is also the sound that was influenced by the following /l/ in words such as "calm" and "palm," and by various nonrhotic pronunciations of words such as "car" and "hard." It is unclear where this sound came from, and it is also unclear how a particular pronunciation (which linguists would call an allophonic variation) became truly phonemic (or not) in certain dialects and registers. Do you say "father" and "farther" the same way? Is this the same sound in your pronunciation of "not" or "hot"? In the Preface to *New Dictionary of the English Language* of 1773 (a work largely borrowing from Samuel Johnson's *Dictionary* of 1755), William Kenrick lists sets of words designed to illustrate proper pronunciation. Sets of different vowel sounds include the following:

Call, bawl, caul, soft, oft, George, cloth
Not, what, gone, swan, war, was
Hard, part, carve, laugh, heart

The sound in the first set most likely approached /ɔː/. In the second set, the sound was most likely /ɑː/. In the third set it was probably /aː/ (Kenrick 1773, p. v). Such distinctions may be hard for us to reproduce or even hear. Whatever is going on here, Kenrick's word lists strongly suggest that some form of a long, low, back vowel had become a key feature of standard British English by this point.

Kenrick was working at the end of over 100 years of fascination with speech sounds. But behind this work was not just linguistics but philosophy. There was a growing fascination with the sounds of speech as somehow entities in themselves, as if speech sound was essentially meaningful. Modern linguistics is based on the concept of the arbitrariness of the sound: the idea that individual sounds do not have essential meanings but have meaning in a language only in relationship to one another. This was the principle behind the concept of the phoneme. In the seventeenth and early eighteenth centuries, however, scholars sought (in the words of modern historian Murray Cohen) "in the physical nature of sound a natural or rational connection between speech and reality" (1977, p. 10). John Wallis argued that there are words "which indicate by their actual sound the different characters of the things they signify" (1972, p. 119). John Wilkins argued:

The Essence of Letters doeth consist in their Power or proper sound, which may be naturally fixed and stated, from the manner of forming them by the instruments of speech; and either is, or should be the same in all Languages.
(1668, p. 357)

From this perspective, the description of sounds was equivalent to the description of reality. Sonic order mirrors the natural order, and the penchant for charts and illustrations in these publications contributes to the belief that studying language is comparable to studying, say, chemistry or mathematics.

People had always been fascinated by language difference and language change. Geoffrey Chaucer recognized that "in forme of speech is chaunge," and that words that once had "prys" (value or meaning) a thousand years before now seem "nice and strange" (curious and odd). Certainly by Shakespeare's time, Chaucer's language was difficult to read, and Thomas Speght's editions of Chaucer's works in 1598 and 1602 for the first time included glossaries of the old words with new equivalents. This kind of work was done for individual writers and texts. What emerges in the mid-1600s, however, is the idea that the study of language is a systematic and empirical inquiry: data and detail appear, and linguistics (even though they did not call it that) could be a science. For these earlier scholars, the most systematically organized and rationally taught language was Latin. In their reforms of English, therefore, they tried to hold English to Latin standards, and reforms in spelling, morphology, and grammar were based on this classical tradition.

In earlier chapters, we saw how institutions such as the Chancery influenced English spelling by creating an official standard, irrespective of the pronunciation or dialect of the scribe or printer. English men and women of the Middle Ages and the early modern period largely still spelled as they spoke. It was not until the late seventeenth and eighteenth centuries that regular spelling became a mark of education and intelligence. If spelling was to be rationally organized – if there were to be rules for spelling – then adhering to those rules was to be rational.

In the mid-1700s, Lord Chesterfield wrote a set of letters to his son, advising him on how to behave well in society. Among his pieces of advice was that good spelling was the mark of a good gentleman:

> You spell induce, ENDUCE; and grandeur, you spell grandURE; two faults of which few of my housemaids would have been guilty. I must tell you that orthography, in the true sense of the word, is so absolutely necessary for a man of letters; or a gentleman, that one false spelling may fix ridicule upon him for the rest of his life; and I know a man of quality, who never recovered the ridicule of having spelled Wholesome without the w.
>
> (quoted in Horobin 2013, p. 1)

Lord Chesterfield is writing at the end of a long period of debates about changes in English spelling. During the sixteenth and seventeenth centuries, there was a move to spell some English words as if they had directly come from Latin. The following words came into Middle English directly from French, and they look like French words:

aventure
avise

cors
dette
doute
faut
langage
neveu
perfeit
receit
samon
sisours
vitaille

Although these words may have come into French from Latin, they came into English from French, and an attempt to respell them as Latin words would not reflect their true word history. Nonetheless, these and other words were respelled to make English look more Latinate and, in the process, raise its status and imagine its greater history:

adventure
advise
corps
debt
doubt
fault
language
nephew
perfect
receipt
salmon
scissors
victuals

During this period, spelling manuals and educational guides proliferated. Some were designed to clarify spelling conventions in words that sound alike. Richard Hodges's *A Special Help to Orthographie: or, the True Writing* (1643) offers lists of what we would now call homonyms:

> To *bow* the knee. The *bough* of a tree.
> To be well *bred*, or brought up. To earn his own *bread*.
> To *pare* the cheese. A *pair* of turtle doves.
>
> (Hodges 1643, pp. 2, 6)

Hodges also presents conventions for early modern pronunciation: noting that the final -e in words "hath no use for sound of it self" but is used to "shewe thereby the vowel going before to bee long" (ibid., p. 21). He distinguishes between words such as *mal, man,* and *mar* from *male, mane,* and *mare.* Like many of his contemporaries, he clarifies that even though "whensoever eth cometh in the end of any word, wee pronounce it sometimes like s & sometimes like z" (ibid., p. 27).

English "grammars" proliferated in the later 1600s to clarify a fundamental feature of modern English: the gap between spelling and pronunciation. By 1700, more than a score had been published, many of them designed to teach children how to write correctly. John Newton, in *School Pastime for Young Children* (1669), advises:

> And certain, if a Child be taught the true and genuine Sound of his Letters, with the customary Spelling of Words and Syllables, as Reason and Art have now for a long time established them, he must needs in a short space be sufficiently instructed in the true spelling and writing of the English Tongue.
>
> (1669, sig. B, verso)

The terms of these grammars are the terms of reason and art: that is, bringing together a notion of spelling, however strange to the uninitiated, as rational and beautiful. Words such as "true" and "genuine" are everywhere in these works: an attempt to find ways of codifying meaningful rules.

English poet and satirist Jonathan Swift (1667–1745) spent a great deal of time arguing for a rational yet historical English spelling system. In his book *A Proposal for Correcting, Improving, and Ascertaining the English Tongue* (1712), he made the point that historical spellings are better than phonetic ones, because they enable people from different dialect regions to read the same words and over time, as pronunciation changed, texts could still be legible to later readers. He called the claim "that we ought to spell exactly as we speak" a "foolish Opinion." He went on: "several Towns and Countries of England have a different way of Pronouncing ... All which, reduced to writing would entire confound Orthography" (quoted in Horobin 2013, pp. 152–3). By the mid-eighteenth century, Lord Chesterfield could, as we saw, equate good spelling with good breeding and judgment. The idea here is that "custom" – a word in the eighteenth century that meant practice based on the judgment of the best educated – should dictate linguistic usage. Thomas Sheridan published a *Course of Lectures on Elocution* in 1763, stating that "It is a disgrace to a gentleman, to be guilty of false spelling" (1803, p. 28). Even when custom preserved various spellings that seemed inconsistent, no less an authority than Samuel Johnson advised people to "sacrifice uniformity to custom" (1755, p. 2).

This distinction between uniformity and custom drives Johnson's work on the English language, along with that of later eighteenth-century teachers. To read through Johnson's *Dictionary* is to watch him try to balance between the two and skirt a fine line between describing how the language is and prescribing how it should be.

Samuel Johnson and His Dictionary

Few books have had the impact on the English language as the *Dictionary* by Samuel Johnson (1709–84). First planned in the 1740s and first published in 1755, Johnson's *Dictionary* created the idea of the dictionary as the arbiter of language use. It regularized spelling and grammatical forms. It codified and judged pronunciations. It broadened the vocabulary of everyday speech, while at the same time identifying (and judging) certain words that were "low" or "vulgar." Although based on the work of dictionary makers for the previous century, Johnson's *Dictionary* differed from his predecessors in that he used literary quotations to illustrate word forms, meanings, and histories. In this practice, he created a canon of English literature: a collection of authors who were to be valued for more than just their imaginative content, fictional characters, or plot lines or drama, but also for their linguistic exemplarity. Good English and good writing come together in Johnson, and the true lesson of his *Dictionary* is that the history of the English language and the history of English literature are intertwined.

Johnson's original aims were personal and commercial. He hoped to produce a dictionary that would sell, and he hoped to write a book that would enhance his professional status in the emerging life of English letters in the 1700s. "No man but a blockhead ever wrote except for money," he famously announced. He needed to work closely with the publishers and booksellers of his time. But he also needed patronage. His initial *Plan of a Dictionary of the English Language* (published in 1747) was dedicated to Lord Chesterfield. It set out a program of describing and fixing the English language, a project as hierarchical and class-driven as the patronage project. Johnson wrote: "I had read indeed of times in which princes and statesmen thought it part of their honour to promote the improvement of their native tongues, and in which great dictionaries were written under the protection of greatness."

The making of the *Dictionary*, then, was part of a larger social ideal of ordering and regulating. There was a politics to this process. Working at a time when England was expanding its imperial reach throughout the world, Johnson saw the study of language as an analogy to colonization. Words were like people. Some were foreign, some were native, and some could be admitted on judgment and reflection. Thus, he wrote, some words "are not equally to be considered as parts of our language, for some of them are naturalized and incorporated, but others still continue aliens, and are rather auxiliaries than subjects." Note his word use here: equally, naturalized, aliens, subjects. This is the language of colonial power, and he returns to it at the close of the *Plan of the Dictionary*:

> When I survey the Plan which I have laid before you, I cannot, my Lord, but confess, that I am frighted at its extent, and like the soldiers of Caesar, look on Britain as a new world, which it is almost madness to invade. But I hope, that though I should not complete the conquest, I shall at least discover the coast, civilize part of the inhabitants, and make it easy for some other adventurer to

proceed farther, to reduce them wholly to subjection, and settle them under laws.

(Johnson 1970 [1747])

In the seven years after this, Johnson labored, largely on his own, to make this dictionary. Upon its publication in 1755, however, he realized that his original plan to conquer, subjugate, civilize, and settle the vernacular was impossible. He realized that no book could fix the language. English was continually changing, flowing like a great river. The Preface to the *Dictionary* has a different tone: "When I took the first survey of my undertaking, I found our speech copious without order, and energetick without rules: wherever I turned my view, there was perplexity to be disentangled, and confusion to be regulated." In the end, he "saw that one enquiry only gave occasion to another, that book referred to book, that to search was not always to find, and to find was not always to be informed."

To understand what happened in between the *Plan* and the *Dictionary*, we need know what changed Johnson's mind and which writers influenced him. Many things happened, but in the eighteenth century, there were two earlier writers who became the models for language use and language theory. These writers were the philosopher John Locke (1632–1704) and the poet John Milton (1608–74). How the eighteenth century read and understood these seventeenth-century writers is a key to how they understood the relationships of word and deed, word and world.

Locke's theory of knowledge was empirical. He held that when we are born, we are blank slates: there is nothing essential or inherent in our minds, and as we learn and grow, we acquire knowledge through sensory experience. At the heart of Locke's theory of education was exposure to objects. Children, he argued, learn best through pictures and things. Learning the alphabet, learning how to write clearly, and learning how to sound out the letters lay at the heart of his pedagogy. His *Essay Concerning Human Understanding* (1690) and *Some Thoughts Concerning Education* (1692) had an immense impact on a later century of teaching and book publishing. These works gave rise to the genres of children's literature coming from English printing presses. They provoked a study of language as something to be learned through particulars. They stand behind Johnson's practice of identifying individual words, discriminating among their particular meanings, and giving examples of their use. Locke permeates Johnson's *Dictionary*. Almost every page has at least one quotation from his works, illustrating a word's meaning. The first volume of the first edition alone has 1,674 quotations from Locke, a fifth of all its illustrative texts.

If Locke is the philosophical father of the *Dictionary*, Milton is its poetic one. Johnson spent a lifetime reading Milton: "I think more highly of him now than I did at twenty." Milton's poetic voice, his immense vocabulary, and his rich scriptural and philosophical subject matter made him a popular authority for later readers. The questions of Satan's fall, of Adam and Eve's sin, and of the nature of human redemption preoccupied generations of Milton's readers, and *Paradise Lost* became a kind of textbook for the eighteenth-century colonist. Was America a new Eden? Was colonial expansion satanic?

Johnson's words in his *Plan* and Preface may have had a strong political cast. But they have a powerful Miltonic one as well. One of the best ways of understanding Johnson is to see how he defines and illustrates the words he uses in his writing. If we go back to the quotations from the *Plan*, we recognize that words such as "invade," "conquest," "civilize," "subjection," and "settle" are all illustrated in the *Dictionary* with quotations from Milton. The word "survey," which Johnson uses significantly in the *Plan* and the Preface, is a powerfully marked word. "Survey" is one of the most significant verbs of *Paradise Lost*. It applies to the benign grace of God's creation ("God saw, surveying his great work, that it was good") and to Satan's bad imperial ambitions ("he then survey'd Hell, and the gulf between"). Here is the entry for "survey" from Johnson's *Dictionary*.

To SURVE'Y. *v.a.* [*surveoir*, old French.]

1. To overlook; to have under the view; to view as from a higher place.
    Round he *surveys*, and well might where he stood,
    So high above.   *Milton.*
        Though with those streams he no resemblance hold,
    Whose foam is amber and their gravel gold;
    His genuine and less guilty wealth t'explore,
    Search not his bottom, but *survey* his shore.   *Denham.*
2. To oversee as one in authority.
3. To view as examining.
    The husbandman's self came that way,
    Of custom to *survey* his ground,
    And his trees of state incompass round.   *Spenser.*
    Early abroad he did the world *survey*,
    As if he knew he had not long to stay.   *Waller.*
    With such alter'd looks
    All pale and speechless, he *survey'd* me round.   *Dryden.*

In the first quotation from Milton, it is Satan who is doing the surveying (*Paradise Lost*, 3, 555). In the other literary quotations from John Denham, Edmund Spenser, Edmund Waller, and John Dryden, there is a sustained link between the political and the geographical. "Survey" may be a word of mapmaking or conquest. But it is also a word of powerful literary resonance.

This is precisely the point of Johnson's view of English. Words come not just with their literal or everyday meanings but with a wealth of literary echoes. One way that language changes, according to Johnson, is through this shift from the literal to the figurative:

> The original sense of words is often driven out of use by their metaphorical acceptations, yet must be inserted for the sake of a regular origination. Thus, I know not whether ardour is used for material heat, or whether flagrant in English ever signifies the same with the burning. Yet such are the primitive ideas of these words.
>
> (Johnson 1755)

Look up "flagrant" in Johnson's *Dictionary* and this is what you find:

FLA'GRANT. *adj.* [*flagrans*, Latin.]

1. Ardent; burning; eager.
   A thing which filleth the mind with comfort and heavenly delight, stirreth up *flagrant* desires and affections, correspondent unto that which the words contain. *Hooker, b.* v. *s.* 39
2. Glowing; flushed.
   See Sapho, at her toilet's greasy task,
   And issuing *flagrant* to an evening mask:
   So morning insects, that in muck begun,
   Shine, buz, and fly-blow in the setting sun. *Pope's Epistles.*
3. Red; imprinted red.
   Their common loves, a lewd abandon'd pack,
   The beadle's lash still *flagrant* on their back. *Prior.*
4. Notorious; flaming.

   When fraud is great, it furnishes weapons to defend itself; and at worst, if the crimes be so *flagrant* that a man is laid aside out of perfect shame, he retires loaded with the spoils of the nation. *Swift.*

   With equal poize let steddy justice sway,
   And *flagrant* crimes with certain vengeance pay;
   But, 'till the proofs are clear, the stroke delay. *Smith.*

First, we get the source of the word from Latin. Then he ranges the meanings from the physical to the emotional. Burning, glowing, red, notorious: the quotations balance the outer and the inner world. These quotations not only hone the meaning of the word, they offer ethical instruction on their own. The quotation from Swift, for example, could come from a common book of political instruction: "When fraud is great, it furnishes weapons to defend itself."

In earlier chapters, we saw how Shakespeare and the King James version of the Bible bequeathed memorable maxims to the history of English. Growing out of education in rhetoric and oratory, these works (and others of the English Renaissance) fostered the skill of distilling experience into aphorisms. This is what Johnson learned from these writers, and his own habits of pronouncing on the world came from this tradition:

> When a man is tired of London, he is tired of life.
> Patriotism is the last refuge of the scoundrel.
> Self-confidence is the first requisite to great undertakings.
> The true art of memory is the art of attention.
> Books, like friends, should be few and well chosen.

This habit of aphoristic living shapes the *Dictionary*, too. Many of Johnson's definitions are aphoristic in this way, and the aim of his lexicography is to get the reader to attend and remember. Some of his most memorable definitions include:

> Cough: A convulsion of the lungs, vellicated by some sharp serosity.
> Distiller: One who makes and sells pernicious and inflammatory spirits.
> Oats: A grain which in England is generally given to horses, but in Scotland appears to support the people.
> Politician: One versed in the arts of government. One skilled in politics. A man of artifice, one of deep contrivance.

But nowhere are Johnson's aphorisms more memorable than in describing his own work:

> Lexicographer: A writer of dictionaries; a harmless drudge that busies himself in tracing the original, and detailing the signification of words.
> Dull: Not exhilaterating [*sic*]; not delightful; as, to make dictionaries is dull work.

The man of judgment is everywhere here. He who can pronounce on London or patriotism can also pronounce on words. He will call words "low" (by which he means colloquial or lower class), "cant" (by which he means restricted to a certain group), "ludicrous," "barbarous," "affected," "vulgar."

> Far-fetch: a ludicrous word.
> Bamboozle: a cant word not used in pure or in grave writings.
> Job: a low word, now very much in use.
> Lesser: a barbarous corruption of less.
> Gambler: a cant word.

Often, he dismisses such words by remarking that he does not know their etymology.

What Johnson means by etymology is something different from what we mean today. The history of words is a matter of semantics and phonology. As we have seen, the methods of comparative philology established relationships of sound among languages that descend from a common ancestor. Charting those relationships enables the reconstruction of earlier forms of a word – both its sound and its social meaning. This method was unknown before the nineteenth century. But Johnson's work is not without historical value. He was writing when Old English was being rediscovered. Literary and religious texts of pre-Conquest England had been studied and printed since the mid-1600s. Grammars of Old English had been published since the 1690s, and there was an increasing awareness, as Johnson himself says in the *Dictionary*, that "the whole fabrick and scheme of the English language is Gothic or Teutonick." Thus, Johnson often accompanies words in his dictionary with Old English (what he calls "Saxon") and other Germanic forms.

Fire: fyr, Saxon; fewr, German.
Heart: heort, Saxon; herz, German.
Head: heafod, Heafd, Saxon; hoofd, Dutch; heved, old English, whence by contraction head.
Lord: hlaford, Saxon.

Sometimes, his learning gets the better of him, as he speculates on word origins in a social or philosophical sense:

Gold: gold, Saxon; *golud*, riches, Welsh. It is called gold in our English tongue either of *geel*, as Scaliger says, which is in Dutch to shine; or of another Dutch word, which is *gelten*, and signifies in Latin *valere*, in English to be of price or value: hence cometh their ordinary word *gelt*, for money.

For Johnson, such etymologies ground words in their heritage. They provide a sense of linguistic origin and of rightful belonging to the language. One of the most dismissive things he can say about a word is that he does not know or cannot find its etymology. Of the word "job," he sates: "I cannot tell the etymology." Another moment of dismissive philology is when he identifies a word from a "foreign" language (invariably French) and marks it as alien: "Finesse: [French.] Artifice; stratagem: an unnecessary word which is creeping into the language." Take the word "transpire," which has a modern, post-Johnsonian meaning of "happen," but which Johnson understands not so much etymologically (from the Latin, *trans* + *spirare*, to breathe across) but rather as a loan from French. "To escape from secrecy [*sic*] to notice: a sense lately innovated from France, without necessity."

Behind these judgments and aphoristic pronouncements is more than humor or eccentricity. Underlying them is a fundamental notion about language use and language value. Words without histories are like people without genealogy: fugitive, outside of class or good breeding. They are not part of what he calls "the wells of English undefiled." People should not use them. And yet they do. The fact that they do is the reason they are found in Johnson's *Dictionary*.

This is the basic challenge of the lexicographer. By recording and admitting words, any dictionary *describes* usage. But by judging those words, a dictionary *prescribes* usage. Modern dictionaries may aspire to objectivity. But from Johnson through the *OED*, judgment is always there. In fact, one of the definitions of the word "judgment" in Johnson's *Dictionary* is: "The quality of distinguishing propriety and impropriety; criticism." To illustrate this definition, he offers a quotation from John Dennis: "Judgment, a cool and slow faculty."

For Johnson and for those he influenced, judgment was everywhere. It generated canons of literature, syllabi of study, acceptable notions of what to say and what to wear. For the grammarians who followed him, making judgments about language was what being a grammarian was all about.

Robert Lowth and Prescriptivism

Robert Lowth (1710–87) was the Oxford-educated Bishop of Oxford and then of London who published a widely read handbook of English: *A Short Introduction to English Grammar*. First printed in 1762, it went through many editions and had an impact on English language teaching well into the late nineteenth century. Lowth is a classic prescriptivist. He is concerned with what is right. Grammar "is the art of rightly expressing our thoughts by words." His aim is "To teach what is right by showing what is both right and wrong." Whatever problems may arise in English usage are the problems of its users: "It is not the Language, but the practice, that is in fault."

His book begins with sounds and letters, then the parts of speech, and moves on to aspects of grammar, using literary examples for best linguistic practice. While he does not make English look like Latin, he certainly betrays a classical education in how he handles English verbs. English tenses do not necessarily correspond to "distinctions in Time," he writes. Nonetheless, he takes the Latin tense system and effectively translates it into English. Table 7.1 is what his chart of the tenses for the verb "love" looks like:

Table 7.1 Lowth's tenses of the verb "to love"

	Time	
Present	Past	Future
I love	I loved	I shall love

Definite, or Determined	
Present imperfect:	I am (now) loving
Present perfect:	I have (now) loved
Past imperfect:	I was (then) loving
Past perfect:	I had (then) loved
Future imperfect:	I shall (then) be loving
Future perfect:	I shall (then) have loved

Lowth wants English to be systematic, rational, and consistent. His argument against double negatives is that "Two Negatives in English destroy one another, or are equivalent to an Affirmative." No matter that Shakespeare and earlier writers used multiple negation. "It is a relique of the antient style, abounding with Negatives, which is now grown wholly obsolete." He also addresses that bugbear of modern English teachers: ending a sentence with a preposition.

> There is an idiom which our language is strongly inclined to; it prevails in common conversation … But the placing of the Preposition before the relative is more graceful, as well as more perspicuous; and agrees much better with the solemn and elevated style.
>
> (Lowth 1762, pp. 127–8)

Of course, in the first clause of this passage, Lowth ends with the preposition "to" (instead of writing what he would advise, "to which our language is strongly inclined").

Lowth develops a set of judgment terms for language use that are both social and aesthetic. He wants English to be graceful and perspicuous (look up "perspicuous" in Johnson's *Dictionary* and you get, "Transparent; clear; such as may be seen through; diaphanous, translucent; not opake"). He uses the word "solemn" to mean a register of language that is serious (Johnson defines it as "religiously grave," and "striking with seriousness"). "Solemn" as a marker of linguistic register later comes to characterize not only usage at a given moment but usage over time: past writers, and especially past religious writers, are more solemn than those of the present.

But Lowth does not favor archaism. He recognizes that the thou-forms of the second person are passing out of fashion:

> Thou in the Polite, and even in the Familiar Style, is disused. And the Plural You is employed instead of it: we say, You have, not, Thou hast. These two distinct forms of Thou and You are often used promiscuously by our modern Poets, in the same Poem, in the same Paragraph, and even in the same Sentence, very inelegantly and improperly.
>
> (ibid., p. 48)

Although Lowth's word "promiscuously" does not carry its modern sense of sexual indiscrimination, it was nonetheless a word of opprobrium (Johnson: "mingled, confused"). His concepts of elegance and propriety are as much grammatical as they are aesthetic, and at the heart of Lowth's prescriptivism is an ideal of linguistic regularity and formal beauty that goes back, half a century, to the age of Swift and Pope and Addison: to an time of classicism and balance.

Joseph Priestley and Descriptivism

By the time Lowth was writing, Swift and his contemporaries were already seen as old. Classic though they may have been, and influential though their writings remained, they were increasingly perceived to be unrepresentative of current usage. Joseph Priestley (1733–1804), in his *Rudiments of English Grammar* (first published in 1761) takes his examples

> from modern writers, rather than from those of Swift, Addison, and others, who wrote about half a century ago, in what is generally called the classical period of our tongue. By this means we may see what is the real character and turn of the language at present.

Once again, the phrase "real character" appears. "Real" is not an intensifier but a specific term of natural philosophy. For Priestley, the study of language is one of the "real sciences." Behind this term lies the British empiricist trajectory beginning with John Locke. Rules can be deduced from experience. They are not (as Lowth would have had it) pre-existing forms keyed to a universal structure that must be imposed on behavior. Priestley's definition of grammar is not a matter of right and wrong but a matter of observation and deduction: "The grammar of any language is a collection of observations on the structure of [language], and a system of rules for the proper use of it."

Priestley embodied the scientific empiricism of the late 1700s. Among his many activities was contributing to founding Unitarianism and the discovery of oxygen. For him, the study of language was a comparable enterprise. He looks for "the true symmetry of ... grammar," as if he were a crystallographer examining a specimen. Observation, while sensitive to beauty and propriety, should not, then, lead to prescription. "Our grammarians appear to me to have acted precipitately in this business, and to have taken a wrong method of fixing our language." Priestley favors observation and consensus: he wants to have its "varieties. held forth to public view, and the general preference of certain forms [to] have been declared, by the general practice afterwards."

He rejects Lowth's attempts to map Latin verbal systems on to English, noting that terms such as "the optative mood, and the perfect and pluperfect tenses of the passive voice" were "absurdly transferred from the Greek language into the Latin" by ancient grammarians and have been no less absurdly transferred into English. "Verbs have two tenses: the Present Tense, denoting time present, and the Preter [*sic*] tense, which expresseth time past." And that is it.

Priestley acknowledges Lowth by name, noting his indebtedness to his predecessor's examples and arguments. "I have taken a few of his examples (though generally for a purpose different from his)." He quarrels with Lowth's notion that expressions of greater gravity or solemnity or formality are better:

There is still a greater impropriety in a double comparative, or a double superlative. Dr. Lowth thinks there is a singular propriety in the phrase *most highest*, which is peculiar to the old translation of the Psalms. But I own it offends my ears, which may, perhaps, be owing to my not having been accustomed to that translation.

By the complaisance of modern times, we use the plural you instead of the singular thou, when we mean to speak respectfully to any person; but we do not use ye in this manner. However, in very solemn style, and in particularly in address to the Divine Being, we use thou, and not you.

Formerly, mine and thine were used instead of my and thy before a vowel. They are generally retained in our present English version of the Bible; and, perhaps, for this reason, give a peculiar solemnity to the style.

(Priestley 1761, p. 78)

In the end, Priestley writes,

It is not the authority of any one person, or of a few, be they ever so eminent, that can establish one form of speech in preference to another. Nothing but the general practice of good writers, and good speakers can do it.

Priestley's claims are as much political as they are grammatical. In a moment of great emotional power, resonant with the Revolution happening across the Atlantic, he writes: "I think it not only unsuitable to the genius of a free nation, but in itself ill calculated to reform and fix a language" (ibid., p. vi).

New Concepts of Register: Grammar, Gender, Class

What emerges in the work of Johnson, Lowth, Priestley, and their contemporaries is a new concept of linguistic register. As we have seen, register is a sociolinguistic concept that can take many forms. For the sixteenth and seventeenth centuries, register was largely a matter of vocabulary: choosing words of different origins or juxtaposing familiar and new words to create particular effects or enhance the writer's authority. By the end of the eighteenth century, register was largely a matter of grammar and style. Choosing between old and new forms, or what Priestley called "solemn" and "common" forms, became a matter of establishing tone. Differences between "you" and "thou," between "hath" and "has," between "me" and "mine," and between "who" and "whom" could be a matter of register in certain cases. They can be identified as a conscious choice to sound "solemn." This is a key word for the age. It does not simply mean serious or humorless. As Johnson defined it, it means "affectedly serious." It is a performance, a register of language taken on for a specific purpose.

What also emerged in the 1700s was a notion of register keyed to gender. Women were increasingly being educated outside of the home. Women's literacy was growing through the century, and the rise of the novel, the proliferation of daily journalism, and the rise of the profession of the personal writing master all responded to and helped shape the social reality of a female public living actively in language.

A book such as James Robertson's *The Ladies Help to Spelling* (1722) exemplifies responses to these trends. Written as a dialogue between a teacher and a student, the book begins by trying to "make Spelling a work of no difficulty." But the young female student protests: "I know nothing of these Rules, for my Education was too like to that bestowed on most of my Sex." She worries that the "bad spelling" of her fellow women will "afford matter of Laughter to the Reader" (quoted in Horobin 2013, p. 155).

For novelist Sarah Fielding (1710–68), such worries motivate the publication of her book, *The Governess, or The Female Academy* (1781 [1749]). Long considered the first novel expressly written for children, the book describes a school for girls (some as young as 9 years old), teaching them "Reading, Writing, Working, and … all forms of proper behavior" (by "working," Fielding means needlework). The girls are visited by a writing master, though exactly what he teaches them is not described in the novel.

A better description of attitudes toward women writing in the mid-eighteenth century may be the responses of Sarah's brother, the more famous novelist Henry Fielding (1707–54), to her work. Henry supported his sister's literary activities, but in his Preface to the revised edition of her earlier novel, *David Simple* (1744), he was not above correcting what he believed to be her "Grammatical and other Errors in Style." Henry objected to Sarah's apparently irrational punctuation (her overuse of the dash to separate clauses and quotations, for example), and he made some changes that give us insight into the practices of standard English at mid-century. He changed the relative "that" to "which." He changed "think" to "guess." He changed "whoever is" to "those that are." He changed "those that" to "those who." Details like these may seem minor, but they represent a strong sense that correctness in grammar and usage reflects authority. In his brotherly correcting, Henry re-enacted the master/student relationships of a book such as Robertson's *Ladies Help*: we watch the man teaching the woman how to write, spell, and punctuate (see the discussion in Barchas 1996).

Whether Henry Fielding was correct in his gendered view of grammar, others shared his opinions. The famous Horace Walpole (1717–97) complained of what he called the "female inaccuracy" of such constructions as "between you and I," even though men and women used this phrase equally (at stake here was the teaching of Latin to boys, which would have supposedly taught them the correct phrase "between you and me").

By the end of the eighteenth century, the education of young women had become a basic concern for socially aspiring families. Educated girls were a commodity, a source of marriageable value that enhanced a family's economic and social status. Grammars for and by women began to proliferate. Anne Fisher (1719–78) may have been the first woman to publish a general grammatical work in English (Elizabeth Elstob had published a grammar of Old English in 1715). Fisher's work survives only in the second edition of 1750. It may well be the first grammar that states the rule for what is called the sex-indefinite "he." "The Masculine person answers to the general Name, which comprehends both Male and Female; as, any Person who knows what he says" (Fisher 1750, 117n). For modern students who increasingly use the singular "they" to signal a sex-indefinite referent, this statement is fascinating, illustrating how even women writers privileged male grammatical categories (the singular "they" had been in use since the late Middle English period; it only came to be criticized and proscribed in the 1700s).

Half a dozen women followed Fisher in preparing grammars in the later eighteenth century, the most popular of which was Ellin Devis's *The Accidence; or First Rudiments of English Grammar. Designed for the Use of Young Ladies* (1775, frequently reprinted). Her purpose is not to offer anything new but to recycle familiar material in a way that would have new "Perspicuity and Simplicity," rendering it "of Use, particularly in Schools." Men were getting into the business, too. George Ussher's *The Elements of English Grammar* (1785) showed that "a grammatical knowledge of English was becoming essentially necessary in the education of ladies." His gender biases are obvious, however, as he seeks to make his book "as easy and as useful to them [i.e., women] as possible." He thus rejects "abstract terms," trying to present grammatical rules "in the plainest manner possible" (see Van Ostade 2000).

Women's voices and women's writings come to proliferate in the 1700s, as an education in the regulated use of English came to be a mark of social acceptance. The voices of other women increasingly came to be written down. Novels, plays, and journals transcribed (often for humorous or condescending effect) the language of servants and tradeswomen. Court proceedings from the Old Bailey (the main courthouse in London) offer what may be more accurate transcriptions of women's voices. One trial in 1734 concerned a certain Abigail Nutsford, who was charging another woman, Mary Campion, with stealing some of her things (Sutherland 1953, pp. 225–6). Mary had owed Abigail money, and Abigail suggested that she work it off by cleaning her room. When Abigail found the room, it was cleaned but robbed. Abigail testified: "And so I goes out and leaves her to clean this room; and while I was gone, she pulls open my drawers and takes my things, and breaks me as much crockery as comes to three or four shillings." Here we see the grammatical use of the narrative present tense with mistaken number as a marker of class difference ("so I goes out"). We see an old reflexive use of the first person: "breaks me" is a relic of a dative case construction, best rendered now as "breaks for me." Mary also seems to steal some of Abigail's "pattins," a kind of thick-soled overshoe. "Give them back," Abigail reports she had said, but Mary responds: "'No,' says she, 'I'll give you none of them. Nap my cuckold for 'em.'"

For the student of the history of the English language, this line should make us work and wonder. If you look up the words "nap" and "cuckold" in the *OED*, you will get nothing: take my cuckold for them? Probably like the readers of this transcript in the 1730s, we must rely on a growing body of lexicography devoted to the "cant" and "argot" of the lower classes. Nathan Bailey, who had published a dictionary of English that Samuel Johnson used in making his own, also published *A Collection of the Canting Words and Terms, both ancient and modern, used by Beggars, Gypsies, Cheats, House-Breakers, Shop-Lifters, Foot-Pads, Highway-Men, &c.* (1736). Bailey's book reflects a growing interest in the different registers of English and, for Londoners in particular, a recognition that they were living among others whom they could not understand.

This canting developed out of earlier slang and colloquial terms. It grew into a complex language of belonging and exclusion: a way of talking so that none outside the group could understand. Its legacies were the Cockney rhyming slang (emerging in the mid-nineteenth century) and later carny talk. It makes for wonderful reading, now, and when we find the word "nap" we get: "To NAP, by cheating with the Dice to sure one change; also a Clap or Pox, and short sleep. *Nap the Wiper*, steal the Hand-kerchief. *You have napt it.* You are Clapt." To nap, then, is to come down with a sexually transmitted disease (the clap, gonorrhea). What Mary Campion is saying, then, is something like: go screw my husband (who would become her cuckold), with the implication that, were Abigail to do so, she would infect him (Bailey 1736).

The seventeenth and eighteenth centuries had been an age of linguistic regulation, codifying and judging grammar, spelling, and pronunciation. It was also an age of vivid colloquialism and disarming obscenity. To understand the English of this time is not just to recall its sounds and forms but to appreciate the vigor of its creativity, its "real character," not only on the page of the learned but in the speech of everyday people.

Sources and Further Reading

Bailey, N. (1736). [Canting Dictionary]. Available at: https://www.gordsellar.com/wp-content/uploads/2014/06/Canting-Dictionary-1736-Nathan-Bailey.pdf

Barchas, J. (1996). "Sarah Fielding's Dashing Style and Eighteenth-Century Print Culture." *ELH* 63: 633–56.

Cohen, M. (1977). *Sensible Words: Linguistic Practice in England, 1640–1785.* Baltimore, MD: Johns Hopkins University Press.

Fielding, S. (1781 [1749]). *The Governess; or, the Little Female Academy.* 6th edn., revised and corrected. London: T. Cadell.

Fisher, A. (1750). *A Practical New Grammar.* Newcastle: Thompson.

Fix, S. (1985). "Johnson and the Duty of Reading *Paradise Lost*." *ELH* 52: 649–71.

Hedrick, E. (1987). "Locke's Theory of Language and Johnson's Dictionary." *Eighteenth-Century Studies* 20: 422–44.

Hickey, R. (Ed.) (2010). *Eighteenth-Century English: Ideology and Change*. Cambridge: Cambridge University Press.

Hodges, R. (1643). *A Special Help to Orthographie: or, The True-vvriting of English*. London: Richard Cotes.

Horobin, S. (2013). *Does Spelling Matter?* Oxford: Oxford University Press.

Johnson, S. (1755). *A Dictionary of the English Language*, 2 vols. London: W. Strahan. On-line facsimile text available at: https://johnsonsdictionaryonline.com/index.php

Johnson, S. (1970 [1747]). *The Plan of a Dictionary* (London, 1747). Facsimile Reprint, English Linguistics 1500–1800, No. 223. Menston: Scolar Press.

Kenrick, W. (1773) *A New Dictionary of the English Language*. London.

Locke, J. (1690). *Essay Concerning Human Understanding*. London:

Locke, J. (1692). *Some Thoughts Concerning Education*. London.

Lowth, R. (1762). *A Short Introduction to English Grammar*. London: J. Hughes.

Mack, R. (2001). "The Historicity of Johnson's Lexicographer." *Representations* 76: 61–87.

Newton, J. (1669). *School Pastime for Young Children or The Rudiments of Grammar*. London: Robert Walton.

Percy, C. (2010). "Women's Grammars." In R. Hickey (Ed.), *Eighteenth-Century English: Ideology and Change*. Cambridge: Cambridge University Press, pp. 38–58.

Priestley, J. (1761). *The Rudiments of English Grammar*. London: Becket and De Hondt.

Reddick, A. (1996). *The Making of Johnson's Dictionary, 1746–1773*. Rev. edn. Cambridge: Cambridge University Press.

Sheridan, T. (1803). *A Course of Lectures on Elocution*, 2nd American edn. Troy, MI: Obadiah Penniman.

Sutherland, J. (1953). *The Oxford Book of English Talk*. Oxford: Clarendon Press.

Van Ostade, I. T-B. (2000). "Female Grammarians of the Eighteenth Century." Available at: https://www.let.leidenuniv.nl/hsl_shl/femgram.htm

Van Ostade, I. T-B. (2010a). "Lowth as an Icon of Prescriptivism." In R. Hickey (Ed.), *Eighteenth-Century English: Ideology and Change*. Cambridge: Cambridge University Press, pp. 73–88.

Van Ostade, I. T-B. (2010b). "Eighteenth-Century Women and Their Norms of Correctness," in R. Hickey (Ed.), *Eighteenth-Century English: Ideology and Change*. Cambridge: Cambridge University Press, pp. 59–72.

Wallis, J. (1688). *Grammatica Linguae Anglicanae*. Hamburg. Gottfried Schultzen.

Wallis, J. (1972). *Grammar of the English Language*, with an Introductory Grammatico-physical Treatise on Speech. Translated with commentary by J. A. Kemp. London: Longman.

Wilkins, J. (1668). *An Essay Towards a Real Character, and a Philosophical Language* London: Gellibrand.

Wimsatt, W. K. (1948). *Philosophic Words: A Study of Style and Meaning in the Rambler and the Dictionary of Samuel Johnson*. New Haven, CT: Yale University Press.

8 The Sounds and Shapes of English in Great Britain, 1800–2000

In the nineteenth and twentieth centuries, the English of the British Isles remained a study in contradictions. New words were coming in from colonial expansion, from industry and science, and from US popular culture, while schools and public media sought to provide a standard based on education, class, and region. English writers explored the possibilities of regional and class pronunciations, seeking to texture novels, plays, and eventually films with different varieties of the vernacular. Certain ideals of Received Pronunciation (RP) began to be consolidated, and the British Broadcasting Corporation (BBC), aided by the royal family's embrace of radio and television, gave the sense that there was a true English. However, the language of the urban street and the village lane increasingly departed from these apparent models. A history of the language at this time and place is more than a through-line to standard English; it is a history of differences of performance and of institutions of regulation.

Not since the late Middle English period did English writers record such varieties of dialect as they did in the nineteenth and twentieth centuries. The talk of men and women fascinated novelists from Charles Dickens to Virginia Woolf to Martin Amis.

Beginning in late 1880s, English came to be audio recorded, and we can use this evidence to chart changes in pronunciation and idiom. We can also recognize that, increasingly, English came to be something performed: the music hall, the comic and dramatic stage, the cinema, and the celebrations of street fairs all contributed to an English that was not just a medium of personal communication but a means of display.

This chapter is about variety. It charts the changes in pronunciation, grammar, and vocabulary over time and across space. Later chapters explore the effects of colonial expansion, American culture, and global communication on the English vernacular. Linguistic change is often motivated by contact with others. We will look at how linguistic change grew out of practices of class and region. Such change often comes more from below than from above, that is, from the strata of society deemed to be outside standard, regulated speech. As we saw earlier, the tensions between regulation and variety, prescriptivism and descriptivism, shape

DOI: 10.4324/9781003227083-9

what is acceptable. We look at how the sounds and shape of English moved between acceptance and rejection, and, in turn, how differences between the standards of an elite were often not so far from the habits of the everyday.

To Received Pronunciation and Beyond

The nineteenth and twentieth centuries saw a scholarly and public fascination with the sounds of English. Scholars, writers, and public educators took a new interest in the histories of pronunciation, seeking the origins for modern speech. Novelists like Charles Dickens were influenced by the developments in philological and lexicographical research, and they tried to reproduce the regional and class dialects of the British Isles by using spelling and pronunciation to evoke sound. George Bernard Shaw's *Pygmalion* (1912), familiar to many through its American musical adaptation, *My Fair Lady* (on stage in 1956, on film in 1964), dramatized the recognition that social advancement had become increasingly dependent on patterns of speech. Yet what Shaw's play, and later phonographic and film recording, also did was to theatricalize the different sounds of class and region – making linguistic variation into something to be curated and even treasured.

We tend to think of Received Pronunciation (RP) as the speech of the upper classes, the educated urban elite, and the professionals and public figures of London and southeast England. Alexander Ellis, in *On Early English Pronunciation*, considered RP to be "the educated pronunciation of the metropolis, of the court, the pulpit, and the bar" (Ellis 1869, vol. 1, p. 23). But he declined to call this a standard, preferring to see this as a form of public language, variable through the nation.

To modern ears, RP may sound "posh," "educated," or "aristocratic." We can hear it in the recordings of English monarchs from the time of George V, in the Christmas addresses of Queen Elizabeth II, and in the films and TV shows trying to evoke a world of country houses and the hunt. There is nothing inherent in this form of speech that makes it posh. It was the set of pronunciations, stress patterns, and idioms that emerged in southeastern England in the earlier nineteenth century that happened to be the patterns of the upper classes.

Linguists would call RP a supralocal form of English. It could be learned and spoken by residents of different areas. Even though its major features may derive from southeastern British English, its performance crosses traditional regional dialect boundaries. While it may have been used regularly by only a small fraction of the British population, it did have an important effect on the reception of what constituted British English for many outside of Great Britain. Some of its key features include the following.

Words such as "bath," "path," and "cast" had been pronounced with a short mid-vowel well into the late eighteenth century. A phonetic representation of these words would be [bæθ], [pæθ], and [kæst]. By the middle of the nineteenth century, and certainly by the early twentieth, the RP version of these words would have had a low back, long vowel: [ba:θ], [pa:θ], and [ka:st].

The long vowels /o:/ and /e:/ increasingly came to be pronounced as diphthongs. Thus, a word such as "note," which would have been pronounced [no:t] at the end of the eighteenth century, came to sound more like [nəʊt] in RP. A word such as "face," which would have been pronounced [fe:s] at the end of the eighteenth century, came to sound more like [feɪs] in recordings of educated speakers in the early twentieth century.

The status of vowels before the letter r changed dramatically. In earlier chapters, we saw how many of the differences between early and Modern English (and, as we will see, between British and American English) is the difference between rhotic and nonrhotic pronunciations. British English increasingly becomes nonrhotic in the nineteenth and twentieth centuries. Thus, words such as "car," "nurse," and "ford" came to be pronounced as: [ka:], [nəs], and [fɔ:d].

But how that r was pronounced was a matter of great debate. There is some evidence that the r may have been trilled or flapped, using the tip of the tongue against the alveolar ridge. We can hear this rolled or flapped r in many recordings of British people born in the mid-nineteenth century.

Sometimes the r came out sounding more like a glide, say, [w], than the liquid [r]. Alexander Ellis quotes a certain Reverend A. J. D. Dorsey, who commented in 1882 on the challenges of teaching pupils proper elocution: "Most pupils cannot trill the r, burring it in the throat, or making it a w, as dwink for drink" (Ellis 1889, vol. 5, p. 226). The sound of the r pronounced in this way is called **rhoticism** (not to be confused with rhotic and nonrhotic languages). Rhoticism is a term used in speech pathology to describe an impediment in pronouncing r. More likely, this sound would have been more like a labio-dental sound between an r and a w. In the spellings of novelists and the caricatures of cartoon and musical hall, it comes off as a w. This rhoticism was a feature of both lower- and upper-class dialects of southeastern and London English.

Linguist Daniel Jones, who styled himself a speaker of RP, distinguished between two different kinds of r sounds in his book, *The Pronunciation of English* (1909). Jones indicates them with an upright letter r and an upside-down letter r. The first is what he calls the rolled, dental r: this would be a sound produced by the tip of the tongue against the teeth. The second is what he calls a fricative, dental r. This sound would most likely have been produced by the top teeth against the back of the lower lip. More recent linguistic work defines this upside-down r, in the words of Geoff Lindsey, as a "post-alveolar approximant, ... articulate with the tongue just behind the alveolar ridge" (2019, p. 61).

People recorded in the first years of the phonograph and film exhibit these sounds. They also exhibit features of rhoticism, the long back vowel /a:/, and several other sounds no longer common in early twentieth-century British English. Recordings of Virginia Woolf (1882–1941), born into the intellectual and artistic world of late nineteenth-century southern England, offer the following features of RP (MacDonald 2016):

- Nonrhotic: she does not pronounce the r sound when it follows a vowel.
- Low central pronunciation of the vowel in "strut": this sound is somewhere between the [ʌ] and the [ə] pronunciations.
- The central onset of the diphthong in words such as "goat": this sound differs from what many modern speakers would pronounce as [gəot], and might be represented as [gɛot].
- The raising of the back vowel in words such as "trap": for many modern listeners, this word would sound closer to "trepp" than "trap," thus [trɛp].
- The lax vowel at the end of words such as "happy": rather than pronouncing this word as [hapi], it sounds more like [hepɪ].

Beginning roughly in the 1960s and 1970s, RP came to be associated increasingly with the rarefied worlds of the aristocracy and the southeastern upper classes. The political upheavals and social reactions of these decades, along with the influx of regional speakers into British popular media and politics, have led to a set of pronunciations that, far from universal, may be understood as characteristic of late twentieth- and early twenty-first-century British speech. Although there are many specifics, we can make some general observations.

High and front vowels have tended to be lowered and retracted. Back vowels tend to be raised. Mid-vowels tend to be fronted. For example, a post-RP pronunciation of the word "trap" would no longer be Woolf's [trɛp], but rather [trap]. The RP pronunciation of the word "lot" [lɑt], sounds more like [lɔt] today.

Diphthongs have also changed. A general principle is that RP centering diphthongs have been lost. RP had four of these sounds: /ɪə/, /eə/, /ɔə/, and /ʊə/. Centering diphthongs get this name because when you pronounce them, you progressively move from the far front or back of the mouth to the center. A good example of this change is the pronunciation of "force." Early twentieth-century recordings and guidebooks indicated that this word would have been pronounced [fɔəs]. Late 1900s and early 2000s evidence indicates that this word is pronounced more like [fɔs]. The tendency to pronounce the vowel as a diphthong, with the second element of the sound moving to the center of the mouth, has disappeared. A word such as "force," then, has a vowel sound closer to a word like "thought" than before. The initial sounds in the diphthongs in the words "fleece" and "face" have been lowered in the mouth:

fleece: RP [flis] > post-RP [flɪs]
face: RP [fes] > post-RP [fɛs]

There are also changes in consonants. Traditional RP had aspirated stops, p, t, and k. These sounds, at the beginnings of words, would have had an extra breath of air. We can represent this pronunciation with the superscript h in transcriptions such as:

kiss /kʰɪs/
take /tʰek/
posh /pʰaš/

This feature has become one of the most parodied of upper-class RP. Modern speakers would say a word such as "carpet" with a simple initial stop: [kapɪt]. RP speakers, and speakers of a highly rarefied RP (listen to the speeches of the royal family, for example), would add an additional breath after the initial stop: [kʰapit].

Another feature of modern British pronunciation is the increasing use of glottal stops in medial positions. Although this had long been considered a feature of regional or lower-class speech, it has become increasingly accepted throughout Britain. Thus, by the end of the twentieth century, words like

little
bottle
platform
Scotland

could be heard as

[liʔl]
[baʔl]
[plæʔfɔm]
[skaʔlɪn].

A word such as "British" can be heard every day as [brɪʔɪš] (though probably not on the BBC). The glottal stop appears between words in certain phrases, often replacing the t sound. Thus, phrases such as

Get out
That is
Support each other
What else?

will have the glottal stop in place of the t, with an added emphasis on the vowel sound after the glottal stop.

Syntax and Grammar

The syntax and grammar of spoken and written English changed in subtle, distinctive ways during the 1800s and 1900s. Among these changes were features that distinguished English by the end of the twentieth century.

First was the increased use of prepositions and prepositional phrases and the use of prepositions in verb phrases. Thus: get up, get over, get into, get out of; speak up, speak out; make up (meaning comprise), make up (meaning reconcile); make out (meaning discern), make out (meaning kiss). While these and many other phrases were available to speakers and writers from the 1700s on, it is in the 1800s and 1900s that they contribute to the distinctive feel of literary and colloquial English.

The simplification of sentence structure, with the pattern of noun + verb + object, became almost universal. The long, sinuous sentences of, say, Samuel Johnson in the Preface to his *Dictionary* – with their strings of subordinate clauses and deferred verbs – may appear difficult to modern readers. Compare this sentence from Johnson's Preface with a passage from the introduction to the *Oxford English Dictionary*'s first volume, written by James A. H. Murray in 1888:

> I have, notwithstanding this discouragement, attempted a dictionary of the *English* language, which, while it was employed in the cultivation of every species of literature, has itself been hitherto neglected, suffered to spread, under the direction of chance, into wild exuberance, resigned to the tyranny of time and fashion, and exposed to the corruptions of ignorance, and caprices of innovation.
>
> (Johnson 1755, p. 1)

> The story of the origin and progress of the New English Dictionary has been told at length in various literary journals and magazines, and is familiar to most persons interested in the study of the English language. The scheme originated in a resolution of the Philological Society, passed in 1857, at the suggestion of the late Archbishop Trench, then Dean of Westminster. It was proposed that materials should be collected for a Dictionary which, by the completeness of its vocabulary, and by the application of the historical method to the life and use of words, might be worthy of the English language and of English scholarship.
>
> (Murray 1888, p. 1)

Johnson is a distinctive prose stylist. But his stylistic habits come from eighteenth-century literary practice. Similarly, Murray's style is one of late Victorian restraint. Johnson cannot start a sentence without interrupting it with a qualifying clause. His sentence structure builds on parallel phrases. Murray's sentences are more direct. He uses compound sentences (clauses linked with "and") more frequently than Johnson. His vocabulary is less exuberant than Johnson's. He uses the passive voice more often. This use of the passive voice, in particular, has become characteristic of present-day English academic, journalistic, and narrative writing.

One of the most notable features of Modern English has been the progressive construction: the use of a form of the verb "to be" with a following verb with an -ing ending. This feature is noticeable from the sixteenth century onward, and during the nineteenth century it becomes increasingly prominent in personal and literary prose. There is a difference, for example, between saying "it rains" and "it is raining." The first statement presents a condition of the present, the second statement presents an activity. A different distinction can be made between the sentences "I ate" and "I was eating." The first sentence simply presents a moment in time; the second presents a continued action. This construction can also create the sense of something transitory or potentially changeable. "I lived at home" is a statement of a condition in the past. "I was living at home," implicitly has the sense that at some point I did not live at home and, at the moment of speaking, I no longer lived at home. A sentence like "he is mean" offers a description of a person, irrespective of time. A sentence like "he is being mean" offers a description of a condition that may change (that is, he is being mean now, but may not have been in the past or may not be in the future).

The increasing use of verb forms ending with -ing becomes a feature of narrative prose throughout the nineteenth and twentieth centuries. In the narrative quotations offered at the end of this chapter, we can see how this grammatical feature expresses continuity, movement, or sometimes a sense that more than one thing is going on at the same time:

- Charlotte Brontë: "*gathering up* my feet, I sat cross-legged like a Turk; and *having drawn* the red moreen curtain nearly close, I was shrined in double retirement."
- Bram Stoker: "I thought that the Professor *was going* to break down."
- Virginia Woolf: "said Mr. Bankes, *replacing* the receiver and *crossing* the room to see what progress the workmen *were making* with an hotel which they *were building* at the back of his house."
- Martin Amis: "I stretched out, *calling* piteously and frequently to the stewardess."

In a quotation from the BBC recording of Lilian Balch from 1949, we can also see this use of -ing forms to create a sense of a kind of progressive present in the narrative past:

> I was busy *dishing* dinner up.
> What's wrong with you *taking* the day off and *going* down to the coast?

These constructions have led to a rise in the passive voice. The passive is not just a grammatical or stylistic feature. It has increasingly become a way of removing agency from actions, creating (rightly or wrongly) a sense of descriptive objectivity rather than of judgment. Such uses will be familiar from news media. To say "hundreds were killed" is a way of creating the impression of dispassionate observation. There is no grammatical subject doing the killing. To say, "my tires were changed" removes any mention of who was changing the tires (a mechanic? a friend?).

Among the many features of Modern, public English, the use of the verb "to be" in passive constructions seems characteristic of the period, especially in what is called the progressive passive. In the eighteenth century, a phrase such as "the house is building" would have been perfectly acceptable. A century later, "the house is being built" was the norm.

A look at news reporting of world crises in the British press gives a good sense of how the passive has emerged as the grammar of journalism. Here is Angus Hamilton, reporting to *The Times* on the siege of Mafeking, January 3, 1900 (emphases indicate the key features discussed):

> The resistance of the garrison *is goading* the Boers to commit various atrocities. Despite innumerable warnings they have concentrated their fire during the last two days upon the women's laager and hospital. Children have been killed and women mutilated by the bursting of shells. These occurrences *are fanning* a spirit of revenge in the breasts of the townspeople.

Here is *The Times* reporting on the Suez Crisis, Wednesday, August 2, 1956:

> The first instinct last weekend was to take the strongest action to ensure that the Canal was in proper hands, and that instinct was right; but *time is passing, consultations are going on, and now the idea seems growing of calling a conference of the chiefly interested powers.*

In these passages, half a century apart, we can see how journalistic reporting creates a sense of present happening by using the construction of the verb "to be" plus the verb ending in -ing. In *The Times* report on the Suez Crisis, the final clauses take this to an extreme, building the impression of things happening almost without the control of named subjects (Who is consulting? Where is the idea growing? Who is calling the conference?).

These style features have become features of grammar and syntax. It is not that they could not have been used by earlier writers. It is that they have become characteristic, defining features of the look and feel of Modern English. Other grammatical and syntactic developments that contribute to this look and feel include the virtual elimination of the subjunctive mood in everyday conversation and the increased use of "to be" in verb phrases.

English long had (and still grammatically has) a conjugated subjunctive mood for verb forms to indicate conditions contrary to fact, wished-for outcomes, or phrases of an if/then meaning. It remains perfectly grammatical to say:

> If I were to go home, I would eat.
> Be he alive or be he dead, I'll grind his bones to make my bread.

For the first sentence, most speakers would say, "If I was to go home." For the second, we would probably hear, "If he was alive or if he was dead," or more pedantically, "If he were alive or if he were dead." A fully conjugated subjunctive has largely disappeared from casual use.

In the case of "to be" phrases, one of the features of an English that looks archaic to us is its absence in verb phrases. Thus, the following sentences from late eighteenth- and nineteenth-century writers, while perfectly understandable today, seem old-fashioned.

> How came you and Mr Surface so confidential? (Sheridan, 1777)
> The Earl seemed much annoyed. (Sewell, 1877)
> She appeared sleeping soundly. (Gaskell, 1848)

These examples (Dennison 1998, pp. 230–1) would now be:

> How did you and Mr. Surface come to be so confidential?
> The Earl seemed to be much annoyed.
> She appeared to be sleeping soundly.

As with the use of the subjunctive, this change may be more a matter of style and idiom than grammar. But it has come be represent a norm of conversational English that enables us to distinguish contemporary from historical statements.

The Growing Vocabulary

During the 1800s and 1900s, the English vocabulary increased dramatically. New words from exploration and colonization, science and technology, and literary writing entered the language – but often in restricted registers. The words for medical conditions, scientific principles, or newly created objects all may be found in modern dictionaries. They are not part of the everyday speech of most people. They contribute to the stratification of register based on profession, class, or region. Moreover, words that were already common or familiar parts of the English lexis took on new meanings or new grammatical functions, in effect, becoming new words. Finally, what we might call a culture of linguistic inventiveness took hold in the English-speaking world. Not since the time of Shakespeare has there been such a cultural fascination with making up words or using them in different ways.

The growth in the Modern English vocabulary can be understood according to several broad categories.

Loan Words

Colonial expansion, trade, migration, and global media have brought words from non-European languages into English. Often these are words for food, dress, architecture, social organization, and commerce. Many such words entered English, beginning in the seventeenth century. The following lists offer words or word forms new in the nineteenth century (dates from the *OED*):

atoll (in this form, first 1832): from the Maldivian language, originally applied to the Maldive islands themselves.

batik (1880): from Javanese, meaning "painted."

chutney (1813): from Hindi.

cola (1887): from West African languages, referring to the kola nut, applied to the American soft drink that used its flavoring.

curry (noun, 1598; verb, 1839): originally from Tamil, *kari*, meaning a sauce or relish for rice; borrowed into Portuguese as *caril*, and first used in English as a Portuguese term.

guerrilla (1809): from the Spanish diminutive of *guerra*, meaning "war."

juggernaut (in its figurative sense, 1854): originally from Sanskrit, Jagannatha, "lord of the world," passed into Hindi, referring to a title of the god Krishna; first used figuratively, and with this English spelling, to mean an institution or a force to which people are devoted or which runs over them.

pajamas (1801): a term in Persian and Urdu referring to loose-fitting trousers.

pidgin (1869): from the Chinese approximated pronunciation of the English word "business," coming to mean a form of a language sharing features of several languages, often simplified, to facilitate communication.

pundit (in general use, not specific to Indian culture, 1816; punditry, 1926): from Sanskrit *pandit*, by way of Hindi, meaning a wise man; in use in English from the mid-1600s, but only much later applied generally to a wise man.

shampoo (noun, 1838): from a Hindi verb meaning "to press" or "massage." First used to describe the act of washing the hair alone in a citation from 1860.

safari (1860): from Swahili, meaning a journey or a tour.

thug (1810): from a Hindi word originally meaning a member of a particular gang or cult; first attested in a general sense in 1838.

Scientific, Technical, and Professional Terms

These are words, often based on Latin and Greek roots, designed to describe objects and phenomena and to create a register of professional knowledge:

computer (1869): originally someone who performs calculations; in the sense of a machine designed to do so.

coronary (noun, 1893)

digital (of signals, information, or electronic displays, 1940)

ecology (1875)

electron (1891)
neutron (1899)
proton (1920)
radio (noun, 1903; verb, 1919)
radioactivity (1899)
telephone (noun, 1832; verb, 1879)
television (1900)
thrombosis (1857)
wireless (as an adjective for a system of communication, 1887; as a noun,
     now replaced by "radio," 1899)

Some of these words have become part of the everyday vocabulary. But many of them exist to separate the professional from the nonprofessional. We may know what a coronary thrombosis or a myocardial infarction may be, but we would probably just call it a heart attack (first attested 1836).

Compounds and Affixes

Newly created or discovered objects may be given names made up of already existing words or morphemes. Some of these will be very familiar; others may be from restricted registers or uses:

aeroplane (1868); airplane (1906).
back-bencher (1910): a member of the British House of Commons, not en-
     titled to sit at the front; generally applied to such politicians of little
     influence.
backroom (1941): a compound originally describing a room at the back of
     a house; figuratively coming to mean an area behind the scenes where
     decisions are made and power exercised in a political sense.
motorcar (1895)
paperback (1843)
stonewall (as a verb, 1876): a word probably of Australian origin to describe
     the process of impeding political action or obstructing legislation.
typewriter (1868)

Words may be created by adding prefixes and suffixes to create new forms. These words tend to contribute to professional or specialized vocabularies or to come from psychology, politics, science, and other disciplines:

amoral (1882)
asocial (1883)
categorization (1886)

microorganism (1882)
privatization (1942)
privatize (1923)
unsympathetic (1823)

Shifts in Function

Nouns had been turned into verbs since the time of Shakespeare. It is a common feature of English in many periods and places. These expressions contribute to the distinctive flavor of nineteenth- and twentieth-century colloquial English:

audition for role (1935)
chair a meeting (in this expression, 1921)
headquarter a leadership (1838)
highlight a point (1881)
mastermind a plan (1923)
medal in a sport (1860)
motor along the road (1892)
referee a contest (1883)
table a motion (originally US expression, 1849)

Verbs can become nouns, a familiar feature of English in all periods. These expressions contribute to the distinctive feel of late twentieth-century colloquialism, often giving the impression of attempting to simplify the vernacular:

make the ask (in the sense of making a large request, 1975)
disconnect, used for "disconnection" (in the sense of consistency of argument or experience, 1982)
a great read ("read" as a noun appears in OE and ME, but disappears, and, according to the *OED*, is reformed in the nineteenth century)
the big reveal (with the definite article, standing in for "revelation," 1952)

Truncation

Words that were formed as compounds can be shortened in colloquial speech. Some of these forms have replaced their originals (e.g., "bus" for "omnibus"); others have become marked by class, region, or register (e.g., "telly"); others have taken on new meanings entirely (e.g., "prom" and "promenade," or the connotation of "retro").

airplane > plane
chatter > chat

fanatic > fan (admirer or zealot)
mitten > mitt
omnibus > bus
promenade > prom
retroactive > retro
television > telly

Words from the Names of People

boycott: originally referring to the isolating of Irish tenants by withholding food or labor, named after Charles C. Boycott (1832–97), an Irish land agent.

Braille: the raised dot method of writing for the blind, named after Louis Braille (1809–52).

diesel: after Rudolf Diesel (1858–1913), inventor of this particular internal combustion engine.

leotard: the garment named after Jules Léotard (1838–70), French trapeze performer.

maverick: originally named after Samuel Augustus Maverick (1803–70), an American politician and rancher, famous for refusing to brand his cattle.

Roentgen: a unit of X-ray exposure, named after the discoverer of X-rays, Wilhelm Roentgen (1845–1923).

sandwich: the food named after John Montagu, Fourth Earl of Sandwich (1718–92), who supposedly invented it as a way of conveniently eating while gambling.

saxophone: invented by the Belgian instrument maker Adolphe Sax (1814–94) in 1840. The suffix is based on a Greek word meaning voiced or sounding. Other instruments named on this model include the sousaphone, a smaller brass tuba featured in the marching band of the American musician, John Philip Sousa (1854–1932), first attested in 1925.

silhouette: a term based on the name of Étienne de Silhouette (1709–67), a French politician known for his petty economic policies.

One of the defining features of spoken English in the second half of the twentieth century (and, as we will see later, in the early 2000s) was a set of pragmatic shifts in word use. Words once considered taboo became accepted, losing their socially transgressive force. The British word "bloody," used as an intensifier from the mid-sixteenth century on, was considered unacceptable in polite or educated society well into the mid-twentieth century. As its taboo status evaporated, other intensifying words came to fill its semantic and syntactic place. Prominent among them would be "damned" and "fucking." The word "fucking" has become so ubiquitous in everyday speech (fucking idiot, fucking fantastic, fucking hell) that it may have, by the late twentieth century, lost some of its shock value (as an intensifier, it is recorded first in the mid-nineteenth century; as a word that splits up another word for effect, such as "fan-fucking-tastic," first recorded in the 1960s). The word "shit" (an Old English word) has increasingly come to refer not just to excrement but to any undifferentiated collection of things (from the 1890s as a general term for something worthless). It may function as a synonym for "stuff," as in, "who moved my shit?", or "get your shit out of here" (most likely an Americanism, beginning in the 1930s).

One feature of idiomatic English speech, then, has been the increasing use of taboo words to create emphasis in conversation, exercise power or verbal violence between speakers, and separate speakers by register. The use of slang words for body parts (especially genitalia) may be another example, at times extending to a general term of opprobrium irrespective of the literal or physical feature of the individual named. By the end of the twentieth century, a woman could refer to herself or another woman as a "dick" or as "ballsy" ("dick" as a slang term for "penis" appears as early as the 1500s; as a general term of abuse, however, first attested in 1966; the *OED* records this quotation for "ballsiness" from 2001: "He admired Mom for her sheer ballsiness"). A man may be called a "twat" or worse with little concern for the original gender specificity of those words (first use in this form from 1929).

Variation as the Mark of Region and Class

Before the twentieth century, the evidence for regional variation in the spoken English of the British Isles came from written sources. These included the spelling habits from writers literate enough to have correspondence, journals, and personal annotations in English, but not schooled in the standards of spelling. They include literary representations of regional dialects in novels, poems, and plays, as well as documentary evidence from public speech and courtroom transcription. In the 1800s, scholarship on the history of the English language dovetailed with scholarship on regional variation (at times, seeking to illustrate how regional varieties preserved earlier forms). W. W. Skeat and J. O. Halliwell are primarily known today as philologists and editors of Early English texts. But they were also cartographers of dialect, and their dictionaries of regional expressions give us a sense of what at least a certain class of educated academics thought the English language sounded like outside their purview. In the twentieth century, recordings and fieldwork in dialectology enabled more fine-grained descriptions of regional variation, often with the production of linguistic atlases designed to mark certain pronunciations or grammatical or lexical features using lines of demarcation, looking like the isobars of a weather map.

A complete and detailed description of regional variety in Great Britain is beyond the scope of this book, but we will cover the broad demarcation of the major lines of difference in regional British English, along with a commentary on how dialectical self-awareness came to be a central feature of the spoken world of Britain in the nineteenth and twentieth centuries.

In describing regional variation, several criteria have emerged over the past two centuries. The first is phonological. How were the long vowels and diphthongs pronounced? What relationship do these regional variations have to historical dialect differences?

Since Chaucer's time, the major distinction among regional varieties of English has been the distinction between northern and non-northern dialects. Even though there are many varieties of spoken English north of the Humber River, what characterizes northernisms is the retention of the unrounded long /a:/ that ultimately came from Old English words. Thus, words such as "stone," "home," and "bone" (with the rounded vowel) as we saw in Chapters 3 and 4 on Old and Middle English, often remained "stan," "ham," and "ban" in northern dialects (an easy caricature for Chaucer in the *Reeve's Tale*). What linguists heard in the nineteenth and twentieth centuries were descendants (or reflexes) of this unrounded vowel. Thus, "stone" would have sounded like [stɪən] or [stiən]. Other vowels that had become rounded in earlier Midland and southern dialects also remained unrounded in the north. In the mid-twentieth century, researchers came up with a set of words that could be used as general markers distinguishing Northern speech from that of other areas in England.

Word	Northern pronunciation
bone	[biən]
cow	[ku:]
eat	[iət]
foal	[fʊəl]
spoon	[spiən]

This list represents some major features of northern English and illustrates how linguists have sought to come up with representative words as markers of regional variation. These tests have been listed, and they have been mapped. Table 8.1 is a list of representative words, ranged according to a more fine-grained set of regional variations than simply north, Midlands, and south (from Ihailinen, 1994, p. 255).

In addition to these vowel sounds, certain grammatical features have been associated with regional dialects. Linguist Ossi Ihalainen describes the "northern subject rule" as follows: plural present-tense verbs take -s, unless they are immediately preceded by a personal-pronoun subject. Thus, northernisms would be "They peel them and boils them" and "birds sings." The difference is that the word "they" in the first example governs the number of the immediately

Table 8.1 Representative regional variation words

	Long	Night	Blind	Land	Arm	Hill	Seven	Bat
Northumberland	lang	neet	blinnd	land	arrm	hill	seven	bat
Lower North	lang	need	blinnd	land	ahm	ill	seven	bat
Lancashire	long	neet	blined	lond	arrm	ill	seven	bat
Staffordshire	long	nite	blined	lond	ahm	ill	seven	bat
South Yorkshire	long	neet	blinnd	land	ahm	ill	seven	bat
Lincolnshire	long	nite	blinnd	land	ahm	ill	seven	bat
Leicestershire	long	nite	blined	land	ahm	ill	seven	bat
Western Southwest	long	nite	blined	land	arrm	ill	zeven	bat
Northern Southwest	long	nite	blined	lond	arrm	ill	seven	bat
Eastern Southwest	long	nite	blined	land	arrm	ill	seven	bat
Southeast	long	nite	blined	lænd	arrm	ill	seven	bæt
Central East	long	nite	blined	lænd	ahm	ill	seven	bæt
Eastern Counties	long	nite	blined	lænd	ahm	hill	seven	bæt

following verb, but not the second verb (peel, boils). In the second example, the noun (not a pronoun), even though it is in the plural, still takes the verb ending in -s. There are other regional dialects in which this distinction does not apply. In the southwest of England, expressions such as "they peels them" and "farmers makes them" would be heard (ibid., pp. 221–2).

Regional British English is also full of distinctive lexical and idiomatic expressions. Words associated with northern dialect areas include:

aye: yes
bairn: child
canny: pleasant
ket: sweets
pet: a term of affection or endearment
snek: nose

Words associated with the dialect of the county of Cumbria, in the northwest of England include:

barrie: good
bog: toilet
clarty: messy
fratch: argument
hossing: raining heavily
ladgeful: embarrassing
lugs: ears
scower: look at
twine: to complain

Expressions associated with the Scouse dialect of Liverpool and Merseyside include:

giz: "give us"
made up: very happy
yous: the second person plural

Words associated with the vernacular of the city of Manchester include:

bobbins: rubbish
gaff: a house or residence
scran: food
scrote: something worthless
sound: good, trustworthy
the dibble: the police

These lists of words may be amusing. But what they and many others reveal is a conception of regional identity as being grounded in words. In effect, lexis becomes curated: it stands as an example of regionalism, much as dress or food might be associated with a certain town or shire. What is new during the past century is not so much a simple distinction between metropolitan and regional speech but a cultivation of regional speech as doing several things: marking insiders from outsiders, creating a kind of private language, and even adding, self-consciously, to the "exotic" feel of certain geographical and social areas.

Perhaps the most noticeable variant of British English – and the one most associated with a certain kind of essential or unrefined Englishness – is and has been Cockney, the vernacular of the East End of London. Working-class men and women, since the late eighteenth century, have been identified with the Cockney dialect on the basis of distinctive pronunciations and grammatical forms. For many people, within and outside of Great Britain, Cockney has come to stand for the British dialect *par excellence*: the furthest thing from Received Pronunciation and the epitome of English working-class authenticity.

Charles Dickens, in his first major novel, *The Pickwick Papers* (1836), has the character Sam Weller speak a Cockney that, by the time of the novel's publication, may have already seemed old-fashioned. In fact, Dickens's character largely speaks in caricature (much as Chaucer's students in the *Reeve's Tale* did). But behind the caricature are some key features of a particular dialect (see Baer 1983).

Sam switches w and v: saying "wery" for "very," and "avay" for "away." He will say "circumwented" and "ven" for "when." The character has given rise to the concept of "Wellerisms" – familiar proverbs, often misunderstood or misapplied, and often spoken with his Cockney accent. Dickens uses eye-dialect spellings to convey the sound and sense of such Wellerisms: "Vich I call addin' insult to injury, as the parrot said ven they not only took him from his native land, but made him talk the English langwidge arterwards."

Aspects of Sam Weller's English survived in the stagings of the English music hall. Actors (some of whom were East Enders, but many of whom were not) created a kind of stage Cockney for humor. One of the earliest of these performers was Gus Elen (1862–1940), who was 8 years old when Dickens died and who lived long enough to make recordings and films in the 1930s. As with Sam Weller, Elen's language verges on caricature (he was not born in the East End but in Pimlico in a modestly lower middle-class family). Again, it does represent what many have come to think of as a distinctive variety of English, associated with place and class (see Roper 2022).

A song from one such film has been phonetically transcribed, and its opening lines look like this.

> Well it's a great big shame, and if she belonged to me
> I'd let her know who's who
>
> [wɛl ɪts ə graɪʔt bɪg šaɪm ənd ïf šeɪ be'lɒŋd tʰə mɪi
> (w)aɪd let ɐ nau ʊus ʊu]

These transcriptions offer symbols designed to represent sound in great detail, and they go beyond the basic International Phonetic Alphabet we have been using to this point. We can see, even at first glance, what makes this form of English distinctive.

The words "great," "shame," "she," "me," "I'd," and "who," all have diphthongs that begin low or back in the mouth and then move forward. Unstressed vowels are mostly reduced to the schwa sound. Here and throughout his performance, Elen does not produce the r after vowels. The symbol ɐ indicates a slightly fronted and raised lax sound (somewhat higher than the schwa) for the word "her." This transcription also indicates that the initial h was unpronounced, a classic feature of Cockney (and of many other regional varieties).

Another feature of Elen's speech is the pronunciation of the interdental continuant written as th as an f sound. He says the word "month" as [mɐnf]. He says the word "thumb" as [fɐm], and the last syllable of "underneath" as [nɪif]. He also pronounces the initial v sound more like a w: "vex" sounds like "wex."

What does this tell us about key features of British English in the 1800s and early 1900s? It tells us that class and regional dialects could be broadly distinguished by the pronunciation of diphthongs that had descended from older, long monophthongs. It also tells us that certain consonant pronunciations may have been shared by different class dialects, especially the pronunciation of r as a labiodental approaching w. It tells us that certain pronunciations associated with lower-class London English, particularly the pronunciation of th as f, survive as features of many dialects in modern Britain.

Such information also tells us something about how late twentieth-century British English had developed new forms that crossed original regional and class boundaries. What came to be identified in the 1990s as Estuary English was a vernacular associated with the rising middle classes of London, and it came to be associated with the political and social elites of the last years of the twentieth century. Estuary English can be thought of as a kind of synthesis, bringing together aspects of RP, Cockney, and some regional forms into a performative dialect. No matter whether this form remains a truly distinctive dialect, it captured the attention of linguists. We might best think of it as another "performative" form of English, in the way that Cockney had become performative. As Lynda Mugglestone puts it:

> Estuary English [is] a *style*, one which evidently need not displace a speaker's habitual forms but which can be adopted as part of the repertoire of possibilities which individual speakers may have at their command. Hence Tony Blair's facility in the use of glottal stops in the context of, for example, the popular television interview, need not countermand his equal facility in their absence in Prime Minister's Questions. Language and language use are ... inherently variable, and such variability inevitably extends to the wide range of contexts and situations in which speakers move.
>
> (2003, p. 286)

This statement characterizes modern British English as well as any does. It helps us understand why novelists became fascinated with, and tried to reproduce, vernaculars through spelling and typography – as if the novel could move back and forth between the "range of contexts and situations in which speakers move." It helps us understand how the regional and class dialects of Britain have become (for lack of a better term) fetishes. For Great Britain from the mid-nineteenth century on, the stock of regional and class accents became as much a natural treasure as Big Ben, the crown jewels, or the Lake District.

Narrative Voices in Modern British English

The quotations in this section illustrate how writers and speakers responded to changes in the English language in the nineteenth and twentieth centuries. Some of these quotations are from canonical literary works. Others are from radio recordings and popular media. In every case, there is a vernacular consciousness to the narrator: an awareness that sound, syntax, lexis, and idiom all contribute to identifying the narrator and, in turn, how the narrator's idiolect shapes the world of experience.

Key features of each passage follow each quotation, and students are encouraged to discover resources to understand these features: are they words and expressions that would have been new at the time of writing; are they colloquialisms of speech that find themselves newly canonized in writing; and how do they contribute to the distinctive voice of the narrator in each passage?

> A small breakfast-room adjoined the drawing-room. I slipped in there. It contained a bookcase: I soon possessed myself of a volume, taking care that it should be one stored with pictures. I mounted into the window-seat: gathering up my feet, I sat cross-legged like a Turk; and, having drawn the red moreen curtain nearly close, I was shrined in double retirement.
>
> (Brontë 1846)

- Compound words: breakfast-room, drawing-room, bookcase, window-seat, cross-legged
- Technical terms: moreen
- Historical idioms: possessed myself of a volume; shrined in double retirement

> I thought that the Professor was going to break down and have hysterics, just as he had when Lucy died, but with great effort he controlled himself and was at perfect nervous poise when Mrs Harker stepped into the room, bright and happy-looking and, in the doing of work, seemingly forgetful of her misery. As she came in, she handed a number of sheets of typewriting to Van Helsing. He looked over them gravely, his face brightening up as he read.
>
> (Stoker 1897)

- Medical vocabulary: break down, hysterics, nervous
- Technology: typewriting
- Historical idioms: in the doing of work

> "But she's no more aware of her beauty than a child," said Mr. Bankes, replacing the receiver and crossing the room to see what progress the workmen were making with an hotel which they were building at the back of his house. And he thought of Mrs. Ramsay as he looked at that stir among the unfinished walls. For always he thought, there was something incongruous to be worked into the harmony of her face. She clapped a deerstalker's hat on her head; she ran across the lawn in galoshes to snatch a child from mischief.
>
> (Woolf 2006 [1927], p. 82)

- Technology: receiver
- Pronunciation keyed to class: an hotel
- Vocabulary used in metaphorical ways: incongruous, harmony
- Specialized vocabulary: deerstalker, galoshes
- Idiom: snatch

It all happened on Monday morning. I was busy dishing dinner up for all my gang, and I just happened to say how fed up I was. It was washday and I'd rather be at the seaside than washing over the dolly-tub. And father said to me 'What's wrong with you taking a day off and going down to the coast with your youngest boy?' That properly put the cat among the pigeons because everybody wanted to come as well. So we argued it this way and we argued it that way and we dived in among the money boxes, and in the end we all went down for the day.

(in Sutherland 1953, p. 439)

- Colloquialisms: dishing dinner up, my gang, fed up, put the cat among the pigeons
- Class vocabulary: dolly-tub

Three days ago (is it?) I flew in on a red-eye from New York. I practically had the airplane to myself. I stretched out, calling piteously and frequently to the stewardesses for codeine and cold water. But the red-eye did what a red-eye does. Oh, my. Jesus, I look like the Hound of the Baskervilles. Shaken awake to a sticky bun at 1.30 in the morning, my time, I moved to a window seat and watched through the bright mists the fields forming their regiments, in full parade order, the sad shires, like an army the size of England. Then the city itself, London, as taut and meticulous as a cobweb. I had the airplane to myself because nobody in their right mind wants to come to Europe, not just now, not for the time being; everybody wants to go the other way, as Heathrow confirmed.

(Amis 1989, p. 1)

- Specialized vocabulary: red-eye, window seat, sticky bun
- Vocabulary used in new or metaphorical ways: regiments, parade order, shires, taut, meticulous, cobweb
- Idiom: had the airplane to myself
- Use of the plural to refer to an unnamed third-person singular: nobody in their right mind

For over a year, when I was nine or ten, I was waylaid, Dartford-style, almost every day on my way home from school. I know what it's like to be a coward. I will *never* go back there. As easy as it is to turn tail, I took the beatings. I told my mum that I had fallen off my bike again. To which she replied, "Stay off your bike, son." Sooner or later we all get beaten. Rather sooner. One half are losers, the other half bullies. It had a powerful effect on me and taught me some lessons for when I grew big enough to use them. Most to know how to employ that thing little fuckers have, which is called speed. Which is usually "run away." But you get sick of running away. It was the old Dartford stickup. They have the Dartford tunnel now with tollbooths, which is where all the traffic from Dover to London still has to go. It's legal to take the money and the bullies have uniforms. You pay, one way or another.

(Richards 2010, p. 19)

- Specialized vocabulary and idiom: waylaid, losers, bullies, turn tail, fuckers, get sick of, tollbooths, traffic, uniforms

Sources and Further Reading

Amis, M. (1989). *London Fields*. London: Cape.

Baer, F. E. (1983)."Wellerisms in *The Pickwick Papers*." *Folklore* 94: 173–83.

Brontë, C. (1846). *Jane Eyre*. Available at: http://victorian-studies.net/Bronte-Jane-1.html.

"Changes in British English Pronunciation in the Twentieth Century." Available at: http://www.yek.me.uk/changestwe.html.

Dennison, D. (1998). "Syntax." In S. Romaine (Ed.), *1776–1976. CHEL*, vol 4. Cambridge: Cambridge University Press, pp. 92–326.

Ellis, A. J. (1869–1889). *On Early English Pronunciation*, 5 vols. London: Trubner.

Hickey, R. (Ed.) (2017). *Listening to the Past: Audio Records of Accents of English*. Cambridge: Cambridge University Press.

Ihalainen, O. (1994)."The Dialects of England since 1776." In R. Burchfield (Ed.), *English in Britain and Overseas. CHE*, vol. 5. Cambridge: Cambridge University Press, pp. 197–276.

Johnson, S. (1755). *A Dictionary of the English Language*. London: Strahan.

Jones, D. (1909). *The Pronunciation of English*, vol. I, *Phonetics*, vol. II, *Phonetic Transcription*. Cambridge: Cambridge University Press.

Lindsey, G. (2019). *English After RP: Standard British Pronunciation Today*. London: Palgrave.

Macdonald, F. (2016). "The Only Surviving Recording of Virginia Woolf." Available at: https://www.bbc.com/culture/article/20160324-the-only-surviving-recording-of-virginia-woolf

Mair, C. (2009). *Twentieth-Century English: History, Variation and Standardization*. Cambridge: Cambridge University Press.

Mugglestone, L. (2003). *Talking Proper: The Rise and Fall of the English Accent as a Social Symbol*. 2nd edn. Oxford: Oxford University Press.

Murray, J. A. H. (1888). *A New English Dictionary on Historical Principles*, vol. 1. Oxford: Oxford University Press.

Richards, K. (2010). *Life*. New York: Little, Brown.

Roper, S. (2022). "19th-Century Cockney and RP." Available at: https://www.youtube.com/watch?v=V29OhkbzwuQ

Stoker, B. (1897). *Dracula*. Available at: https://jmc.msu.edu/r/Stoker_Dracula.txt

Sutherland, J. (1953). *The Oxford Book of English Talk*. Oxford: Clarendon Press.

Times of London (1900). [Report on the Siege of Mafeking]. July 3.

Times of London (1956). [Report on the Suez Crisis]. August 2.

Trudgill, P. (2000). *The Dialects of England*. 2nd edn. Oxford: Wiley-Blackwell.

Woolf, V. (2006 [1927]). *To the Lighthouse*. (Ed.) David Bradshaw. Oxford: Oxford University Press.

Wright, P. (1981). *Cockney Dialect and Slang*. London: Batsford.

9 American English
Origins, Varieties, and Attitudes

The English language came to North America with the initial settlements of English people in the early seventeenth century. The first permanent English colony in the Americas was at Jamestown, Virginia, established in 1607. Plymouth, Massachusetts, was established in 1620. Boston was founded in 1630. By the middle of the century, colonies were taking hold in Rhode Island, the Hudson River estuary, Virginia, and the Delaware Valley. Each settlement area had a distinctive heritage in the class, regions, and religious sects of England. Puritans from East Anglia dominated in Massachusetts, Catholics in Rhode Island, southern English gentry in Virginia, Quakers from the Midlands to the Delaware Valley. In the eighteenth century, settlers came from northern England, Ireland, Scotland, and Wales to the mountainous areas of Appalachia and the Ohio River basin. From 1619 onward, people of African origin were brought against their will to work as forced labor in agriculture, bringing with them their languages and cultural heritages.

In many ways, American English has become an international language, and American popular culture and online communication have contributed to the structure and flavor of global English. But long ago, really from the very beginning of European settlement, American words and expressions inflected English speech. Alexander Gil, the early-seventeenth-century linguist and pedagogue, published *Logonomia Anglica* in 1619. We have seen something like it before: a Latin treatise arguing for a purer, historical English, shorn of Romance and Latinate coinages. Gil noticed how people were already beginning to borrow words from what he called Americanis. He calls attention to the word "maiz," which he calls *triticum Indicum*, or Indian grain (most likely an indigenous term borrowed through Spanish). The word "canoe," which he records as "Kanoa," is there too, as are "moose," "raccoon," and "opossum." By 1755, Samuel Johnson could record such American words as "tobacco," "chocolate," "barbecue," and "squash." By 1781, Reverend John Witherspoon (who emigrated to North America in 1768 and became president of what is now Princeton University) had coined the term "Americanism" to express the relationship between linguistic and regional identity (Cassidy and Hall 2001, p. 185).

DOI: 10.4324/9781003227083-10

New vocabulary terms, changes in pronunciation and grammar, and particular idioms came together to make American English markedly different from British English. They also contributed to the regional and class stratification of the language. Visitors to colonial America often remarked on how uniform the English language was across those class and regional boundaries. Everyone, some noted, seemed to speak well and with the same care and "propriety" (in the eighteenth century, a word that meant grammatical agreement – that is how Johnson primarily defines it in his *Dictionary*). Nonetheless, by the late eighteenth and early nineteenth centuries, regional differences were being recognized. By the late 1800s, such differences crystallized into recognizable dialects, increasingly represented in literary and journalist works for dramatic or satiric effect. Mark Twain, Stephen Crane, Joel Chandler Harris, Sarah Orne Jewett, and many other nineteenth-century writers reveled in displaying their ability to reproduce the sound and sense of local vernaculars. While these regional varieties were not mutually unintelligible, they were recognizable, and they contributed to a new sense of regionalism in American literature by the early twentieth century.

The study of phonology, morphology, grammar, and lexis in American English is inseparable from the study of the attitudes toward language, the guidelines of teaching, the making of new dictionaries, and the making of the United States as a nation. As Noah Webster put it, in his *Dissertations on the English Language* (1789), "As an independent nation, our honor requires us to have a system of our own, in language as well as government." He continued: "A national language is a band of national union" (quoted in Simpson 1986, p. 82). How that national language emerged is the theme of this chapter.

Sound and Sense

One of the founding presuppositions (if not myths) about American English is that it preserves forms of the language from the age of early settlement. The beliefs that somehow rural communities were still speaking "Elizabethan" English into the twentieth century or that linguistic developments were somehow frozen at the moment of colonization have long been popular notions. Although it is true that American and British English diverged, and it is true that there are some features of American that would appear to be archaic when compared to British, both are living, changing vernaculars.

There are features of American English, broadly defined, that hearken back to earlier forms of British, just as there are unique features that developed over time. We can begin with a few of these specifics.

Early Modern English /a/, as we have seen, became a long vowel, retracted in the mouth in British English from the late eighteenth century onward. In America, this vowel became /æ/ in words such as "cat" and "hat," but remained /a/ in "father." This difference was noticed as early as Webster's *Dissertations* of 1789. American pronunciations of historical /æ/ in words such as "fast," "calf," and "bath" kept the /æ/ sound, whereas in Britain this sound came to be more like a short /a/.

Other vowel sounds were changing in the late 1700s. The sounds of the words "pen" and "pin" (/ɛ/ and /ɪ/) were apparently not distinguished in colonial America. The short /o/ in words such as "not," "hop," and "hot" was often unrounded to an /a/ sound in American pronunciation (but kept as a rounded vowel in British).

Most complex is the pronunciation of /r/ and the status of American as a rhotic language. As we have seen, British pronunciation, leading up to Received Pronunciation, increasingly became nonrhotic. The /r/ sound was almost never pronounced, except before vowels. Colonial examples of r-dropping include such words as "cuss" for "curse," "bust" for "burst," and "hoss" for "horse." In New England, the prestige dialect became largely nonrhotic ("pahk the cah in Havahd Yahd" remains the parody example), but in the rest of the colonies, and later in middle America, rhotic pronunciations became the norm. Evidence suggests that in the late nineteenth century, rhotic pronunciations were associated with class superiority and political power. One explanation may be that as cultural and political power shifted from the older New England and Virginia families (largely nonrhotic speakers) to New York, Philadelphia, and then Chicago and the Midwest, the rhotic speech of the newer elites became the prestige standard.

Early Modern English speakers tended to pronounce all syllables in polysyllabic words (based on evidence from rhyme and meter in poetry). Webster argued that all syllables in polysyllabic words should be pronounced, clearly recognizing that by the late 1700s, British speakers were beginning to shorten these words. Thus:

American		*British*
necessary	sounds like	necessry
secretary	sounds like	secretry
literature	sounds like	litrature

Other features were noticed as early as Webster in 1789, and the 1829 edition of his *American Dictionary* featured a "Synopsis of Words Differently Pronounced by Different Orthoepists," put together by Joseph Worcester. Among these differences, often along American/British lines, were the pronunciation of the initial /h/ sound in words such as "human" and "hospital"; the vowel sound in the word "again" as either /ɛ/ or /e:/; and the pronunciation of the medial sibilant in words such as "design" as an unvoiced /s/ or a voiced /z/.

There were also certain expressions that came to be seen as American early on. A traveler in 1839 argued that the English language had become "debased" in the new nation. Examples given include the phrase "right away," the use of the word "admire" in everyday speech, and the verb "to fix" used to mean "to prepare a meal."

At the heart of early discussions of American English was the question of whether the language had become debased or whether it had become new and vital. John Witherspoon argued that the new Americanisms were no "worse in themselves," but rather "merely that they are of American and not English growth." "It does not follow," he noted, "from a man's using these that he is ignorant or his discourse upon the whole inelegant." Witherspoon was not above correcting his fellow colonists, though. Every day he heard and read "errors in grammar, improprieties and vulgarisms, which hardly any person of the same class in point of rank and literature would have fallen into in Great-Britain." Again, he noted,

> The vulgar in American speak much better than the vulgar in Great-Britain, for a very obvious reason vis., that being much more unsettled and moving frequently from place to place, they are not so liable to local peculiarities either in accent or phraseology.
>
> (quoted in Cassidy and Hall 2001, p. 185)

Witherspoon's observation about the mobility of American English speakers is key. Because the colonies were founded with the idea of geographical control, and because the vastness of the American West (in Witherspoon's day, this meant west of the Hudson River) seemed open for the taking, migration was central to the early American ideal. Even though dialect boundaries took shape early on, and even though today we may observe regional differences in lexis and pronunciation, everyone recognized that the varieties of English in North America were mutually intelligible.

Writing in 1919, H. L. Mencken looked back on a century and a half of Americanism to codify what he called "the Hallmarks of American:"

> The characters chiefly noted in American English are, first its general uniformity throughout the country; second, its impatient disregard for grammatical, syntactical, and phonological rule and precedent; and third, its large capacity (distinctly greater than that of the English of present-day England) for taking new words and phrases from outside sources, and for manufacturing them of its own materials.
>
> (Mencken 1977, p. 98)

These three features were and still are a useful way to organize the study of American English. Certainly, they stood (at least implicitly) behind Noah Webster's attempts to describe and prescribe the vernacular of the new nation.

Webster had philosophical and political goals more explicit than Mencken. His notion of language is deeply indebted to John Locke's theories of knowledge, which had had a great influence on Samuel Johnson and, through Johnson, gave

Webster guiding principles about how words were loosely tethered to things. In the Preface to his *American Dictionary*, Webster claimed:

> Language is the expression of ideas; and if the people of our country cannot preserve an identity of ideas, they cannot retain and identity of language. . . . No person in this country will be satisfied with the English definitions of the words congress, senate, and assembly, court, &c, for although these are words used in England, yet they are applied in this country to express ideas which they do not express in that country.
>
> (1828, "Preface")

This is pure Locke. In the *Essay on Human Understanding*, Locke stated that words "stand for nothing but the Ideas in the mind." Johnson adapted this view when he wrote, "Difference of thoughts will produce difference of language." For Locke and Johnson, the mind was a blank slate at birth, and ideas came to be imprinted on it through the impressions of the senses. For Johnson, then, a notion of linguistic change necessarily followed from the conviction that changes in the lived environment altered the impressions of the senses. As people changed, so would language. "To enchain a syllable," wrote Johnson, "and to lash the wind, are equally the undertakings of pride" (Johnson 1755, p. 7).

Webster took this imagery and shot it through with an explicit political purpose. Johnson's chains and lashes – like the words "senate," "congress," and "court" – take on a new particular meaning in a nation seeking to throw them off:

> [Americans] had not only a right to adopt new words, but were obliged to modify the language to suit the novelty of the circumstances, geographical and political, in which they were placed ... It is quite impossible to stop the progress of language—it is like the course of the Mississippi, the motion of which, at times is scarcely perceptible yet even then it possesses a momentum quite irresistible. Words and expressions will be forced into use in spite of all the exertions of the writers of the world.
>
> (Webster 1828, "Preface")

Webster blends a language of linguistics and liberty here. Johnson had already noted that new words "are readily adopted by the genius of our tongue." Early America was all about adoption. The US Constitution explicitly referred to its approval as an "adoption." Ben Franklin had used the phrase "A Plan of Union adopted by the Convention at Albany." That adoption, for Webster, was a "right," for the United States was a nation of rights. The Declaration of Independence avers a set of "unalienable Rights." The Constitution has a Bill of Rights. Thomas Paine published "The Rights of Man" in 1791.

Webster uses familiar words in the new ways for which he had argued. Progress and flow, notions central to Johnson's view of language change, now become localized into the image of the Mississippi River. A word such as "irresistible," which readers today might hear as a term of desire or pleasure, was charged with geographical and political power for Webster. His definition of "resist" in his own *Dictionary* goes right to the image of flowing water: "a dam or mount resists a current of water by standing unmoved and interrupting its progress." Resistance against political change was similarly futile. Thomas Jefferson wrote in his autobiography in 1821, in ways that echo behind Webster:

> The appeal to the rights of man, which had been made in the United States, was taken up by France, first of the European nations. From her, the spirit has spread over those of the South. The tyrants of the North have allied against it; but it is irresistible.

> (Jefferson 1914, p. 156)

Webster's impact on American English was greater than that of any other writer or teacher. He sought to reform American spelling, making it more concise, more logical, and free of unpronounced letters. Thus, he spells the British -our words as -or words:

colour > color
honour > honor
labour > labor

He removes the final -k in words such as the following:

musick > music
logick > logic
physick > physic

He respells British -re endings to -er endings, to reflect pronunciation:

centre > center
metre > meter
theatre > theater
sabre > saber

He replaces British c in words such as "defence" and "offence" with an s:

defense
offense
pretense
license

He advocated uniform pronunciation of syllables, codifying such pronunciations as we saw already:

necessary
secretary
literature

Webster's impact on American English went beyond simple details of spelling and pronunciation. In his many instructional books and his *Dictionary*, he set forth a conviction that uniformity in speech should mirror a shared national identity (see Montgomery 2001, p. 99). His influence on generations of public orators and literary writers contributed to a shared verbal purpose in American belonging. Frederick Douglass turned to Webster's spelling books during his enslavement. Seeking to improve his handwriting, he copied the letters, and in his slaveholder's copy, "in the ample spaces between the lines I wrote other lines as nearly like his as possible."

Webster shaped the poetic imagination, too. Emily Dickinson spent days with the 1844 edition of his *Dictionary*, finding meanings and word associations that she incorporated into her poetry. Scholars have found what has been called a "lexical cohesion" between Webster and Dickinson. One of her poems reveals word associations from the *Dictionary*:

> Perhaps you think me stooping
> I'm not ashamed of that
> Christ—stopped until He touched the Grave—
> Do those at Sacrament
> Commemorate Dishonor
> Or love annealed of love
> Until it bend as low as Death
> Redignified, above?
>
> (Johnson 1958, poem number 833)

This enigmatic text (with its characteristic asides, dashes, half-rhymes, and hymn-like meter) opens up when we place Webster alongside it. He defined "stooping" as "bending the body forward," generating the association between "stoop" and "bend" in Dickinson's poem. The words "commemorate," "death," "love," and "Christ" all appear in Webster's definition for "sacrament." Webster's etymology of "anneal" as coming from "to anoint with oil" (a word history we now know to be inaccurate) led to a string of associations leading to Christ (whom Webster defines as "the anointed").

This is the work being done by the Emily Dickinson Lexicon project at Brigham Young University, and it says something important about the intersections of linguistic history and the literary imagination. It illustrates what became a distinctively American view of language: a way of reading the inheritances of English and transforming them into imagined landscapes.

For scholars of American English, those landscapes remained regional and distinct. In spite of Webster's urge for uniformity, American dialects have proliferated, and their origins have been traced in the original settlement patterns of the Eastern Seaboard, the Southern coast, and the Midwestern migrations. As early as 1832, Reverend Jonathan Boucher tried to argue that "there is no dialect in America." But even he recognized differences:

> Unless some scanty remains of the croaking, guttural idioms of the Dutch, still observable in New York; the Scotch-Irish, as it used to be called, in some of the back settlers of the Middle States; and the whining, canting drawl brought by some republican, Oliverian and Puritan emigrants from the West of England, and still kept up by their unregenerated descendants of New England—may be called dialects.
>
> (quoted in Montgomery 2001, pp. 97–8)

Boucher's characterizations remind us of John of Trevisa, writing at the end of the 1300s, on the "scharp, slitting, frottyng" and "harrying, garrying, grisbyting" sounds of the north of England to a southerner's ear. Like Trevisa, Boucher associates dialectical difference with social status and linguistic corruption. Just as the northerners of medieval England had a speech shaped by "aliens" (what Trevisa thinks of as the Scandinavian and Celtic peoples), so the different spaces of America bear the scars of other tongues.

North American dialects and the study of dialectology have taken on a very special status in the history of the vernacular and its literatures. Recognition of regional and class difference sparked the rise of sociolinguistics and corpus linguistics in the 1950s and 1960s. The work of William Labov on New York City speech, and the great project of the *Dictionary of American Regional English* are just two of the many ongoing studies seeking to use living, regional informants as sources of linguistic evidence.

All of this had more than scientific or sociological interest. By the mid-1800s, American regional speech became associated with proverbial wisdom and the unadulterated voice of experience. American dialectology took on much of the purpose of American lexicography. The heart of the nation was found in its folklore: myths of Paul Bunyan, songs of the field, homespun maxims in the descendants of Ben Franklin's *Poor Richard*. After the Civil War, scholars and writers became fascinated by sources of cultural difference. Some saw regional variation as a sign of "moral obliquity" (Jones 1999, p. 20). Others saw "standard English" as really nothing more than a socially accepted dialect. Philologist E. S. Sheldon, writing in 1902, averred that "the natural, careless, unconscious, colloquial speech furnishes the philologist with his best illustrative and explanatory material" (ibid., p. 17).

The American Dialect Society was founded in 1889. A century later, the *Dictionary of American Regional English* (DARE) opened with a quotation from that society's founder, William E. Mead, advocating for "an adequate dialect map of our vast country and ... bringing together a sufficient amount of trustworthy material for an *American Dialect Dictionary* worthy to stand beside the *English Dialect Dictionary*" (Cassidy 1985, vol. 1, p. xi). Mead's challenge was met by the DARE in several ways. Its compilers developed a set of questionnaires designed to elicit responses from living speakers. The data from these questionnaires were then mapped on to geographical regions.

The first thing one notices when opening the DARE is the reliance on lexical variation to determine dialect boundaries. For example, one question asked of informants was: "what other names do you have around here for the dragonfly?" Fieldworkers got two answers: "mosquito hawk" and "skeeter hawk" (Figure 9.1). Plotted on to a map of the United States, we see clusters of data points on the East Coast and in the South. But plotted on to a map with the states distorted into shapes keyed to their population density, we can see something else. The editors describe this kind of map as "essentially a scatter diagram that economically illustrates degrees of clustering – that is, degrees of regionality."

This notion of degrees of regionality lies at the heart of the DARE project and much study of North American dialects. Certain dialects are distinguished not just by their phonology or their lexis. They are distinguished by their aggregate departure from a national norm. Thus, the more distinctive terms used by a group of speakers, the more regional, as it were, their language appears to be.

This is a complex notion of dialectology that works in tandem with (and sometimes in conflict with) other versions of dialect mapping, notably those by the linguist William Labov. Labov's project, *The Atlas of North American English*, establishes its boundaries according to "the systematic study of phonological relations in the vowel system." Sometimes, he and his collaborators note, there may be "a high degree of convergence" between maps "based on regional vocabulary" and those based on sound. Sometimes there will be differences.

Labov's version of sociolinguistics was designed to chart the stratification of American speakers by class, education, and wealth, as well as region. One anecdote illustrates his approach. In the 1960s, Labov explored the speech of floor walkers (the supervisory, senior staff) at some of New York City's major department stores. The most prestigious of these stores was Saks Fifth Avenue. There, the floor walkers pronounced the r-sounds in "fourth floor" prominently. At Macy's, a more general, middle-class store, the r-sounds were less prominent. And at S. Klein's on the Square (a bargain basement shop, frequented by working-class shoppers and recent immigrants), the r-sound could be heard hardly at all (Labov 1965).

Labov's inquiries were chosen to illustrate how pronunciation was keyed to class (in a sense, a project akin to Lynda Mugglestone's in her *Talking Proper*). In the case of vocabulary, the DARE inquiries were chosen to illustrate geographical difference and historical inheritance. Labov commented on such

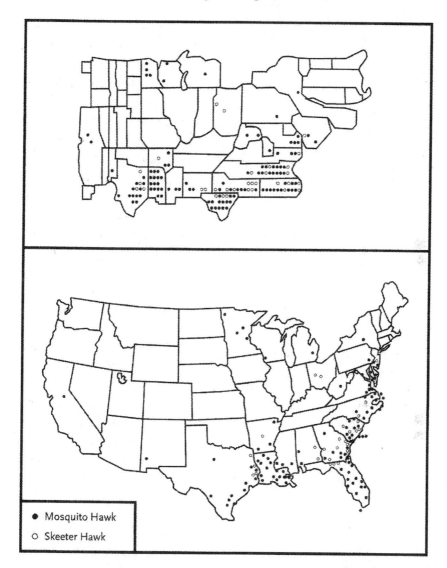

Figure 9.1 Distribution maps, from *The Dictionary of American Regional English*. These illustrate the distribution of regional phrases "mosquito hawk" and "skeeter hawk"

Source: Cassidy (1985, vol. 1, p. xxviii)

linguistic inquiries: "Words are selected for study on the basis of their regional heterogeneity and their possible connection with settlement history." Thus, the dialectologist looks for differences across space (synchronic variation) and evidence for historical survival (diachronic change).

Any mapping of language variation in real time is, in the words of Craig Carver, "merely a static representation of a phenomenon whose most salient characteristic is its fluidity." A dialect map is a snapshot of a moment, or something of a methodological fiction.

A Guide to American Regional Variety

American dialectology is a complex subject, and the details go far beyond the scope of this book. Nonetheless, we can identify some major features of regional American and approach their representation in literary and linguistic terms.

The *Atlas of North American English* characterizes regional variations according to patterns of pronunciation.

Inland North American English

This is the language of the northern tier of the United States, running from New England through upper New York state and the upper Midwest. Some representative features of this variety include:

- The pronunciation of words such as "bath," and "trap" with sound [æ] rather than [a].
- The pronunciation of words such as "dog," "all," "taught," "loss," and "saw" with the sound [ɑ].
- The pronunciation of words such as "bus," "flood," and "what" with the sound [ʌ].
- What is known as the coloring of vowels before r: that is, the influence of postvocalic r in certain words, effectively making rhyming groups out of such groups as "north" and "force"; "marry," "merry," and "Mary"; "mirror" and "nearer"; "hurry" and "furry."

New England English

There are a variety of forms throughout New England, ranging from features distinctive to Boston, to those of Maine. These forms are characterized by some representative features:

- The merger of the sounds in the words "cot" and "caught."
- The nonrhoticity in words such as "far," "heart," and "care."
- The raising and fronting of certain vowels, especially before unvoiced consonants. In practice, this means that the words "writer" and "rider" would sound different from each other.
- Replacing a medial t sound with a glottal stop. Thus, a word such as "sitting" often sounds like [sɪʔn], or sometimes [sɪʔən].

The effect of nasal sounds on previous vowels. Words such as "fan" and "pan" will have highly raised vowels.

New York City English

Many varieties depend on social status, class, and region in New York. The old-fashioned Brooklyn accent, with the oi sounds in "third," the er sounds in "oyster," and the d sound for "this" and "that," largely remains a caricature. Older pronunciations such as the aw sound in the name "Paul" and in the word "water," may be disappearing. This author grew up in the Brooklyn in the 1950s and 1960s, pronouncing the words "orphan" and "often" as homonyms. Broadly speaking, New Yorkers speak a nonrhotic variety of English, with some distinctive pronunciations of words with a short [a] and [æ]. Social stratification remains pronounced in New York City. Labov commented on the pronunciation of the first responders on September 11, 2001: "The dialect spoken by all those firemen on TV after September 11 was pure, unmodified New York speech from the nineteen-fifties."

The Mid-Atlantic Region

This region includes the speech of the cities of Philadelphia and Baltimore. It is largely characterized by rhotic pronunciations, with distinctive vowel sounds. For example, the word "on" tends to be pronounced to rhyme with "dawn." Words spelled with an a, ranging from "bath" and "bag," to "dragon" and "locality" are usually pronounced with the [æ] sound. Again, social stratification contributes to variety in the Mid-Atlantic region, with characteristics of the Baltimore and Philadelphia accent largely associated with white, working-class speakers. Some distinctive sounds here are the pronunciation of the word "water" as if it were "wooter" or even "warter"; the pronunciation of words such as "window" and "pillow" as if they were "winda" and "pilla"; and the pronunciation of "Baltimore" as if it were "Ballmer."

The South

Southern American English varies markedly from coastal to inland groups. There are distinctive local varieties (e.g., the English of the islands off the coast of North Carolina; the French-influenced speech of Louisiana, particularly, New Orleans; and the dialects of Texas, Appalachia, and the Ozarks). Most familiar to non-Southern speakers will be the "drawl" of Southern vowels. The drawl may be more precisely described as the breaking of monophthongs into diphthongs, where one element of the diphthong is a glide.

"pet" pronounced as if it were "pay it"
"pit" pronounced as if it were "pee it"

"Yale" pronounced as if it were "yay ell"
"yep" pronounced as if it were "yay up"
"fan" pronounced as if it were "fay un"

Other features of Southern English, broadly described, include maintaining the distinction between words such as "cot" and "caught," but not maintaining a distinction between words such as "pin" and "pen" and words like "feel" and "fill." Also distinctive is the accenting of polysyllabic words on the first (rather than the second) syllable. Thus, the following words may be pronounced: pólice, ínsure, Júly, úmbrella.

Midland English

The language of the large swath of the American Midwest, traditionally thought of as a kind of baseline of American English. As with other regions, the boundary lines are fluid, and there are variants within the region. Its major features may be identified as:

a rhotic dialect: the pronunciation of the r sound in "car," "heart," "party," and the like.
the occasional intrusion of the r sound in certain sequences. Thus, many words with wa spellings may be affected:

- "wash" may sound like "warsh."
- "Washington" may sound like "Warshington."
- "squash" may sound like "squarsh."

The varied pronunciation of the word "on." Pronunciations may range from [an] to [ɔn].

Western English

The pronunciation of English in the western US states may not seem as regional as Southern or New England English, but there are some distinctive phonological features. Words such as "cot" and "caught" tend to be pronounced the same way. Some distinctive features of California English include the pronunciation of words such as "rang" and "rain" with the same vowel sound, and what many consider the distinctive pronunciation of the word "strawberry" as close to "strahburry."

In all of these regions, phonology has been strongly influenced by contact with immigrants. Thus, New York and Boston English have been shaped by the influx of Irish immigrants in the later 1800s. New York English has long been colored with Yiddishisms from the Jewish immigrant community (e.g., "schmuck," "bupkes," "dreck"; and the syntactic pattern in "You want I should go now?"). Upper Midwestern English has been influenced by the Scandinavian and Eastern European immigrants of the nineteenth and twentieth centuries (e.g., the pronunciation of the penultimate vowel in "Minnesota" or the second vowel in "Wisconsin"). Southern English and the varieties of speech in many large cities have been transformed by long-standing contact with African Americans and, after the 1920s and 1930s, by the great migration of African Americans to western and northern urban and industrial centers. Western English has long had contact with Spanish speakers (Spanish-speaking Europeans had been colonizing the southwest since the early 1500s), and twentieth-century Mexican and Central American immigration has inflected aspects of New Mexico, Texas, and California speech (notably in the merging of the vowel sounds in "pin" and "pen" and "fill" and "feel").

American regional English is more than the sum of phonological differences. Distinctive grammatical usages and distinctive vocabularies mark the speech of different regions. In the American South, grammatical forms may have been influenced by African American English and by historical survivals of earlier constructions. Thus, the use of the verb "do" in its various forms has come to represent differences in tense and aspect. This is different from the use of "do" forms as intensifiers. In some varieties of Southern English, the following sentences may have different aspects:

I told you.
I done told you.

The first is a statement of the simple past. The second implies an action begun in the past and repeated in the past, and now reaffirmed in the present. "Done" may also replace the word "did" in statements such as "I done what you told me." This is an example of what are called nonstandard preterits: that is, expressions of actions in the past by using verb forms in distinctive ways. Expressions like the following are examples of nonstandard preterits:

"I knowed that" for "I knew that."
"You was sitting there" for "You were sitting there."
"I been waiting all morning" for "I have been (or I had been) waiting all morning."

The verb "fixing" has been idiomatically used to mean preparing, getting ready, or planning a future action. This usage differs from the idiom "fixing dinner," and often appears with the preposition "to." Thus: "I've been fixing to drive home," "I'm fixing to ask her out." Southern English also seems to preserve an older form of a reflexive dative pronoun. In the Old English text of Bishop Aelfric's *Colloquy* (from about 1100), the student playing the fisherman says: "Ic bregde me max," I weave a net for myself. In colloquial American and characteristically Southern English, this statement would be perfectly grammatical: "I weave me a net." Finally, what may be most familiar to listeners is the Southern restoration of the second-person plural pronoun. "Y'all" (a contraction of "you all") functions not simply as an address to a group of people, but may be used in statements that distinguish addressing a group from addressing all individuals in the group. A sentence such as, "I gave y'all a speech" implies that I spoke to a group as a whole. A sentence such as, "I gave all y'all a T-shirt," implies that I handed out a T-shirt to each individual in that group.

All regional varieties of American English have their grammatical and idiomatic distinctive features. In western Pennsylvania (especially Pittsburgh), expressions such as "your hair needs washed" are marks of regionalism. Characteristic of some Midland dialects is the retention of old strong verbs in the preterit tense. A famous example was the baseball player and sportscaster Dizzy Dean, who is said to have announced, at a moment of high drama during a game, "he slud into third." Other attested examples of this feature include "climbed" said as "clum" or "clim."

All regional varieties have their own distinctive vocabularies. Examples that will be familiar to travelers in the United States are terms for items of food:

hero, hoagie, grinder, sub
pop, soda, Coke
pancake, flapjack
crayfish, crawdad
taters, spuds, potatoes

Distinctions among household items will also be familiar. Linguists have drawn lines across America distinguishing regions that say "pail" and those that say "bucket."

Different idioms mark regionality: "on line" or "in line" has long been used as marker of New York speech. In California, the labeling of numbered highways distinguishes speakers from Los Angeles: Interstate 5 will be "the five" and US route 101 is just "the one-o-one."

Literary representations of American dialects often try to represent these features. In many ways, the rise of dialect literature and the study of dialectology are shared developments in late nineteenth-century America. Both contribute to what the critic Gavin Jones has called "popular debates about the national significance of the nonstandard voice" (Jones, 1999, p. 66). As Easterners traveled west after the Civil War, they encountered new words and new sounds. William Chauncey Fowler noted, in his *English Grammar* of 1868:

As our countrymen are spreading westward across the continent and are brought into contact with other races, and adopt new modes of thought, there is some danger that, in the use of their liberty, they may break loose from the laws of the English language.

(quoted in ibid., p. 55)

Fowler's warning sounds very much like Webster's praise turned on its head: "adopt" is no longer a positive term, and "liberty" is something that may need to be restrained.

Linguist Maximilian Schele de Vere wrote in *Americanisms: The English of the New World* in 1872:

> The student of English finds in the West a rich harvest of new words, of old words made to answer new purposes, often in the most surprising way, and of phrases full of poetical feeling, such as could only arise amid scenes of great beauty, matchless energy, and sublime danger.

(quoted in Jones 1999, p. 56)

Was linguistic regionalism a good thing or a bad thing? Did it contribute to the decay of English or to its potential beauty?

For Mark Twain, American regionalism lay at the heart of realist fiction and, in turn, his representation of US identity. In novels like *Tom Sawyer* and *The Adventures of Huckleberry Finn*, Twain creates a kind of eye-dialect spelling to represent a variety of speech sounds. He has Tom Sawyer say that he was "drownded with sweat," as well as saying "warn't" for "weren't," and "knowed" for "knew." But there is more than just detail. In the Preface to *Huckleberry Finn*, which he titled, "Explanatory," he wrote:

> In this book a number of dialects are used, to wit: the Missouri negro [*sic*] dialect; the extremest form of the backwoods South-Western dialect; the ordinary "Pike-County" dialect; and four modified varieties of this last. The shadings have not been done in a hap-hazard fashion or by guess-work; but pains-takingly, and with the trustworthy guidance and support of personal familiarity with these several forms of speech.

(Twain 1884)

Twain's remarks are valuable for what they say about his methods and for what they say about his own use of language. He loved to bring new words into literary life. The word "painstakingly," which he hyphenates to reveal its etymology, is first recorded only from the 1850s. Much older words such as "hap-hazard," and "guess-work," are hyphenated too, as if Twain wished to expose their histories as well. Twain's own work is full of words entering into American English literary writing for the first time: words such as "dude" and "hello," so common now that we may not give them a second thought.

Twain exemplifies a growing trend in US literature in the late nineteenth and early twentieth centuries. Eye-dialect spelling was coming into fashion, and the

American landscape was increasingly filled not just with mountains and cities and rivers and railroads but new spellings. Writer Ring Lardner has his Midwesterners say "ast" for "asked," and he represents the unstressed form of the word "of" as "o'." Jesse Stuart wrote stories in the Kentucky Piedmont dialect, and he spells "join" as "jine," indicating what some scholars believe to be a holdover from an archaic (perhaps eighteenth-century) pronunciation that enabled English poet Alexander Pope to rhyme the words "join" and "line."

The New England, late nineteenth-century writer Sarah Orne Jewett is particularly careful in her spellings. Here is a passage from her story, "Andrew's Fortune," originally published in *The Atlantic Monthly* in June 1881:

> "We was dreadful concerned to hear o' cousin Stephen's death," said the poor man. "He went very sudden, didn't he? Gre't loss he is."
>
> "Yes," said Betsey, "he was very much looked up to;" and it was some time before the heir plucked up courage to speak again.
>
> "Wife and me was lotting on getting over to the funeral; but it's a gre't ways for her to ride, and it was a perishin' day that day. She's be'n troubled more than common with her phthisic since cold weather come. I was all crippled up with the rheumatism; we wa' n't neither of us fit to be out," plaintively. "'T was all I could do to get out to the barn to feed the stock while Jonas and Tim was gone. My boys was over, I s'pose ye know? I don' know's they come to speak with ye; they 're backward with strangers, but they 're good stiddy fellows."
>
> "Them was the louts that was hanging round the barn, I guess," said Betsey to herself.
>
> "They're the main-stay now; they 're ahead of poor me a'ready. Jonas, he's got risin' a hundred dollars laid up, and I believe Tim's got something, too, – he's younger, ye know?"
>
> (Jewett 1881)

"Gre't," "be'n," and "wa'n't" evoke the long aesch sound [æ:] characteristic of Maine speech. She spells "sturdy" as "stiddy," indicating the loss of postvocalic r and the fronting of the back vowel. Morphological features of this dialect include the loss of the -ly suffix for adverbs: thus "dreadful concerned." Grammatically we see the nonstandard preterit: "we was," "wife and me was." Jewett also illustrates the confusion of nominative and objective cases for pronouns (a feature not unique to her dialect). Thus, she has characters say, "wife and me" for "wife and I," and "them was" for "they were." In her writing, there are patterns and idioms that the reader is meant to recognize as regionalisms: "very much looked up to"; "all crippled up"; "perishin' day"; "fit to be out."

What literary writers in America recognized was what the DARE recognized: regional variation is not simply a matter of individual differences but a collection of forms that indicate degrees of regionality. The greater the degree of regionality, the more authentic or realistic the dialect seems. The greater degree of regionality, too, the less transparent it is to the non-regional reader.

A good example of a writer who represents a high degree of regionality in literary narrative is Stephen Crane. Writing in the 1890s, Crane captures the sound and sense of the working-class, recent immigrant communities of New York City. In his novel, *Maggie: A Girl of the Streets*, Crane represents an argument between two young boys in Lower Manhattan:

> "Ah, we blokies kin lick d' hull d – n Row," said a child, swaggering.
>   Little Jimmie was striving to stanch the flow of blood from his cut lips. Scowling he turned upon the speaker.
>   "Ah, where was yehs when I was doin' all deh fightin'?" he demanded. "Youse kids makes me tired."
>   "Ah, go ahn!" replied the other argumentatively.
>   Jimmie replied with heavy contempt.
>   "Ah, youse can't fight, Blue Billie! I kin lick yeh wid one han'."
>
> (Crane 1896, p. 6)

This passage represents some key features of American English at a certain time and place: key vowel sounds in spellings such as "hull" for "whole," "kin" for "can," "ahn" for "on," and "wid" for "with"; the use of a plural second person, "yehs" and "youse"; the use of the singular form of a verb with a plural subject, "Youse kids makes me tired." What this passage also does is create a degree of regionality that takes particular marked forms, repeatedly as the representation of difference. What Chaucer did in the "*Reeve's Tale*" is something similar: selecting a few representative forms of a regional variant to stand for that variant as a whole. Neither Chaucer nor Crane writes phonetic transcriptions of lived speech. They write imaginative representations.

Let's look at a representative word of dialect use. Jewett uses the word "phthisic" to mean a pulmonary condition, such as consumption or asthma. Forms of this word (from the Greek *phthisis*) show up throughout late Middle and Early Modern English. By the eighteenth century, it seems to have dropped out of British English use. But it was familiar in the United States. Looking it up in the DARE gives us a mini-essay on identity. We find quotations from Webster, learned publications, folklore, and answers to questionnaires of linguistic fieldworkers. DARE quotes from Gould's *Modern English Lingo* of 1975:

> *Tizzic*—Included here because somebody who didn't now how to spell suggested it was "a good Maine word." Phthisic is in any good dictionary. Its peculiar orthography made it a favorite in old-time spelling bees, and until spelling bees went out of style almost all Mainers could spell phthisic.

This passage reveals a great deal about the history of a word and about how that history gets represented in works of North American linguistic scholarship. We read a story about spelling, a location in region, a claim about "any good dictionary," and (at least in 1975) what is presented as a disappearing American social practice (spelling bees). "Phthisic" is a touchstone for regionalism and its academic study.

The history of English, as we have seen, is a tale of external forces affecting language and, in turn, a story of groups of speakers coming into contact and influencing each other. Primary among these groups is the community of African descent that has lived in North America and the Caribbean since the early seventeenth century. African American English, and the Englishes of the Black Atlantic have had an indelible effect on the vernacular speech, writing, and performance throughout the world, and they deserve a chapter of their own. From this point on, this book takes a global approach to English in its history and its forms: from the Black Atlantic, through the postcolonial landscapes of Africa and the Indian subcontinent, to the age of digital communication.

Sources and Further Reading

Algeo, J. (Ed.) (2001). *CHEL*, vol. 6, *English in North America*. Cambridge: Cambridge University Press.

Bailey, R. (2012). *Speaking American: A History of English in the United States*. Oxford: Oxford University Press.

Carver, C. (1987). *American Regional Dialects: A Word Geography*. Ann Arbor, MI: University of Michigan Press.

Cassidy, F. G. (Gen. Ed.) (1985–2012), *The Dictionary of American Regional English*. 4 vols. Cambridge, MA: Harvard University Press. Available at: www.dare.wisc.edu.

Cassidy, F. G., and Hall, J. H. (2001). "Americanisms." In J. Algeo (Ed.), *CHEL*, vol. 6, *English in North America*. Cambridge: Cambridge University Press, pp. 184–218.

Crane, S. (1896). *Maggie: A Girl of the Streets*. New York: Appleton.

Deppman, J. (2002). "'I could have defined the change': Rereading Dickinson's Definition Poetry," *The Emily Dickinson Journal* 11: 49–80.

Jefferson. T. (1914). *Autobiography of Thomas Jefferson, 1743–1790*. New York: Putnam's.

Jewett, S. O. (1881). "Andrew's Fortune." *The Atlantic Monthly*, June. Available at: https://www.theatlantic.com/magazine/archive/1881/07/andrews-fortune/632746/

Johnson, S. (1755). *A Dictionary of the English Language*. London: Strahan.

Johnson, T. H. (Ed.) (1958). *The Complete Poems of Emily Dickinson*. Boston: Little, Brown.

Jones, G. (1999). *Strange Talk: The Politics of Dialect Literature in Gilded Age America*. Berkeley, CA: University of California Press.

Labov, W. (1965). *The Social Stratification of English in New York City*. Washington, DC: Center for Applied Linguistics.

Mencken, H. L. (1977) *The American Language*. With annotations and new material by Raven I. McDavid, and with the Assistance of David W. Maurer. New York: Knopf.

Metcalf, A. (2000). *How We Talk: American Regional English Today*. Boston: Houghton Mifflin.

Montgomery, M. (2001). "British and Irish Antecedents." In J. Algeo (Ed.), *CHEL*, vol. 6, *English in North America*. Cambridge: Cambridge University Press, pp. 86–153.

Simpson, D. (1986). *The Politics of American English, 1776–1865*. Oxford: Oxford University Press.

The Emily Dickinson Lexicon. Available at: http://linguistics.byu.edu/faculty/hallenc/EDlexicon/nehgrant.html

Twain, M. (1884). *The Adventures of Huckleberry Finn*. New York: Harper and Brothers.

Webster, N. (1783). *A Grammatical Institute of the English Language*. Hartford, CT: Hudson and Goodwin.

Webster, N. (1828). *An American Dictionary of the English Language*. Available at: https://webstersdictionary1828.com

Wolfram, W., and Schilling-Estes, N. (2015). *American English: Dialects and Variation*. 3rd edn. Oxford: Wiley-Blackwell.

Wolfram, W., and Ward, B. (2005). *American Voices: How Dialects Differ from Coast to Coast*. Oxford: Wiley.

10   The English Language and the Black Atlantic

Since their arrival in North America in 1619, people of African ancestry have spoken, written, changed, and indelibly shaped the English language. Words from West African languages have been used to describe foods, social relations, and personal identities. Grammatical features of the various creoles spoken in North America and the Caribbean have influenced the vernacular of twentieth- and twenty-first-century English speakers of all races. The soundscapes of music, dance, and cultural performance have textured the lives of Black people in North America as well as in Great Britain and the West Indies. Quite simply, Black English is everywhere.

Some histories of the English language define varieties of English according to region and heritage. What has come to be called African American English (AAE), or African American Vernacular English (AAVE), represents a mix of different sounds and forms. The speech of people from the rural American South, the urban North, the outer islands of North Carolina, Jamaica, Barbados, London, and many other areas differs. What has emerged in the twenty-first century is a recognition not that all people of African ancestry speak in the same way, but people of African ancestry throughout the Atlantic world have a shared vernacular culture, where influences move back and forth among North America, Britain, and the Caribbean. This chapter introduces the range and variety of Black Englishes. The aim is to illustrate the challenges of studying a form of language traditionally defined by the skin color of its speakers.

This chapter takes its title from the work of the historian Paul Gilroy, whose *Black Atlantic* (1993) argued for a "black vernacular culture" shaped through political action, musical performance, and diasporic sensibility (Gilroy 1993). Since the publication of that book, much research has been conducted on this vernacular culture. Salikoko S. Mufwene has analyzed African American English and identified the phonological, grammatical, and lexical features shared by many speakers of African heritage, almost irrespective of current geographical location (Mufwene et al. 1998; Mufwene 2001). John Rickford has charted the inheritance of West African linguistic and cultural practices on the performative qualities of the Black vernacular (Rickford and Rickford 2000).

DOI: 10.4324/9781003227083-11

John McWhorter has made a case for Black English as a new "American lingua franca," a way of using language that has transcended identity and class and has become identified with many forms of popular culture and youthful expression, irrespective of the origin of its speakers (McWhorter 2017). Miles Ogborn has illustrated how speech was a marker not only of heritage but also of status: free and enslaved people spoke differently in the Anglo-Caribbean world (Ogborn 2019).

Given this variety – across region, age, and social position – it is difficult to define a distinctive "Black English." Moreover, much of Black English has come to be perceived through theatrical, musical, and comic performance. In ways very much like British regional dialects such as Cockney or Geordie, the perception of Black English is often shaped through caricature. Writing Black speech – from Mark Twain through Joel Chandler Harris, Zora Neal Hurston, Richard Wright, Toni Morrison, and Colson Whitehead – often involves spelling conventions that create an exaggerated sense of difference. Where can we begin, and how shall we end?

Origins and Debates

Salikoko S. Mufwene writes about the phonological features of African American English with the following qualifiers: "one of the most common stereotypes"; "often characterized"; "noteworthy in some varieties"; "some speakers" (Mufwene, 2001, in *CHEL*, vol. 6, pp. 295–7). In the early 2000s, there is no uniform set of features shared by all English speakers of African descent. There was a time when linguists believed they could identify a common core of African American vernacular. Writing in 1972, William Labov said this language has a "relatively uniform grammar found in its most consistent form in the speech of the black youth from 8 to 19 years old who participate in the street culture of the inner cities" (quoted in Mufwene, 2001, in *CHEL*, vol. 6, p. 291). Ten years later, Labov identified the following characteristics of the language:

A distinct set of phonological and syntactic rules that are now aligned in many ways with rules of other dialects;
Incorporates main features of Southern phonology, morphology, and syntax; Shows evidence of derivation from an earlier Creole;
Has a highly developed aspect system, quite different from other dialects of English.

(Labov 1982)

Linguists have since qualified and sometimes challenged parts or all of these statements.

The origins of African American English are contested. One school of thought holds that the enslaved peoples in North America and the Caribbean learned

English at the times and places of their enslavement and passed it on to future generations. This view is called the English origins hypothesis: that African American English historically represents origins and developments of regional and social forms of English. The other major school of thought, known as the creole origins hypothesis, argues that Black speech emerged out of the mix of English, French, Spanish, and African languages, all at work along the West African coast, the Middle Passage, and the Caribbean and American South. As a **creole**, African American English is thus held to demonstrate features of creoles in general: an outgrowth of sustained contact between two or more languages; a vocabulary that blends the lexis of an original language and a host, or dominating language; a syntax that retains features of an original language.

In addition to this debate about linguistic origins, the social formation of African American English speech varied from place to place. Plantations that specialized in tobacco, rice, and cotton had different forms of social and economic organization and often drew on groups of different African ancestry for their forced labor. The colonial and early US republican speech of South Carolina, Virginia, and Louisiana (to name three states prominent in their historical Black populations) also varied significantly, and each would have influenced Black speech locally. Finally, the speech of enslaved people varied greatly according to social situation. How Black people spoke to their enslavers differed from how they spoke among themselves (Winford 2015).

Evidence of historical forms of African American speech remains tantalizing. Court transcripts from the Salem witch trials in Massachusetts in 1692 reveal at least one African person speaking in ways indistinguishable from the English settler community. Literary representations of Black speech in the 1800s often shade into caricature (major features may be represented, but as with other representations of dialects in literature, they may be limited or exaggerated). During the 1930s, recordings were made of formerly enslaved people. Fascinating though these documents are for many reasons, they recorded people of advanced old age, in different parts of the United States, and in highly artificial, curated contexts.

This textbook shares with Mufwene the position that African American English has no single point of origin. It is the product of what Mufwene calls a "polygenesis" from different communities at different times. That mid-twentieth-century linguists could identify shared features and common forms may be a function of how they defined African American communities as much as language – that is, looking at a largely urban population, economically less well off than others, with less access to social advancement (higher education, European cultural models, and the like). In the twenty-first century, middle- and upper-class African American people may speak differently from urban and rural working-class people. Just as there is no homogeneous "African American" population, there is no homogeneous African American English (Mufwene 2015).

Sounds, Syntax, and Grammar

Nonetheless, there are phonological, lexical, and grammatical features of the speech of African Americans that, historically and culturally, have been identified as characteristic of the population and have influenced other forms of English with an awareness that they are of Black origin. We may identify these features, most broadly, in the following ways.

The interdental continuant represented by the letters -th- often may be pronounced with an initial [t] or [d] sound. In medial or final positions, this sound may be pronounced as an [f] or a [v]. Put more generally, the interdental continuant may appear as a stop in an initial position and as a labio-dental continuant in medial and final positions. "This" may sound like "dis." "Mouth" may sound like "mouf." "With" may sound like "wiv." Some words are exceptions: "three" may sound less like "tree" than like "free."

African American English often appears to be nonrhotic. Words such as "floor" and "four" may sound like "flow" and "foe." Final stops may be dropped in certain words: "guest," "desk," and "wasp" may sound like "guess," "dess," and "wass." In the case of verb endings, some features may be phonological rather than grammatical. Saying "she jump" instead of "she jumped" is most likely a matter of pronunciation, dropping a final stop, than it is a feature of the preterit form of the verb "jump."

There are many features of African American English that are shared with Southern American English generally. The words "pen" and "pin, "ten" and "tin," and "get" and "git" may be pronounced the same. The diphthongs in words such as "cry" and "toy" may appear as long monophthongs: more like "crah" and "tah." Like Southern American English as well (and like other regional dialects), certain words will be prosodically distinctive: that is, the stress on syllables will differ from the stress patterns in "standard" English. Words such as "Detroit," "umbrella," and "police" may be stressed on the first syllable.

Grammar and syntax may be distinctive and shared with other regional dialects. What Labov identified as the "aspect," rather than the tense system, of African American English can be defined as follows: the verbal system describes actions in terms of origin and continuance, rather than simply by time relative to the present. Speakers of African American English have traditionally used forms of the verb "to be" and the verb "do" as what are called aspectual markers (Lanehart, p. 361). For example, they can signal repetition or habitual action. They can signal actions that are remote in time. And they can signal actions that continue.

Not everyone of African American ancestry will use these expressions. Individuals who do use them may not use them consistently in all situations. These are grammatical features that have been identified over time as largely characteristic of the performative vernacular of African Americans and that contribute to the point that African American English is not a debased or simply regional dialect or variety of English, but a pattern of linguistic behavior with rules, structures, and conventions. These rules, structures, and conventions make up the verbal system of African American English.

Here are some representative sentences that illustrate the aspectual, verbal system of African American English as it has been described and analyzed by linguists:

"She sick"; "she go": a condition that expresses her sickness or her movement as without defining when she got sick or left.

"She be sick"; "she be going": an action that began in the past and continues through the present.

"She be tired after work"; "She be crying after I leave": expressions of habitual action; she is usually tired after work, or she usually cries after I leave.

"She been working": an action begun in the past and long continuing.

"She done eat": an action begun and completed in the past.

"She been done gone": an action begun and completed in the past, more remotely than the previous sentence.

"She done her homework": not simply that she has completed her homework, but that she began it in the past and finished it in the past.

Other features of this verbal system emerge when we change the subject of the sentence. Look at the following three sentences (Green and Sistrunk 2015, p. 363):

The dog be barking.
A dog be barking.
Dogs be barking.

The first sentence describes an action that began in the past and continues through the present. It may carry with it a sense of habitual action, that this particular dog is in the habit of barking often. The second sentence may mean not simply that a particular dog is barking but that it is the characteristic feature of all dogs that they bark: in other words, it is in the nature of dogs to bark. The third sentence may describe an action in the present, but it may carry with it a habitual or essential quality.

African American English has also been seen as marking futurity in distinctive ways. Using forms of the verb "go," a speaker may announce a predictive action that has not yet happened. A sentence such as, "We gon have dinner," means that we are about to have dinner or we are planning to have dinner sometime in the future.

Expressions of actions in the past can also appear, superficially, to use present tense forms of verbs. Thus, the sentence, "I cook dinner," can mean, "I cooked dinner." Here, the question is whether the form of the verb "cook" is actually morphologically distinct or if it is a question of phonology: whether the final -ed is dropped as a matter of pronunciation (ibid., p. 372).

Exploring these features of African American English engages with the methodologies of sociolinguistic research. Much of that research involves studying the lived and recorded speech of African Americans. Much of it is site-specific, that is, recognizing that particular regions and cities in North America have distinctive speech patterns. Reading through this scholarship reveals phrases such as "intonational distinctiveness," "autosegmental metrical analysis," and "multi-modality" (Thomas, 2015, p. 433). What these technical terms mean is that we need to listen to speech patterns of individual people; those speech patterns may be characterized not only by the pronunciation of vowels and consonants but also by stress patterns in words and sentences. The nature of the African American vernacular is, by and large, one of oral performance in social situations.

For these reasons, it is a challenge to find written, literary representations of African American speech. In the nineteenth century, Frederick Douglass, Mark Twain, and Joel Chandler Harris, among others, developed spelling conventions to evoke Black speech. Are these caricatures, or are they representations?

Douglass writes a highly rhetorical American English of the mid-nineteenth century, rich with polysyllables and Shakespearean allusions (Douglass 2008, p. 111):

The reader can have little idea of the phantoms which would flit, in such circumstances, before the uneducated mind of the slave … This dark picture, drawn by ignorance and fear, at times greatly shook our determination, and not unfrequently caused us to

Rather bear the ills we had,
Than flee to others which we knew not of.

Then again, Douglass can give examples of the songs of the enslaved, with "fiddling, dancing, and jubilee beating," in spellings that are designed to evoke the key features of slave speech (Douglass 2008, p. 99):

We raise de wheat,
Dey gib us de corn;
We bake de bread,
Dey gib us de crust.

In these passages, Douglass offers the two poles of the African American vernacular experience. On one hand, there is the rhetorical force of the narrator, the preacher, and the politician – linguistic techniques Douglass learned from Webster's handbooks and *Dictionary* and from Caleb Bingham's *The Columbian Orator* ([1797] 2011). This latter work was the major instructional text for public verbal performance and for an emerging sense of American rhetorical identity in the late eighteenth and nineteenth centuries. It had an immense effect on promoting ideals of a "republican" America based on classical Roman models, and in its rhetorical modeling and ideological content influenced antislavery writings from those of Ralph Waldo Emerson and Harriet Beecher Stowe through Douglass and his heirs.

There is a through-line from Douglass to Booker T. Washington, W. E. B. Du Bois, Martin Luther King Jr., and Barack Obama. Follow the rhythm of these passages and see in them the instructions going back to Caleb Bingham: the cultivation of eloquence as a virtue, what he called a "proper attention to accent, emphasis, and cadence," and a need to "fill the place in the natural key of the voice" (Bingham 2011, p. 14).

> When I get to the head of the bay, I will turn my canoe adrift, and walk straight through Delaware into Pennsylvania. When I get there, I shall not be required to have a pass; I can travel without being disturbed. Let but the first opportunity offer, and, come what will, I am off. Meanwhile, I will try to bear up under the yoke. I am not the only slave in the world. Why should I fret? I can bear as much as any of them. Besides, I am but a boy, and all boys are bound to some one. It may be that my misery in slavery will only increase my happiness when I get free. There is a better day coming.
>
> (Douglass 1849, p. 65)

> Our greatest danger is that in the great leap from slavery to freedom we may overlook the fact that the masses of us are to live by the productions of our hands, and fail to keep in mind that we shall prosper in proportion as we learn to dignify and glorify common labour, and put brains and skill into the common occupations of life; shall prosper in proportion as we learn to draw the line between the superficial and the substantial, the ornamental gewgaws of life and the useful. No race can prosper till it learns that there is as much dignity in tilling a field as in writing a poem. It is at the bottom of life we must begin, and not at the top. Nor should we permit our grievances to overshadow our opportunities.
>
> (Washington 1895)

> The nation is sick. Trouble is in the land. Confusion all around. That's a strange statement. But I know, somehow, that only when it is dark enough, can you see the stars. And I see God working in this period of the twentieth century in a way that men, in some strange way, are responding – something is happening in our world. The masses of people are rising up. And wherever they are assembled today, whether they are in Johannesburg, South Africa; Nairobi, Kenya: Accra, Ghana; New York City; Atlanta, Georgia; Jackson, Mississippi; or Memphis, Tennessee – the cry is always the same – "We want to be free."
>
> (King 1968)

The road ahead will be long. Our climb will be steep. We may not get there in one year or even in one term. But, America, I have never been more hopeful than I am tonight that we will get there.

(Obama 2008)

At the heart of these speeches, and the traditions of American Black oratory, is the King James Bible. Patterns of repetition, cadences shaped by alternating strong and weak stressed syllables, oppositions of polysyllabic and monosyllabic words, lists of places, and the sustaining image of the journey along the river and the road – these are the key markers of the public, American Black vernacular. We can see the rhetorical devices of juxtaposing short sentences of statement ("the nation is sick," "the road ahead will be long," "there is a better day coming") with longer compound and complex sentences.

These oratorical traditions owe much to what Douglass learned and passed on from his reading and study. But they also owe much to the preaching of the Black Church in North America. They share that combination of what has been called "musicality, audience participation, and improvisation" – even though they may be highly scripted, formal performances. Watching recordings of Martin Luther King Jr.'s, "I have a dream" speech, we can see how call and response are central to the participatory quality of Black sermons. We can see how patterns of alliteration and repetition, internal rhyme and rhythm, all contribute to the "identity markers produced in talking Black as a marked choice" (DeBose 2015, p. 688).

Behind the rhetoric of the pulpit are the songs of the street and the memories of rural labor. What W. E. B. Du Bois called the "Negro spiritual" made up, as he put it in *The Souls of Black Folk*, "sorrow songs" of a people. Douglass also remembered these songs: "Every tone was a testimony against slavery, and a prayer to God for deliverance from chains." Du Bois rephrases this memory as follows: "They that walked in darkness sang songs in the olden days ... Ever since I was a child these songs have stirred me strangely." Du Bois's phrasing is powerfully biblical, alluding to Isaiah 9:2: "The people that walked in darkness have seen a great light" (Du Bois 1904, pp. 250–64).

This biblicism became part of the American Black vernacular through such spirituals as "Swing Low, Sweet Chariot," and "Let My People Go," both of which appear in printed texts by the mid-1800s. Such spirituals, and the newly composed poetry by African American writers in the late nineteenth and early twentieth centuries, contributed to the larger literary movement in American letters known as regionalism. It became one more aspect of a purportedly authentic voice – in dialect, in vocabulary, and in rhythm that was seen as kin to such other examples of regional poetry as James Whitcomb Riley's (1853–1916) so-called Hoosier poetry of the Midwest. Here are Riley's most famous lines:

When the frost is on the punkin and the fodder's in the shock,
And you hear the kyouck and gobble of the strutt' turkey cock ...

Compare these lines with those of the African American poet Daniel Webster Davis (1862–1913), whose poem "Hog Meat" appeared in James Weldon Johnson's *Book of American Negro Poetry* of 1922:

> When the fros' is on de pun'kin an' de sno'-flakes in the ar',
> I den begin rejoicin'—hog-killin' time is near.

It is not simply that Davis borrows or plays off of Riley's lines; it is that he uses them as a touchstone for dialect regionality. Davis changes the spelling, using apostrophes to illustrate characteristic (or stereotypical) dropping of final stops in certain words (fros', an'), the final -g (rejoicin', killin') and also to suggest a particular pronunciation of preceding vowels (sno' as having an exaggerated quantitative length, perhaps, and ar' rhyming with the word "near").

Davis's wordplay offers an example of what Henry Louis Gates Jr. identified as the practice of signifyin' in African American culture. Signifyin' (without the final -g) represents how one community, traditionally oppressed or disenfranchised, adopts the language of the controlling, enfranchised community for playful subversion. To signify was to take the master's language and use it to dismantle the master's house. It enabled, as Gates put it, "the black person to move freely between two discursive universes." In the words of linguist Claudia Michell-Kernan, "it incorporates essentially a folk notion that dictionary entries for words are not always sufficient for interpreting meanings or messages" (quoted in Rickford and Rickford 2000, p. 82).

In the 1930s, musician Cab Calloway effectively took this idea of a dictionary and created his own lexicon of signifying. The lyrics to his song, "Jive-Talk Dictionary," playfully define words such as "hepcat" as a "student of the Calloway vocab." As students of the Calloway vocab, we too should be aware of how jive talk manipulates the everyday. "What's the twister to the slammer?" Calloway asks in the course of his song, and he answers that it is the key to his "chicken fricassee." Look up the phrase "twister to the slammer" in the *OED* and you see a definition from 1939: "key to the door." But Calloway's key is no mechanical contrivance to open a physical door. It is a metaphor, a figure for sexual conquest, with the woman's sexuality represented here (as elsewhere in popular American verse) as a dish to be had. Dictionary entries for words are not always sufficient.

This brilliant play on lexicography shows us signifyin' at its most exuberant and defiant. Much of the play of African American jive, rap, and hip-hop carries the force of sexual threat. Gates quotes from the poetry of H. Rap Brown:

> Man, you must don't know who I am
> I'm the sweet peeter jeeter the womb beater
> The baby maker the cradle shaker
> The deerslayer the buckbinder the women finder.

(Gates 1988, p. 72)

This is what linguist David E. Kirkland calls Black masculine language. It is a form of coding, but also a form of pronouncing. Kirkland identifies a definite phonology to Black masculine language:

"the" pronounced as "de"
"father" pronounced as "faduh"
"with" pronounced as "wif" or "wid"
"cipher" pronounced as "cypha"

(Kirkland 2015)

Perhaps the most defiant and challenging of these phonological practices is the pronunciation of the n-word without the final -r. This difference was highlighted by American comedian Larry Wilmore in a speech at Barack Obama's White House Correspondents' Dinner in 2016: a speech that distinguished between white people who use the n-word as a form of disparagement and Black people who use the word, pronounced without the final -r, as a form of bonding (Wilmore 2016).

The vernacular of African Americans goes beyond these masculine posturings, of course. Tracey Weldon has defined a middle-class African American English: different from but sharing features with the broadest forms of African American speech (Weldon 2021; Britt and Weldon 2015). The point of her research is social as well as linguistic. Traditional accounts of Black American speech have focused on working-class, urban, and rural communities. They have addressed the imaginative world of subversion and resistance. They have explored the place of the obscene in public life. By contrast, Weldon sees a spectrum or continuum of Black American vernacular performance, and in the case of middle-class and prominent public figures, there may be a carefully curated form of pronunciation and grammar that marks this language from what we might call mainstream, white American speech. Weldon identifies hallmarks of this speech as including the reduction of final consonants and the use of "be" in its various forms to indicate aspect. Multiple negation ("they didn't have no food") frequently appears as a marker in speech irrespective of education or class – not because of inability or failure, but precisely because such phrasing has come to be taken as an identity marker of African American-ness, of belonging to a particular group with a particular heritage. Working from the research of Geneva Smitherman, Weldon and Erica Britt summarize:

African American public figures often tap into the sacred-secular continuum of African American speech. This continuum, with its emphasis on verbal performance and its foundation in a spiritual worldview, is the thread that unifies the speech styles of a wide array of African American public speakers ... the use of hallmark vernacular features of AAE (such as copula deletion and invariant be) [allows] them to take controversial political stances as they expressed their ethnic, religious, and philosophical affiliation with members of the African American community.

(Britt and Weldon 2015, p. 808)

Vocabulary

The lexis of African American and Black Atlantic speech draws on a variety of sources. Some expressions have been identified as translations of West African expressions.

"Big-eye," meaning greedy
"Bad-mouth," meaning to speak ill of someone
"Bad-eye," the evil eye or a curse

These expressions can be traced to Mandinka, Hausa, Igbo, Wolof, and other languages. Some have argued that the words "cool," "cat," and "dig" also come from West African origins. Words for foodstuffs and forms of artistic expression have been traced to these origins: gumbo, okra, yam, banjo, jazz. The Rickfords have noted the following sources for words characteristic of the Black American idiom:

Music and performance: gig, funky, boogie
The church: shout, Amen corner
Sex: grind
Conjure: voodoo, mojo
Street life: trick, numbers, hog
Youth culture: fresh, phat, def

(Rickford and Rickford 2000, p. 96)

Black speech is not limited to new words or expressions. At the heart of verbal performance is, as we have seen, the practice of signifyin' and the creative use of familiar terms in new ways.

Perhaps the best and most complex example (and the one with some of the greatest impact on spoken American English generally) is the use of the word "down." Readers of this textbook will be familiar with expressions such as: "I'm down with (or for) that," "I'm down to do that," and "get down." Several different etymologies may stand behind these expressions. One is the appearance of the word "down" in eighteenth- and nineteenth-century thieves' slang. The *OED* offers a definition: "aware of or possessing knowledge about something, esp. of illicit or criminal activity; alert; suspicious." They cite a range of British sources from the 1770s through the 1920s (a representative quotation from 1850: "You're down to every move, I see, as usual"). Following the *OED*'s links, we find the word "downy" used to mean "aware, alert, savvy; cunning, crafty."

Here the word comes from the expression "downy bird," as in this quotation from 1873: "Hilda, you are the downiest bird—I beg your pardon, the cleverest woman I ever met with."

The *OED* lists two slang forms of "down," associated with the United States and especially African American usages: "Eager, ready, and willing," with citations from 1952; and "smart, well-informed, hip, up-to-date, cool," from 1967. They also have a separate entry for the phrase "down with something," meaning to go along with or approve. This, too, they list as an African American usage, first cited in 1944.

Going beyond the *OED*, sources find uses of the word "down" coming from elsewhere. Robert S. Gold's *A Jazz Lexicon* offers the following (Gold 1964, pp. 87–8):

> A few terms, perhaps because of their simplicity and widespread applicability, have survived from the early jazz life ... The jazz slang speaker's aloofness is tacitly justified by his feeling that only those who are down with the action (aware of what is going on) should have access to the speech of those who have paid their dues (suffered an apprenticeship in life generally and in the jazz life in particular).

This *Lexicon* offers a potential source from the language of gambling: putting a bet down. Here is the entry:

> down with, [poss. from gambling slang to be down (i.e., to have one's bet placed) and poss. from general colloquial down to his toes (or socks); current esp. among Negro jazzmen since c. 1935]. See 1957 and second 1959 quotes. —1944 Dan Burley's Original Handbook of Harlem Jive, p. 15. "I'm down with the action."—p. 41. Othello, the spade stud, pops in port, "down with it, cause he can't quit it."—p. 47. Iago is down with the action.—1946 Really the Blues, p. 369. down with it: top-notch, superlative.—1955 Down Beat, 5 Oct., p. 51. I don't know who the singer is, 'cause I'm not down with all the singers now.—1957 The Book of Negro Folklore, p. 483. down with it: to get acquainted with, to understand.—1959 Diggeth Thou?, p. 23. Let's see what's down with the deal.—1959 Esquire, Nov., p. 70I. down with something, to be: to know something thoroughly.—1960 Beat Jokes Bop Humor & Cool Cartoons, p. 57. The Ham wasn't down with the action.

These examples do not limit or definitively explain the origin of these uses of "down" as much as they reveal the many different colloquial and specific social and professional contexts in which a familiar word was used in a newly private way. Whatever its origin, "down" has become the marker of a distinctive Black usage that has, by the early twenty-first century, become largely unmarked in everyday discourse. Undergraduates can be "down with" or "down for" something irrespective of their origin or identity.

Perhaps these expressions have now come to be associated with other collo-quial expressions, such as "lowdown" and "down-low." Getting the "lowdown" on something, from the first years of the twentieth century, was a way of get-ting information, getting to the bottom of a person or an action. By the 1920s, "lowdown" could also refer to musical performance. The *OED* considers this ex-pression to refer to rough or rasping performance. But it is clear from their quo-tations that this term is not a criticism but praise, as in this citation from the *New York Times* from 1922: "From that time on the highest compliment you could pay to the music at the party has been to mutter admiringly, 'That's a low-down band.'" Even the quotation from 1994 – "But the lengthy final straight is an in-consistent grab-bag of lowdown, sleazy, horn-infested swamp rock" – suggests something good and enjoyable. "Down-low" may have come from "lowdown," but it has now become associated with behavior to be kept quiet or secret. In the early 2000s, "on the down-low" may connote activities kept private, but in its origin this phrase came from African American ways of describing gay behavior (the *OED* cites this usage as beginning in the early 1990s). "On the DL" emerges at the same time.

Caribbean English and the Black Atlantic

English speakers came to the islands of the Caribbean and to the north coast of South America as early as the late 1580s. By the end of the sixteenth century, a combination of British-born landowners, indentured servants, sailors and pi-rates, and African-born and African-descended speakers were living side by side with people of French, Dutch, Portuguese, and Spanish ancestry. The languages of the Caribbean have traditionally been described as creoles, and these creoles may have had a formative influence on the speech of North Americans of Afri-can ancestry.

At this point, it is important to redefine a creole, its difference from a pidgin, and the possible nature of creolization on the English of the Black Atlantic.

A **pidgin** is a form of language designed to enable communication between two mutually incomprehensible groups of speakers. The word in English comes from the pronunciation of the word "business" by Chinese speakers in the nineteenth century. Pidgins were often ad hoc or improvisational. They took words from different languages to describe things. But they often retained the grammatical structures of the language of the speakers of prestige or power. Thus, pidgin English, in areas such as China, Southeast Asia, and the Carib-bean, often took the form of English-looking sentences with particular words or phrases from other languages brought in. The pronunciation of a pidgin was often grounded in the phonology of the non-English language group. Pidgins are always recognized by their speakers as accommodations. They are understood not to be formal languages to be passed on to children, but as forms of commu-nication for particular purposes or occasions.

By contrast, **creoles** are languages that are passed on to children. They are considered by their speakers to be a language learned or acquired. No one is a "native" speaker of a pidgin, but creoles do have native speakers. Creoles emerge over time when pidgins come to be accepted as first languages of a group of speakers. "Creole English" describes a language in which much of the vocabulary and much of the basic grammar may be English, but the sound system, the semantics of a sentence, and sometimes the forms of words owe much to languages of West Africa and other Europeans living and working in the Caribbean over time.

The status of African American English as a creole in origin, as we have seen, has been debated. The status of Caribbean English and ultimately of British English of West Indian originating as a creole is largely confirmed. Nonetheless, there are many varieties of Caribbean English that vary in pronunciation, syntax, and idiom. The English of twenty-first-century Jamaica, Barbados, Trinidad (as well as the Black English of Britain today) remains in flux, responding to influences from US popular culture, African Anglophone music, and changing British idiom.

Many speakers of Caribbean and Atlantic English preserve forms and expressions that, for modern British and American speakers, would seem archaic:

A distinctive use of the word "from" to mean "since." A sentence such as "from I was a boy" is recorded in the *OED* in the early seventeenth century, but not afterward. Such expressions, common in Caribbean English, may be historical.

Some forms of Caribbean English preserve forms of or descendants of earlier English pronunciations. Thus, a word such as "join" may rhyme with "line" (as it did in the poetry of the early 1700s).

Some forms of Atlantic creoles preserve influences from the vocabulary of West African languages. An expression such as "big eye" can mean "greedy," and it may derive from phrasings in West African languages that translate as exactly that.

The place of African languages in African American English, as well, has been suggested. Thus, a word such as "hip" or "hep" may come from the Wolof language of Nigeria: "hepi, hipi," meaning "to open one's eyes, to be aware of what's going on." The verb "dig," meaning "enjoy" or "understand" may also come from a Wolof word, "deg," meaning "understand" or "appreciate."

Creole Englishes have a tendency toward nasalized vowels. This means that a vowel preceding a nasal consonant, n, m, or ng, may be pronounced more in the nose than in the mouth. Such nasalization would affect the vowel quality and the pronunciation (or lack thereof) of the following consonant. The stereotypical pronunciation of the word "man" in Jamaican English, for example, as [mɔn] may be a feature of this nasalization.

Some Creole Englishes are rhotic and others are nonrhotic. Thus, a speaker of Jamaican English might say [weɪ ɪz dæt] for "where is that." A speaker of Barbadian English, however, would most likely say [hwer iz dæt], with a noticeably pronounced -r at the end of "where."

In the mid-twentieth century, Great Britain saw the influx of a new generation of Black English speakers from the Caribbean. Known as the Windrush generation (after the name of one of the ships that brought hundreds of people across the Atlantic), they were not immigrants, as such, to the United Kingdom, as they had held British citizenship. Many had served in World War II. From 1948 until 1971, hundreds came to the British Isles, and they brought with them varieties of English and Caribbean Creoles that had an indelible impact on the speech of late-twentieth century Britons. Multicultural London English (MLE) remains, to a large extent, the beneficiary of this linguistic mix. Vocabulary is an obvious place to go: words such as "peng" meaning "beautiful" or "attractive," "bare" meaning "very," and "innit" meaning "isn't it" can be traced to this mid-twentieth-century movement of population.

The Windrush generation was not the only movement of Black people, culture, and speech back from the New World to the Old. Commerce across the Atlantic – from east to west, from Africa to North America to Great Britain – continued and continues through our time. West African musical and performative practices, for example, have had a great impact on Atlantic English popular culture. To some extent, these practices were influenced by the Rastafarian movement in Jamaica, beginning in the 1930s. This movement offered a blend of religious, social, and imaginative worldviews, keyed to a focus on Ethiopian inheritances and a growing Afrocentric sensibility. Ska, reggae, and dub emerged as musical styles in this environment. A self-consciously developed Rastafarian way of speaking also developed: largely a blend of Jamaican English creole and concepts drawn from West African belief. In the 1970s, the Rasta idiom came to be associated with the world voice of the Black experience. The film *The Harder They Come* (1972) starring musician and actor Jimmy Cliff brought reggae and Rasta culture to a wide audience. Songs such as Bob Marley's "I Shot the Sheriff" (first released in 1973) and Peter Tosh's "Pick Me Up" (released in 1977), used Jamaican English to tell stories about oppression and release. Marley's song ends in ways that resonate with oratory from Douglass to Obama: "Freedom came my way one day." Marley interrupts his lyrics here with interjections – "yeah! – and repetitions: "So I shot, I shot, I shot him down." We can see features of what has been called the "singjay" style of Jamaican performance. This term, coined after the model of the word "deejay" (itself, a word made out of the initials of the term "disc jockey") connotes a kind of middle-ground between notated melody and spoken or shouted word. The practice is also known as "toasting" (a term that looks back to the traditions of spoken praise over a drink) and it shares with American rap and the scat singing of the

1930s and 1940s, a way of dismantling official language into subversive parody and defiant shout. Both terms can be found in the *OED* now, and the *Dictionary* offers this exuberant quotation from 1976 to illustrate the practice: "Another bass riff that cracks foundations, knocks down walls, and brushes aside nine stone weaklings, but this and all the dubwise trickery in Trenchtown can't hide the absolute ordinariness of Woosh's toasting." Words such as "singjay," "toast-ing," and "reggae" may have traceable etymologies (the *OED* offers several possibilities for "reggae"), but they represent how a performative vernacular wrests originality from earlier verbal templates. They contribute to Gates's idea of signifyin', and even if we find them in a dictionary, we can be sure, to quote Claudia Michell-Kernan again, "that dictionary entries for words are not always sufficient for interpreting meanings or messages."

Such cultural productions contributed to the larger Black Atlantic vernacular that Gilroy has identified as one of the defining features of the post-African experience. Language and narrative are inseparable from that experience. To consider the linguistic condition of the Black Atlantic is not to make essentialist associations between African American and other Black cultures. Nor is it to argue that just because people may have shared a heritage or a skin color, their linguistic practices should necessarily be shared. It does illustrate how debates on creolization inform the study of Black Atlantic English. It also illustrates how the African American and the Caribbean experiences find their voices in narra-tives of captivity and release and in music that synthesizes Western and non-Western traditions. What John Rickford has called "spoken soul" brings together language and identity in a unique way, helping us understand the sociocultural and sociolinguistic features of the Black Atlantic.

Sources and Further Reading

Alim, H. S. (2006). *Roc the Mic Right: The Language of Hip Hop Culture*. London: Routledge.

Alim, H. S., et al. (2016). *Raciolinguistics*. Oxford: Oxford University Press.

Alim, H. S. and Smitherman, G. (2012). *Articulate While Black: Barack Obama, Language and Race in the United States*. Oxford: Oxford University Press.

Bingham, C. (2011). *The Columbian Orator*. New York: Cosimo.

Britt, E. and Weldon, T. (2015). "African American English in the Middle Class." In S. Lanehart (Ed.), *The Oxford Handbook of African American Language*. Oxford: Oxford University Press, pp. 800–16.

Calloway, C. (1945). "Mr. Heptster's Dictionary – Performed by Cab Calloway." Available at: https://www.youtube.com/watch?v=b3rjQnfm6Yk

Davis, D. W. (1922). "Hog Meat." Available at: https://poets.org/poem/hog-meat

DeBose, C. (2015). "African American Church Language." In S. Lanehart (Ed.), *The Oxford Handbook of African American Language*. Oxford: Oxford University Press, pp. 677–90.

Dillard, J. L. (1972). *Black English*. New York: Random House.

Douglass, F. (1849). *Narrative of the Life of Frederick Douglass, an American Slave.* Boston: Anti-Slavery Office.

Douglass, F. (2008). *The Life and Times of Frederick Douglass.* New York: Cosimo.

Du Bois, W. E. B. (1904). *The Souls of Black Folk.* Chicago: McClurg.

Gates, H. L., Jr. (1988). *The Signifying Monkey.* New York: Oxford University Press.

Gilroy, P. (1993). *The Black Atlantic: Modernity and Double Consciousness.* Cambridge, MA: Harvard University Press.

Gold, R. (1964). *A Jazz Lexicon.* New York: Knopf.

Green, L. (2002). *African-American English: A Linguistic Introduction.* New York: Routledge.

Green, L. and Sistrunk, W. (2015). "Syntax and Semantics in African American English." In S. Lanehart (Ed.), *The Oxford Handbook of African American Language.* Oxford: Oxford University Press, pp. 355–70.

Holm, J. A. (1994). "English in the Caribbean." In R. Burchfield (Ed.), *CHEL*, vol. 5, *English in Britain and Overseas.* Cambridge: Cambridge University Press, pp. 328–81.

King, M. L., Jr. (1968). "I've Been to the Mountaintop." Available at: https://kinginstitute.stanford.edu/encyclopedia/ive-been-mountaintop

Kirkland, D. (2015). "Black Masculine Language." In S. Lanehart (Ed.), *The Oxford Handbook of African American Language.* Oxford: Oxford University Press, pp. 834–49.

Labov, W. (1972). *Language in the Inner City.* Philadelphia, PA: University of Pennsylvania Press.

Labov, W. (1982). "Objectivity and Commitment in Linguistic Science: The Case of the Black English Trial in Ann Arbor." *Language in Society* 11: 165–201.

Lanehart, S. (Ed.) (2015). *The Oxford Handbook of African American Language.* Oxford: Oxford University Press.

McWhorter, J. (2017). *Talking Back, Talking Black: Truths About America's Lingua Franca.* New York: Bellview Books.

Mufwene, S. (2001). "African-American English." In J. Algeo (Ed.), *CHEL*, vol. 6, *English in North America.* Cambridge: Cambridge University Press, pp. 291–324.

Mufwene, S. (2015). "The Emergence of African American English." In S. Lanehart (Ed.), *The Oxford Handbook of African American Language.* Oxford: Oxford University Press, pp. 57–84.

Mufwene, S., et al. (1998). *African-American English.* London: Routledge.

Obama, B. (2008). "Victory Speech." Available at: https://www.c-span.org/video/?282164-2/barack-obama-victory-speech

Ogborn, M. (2019). *The Freedom of Speech: Talk and Slavery in the Anglo-Caribbean World.* Chicago: University of Chicago Press.

Rickford, J. R. (2015). "The Creole Origins Hypothesis." In S. Lanehart (Ed.), *The Oxford Handbook of African American Language.* Oxford: Oxford University Press, pp. 35–56.

Rickford, J. R. and Rickford, R. J. (2000) *Spoken Soul: The Story of Black English.* New York: Wiley.

Riley, J. W. (n.d.). "When the Frost Is on the Punkin." Available at: https://poets.org/poem/when-the-frost-is-on-the-punkin

Thomas, E. (2015). "Prosodic Features of African American English." In S. Lanehart (Ed.), *The Oxford Handbook of African American Language*. Oxford: Oxford University Press, pp. 420–37.

Van Herk, G. (2015). "The English Origins Hypothesis." In S. Lanehart (Ed.), *The Oxford Handbook of African American Language*. Oxford: Oxford University Press, pp. 23–34.

Washington, B. T. (1895). "Atlanta Compromise Speech." Available at: https://www.loc.gov/exhibits/civil-rights-act/multimedia/booker-t-washington.html#:~:text=Washington%3A%20Mr., and%20reach%20the%20highest%20success

Weldon, T. (2021). *Middle-Class African-American English*. Cambridge: Cambridge University Press.

Wilmore, L. (2016). "Complete Remarks at 2016 White House Correspondents' Dinner." Available at: https://www.youtube.com/watch?v=1IDFt3BL7FA

Winford, D. (2015). "The Origins of African American Vernacular English: Beginnings." In S. Lanehart (Ed.), *The Oxford Handbook of African American Language*. Oxford: Oxford University Press, pp. 105–24.

11 English in the World

How did the mix of West Germanic dialects in a small, northern archipelago become the language of global commerce, culture, and politics after a millennium and a half? At the beginning of the twenty-first century, one-eighth of the world's population has English as its first language. Forty-five nations list English as their official language (or as one of several official languages). English is the language of airline communication, irrespective of an airline's country of origin. English is frequently the medium of communication between speakers of different languages. In Scandinavia, for example, Icelanders will speak English to Norwegians. In the Middle East, Israelis will speak English to Europeans. Much of the internet appears in English. Popular songs and stories are in English. English words come and go in everyday communication between people speaking Hindi, Arabic, Telugu, Japanese, and Korean.

Yet there are many different kinds of English in the modern world. The legacy of British colonialism and American post-war commerce, English is the language of many people in South Africa and India, as well as the primary language in Canada, Australia, New Zealand, Liberia, the Caribbean, and many South Pacific islands. The language varies globally in pronunciation, vocabulary, grammar, and idiom. Someone speaking English in New Delhi will generally understand someone speaking English in Montreal. To an American, though, these may sound like very different forms of speech. English has become a world language for journalism and commerce, but it has also become a world language for imaginative literature. In the late twentieth and early twenty-first centuries, English fiction has been vivified (if not completely redefined) by writers such as Salman Rushdie (born in India), Alan Paton (born in Australia), Keri Hulme (born in New Zealand), J. M. Coetzee (born in South Africa), Ben Okri (born in Nigeria), Edwidge Danticat (born in Haiti), Jamaica Kincaid (born in Antigua), Namwali Serpell (born in Zambia), and many others.

This chapter presents a synthesis of current work on English as a world language to explore its variety and impact. It begins with a brief review of patterns of colonial movement before outlining the distinctive features of English in South Asia, Australia and New Zealand, Canada, and South Africa. It then

DOI: 10.4324/9781003227083-12

explores some ways world English has been influenced by American popular culture and how Anglophone culture has moved beyond Hollywood, blue jeans, and Coca-Cola to become a changing and self-generating mix of high and low, learned and lewd.

Origins and Legacies

With the formation of the East India Company in 1600 and the Hudson Bay Company in 1670, English merchants began to trade with and eventually settle in regions far from the British Isles. Such companies were a key feature of early modern European commercial and colonial expansion. Made up of investing shareholders, they originally sought to take advantage of the natural resources of South Asia and North America: spices and textiles, precious gems and metals, furs and timber. Over time, these companies became military and quasi-political entities. The East India Company in particular engaged in military battles with Indian states and confederacies. By the early nineteenth century, much of what is now India, Pakistan, Nepal, Bhutan, Bangladesh, and Burma was effectively run by the company. Education in English was important to the British populations who had relocated and to indigenous populations – English came to be the medium of social and economic advancement and the means of participation in the large bureaucracies of rule. In 1835, British legislator Thomas Macaulay proposed establishing a class of interpreters between the Indians and the English. He developed a curriculum of education, centered on the English literary canon, that had a lasting impact on Indian culture for a century. After uprisings in 1857, the British Crown dissolved the East India Company, and in 1877 Queen Victoria became Empress of India. With Independence and the Partition of India and Pakistan in 1947, the independence of Sri Lanka (formerly Ceylon) in 1948, and the establishment of Bangladesh as an independent nation in 1972, English remained one of the official languages of politics and power.

English came to Africa in different ways. North African and Sub-Saharan areas were colonized directly. In the nineteenth century, the so-called scramble for Africa led many European countries to seek a foothold there. British colonial Africa eventually covered the northeastern part of the continent, running from Egypt and Sudan through Uganda and Kenya; the southern part of the continent, from what is now South Africa through Botswana, Zimbabwe, and Zambia; and the eastern part of the continent, centering on Nigeria and Ghana.

The linguistic history of South Africa is unique. Dutch settlers in the seventeenth and eighteenth centuries met with speakers of Bantu and Xhosan. British military operations beginning in 1795 progressively marginalized the Dutch socially and geographically, and by the 1820s English settlers were establishing themselves in the eastern part of the Cape Peninsula. A population of Indian heritage (originally brought as indentured servants) grew as well, especially in the area around Natal. Finally, the discovery of great mineral wealth (diamonds, gold, and later uranium and strategic metals) helped provoke a political environment in which European (white) control became consolidated. In the twentieth century, racial stratification became law, and the system of apartheid shaped what became the Union of South Africa (established in 1910) through the twentieth century. In the twenty-first century, the disestablishment of white rule and the reorganization of South African society have further changed the linguistic landscape. The key point is not simply that South Africa is a place of many different languages with different histories. Central to the history of the region is an ideology of language primacy: the conception of some languages as essentially more developed than others, in particular, the establishment of Afrikaans as a language separate from Dutch, yet part of the European inheritance shared by English.

What distinguishes English in Africa, South Asia, and Oceania from English in North America is the sustained contact with speakers of indigenous languages and, in turn, the borrowings of vocabulary terms and the shaping of pronunciation by speakers of those indigenous languages when they learned English. "White" and "Black" South African English is different. English spoken in India by people of Hindi and Urdu linguistic heritage differs from that spoken by people of Telugu and Tamil heritage. In North America, indigenous languages had minimal effect on the English of the settlers. Place names and a small number of loan words remain largely the only legacy of the rich linguistic cultures of the Algonquin, Iroquois, Sioux, Athabascan, Aztecan, Navajo, and Aleut.

English in South Asia

There are many varieties of English spoken throughout the Indian subcontinent and the islands of the Indian Ocean. BBC listeners may recognize a certain standard "Indian English" diction. Audiences for Bollywood (and Tollywood) film may recognize how English words and phrases take on a distinctive sound and sense. English is as stratified on the subcontinent as much as it is anywhere. Nonetheless, there are features of English in South Asia that contribute to the private and performative nature of vernacular life. As with Cockney and African American English, there is the danger of caricature. But there remain features we should recognize, for linguistic and sociopolitical reasons.

One of the most distinctive features of South Asian English is how its patterns of stress create a particular sonic and rhythmic feel to speech. We need to distinguish between **stress-timed languages** and **syllable-timed languages**. Stress-timed languages have alternating stressed and unstressed syllables in words and in sentences. There is a kind of additive effect: the time spent on stressed and unstressed syllables in sequence remains constant. What this means is that in a language such as English, unstressed syllables tend to be very short, often with the schwa vowel sound, and stressed syllables seem relatively long. In a stress-timed language, especially in modern spoken English, this creates what has been called a Morse code effect. The history of English poetic meter reflects this effect. A poetic line is made up of unstressed and stressed syllables. Take this line from Shakespeare (Sonnet 18): "Shall I compare thee to a summer's day?" Scanned as perfect iambic pentameter, it would come out: "Shăll Í cŏmpáre thĕe tó ă súmmĕr's dáy?" But no one would speak this sentence in this way. In everyday, modern speech, it would sound more like: "Shăll Ĭ cŏm**páre** thĕe tŏ ă **súm**mĕr's dăy?" The syllables in -pare- and sum- receive far more stress, proportionally, than the other syllables in the sentence. It is as if the unstressed syllables are being compressed together, while the stressed syllables are held longer.

By contrast, syllable-timed languages have every syllable taking up the same amount of time in speech. There is little sense of the "dot dash" feel of English. South Asian languages are syllable-timed languages. Speakers of South Asian languages who have learned English may sound as if they are stressing all syllables in a sentence equally or that they are stressing the wrong syllables in certain words (Kachru 1994, pp. 516–18).

How is it possible to convey this feature of South Asian English in writing? Salman Rushdie's *Midnight's Children* (1981) captures what linguists would call these **super-segmental features** of the English language in the speech of characters living in the British Raj. Through subtle displacements of words and arrangement of patterns, Rushdie evokes this rhythm:

> "Again?" Aadam's mother said, rolling her eyes. "I tell you, my child, that girl is so sickly from so much soft living only. Too much sweetmeats and spoiling, because of the absence of a mother's firm hand. But go, take care of your invisible patient, your mother is all right with her little nothing of a headache."
>
> (Rushdie 1981, p. 22)

Rushdie conveys the flow of speech through repetition ("so sickly," "so much"), displacement of the modifier "only" to the end of the sentence, and strings of short words without contractions ("your mother is all right with her little nothing of a headache").

As with other forms of language, it is important to recognize the line between characterization and caricature. For many British writers and readers, Indian English was dismissed as "Babu English" – an exaggerated form of an official, bureaucratese, laden with markers of excessive politeness and indirection. "Being in much need and suffering many privations, I have after long time come to the determination to trouble your bounteous goodness." There was also "butler English," a discourse of household servitude characterized by syntactic patterns possibly influenced by South Indian languages. "Want anybody want mixed tea, boil the water, then I put tea leaves, then I pour the milk and put sugar" (Kachru 1994, pp. 509–12). Bollywood films from the 1960s on often show spoken English as the site of humor or subversion. Trying to speak the language of the colonizers, characters may say things like this, from the 1982 film *Namak Halaal*: "I can talk English, I can walk English, I can laugh English, because English is a very phunny language" (Gaekwad 2017). In the 2021 film, *RRR*, a Telugu-speaking man tries to speak English to a British woman (the film is set in the 1920s), and they go back and forth in a language lesson worthy of Shakespeare's *Henry V*, when the young king tries to teach the French princess how to speak. "I cannot speak your England," Princess Katherine offers in that play, in a revealing moment that associates language and nationality. In the great film *Shakespeare Wallah* (1965), a traveling troupe of performers confronts the changing tastes of a nation asserting its own linguistic and cultural theatricality. "We are all forced," says the melancholy troupe leader, "to make cuts to the text given to us by destiny."

The word *wallah* in the title of that film comes from a word used in a variety of languages descended from Sanskrit (Hindi, Urdu, Bengali) to mean someone identified with a profession or a task: *chaiwallah*, someone who serves tea; *rickshawallah*, someone who drives a rickshaw; *dishwallah*, someone who installs a satellite dish. The title *Shakespeare Wallah* illustrates the ways the English language in India and beyond has been reshaped by contact with subcontinental languages.

The English presence in South Asia brought many words from Hindi, Urdu, Tamil, Sinhalese, and Persian (the language of the Mughal courts) into English. Some of the most familiar words that entered during the periods of East India Company rule and the Imperial Raj include:

bazaar (Persian)
brahmin (Hindi)
bungalow (Bengali)
jungle (Hindi, ultimately Sanskrit)
nabob (Urdu)
pundit (ultimately Sanskrit)

Many words for food, dress, and luxury items also entered English at this time:

chaat (from Hindi, meaning a tasting or delicacy)
chai (a word for "tea," ultimately from Cantonese and related to many words in Asian languages; the modern sense of a "spiced tea" probably came from China through Persian and Hindi)
curry (from Tamil, meaning a sauce or accompaniment for rice)
masala (originally from Arabic and borrowed from Hindu and Urdu, meaning a mix of spices)
pajama (originally from Persian, borrowed into English from Urdu)
pukka (a word meaning absolute or first class, from Hindi)
tikka (a word originally from Arabic and borrowed into Turkic languages, originally meaning a piece of meat)
tourmaline (a gemstone, originally from a Sinhalese word that meant a red form of quartz)

Vocabulary influences were the subject of commentary from the late eighteenth century on, and by the end of the nineteenth century dictionaries of Anglo-Indian English emerged along the lines of the late Victorian lexicography shaping the *Oxford English Dictionary*.

The most influential, and perhaps the most notorious, of such lexicons was the dictionary assembled by Englishmen Henry Yule and Arthur Coke Burnell published in 1886. Titled *Hobson-Jobson*, it offered historical and etymological information about words from Indian languages that had entered English. The title was based on the chant, "Ya Hasan! Ya Hosein," performed by North Indian Shia Muslims during the period of mourning in the month of Muharram. This chant came to be heard through a variety of corruptions: Hoseen Gosseen, Hosein Jossen, and then Hobson Jobson. Of course, the title evokes the rhyming reduplicating sounds that Europeans had always imagined to be characteristic of non-European languages (take, for example, "mumbo jumbo"), and later scholars have critiqued the condescension of the volume's title and the amateurism of its lexicography.

Nonetheless, *Hobson-Jobson* offers a revealing window into Anglo-Indian linguistic relationships in the Raj period. The "Introductory Remarks" are as revealing as Johnson's or Webster's prefaces to their own dictionaries:

> Words of Indian origin have been insinuating themselves into English ever since the end of the reign of Elizabeth and the beginning of that of King James, when such terms as calico, chintz, and gingham had already affected a lodgment in English warehouses and shops, and were lying in wait for entrance into English literature. Such outlandish guests grew more frequent 120 years ago, when soon after the middle of the last century, the numbers of Englishmen in the Indian services, civil and military, expanded with the great acquisition of dominion then made by the Company; and we meet them in vastly greater abundance now.
>
> (Yule and Burnell 1903, p. xv)

The words "insinuated" themselves. They "affected a lodgment." They were "lying in wait." Yule and Burnell use a highly charged, judgmental vocabulary to imagine these loan words surreptitiously and dangerously coming into English (their judgmentalism is no different from that of Alexander Gil, who complained about words of Native American origin entering English in the early 1600s, or that of Samuel Johnson, who marked the various Americanisms and Gallicisms that he saw as diluting the tongue). Later, Yule and Burnell use the same terms as Webster, but with different force, when they write, "There are a good many other [words], long since fully assimilated which really originated in the adoption of an Indian word." "Assimilate" and "adopt" are words of identity passing and belonging. Although this may sound like the vocabulary of Webster and the Americans, it is very different. Rather than adopting a constitution, we are looking at a world in which the ethnic other may be adopted as a child and, in the process, assimilate into a culture.

Reading through *Hobson-Jobson* now is a challenge, but also a charge. Look up "calico," and you get this disquisition on toleration and otherness:

CALICO, s. Cotton cloth, ordinarily of tolerably fine texture. The word appears in the 17th century sometimes in the form of *Calicut*, but possibly this may have been a purism, for *calicoe* or *callico* occurs in English earlier, or at least more commonly in early voyages. [Gallaca in 1578, Drapefs Did. p. 42.] The word may have come to us through the French *calicot*, which though retaining the t to the eye, does not do so to the ear. The quotations sufficiently illustrate the use of the word and its origin from *Calicut*. The fine cotton stuffs of Malabar are already mentioned by Marco Polo (ii. 379). Possibly they may have been all brought from beyond the Ghauts, as the Malabar cotton, ripening during the rains, is not usable, and the cotton stuffs now used in Malabar all come from Madura (see *Fryer* below; and *Terry* under CALICUT). The Germans, we may note, call the turkey *Calecutische Hahn*, though it comes no more from Calicut than it does from Turkey.

(ibid., p. 147)

This is less an etymology than a series of judgments on quality and national identity.

Consider their entry for "curry," a veritable dissertation running for several pages on foodstuffs and dietary history. Yule and Burnell offer an etymology from Tamil, *kari*, and then note that such sauced dishes were mentioned in ancient Greek and Roman writings, in medieval English texts, and through William Makepeace Thackeray's 1848 novel *Vanity Fair*. Here, we find a word of unmistakable Indian identity told as a story of European literary culture (ibid., p. 281). Consider their equally long entry for the word "veranda," a word, they note, "of very perplexing" origins. Is it a word of Hispano-Portuguese origin (*baranda*), or is it a word of Indian linguistic origin (ultimately going back to a word in Sanskrit meaning "to cover")? The word comes into European languages as early as the 1490s, and the entry offers a long string of literary quotations illustrating that the veranda was not simply a part of a house but a meeting place (a liminal space, as it were) where European and Indian people could meet. From 1809, they quote: "In the same veranda are figures of natives of every cast and profession." From 1810: "The viranda keeps off the too great glare of the sun, and affords a dry walk during the rainy season." From 1816: "And when Sergeant Brown bethought himself of Mary, and looked to see where she was, she was conversing up and down the verandah, though it was Sunday, with most of the rude boys and girls of the barracks." These quotations illustrate the social space of the veranda. It is a place where the English and the Indian can mix, literally and symbolically, a place where Europeans can experience the landscape but with covering and shade, a place where a well-born woman can talk with rude boys and girls. The veranda is a figure for this dictionary itself: a place of meeting and observation, a place of judging the "native" from the perspective of the ruling class (ibid., pp. 965–6).

Hobson-Jobson had a great impact on later lexicography. Sir James A. H. Murray used it when compiling the *Oxford English Dictionary*. Rudyard Kipling praised its publication. It remains a valuable artifact of linguistic sociology. But it is also a product of what has come to be called Orientalism – the Western imaginative construction of a non-Western other. Much of early linguistics was Orientalist in this way – from Sir William Jones's first forays into Sanskrit and Indo-European linguistics, through the decipherments of Old Persian cuneiform, to the discovery of Hittite. Twenty-first-century critics have explored how modern South Asian writers, writing in English, develop a productive if at times uneasy relationship with the legacies of Raj English. Salman Rushdie remains the most famous of such writers, and his novels develop a heightened form of English narrative that embraces (often untranslated) words of Indian origin. Rushdie himself published an essay on *Hobson-Jobson*, moving between linguistic and cultural dismissal on one hand and exuberant thrill at the possibilities of wordplay on the other (see Mishra 2009). Rushdie recognized the temptations of linguistic history, and he understood the ways the modern Indian vernaculars have uniquely appropriated English words. Behind it all there is the legacy of colonial power and its past. Are the words left behind legacies or scars?

> A modern appendix might usefully be commissioned to include many English words which have taken on in the independent India new Hinglish meanings. In India today the prisoner in the dark is the *undertrial*, a boss is often an *incharge*, and in a sinister euphemism those who perish at the hands of the law enforcement officers are held to have died in a *police encounter*.
>
> To spend a few days with *Hobson-Jobson* is almost to regret the passing of the intimate connection that made this linguistic *kedgeree* possible.
>
> (Rushdie 1991, p. 81)

The key word here is "almost." The history of English as a global language is a history of power and translation. It is a history of languages in contact, in which words can be both instruments of the imagination and sinister euphemisms.

English in Australia and New Zealand

English speakers settled in Australia in the late eighteenth century. The First Fleet set sail from Portsmouth on May 13, 1787 – 11 ships filled with convicts and sailors, officers, and settlers. The British flag was raised upon landing at

Sydney cove on January 26, 1788, and Australian English effectively began. The first settlers were a socially disparate group. Regional and class dialects mixed together. Immediate contact with indigenous peoples brought new local words into the conversation. The presence of convicts – coming from various places in England and Ireland – offered a range of speech forms but also a shared subversive playfulness with language itself. The so-called flash language of the convicts was full of older thieves' cant, the secret vocabulary of criminals. Convict George Barrington left this account of another convict, known as Black Caesar:

> he was so indifferent about being punished with death that he used to declare if they should scrag [hang] him he would quiz [confound] them all, and show them some gig [fun] at the nubbing-cheat [gallows] before he was turned off.
> (quoted in desidd 2016)

Australian English is most often thought of as distinctive in its vocabulary and its phonology. Words from indigenous languages described animals, geographical phenomena, meteorological conditions, and various personal relationships. The most familiar of these words include:

barramundi (a kind of sea bass)
billabong (a lake formed at the bend of a river)
boomerang (a wooden weapon that returns to the thrower)
kangaroo (the large marsupial animal)
kookaburra (a bird akin to the kingfisher)
wallaby (a smaller marsupial)
wombat (another marsupial)

English words that have taken on a uniquely Australian connotation include:

billy (a cooking pot; probably from Scottish usage)
digger (a soldier, originally applied during World War I)
dinkum (often in the phrase "fair dinkum," probably coming from a regional English phrase for hard work)
g'day (a general greeting)
mate (a general term for friend or buddy)
outback (a remote rural area)
sheila (a general, sometimes dismissive, term for a young woman)
yobbo (an obnoxious person)

Rhyming slang was a feature of lower-class, urban London in the eighteenth and nineteenth centuries. It created, in effect, a kind of parallel vocabulary known only to the initiated and, like thieves' cant, it offered a linguistic way of separating groups by structures of incomprehensibility. The principle of rhyming slang is to take a familiar word, like "mate," and find a rhyme with it, such as "plate." Then the rhymed word is often paired with a familiar descriptor, in this case, "China plate." This phrase is meaningful on its own, but in rhyming slang it has been displaced from its familiar connotation to mean the rhymed original. "China plate" thus means a friend or a partner; sometimes, it might even be reduced to "China." How often rhyming slang appears in everyday, contemporary Australian conversation may be debatable. Does "Bugs Bunny" really mean "money"? Does "ham and eggs" really mean "legs"? Whatever is at stake in rhyming slang, its practice represents a distinctive feature of linguistic differentiation: a way of signaling a kind of private language, a way of decentering the word from the familiar world, and a way of infusing the vernacular with play and resistance.

The phonological features of Australian English are easily recognized (and equally easily caricatured). Variations occur across the country and across social strata, but the main lines of pronunciation may be described as follows:

"beet," and "fleece": these and other words that come from a long stressed monophthong /iː/ are generally pronounced as diphthongs: [ɪiː] and [əiː].

"boot" and "goose": these and other words that come from a long stressed monophthong /uː/ are generally pronounced as diphthongs: [ʊuː] and [əuː].

"face" and "say": these and other words that come from a long stressed monophthong /eː/ are generally pronounced as diphthongs: [ʌɪ].

"goat" and "so": these and other words that come from a long stressed monophthong /oː/ are generally pronounced as diphthongs: [ʌʊ].

"price" and "high": these and other words that come from long stressed diphthongs /aiː/ are generally pronounced as different diphthongs: [ɑi] or [ɒi] – that is, with an initial sound that is lower and rounder in the mouth than in American and British English "mouth" and "how." These and other words that come from long stressed diphthongs /au/ are generally pronounced as different diphthongs: [æʊ] – that is, with an initial sound that is more central and less round than in American and British English.

Variation in Australian pronunciation is often described in terms of differences of "cultivation" – that is, the sound of an urban, educated elite in contrast to a less educated, rural populace. "Broader" forms of pronunciation have a more noticeable diphthongization in long vowels. For example, the pronunciation of the word "mouth" can be described as: [maʊθ], [mæoθ], or [mɛːoθ]. This sequence moves from "cultivated" through "broad." What we can see in these transcriptions is that the distance in the mouth between the first and second element of the diphthong increases. Another way of putting it is to say that the mouth moves more in the pronunciation of the diphthong.

This is only a suggestive outline of Australian English phonology. Its purpose is to help readers recognize that features of pronunciation can be described in detail and that one of the characteristics of the sound of Australian English – the diphthong – can be described in terms of increased movement of the organs of speech production.

Australian English is of course more than the sum of these linguistic details. It has become a global language of its own. Personalities from film and television, poetry and prose, sport and politics, are world figures. In the twenty-first century, one may hear and read Australian English speakers in sports broadcasts, in dramas and comedies, and in prize-winning novels.

On the surface, New Zealand English seems very similar to Australian. Like Australian, it is a nonrhotic language, with many of the same vowel and consonant sounds. Like Australian, its development was shaped by patterns of original settlement (in this case, from the southeast of England) and by sustained contact with an indigenous language group. But New Zealand is unique. The Māori people spoke varieties of Polynesian languages, related to those of other South Pacific island populations. There were established hierarchies of political and social power in New Zealand that the English had to reckon with. Unlike Australia (which was originally settled by a mix of social classes), New Zealand's first settlers were mainly a pastoral missionary community.

New Zealand is sociolinguistically unique in that its political foundation was grounded in an act of linguistic performance. The missionaries who settled in the 1830s believed that they could teach the Māori – a highly complex and politically sophisticated group that relied on oral lore and practice – to be literate. Early attempts at translating the Bible into Māori were designed to foster a focused literacy, one keyed to conversion and spiritual growth. Just how literate the Māori were has long been debated. Certainly, by 1840, when the English sought to establish a treaty with the Māori leadership, some Māori could read their own language in the English transliterations provided for them, and some could read English. They knew that signing one's name was a mark of identity. But what they did not know was precisely what they were signing. The story of the Treaty of Waitangi is one of the great stories of linguistic power politics. Much like Henry III's proclamation of 1258, it remains a test case for how the English language worked, and did not work, in shaping governance in theory and practice. Here is the account of the treaty by Donald F. McKenzie:

> On 6 February 1840 forty-six Maori chiefs from the northern regions of New Zealand "signed" a document written in Maori called "Te Tiriti o Waitangi," "The Treaty of Waitangi." In doing so, according to the English versions of the document, they ceded to Her Majesty the Queen of England "absolutely and without reservation all the rights and powers of Sovereignty" which they themselves individually exercised over their respective territories. That act of assent became the substantive ground of British sovereignty over New Zealand.
>
> (1999, p. 79)

Just what the chiefs were signing was a matter of interpretation. What the words meant in both English and Māori has been contested for nearly two centuries. "Sovereignty," as we have seen, was one of those polysyllabic words of power borrowed from Old French into English during the Middle English period. It is a word of Latin origin, with the root *super*, "above." In Middle English, it meant superiority, not only over someone else but over oneself. Chaucer used it to mean mastery and the opposite of servitude. By 1840, however, the word (especially capitalized, as it was here) came to mean something more specifically political. The *OED* offers a definition, "a territory under the rule of a sovereign," starting in 1815. They offer an additional connotation, "The supreme controlling power in communities not under monarchical government; absolute and independent authority," with a first quotation from 1860. Clearly, the word "sovereignty" in the Treaty of Waitangi means this sense of political control over communities not currently under a monarchical government, which the Māori chiefs held and which they were to transfer to a monarchical government. "Sovereignty" is therefore not just a word that needed to be translated; it was a word that, in the early nineteenth century, was changing in its connotations of political control.

The men who translated this word into Māori based it on a word that they had already devised. The English word "governor" had been transliterated into Māori as *kawana*. The Māori language suffix, *-tanga*, makes a noun into an abstract idea. Thus, the word *kawanatanga* came to mean something like "governorship" or "sovereignty." As scholars have pointed out, there were Māori words for political power: *mana*, which meant personal prestige and its accompanying power, and *rangatiratanga*, which meant chieftainship. By not using these words, the translators of the treaty took an English concept and kept it English. They did not ask Māori rulers to give up status or power that they understood. They asked them to give up something that they never had.

This exercise in political lexicography shows us how the history of the English language can illuminate acts of political appropriation. Treaty-making in colonial societies hinged on finding the right or the wrong words. Colonial treaties sit uneasily between languages, each of which has its own history and resonance. As we saw in Chapter 4 on Middle English, there was a great difference between words such as the Old French *honour* and the Old English *treope*, between the *reaume* and *londe*. In the word "sovereignty," we can see a history of control, moving from the inner to the outer, from the self and society to the political and the royal.

The Challenge of Global English

These examples illustrate the challenges of studying global English. At one level, every post-colonial nation has developed its own form of the language, distinctive in sound and sense. At another level, English words have come into use by people who may have little or no English fluency. Finally, people may mouth the words of songs and stories, advertisements and media, not so much for their lexical meaning but for their social effect, a marking of belonging in popular or professional culture.

Linguist Braj B. Kachru developed a model of world English based on concentric circles of inheritance and use (Kachru 1992) (Figure 11.1).

In our adaptation of this model, the inner circle represents nations where English is a first language, where the historical identity of the nation is wrapped up in the historical development of English. The outer circle represents nations where English was imposed by a colonial rulership, and where it may remain as an official language of politics or commerce but still exists with the legacies of colonialism. The expanding circle represents nations and societies where English is learned as a means of access to economic, political, and cultural engagement. Kachru uses the following terms to characterize these circles. The inner circle is "norm-providing": it establishes the acceptable patterns of speech and writing as developed in these countries. The outer circle is "norm-developing": various nations and national identities continue to develop patterns of speech and writing that are distinctively their own and are often in historical dialogue with the

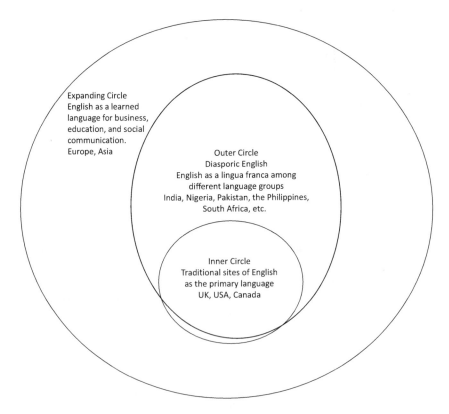

Expanding Circle
English as a learned language for business, education, and social communication.
Europe, Asia

Outer Circle
Diasporic English
English as a lingua franca among different language groups
India, Nigeria, Pakistan, the Philippines, South Africa, etc.

Inner Circle
Traditional sites of English as the primary language
UK, USA, Canada

Figure 11.1 The concentric circles of World English

norms provided by the political group that brought English to them. The outer circle is what Kachru calls "norm-dependent": uses of English in these nations and societies are learned in the lifetime of the speaker through schooling, rather than through the home, and the forms of English that are learned are highly dependent on the forms taught (thus, some may learn American and others may learn British English).

Other models of globalization depend more on historical change than on geographical difference. For example, India, Pakistan, Singapore may seem to be outer circle language groups, but the historical development of colonialism and commerce in these nations, the relationship of language to religion and ethnic identity, and the conceptions of modernization and global political reach differ markedly among them (as among many other nations in which English is at least one official language).

Throughout the world, "business English" has emerged as a medium of commerce. We may think of business English as the language of specific trades or professions. But it has become marketed largely as a matter of colloquialisms and idiom. The book, *Business English Vocabulary Builder*, is largely a collection of idioms, presented with the conviction that speaking in these ways will "help you become more comfortable and fluent in native and natural English-speaking situations" (Mastery 2020):

Bend over backward
Call it a day
Easy come, easy go
Get off on the wrong foot
In the dog house
On the same page
Rule of thumb
The cat's out of the bag
Word of mouth

These are just a few of the phrases this book touts as markers of comfort and fluency. Behind this rough-and-ready instruction, however, is an important feature of Modern English: the conviction that what makes the language natural or native sounding is the use of idiom.

English has always had idioms: phrases that are designed to convey meaning and intention by using words in figurative ways or by referring to particular metaphors or images that stand behind activities. To "table a motion" may be an act performed without any office furniture, but it hearkens back to a time when tables and documents were central to decision making. At the heart of idiomization is the point made by linguist Anatoly Lieberman in *Take My Word for It*: "Native speakers do not always recognize that a certain word group is idiomatic" (2022, p. 6). Sometimes, idiomatic expressions are so old that they are naturalized into the language. For example, early Middle English borrowed certain phrasal verb expressions from French: "do battle," "put to death," "make peace," "take notice." Folklore and proverb have also been the source of idioms whose origins are lost to history. Some expressions may require a level of research to exhume their origins: "kick the bucket," "cock and bull," "sleeveless errand."

Modern linguists have defined idioms more precisely.

> An idiom is an institutionalized and conventionalized sequence of at least two morphemes that is semantically restricted so that it functions as a single lexical unit, whose meaning cannot or can only to a certain extent be deduced from the meanings of its constituents.
>
> (Umar 2019, p. 29)

One of the ways we may distinguish the various circles or strata of world English usage might be according to a speaker's self-conscious recognition of a phrase as an idiom and, furthermore, according to each group's development of new idioms unique to that group. Speakers of Nigerian English, for example, will recognize the phrase "bad belle" as uniquely theirs: "bad belle" comes from "bad belly"; having a "bad belle" about someone or something connotes having a negative view of them, or envy or jealousy. By contrast, the phrase "shout Hosanna" is not unique to Nigerian usage (coming as it does from traditions of Christian practice). But in Nigerian colloquial usage, it has become separated from its original religious context and is often used in everyday speech to signal agreement or praise (ibid.). Jamaican English has its share of distinctive expressions, some transparent to non-Jamaican speakers and some not. "Ya mon" is a general sign of approval, with "yeah, man" visible beneath its phonological surface. "Blouse and skirts," however transparent its lexical components may be, cannot be translated word for word. In Jamaican idiomatic speech, it connotes amazement: something like "wow" or "what the hell?"

Every culture has such forms of speech, and whether we think of Cockney English, Texas English, Nigerian, Jamaican, or Indian Englishes, these kinds of phrases are as much markers of social belonging as they are patterns of sound. If they reveal anything, it is the ongoing vitality of all speakers to bring a metaphorical creativity to the description of the world. In their own way, many of these idioms can take us back to the kennings of Old Germanic poetry: to the road of the whale, to God's candle, to the cauldron of tears.

The worlds of global English, though, should not be confused with the idea of "globish." This term has emerged in the early twenty-first century to mean a form of international communication, grounded in English words and phrases but separate from other, national, or regional Englishes. Identified by French business executive Jean-Paul Nerrière, globish is not so much a language of its own as a body of expressions, based on English words, used in professional communication. Linguist Barbara Cassin (2017) has claimed that this globish is not "a language of culture but a language of service," that is, something designed to get business done rather than a medium of life. National languages, writes linguist Mark Abley, "will continue to act as the bearers of culture and transmitters of identity, whereas the task of Globish is merely to convey English. Nobody is likely to grow up speaking Globish as a mother tongue" (2008, p. 98).

By contrast, Robert McCrum (the author of several popular histories of the English language) considers globish not in its limited sense but more generally as the world's new lingua franca. His arguments recall those of a history of writers on the language. There is what he calls a "demotic energy" to the English of US cities; there is a "world appetite for English language and culture." He goes on: "The great quality of the English language in the contemporary world is that its transactions urge us ceaselessly to engage our imaginations, and express them, on a global scale" (McCrum 2010, p. 19). In moments like these, McCrum recalls Samuel Johnson on the "genius of the tongue."

Somewhere between these extremes – a medium of practical communication and a phenomenon of essential power and beauty – lies the nature of the English language in the twenty-first century world.

Sources and Further Reading

Abley, M. (2008). *The Prodigal Tongue*. Boston: Houghton Mifflin.

Auddy, R. K. (2020). *In Search of Indian English*. London: Routledge.

Bauer, L. (1994). "English in New Zealand." In R. Burchfield (Ed.), *CHEL*, vol. 5, *English in Britain and Overseas*. Cambridge: Cambridge University Press, pp. 382–428.

Branford, W. (1994). "English in South Africa." In R. Burchfield (Ed.), *CHEL*, vol. 5, *English in Britain and Overseas*. Cambridge: Cambridge University Press, pp. 430–95.

Burchfield, R. (Ed.) (1994). *CHEL*, vol. 5, *English in Britain and Overseas*. Cambridge: Cambridge University Press.

Cassin, B. (2017). "The Power of Bilingualism." Available at: https://conversations.e-flux.com/t/the-power-of-bilingualism-interview-with-barbara-cassin-french-philosopher-and-philologist/6252.

Crystal, D. (2003). *English as a World Language*. 2nd edn. Cambridge: Cambridge University Press.

desidd (2016). "Use of Flash Language in Australian English: Background and Evolution." Available at:https://desidd.wordpress.com/2016/04/23/use-of-flash-language-in-australian-english-background-and-evolution/

Gaekwad, M. (2017). "Bollywood Has Always Treated English as a Funny Language." Available at: https://scroll.in/reel/837368/bollywood-has-always-treated-english-as-a-funny-language)

Hickey, R. (Ed.) (2005). *Legacies of Colonial English*. Cambridge: Cambridge University Press.

Jenkins, J. (2007). *English as a Lingua Franca: Attitude and Identity*. Oxford: Oxford University Press.

Kachru, B. B. (1983). *The Indianization of English: The English Language in India*. Oxford: Oxford University Press.

Kachru, B. B. (1992). *The Other Tongue: English Across Cultures*. Urbana, IL: University of Illinois Press.

Kachru, B. B. (1994). "English in South Asia." In R. Burchfield (Ed.), *CHEL*, vol. 5, *English in Britain and Overseas*. Cambridge: Cambridge University Press, pp. 497–553.

Lieberman, A. (2022). *Take My Word for It: A Dictionary of English Idioms*. Minneapolis, MN: University of Minnesota Press.

Mastery, L. (2020). *Business English Vocabulary Builder*. N.p.: Lingo Mastery.

McCrum, R. (2010). *Globish: How the English Language Became the World's Language*. New York: Viking.

McKenzie, D. F. (1999). "The Sociology of a Text: Oral Culture, Literacy, and Print in Early New Zealand." In D. F. McKenzie, *Bibliography and the Sociology of Texts*. Cambridge: Cambridge University Press, pp. 77–130.

Mishra, V. (2009). "Rushdie-Wushdie: Salman Rushdie's Hobson-Jobson." *New Literary History* 40: 385–410.

Mukherjee, A. (2013). *What Is a Classic? Postcolonial Rewriting and the Invention of the Canon*. Stanford, CA: Stanford University Press.

Rushdie, S. (1981). *Midnight's Children*. New York: Avon Books.

Rushdie, S. (1991). *Imaginary Homelands*. London: Granta Books.

Schneider, E. (2007). *Postcolonial English: Varieties Around the World*. Cambridge: Cambridge University Press.

Trudgill, P., and Hannah, J. (2008). *International English: A Guide to the Varieties of Standard English*. 5th edn. London: Arnold.

Turner, G. (1994). "English in Australia." In R. Burchfield (Ed.), *CHEL*, vol. 5, *English in Britain and Overseas*. Cambridge: Cambridge University Press, pp. 277–327.

Umar, A. M. (2019). "The Structure of Idioms in Nigerian English." *English Today* 35: 29–34.

Wiegand, C. (2021). "*Shakespeare Wallah*: Merchant Ivory's Bittersweet Tale of Bollywood and the Bard." Available at: https://www.theguardian.com/stage/2021/mar/30/shakespeare-wallah-merchant-ivorys-bittersweet-tale-of-bollywood-and-the-bard

Yule, H. and Burnell, A. C. (1903). *Hobson-Jobson: A Glossary of Anglo-Indian Words*. New edn, (Ed.) W. Crooke. London. John Murray.

12   Twenty-First-Century English

Writing in the *New Yorker* magazine in 2022, Rebecca Mead recounted how, upon moving back to London after 30 years in the United States, now with a teenage son, the speech of English children had changed noticeably from that of her youth. She described what has been called multicultural London English, an emerging vernacular growing out of contact with speech patterns from immigrants throughout the Anglophone world. She noted, children have "found their way to a new common language." Some of its features are lexical, borrowing words and idioms from Caribbean English. Some of its features are phonological (e.g., the monophthongization of diphthongs in words such as "face," now sounding like "fess"). Other changes cross the boundaries of lexis and grammar: for example, the appropriation of the word "man" in various pronominal forms: "man's gotta calm down" (second person); "man's gotta work hard" (impersonal). Some phrasings bear the impression of other global Englishes, such as dropping prepositions with words of movement or intention. Mead quoted British linguist David Hall on this matter: "It has to be some sort of familiar or institutional goal, like 'I went pub last night,' or 'I went chicken shop,' " he told me. "It can't be 'I went art gallery'" (Mead 2022).

Mead's article calls attention to things we already know: that children speak more like their peers than like their parents, that caregivers from different linguistic backgrounds can affect children's speech patterns, that language varieties in contact can effect long-term linguistic change. American linguist Julie Roberts has published widely on these aspects of child language acquisition and use in rural and urban environments, and she avers that "like gender, ethnicity, and age, the construct of speech community is not fixed, but socially negotiated and continually changing." She concludes: "within the interactions in which children and adolescents participate, with their caretakers, their peers, their community, lie the possibilities of language change" (Roberts 1999).

Linguists primarily concern themselves with charting the details of that change. Developments in corpus linguistics and field survey methods make possible a fine-grained picture of the sounds, syntax, and semantics of emerging communities in the Anglophone world. As we have seen throughout this book,

DOI: 10.4324/9781003227083-13

language change proceeds in many ways: through contact among different kinds of speakers, in reaction to political and social change, in response to pedagogical pressures to conform. Technologies of communication have also had an effect on the shape of English, from the first attempts to write a Germanic language in Latin letters to the attempted regularizations of print and the digital modes of texting, email, internet searching, and the varieties of social media. So many sources and so many forms of English speech and writing exist in the first third of the twenty-first century that it would be impossible to codify them. Anything a textbook like this one might affirm might well be obsolete by the time it reached a student readership.

However, there are several features of twenty-first-century English that distinguish the vernacular of this time from that of even 20 years before, that readers of this book will encounter and use, and that may provoke us to predict what English may look and sound like in the future. These features include the following:

- The breakdown of distinctions between formal and informal language use: the sense that colloquial, slang, and even vulgar diction can appear in such traditionally high cultural or socially regulated venues as business communication, literary prose and poetry, media broadcasting, and journalism.
- The rise of qualifying speech patterns: uses of expressions such as "like" and "you know," forms of the verb "to go," and markers of address such as "man," "girl," "dude," "bro" and others to signal intimacy or bonding.
- The changing function of punctuation and typography: rather than marking breath or emphasis in speech (as punctuation originally developed) or distinguishing grammatical units in a sentence (as punctuation came to be regularized in the 1700s and 1800s), punctuation and typography today are largely emotive. Capitals and exclamation points are signals of sincerity and purpose. Periods have become markers of dismissal.
- The emergence of a global English popular culture: no longer primarily based in American song or speech, the English of world music and performance has been shaped by K-pop and J-pop, by Afro-Caribbean cadences, by Bollywood and beyond.

We have seen many different ideas of English: is there a "genius" to the tongue?; are Americans "ardent rhetoricians"?; is world English something akin to a "kedgeree" of different ingredients? For many students today, a resource such as Urban Dictionary may provide a different set of ideas. Rifle through the entries at urbandictionary.com and you will find strings of synonyms for body parts, sexual activities, drug-induced experience, anger, fear, desire, love, beauty, disgust, pleasure, and pain. If the reader comes away with anything from such a survey, it will be that English (especially American English of those born in the twenty-first century) remains vibrant, playful, and anarchic.

The literary genre of this time is not the epic or the tragedy, the lyric or the novel, but the memoir. Personal voices are everywhere. Mary Karr has offered up a guidebook to the reader and prospective memoirist, *The Art of Memoir*, and her sentences distill the English of this moment in their blend of artifice and irony. Consider her response to Vladimir Nabokov's memoir *Speak Memory*:

> He has shaped the book to highlight his own magnificent way of viewing the world, a viewpoint that so eats your head that you never really leave his very oddly bejeweled skull, and you value things in the book's context as he does, never missing what you otherwise adore in another kind of writer.
>
> (Karr 2015, p. 57)

Consider this concluding move to her book: "We are the inward-looking goof-balls who spill on our blouses and look befuddled in our selfies" (ibid., p. 218). Phrases such as "eats your head," "inward-looking goofballs," and "befuddled in our selfies" offer up the idioms of a distinctively twenty-first-century diction (the Oxford Dictionaries named "selfie" the word of the year in 2013). Their power comes not only from their novelty but from their jarring place against a phrase like "his very oddly bejeweled skull," as if the modern reader were holding up an ancient artifact, something from the age of William Shakespeare or Sir Thomas Browne.

How can we understand the mechanisms of what makes the English language of the twenty-first century unique?

Formal and Informal, Literal and Figurative

In the chapter on slang in volume 6 of *The Cambridge History of the English Language*, Jonathan Lighter identifies a range of figurative devices that have generated modern, colloquial ways of speaking. Lighter finds these slang terms working "at a heightened intensity, like a kind of negative poetry," and he organizes the generating principles of slang along the lines of poetic schemes and tropes. Here are some of his examples (Lighter 2001, pp. 224–5):

Antiphrasis: bad, "very pleasing or impressive"; son of a bitch, "remarkable fellow

Antonomasia: Romeo, "a man noted for his many love affairs"

Burlesque metaphor: gasbag, "boastful or loquacious speaker"; cowboy Cadillac, "pickup truck"

Hyperbole: slam, "criticize"; chew someone out, "rebuke or scold someone sharply"

Meiosis: kid, "child"; heap "automobile"

Metaphor: bread, "money"; gravy, "profit"

Metonymy: tube, "television"; suit, "business executive"

Personification: Uncle Sam, "US Government"; GI Joe, "an ordinary US soldier"

Synecdoche: wheels, "automotive transportation"; tube, "television."

Such modes of figuration still affect the language, and a glance at Urban Dictionary or any other work of popular music, culture, or verbal art will generate comparable examples. Often, these rhetorical devices describe acts of sex, human body parts, or forms of unacceptable public behavior (the lexicon of terms for "vomit" could fill a volume). The various figurative uses of the word "job" write an anatomy of desire. Antonomasia adds new words with every popular film or video: "don't go all John Wick on me." Phrases that were once expressions of social prejudice have extended to connote general experiences of dismissal or distaste: "all back of the bus" recalls the US segregationist practice of seating people of African American heritage at the back of public transportation. Now it can mean any demeaning situation. Although probably no one uses the phrase "cowboy Cadillac," the burlesque metaphor "country Kleenex" can be heard to describe the use of the hand alone to blow the nose.

One of the notable strategies for word formation in the late twentieth and early twenty-first centuries, however, is not through metaphor but through the re-formation of morphemes. As we have seen, **morphemes** are a unit of semantic reference (meaning), signaling a grammatical category (-ly as the morpheme for adverbial modification; -ness as the morpheme for nominalization), or an action (-spire as the morpheme for breathing: "respire," to breathe over and over again; "expire," to stop breathing; "perspire," to breathe through a membrane such as skin; "conspire," to breathe, and hence work secretly, together).

Modern English speakers have developed a practice of breaking words into morphemes that are not historical or etymological. For example, consider words derived from "Watergate." This was the name of the hotel complex in Washington, DC, where the Democratic National Committee had its headquarters, which the minions of President Nixon broke into in 1973. -gate has become the morpheme for scandal, even though it did not mean scandal in the original word. Thus, we have Irangate, Whitewatergate.

The word "hardware" is as old as the fifteenth century. In the mid-1800s, it came to refer to the physical materials of operating machinery. In 1947, the word was applied to the wiring, tubes, and frameworks of the earliest computers. During the computer age, hardware came to be distinguished from "software" ("the interpretive routines, compilers, and other aspects of automotive programming," in the words of a 1958 quotation from the *OED*). "Vaporware" (first recorded in 1983) connotes a product that is still in development. "Wetware" (first recorded in 1963) refers to organic structures that work analogously to computers. Physicist Michio Kaku wrote in 2014: "perhaps the 'mind' was just a software program running on 'wetware'" (quoted in the *OED*). More directly, Urban Dictionary offers this definition: "a soggy meat computer."

"Explain" comes from the Latin roots meaning to open up or display. The morpheme -splain has been invented to refer to an act of speaking instructively to someone. "Mansplain" (first recorded in 2008) means the act of a man talking down, usually to a woman, about something the woman already knows. "Mansplain" has been broken down, again, with the morpheme "man" referring to an activity of intrusive, toxic, or self-indulgent masculinity. Thus, "manscaping" refers to the act of trimming one's pubic hair (unrecorded in the *OED*). "Manspreading" (also unrecorded in the *OED*) refers to the act of taking up too much space on a seat that adjoins others, usually on public transportation.

A word such as "bimbo" offers a different kind of example of false morphemics. Originally referring to a kind of punch, it became a clownish name in the nineteenth century, and it may have merged in sense with the Italian word "bambino," little child, to connote a silly or helpless person by the 1920s. Originally gendered male, it later came to refer to a woman notable for her physical features rather than her intellect. By the 1980s, a new version of the male form had to be found: hence, the coinage "himbo."

In the early years of the internet, people would post personal statements on websites. Weblogs became "blogs." Video logs became "vlogs." "Blogging" and the "blogosphere" emerge from these coinages. Similarly, a word such as "literati" could generate "digerati" (the cognoscenti of the world of digital communication).

Godzilla, the monster from post-war Japanese film, sired the morpheme -zilla, for a monstrous representation of an otherwise familiar character: "bridezilla." Urban Dictionary now defines the -zilla morpheme as a "suffix added to describe the biggest/baddest/meanest/nastiest of its type." My bad cat is now "catzilla."

The morpheme -core has emerged as a generic marker of literary genre and style of life. Originally, "hardcore" referred to solid building material. It developed a figurative usage as strong, intractable, committed (a hardcore member of the Party). By the 1950s, it came to refer to explicit pornography. "Softcore" emerged in the 1960s to designate less explicit adult material. "Mumblecore" is a modern coinage referring to films with improvised or inarticulate dialogue, often designed to represent the everyday speech of young people "Cottagecore" (unrecorded in the *OED*) refers to a style of life built around pretty objects and decoration from rural or country life.

Other examples of false morphemic transformation might include the following. A "hamburger" with lamb is a "lamburger." A vegetarian version is a "veggie burger." A huge disappointment is a "nothingburger" (remember that the morpheme "burger" originally comes from the German word for a city, Hamburg, and not a piece of meat). A "seminar" held virtually is a "webinar." The word "web," referring to the virtual linking of sites and computer users, generates a lexicon of new communications and professions: "webcam," "webcast," "web surf," "webtoon," web-wise" (these are just a few of the more than 40 forms listed by the *OED*, s.v., *web*, def. C.4.b). In many of these terms, we are looking at words being broken up and mixed into ahistorical morphemes ("broadcast" becomes "webcast"; "camera" becomes "webcam"; "cartoon" becomes "webtoon").

In the early 2020s, the COVID-19 crisis had an immediate effect on English. Speakers who had never heard such words before became proficient in using "coronavirus," "quarantine," "pandemic," and "lockdown." Phrases such as "shelter in place," "social distancing," and "brain fog" became common. The playfulness of metaphor and morphemic displacement was everywhere. A "quarantini" became the new "martini." "Zooming" was the activity of the moment (turning a product name, Zoom, into a verb for virtual communication). Deniers of the pandemic or people who kept sloppy hygiene came to be called "covidiots." A badly behaved person became a "maskhole" (Goldberg 2020).

Internet and Social Media English

Since its emergence in the 1990s, forms of digital communication – email, online chat, texting, messaging, and blogging – have changed how written English appears. Most digital forms of communication will affect a studied informality. Traditional rules of punctuation, capitalization, spelling, and grammar will be elided in favor of a carefully curated wrongness. It is not that digital communication is sloppy and uncaring (though sometimes it may be). It is that digital communication seeks to establish a voice of informal colloquialism designed to convey a personal, sincere, and authentic tone. Business-letter conventions, once seen as respectful and professional, are now seen as dismissive and patronizing.

> Dear Sirs:
> Please find enclosed my submission to your journal.
>
> Dear Professor,
> Please accept, as an attachment, this late paper for your consideration.

During the twenty-first century, I have received emails from students designed to convey emotion and personality, rather than reinforce the hierarchies of professional caste. Here is a student email from 2004:

> prof. lerer –
> on my way out to class today i got a piece of glass stuck in my foot. It was bleeding and hurting a lot so I had to come back and clean it up worry about the absense [*sic*], but i'll get the notes from someone.
>   Apologies

The misspellings and run-on colloquialisms are markers of a style of faux simplicity. They are designed to elicit the sympathy of the recipient and create the impression that the writer is writing in the moment, unfiltered by reflection. Many emails today articulate this kind of informality passing for sincerity.

Compare this message with an email from a student from 2023:

> Professor!!!
>   I will likely not be in class tomorrow because I am currently sick 🤒. It's not COVID, the flu, RSV, or strep. 🤧 Other than that, I am well 😊
>   Thanks

What is the difference between these messages, sent two decades apart? They represent a generational difference in digital literacy. The first relies on violating conventions of written communication to create the impression of a voice. The second relies on a form of visual communication designed to create the impression of a text. It represents what linguist Gretchen McCulloch has called "the typographical tone of voice." Emojis, exclamation points, and (in other kinds of communications) capital letters and repeated letters all come from a performative culture of literacy in which typing, rather than handwriting, has become the norm. This is English meant to be seen, rather than heard (McCulloch 2019, pp. 109–54).

The origins of texting and emojis, however, came from the limitations of technology, rather than from their resources. Early cell phones used the traditional telephone push-button set to convey brief texts. Users had to repeatedly press a number on a keypad, say 2, to get the letters A, B, and C (two presses for A, three for B, four for C). Typing in this way was clumsy, and forms of abbreviation and acronyms developed to replace whole words. C U @ 4, BRB, LOL, and the like were strategies of simplification. They worked as word and symbol puzzles. During the heyday of this phone texting (the 1990s and early 2000s), a range of acronyms developed, some serious and some ironic, to express conditions and emotional responses.

BRB: be right back
OMG: Oh, my God
LOL: laughing out loud

The author of this textbook remembers receiving texts with the following acronyms, deliberately complex and humorous:

DWPKOTL: deep, wet, passionate kiss on the lips
ILICISCOMLP: I laughed, I cried, I spilled coffee on my laptop

Once smartphones became equipped with virtual keyboards, such time-saving devices were less necessary. Users familiar with these phones can type as quickly and accurately as they could on a mechanical keyboard. In this environment, abbreviations and acronyms function as discourses of belonging or identity. They became what McCulloch calls "expressive tools," whose meaning lay in their impact rather than their semantic or lexical referents (McCulloch 2019). LOL and OMG, for example, became increasingly used to signal ironic distance from a statement made: a way of reminding the message recipient that something is said in jest. Exclamation points came to be markers of sincerity and attention, to the point where, as one undergraduate reported to me in 2023: "If I got a message with the word 'great' followed by a period I would take it as someone telling me they wanted me to die."

Social media platforms such as Facebook, Instagram, TikTok, and Twitter (now X) have enabled forms of communication keyed to abbreviations and emojis. Although many of these innovations may ultimately be ephemeral (the use of the lizard emoji for sexual activity, the spelling of "sex" as "seggs," the use of the verb "to serve" to mean display or represent a personal condition), these platforms have had a measurable effect on the learning of English by non-native speakers throughout the world. In the near future, social networking may become the medium for English acquisition, more than popular media or a formal classroom.

As a faculty member at a university, I have received many messages of excuse, apology, and requests for tolerance or forgiveness. The rhetorical strategies of such messages come from a form of discourse in which all statements are questions asking for affirmation. The phenomenon known as **uptalk** (sometimes upspeak) developed in Southern California in the 1970s and 1980s to signal indifference or playful insecurity. Uptalk describes a form of speech in which sentences end with a rising rather than a falling voice. The rising voice indicates a question or a moment of insecurity. Uptalk has spread throughout the United States and the Anglophone world. It remains largely a gender-marked form of expression (mostly used by women), a way of saying something as if prefaced by "this may be off-base" or "I'm not sure if this is right." Apology, rather than assertion, seems to mark twenty-first-century conversation, so much so that the BBC noted a global English phenomenon of "the unstoppable march of the upward inflection" (BBC News 2014).

Also marching on is the increasing use of words such as "like," forms of the verb "to go," and interjections such as "you know." Linguists call these phrases **adverbial colloquialisms** and **quotatives**, as well as time-fillers or metalinguistic units. In the words of linguist John McWhorter, words such as "like" have now become "part of the linguistic system" (McWhorter 2016). They are designed to distance the speaker from assertion: to create the sense that everything potentially is a simulacrum rather than a reality:

"I'm, like, all alone here." Is the speaker truly all alone, or is the speaker in an emotional state comparable to isolation?

"So, I go, what are you doing, and he goes, not much." Are these actual quotations, where the verb "go" replaces "say," or are these approximations or paraphrases of what was actually said?

"You know, it's like when you're dating, and the guy goes, hi?" If the listener has not dated in 50 years, the invitation to shared knowledge is lost.

Language and Power, Trust and Authority

This book concludes with the argument that English speakers and writers, especially in North America but increasingly throughout the Anglophone world, have systematically questioned public rhetoric and eloquence as discursive modes of sincerity. The language of political authority was traditionally rooted in eloquence. Roman writer Cicero codified the older, oratorical traditions into an equation of speaking well and thinking well. He advocated a union of *ratio et oratio*, reason and speech. He argued that political power came from those who could hold an audience. He advocated the systematic teaching of the tropes and techniques of public speaking as a means of gaining trust.

English and US politics modeled itself on classical authorities such as Cicero. Eighteenth-century rhetoricians and pedagogues sought to align English with Latin. Political commentators such as Edmund Burke sought to compel an audience through carefully constructed cadences and periods. American politicians, from Daniel Webster and Abraham Lincoln in the nineteenth century, through Franklin Roosevelt and John F. Kennedy in the twentieth, fashioned a rhetorical style grounded in repetition and **chiasmus**: balancing different parts of a sentence, often into echoing patterns of syntax. Lincoln's Gettysburg Address of 1863 stands as a model of American public rhetoric. "Four score and seven years ago, our fathers brought forth on this continent, a new nation, conceived in liberty, and dedicated to the proposition that all men are created equal." This address has been carefully analyzed by politicians and scholars ever since it was delivered. H. L. Mencken saw it as reaching back to the oratorical devices of the 1770s and the 1830s – the rationalisms of the Enlightenment that shaped the Declaration of Independence, and the courtroom arguments of legally trained politicians such as Daniel Webster. Gary Wills has seen it as a classically shaped oration, redolent with echoes of Shakespeare and the King James Bible. There are alliterations (four, fathers, forth; new, nation), biblical allusions (four score and seven echoing the Old Testament "three score and ten" as the life of a human being), and powerful repetition (later on, the statement, "we cannot dedicate, we cannot consecrate, we cannot hallow"). The final phrasing, "of the people, by the people, for the people," has become one of the most familiar cadences in American politics – a way of giving verbal shape to national belonging (Wills 1992).

Politicians since Lincoln have striven to sound equally cadenced. Franklin Roosevelt's line, "the only thing we have to fear, is fear itself" balances and echoes words into a national charge. John F. Kennedy's challenge, "Ask not what your country can do for you, ask what you can do for your country," similarly uses verbal mirroring to drive home a point.

I contend that the wars, social conflicts, and cultural contestations of the 1960s and 1970s undermined public faith in official eloquence. Statements by leaders were seen as lies, the more they sounded resonant. Military language developed a set of euphemisms, resonant with the examples of George Orwell from the 1940s. In "Politics and the English Language," Orwell averred:

> Political language has to consist largely of euphemism, question-begging, and sheer cloudy vagueness. Defenceless villages are bombarded from the air, the inhabitants driven out into the countryside, the cattle machine-gunned, the huts set on fire with incendiary bullets: this is called pacification ... Such phraseology is needed if one wants to name things without calling up mental pictures of them.
>
> (Orwell 1946)

In 1946, Orwell anticipated (even scripted, perhaps) the world of the Vietnam War. "Pacification," "Vietnamization," and the "five o'clock follies" (the term for the daily press briefings from Saigon), evacuated words of any meaning. A new language of conflict – "fragging," "greasing," "getting some," "sack" – wrote a new dictionary of death.

In the 1979 film, *Apocalypse Now*, set in late 1960s Vietnam, the renegade Col. Kurtz becomes the subject of a secret mission. Captain Willard's goal is to find him and take him out. In the words of the mysterious adviser at the briefing: "terminate with extreme prejudice."

Since then, public English has become a site of doubt. US Secretary of Defense Donald Rumsfeld, reporting on activities surrounding the incursion into Iraq in 2002, said:

> Reports that say that something hasn't happened are always interesting to me, because as we know, there are known knowns; there are things we know we know. We also know there are known unknowns; that is to say we know there are some things we do not know. But there are also unknown unknowns – the ones we don't know we don't know. And if one looks throughout the history of our country and other free countries, it is the latter category that tends to be the difficult ones.
>
> (Defense.gov News Transcript, 2002)

This fundamental split between official language and popular trust characterizes changes in English in the twenty-first century. One can find examples from throughout the Anglophone world. Consider the words of the outgoing president of Nigeria, Muhammadu Buhari, delivered in May 2023:

> Young men and women in urban centres were also supported to put their skills into productive use. Our administration also provided an enabling

environment for the private sector to engage in businesses for which their return on investments is guaranteed.

In the course of revamping the economy, we made some difficult choices, most of which yielded the desired results. Some of the measures led to temporary pain and suffering for which I sincerely apologised to my fellow countrymen, but the measures were taken for the over-all good of the country.

(Buhari 2023)

These words could come from almost any world politician: circumlocution, euphemism, and apology mark the tone (a phrase such as "provided an enabling environment" has all the patina of corporate-political indirectness). As we have seen, the passive voice ("were also supported," "measures were taken") has become the grammatical mode for public speech addressing difficult problems.

Words and Things

Some representative examples of language change, of vocabulary development, and of sociolinguistic attitudes may therefore be thought of as matters of trust and identity. For example, what does it mean to be "woke"? Behind this question lies a history of political discourse, weaving through African American resistance, popular culture, and cultural commentary from both sides of the aisle. The term originates in the early twentieth century, with calls to resist oppression and, in addition, movements to return to an African homeland. Activist Marcus Garvey, best known for his "Back to Africa" movement of the 1920s, called: "Wake up Ethiopia! Wake up Africa!" The phrase "stay woke" can be heard in the 1938 recording by blues guitarist Lead Belly (Huddie Ledbetter), calling for action after the killing of black teenagers in Scottsboro, Arkansas. By the 1960s, staying woke became a familiar injunction: be aware of your political rights, act in support of others. In 2008, singer Erykah Badu released a song with the refrain, "I stay woke." By the late 2010s, the call to "wokeness" had become global (in a conversation with one of the editors for this textbook, the author was told over lunch in London: "You're quite woke for a Boomer"). But reaction has set in, and the term "woke," by the 2020s, had come to be used as a criticism by the political right of the political left: marking it as an almost self-parodic virtue signaling.

Readers should notice how, in the preceding paragraph, several words and phrases appear that mark present-day idiomatic English.

- "Both sides of the aisle": this phrase refers to the tradition of seating in the US Congress. Viewed from the back of the chamber, Democrats sit on the left of the speaker, while Republicans sit on the right. In Great Britain, the phrase "crossing the floor" means changing a political party affiliation. In Nigeria, the phrase is "crossing the carpet."

- "Resistance": the word goes back to a French borrowing into Middle English. In the mid-1900s, it took on a specific sense of covert action to defeat a political (typically oppressive) regime (the French resistance of World War II; the resistance fighters of the *Star Wars* films; the anti-Taliban resistance in Afghanistan).
- "Boomer": a short form of "Baby Boomer," a member of the generation born in the 15 years after World War II. By the twenty-first century, the word had become a humorously dismissive way of characterizing an older, out-of-touch generation. The retort, "OK Boomer," emerged in online forums in the early 2000s, becoming widespread after a 2019 TikTok video, and it has become a global English taunt.
- "Virtue signaling": this phrase, probably common in the early 2000s, is first recorded in the *OED* in 2013 to mean a way of announcing one's social conscience to gain external validation.

To take another example, what does it mean to use the pronoun "they" to refer to an individual person? Remember that throughout its history, English had a range of pronouns to signal number, formality, and hierarchies of relationship. "You" forms were plural and formal; "thou" forms were informal and singular. While Old English distinguished regularly between the pronouns and retained the older Germanic dual pronoun (the two of us, you two, and so on), it was not until the Middle English period that "thou" and "you" developed as distinguishing social markers of class and intimacy, probably under the influence of French "tu" and "vous." By the seventeenth century, "thou" had come to seem archaic or mannered: the language of the King James Bible gave it the patina of age, and the habits of the Quakers in England and North America (addressing everyone equally in the "thou" form) further estranged its familiarity. "You" increasingly became the default form in writing (probably as early as the late 1400s and 1500s), as people communicated to individuals they did not know.

Although the singular "they" seems uniquely modern, it is not. Single individuals could be "they" in relative clauses. The *OED* offers this miniature history: "With an antecedent referring to an individual generically or indefinitely (e.g. *someone, a person, the student*), used esp. so as to make a general reference to such an individual without specifying gender." The *OED*'s first example is from 1450. Here is a good example from the writings of Lord Chesterfield from 1759: "If a person is born of a ... gloomy temper ... they cannot help it." The magazine *The Listener*, a model of mid-twentieth-century British prose, offers this example from 1968: "When somebody becomes prime minister they're immediately put on a pedestal."

Today, "they" has come to be used to refer to an individual whose gender identity does not conform to conventional social expectations. People who identify as gay, lesbian, bisexual, transgender, and nonbinary may refer to themselves (and ask to be addressed) as "they." The *OED* offers the first example of this usage from 2009. It has become far more complex, however, than simply another choice. "He/they" and "she/they" identities reflect manners of performative presentation, social construction, and the tensions between somatic appearance and one's inner self. The language of gender has changed markedly in the twenty-first century. AFAB and AMAB mean, respectively, "assigned female at birth" and "assigned male at birth." "Gender envy," sometimes reduced to the word "genvy," has been used to describe several different sets of feelings: on the one hand, the aspirations of a trans person to present their gender in a particular way; on the other hand, to describe cis-gender people with non-normative or ideal gender presentations, envying those with more ideal or normative presentations. Cis, trans, queer, nonbinary, personal pronoun preferences – these are the terms of twenty-first-century being and belonging. They represent how communities of difference try to find words to mean things that they did not mean before. As with the history of Black Englishes and the adaptations of global Englishes, the changing language of gender illustrates how English speakers constantly adapt the old to the new, the central to the marginalized.

This textbook has presented English as a means of communicating and describing, imagining and persuading, including and excluding, being and becoming. It has shown how the history of the language is a history of varieties and contingencies, rather than of standards and evolution. It has argued that the mechanisms of language change operate when different languages and different forms of language come together. It has relied on letters, poems, novels, plays, journalism, and political speechmaking to show that a history of English is not just a narrative of sound changes or semantic shifts or grammatical developments but a story of people speaking and writing in social and artistic environments. In retrospect, some aspects of that history may seem ephemeral: the use of aureate diction and inkhorn terms in the early modern period, the TikTok chatter of the twenty-first century. Some things last, and some things don't. There is nothing in the English language that essentially makes it better or more powerful than any other language. Its worldwide spread has been a result of colonization, commerce, and communication technologies. In the end, if we can say anything about the future of English, it may be that it will always have varieties, that it will always differ in its social and professional uses, and that people will always make it their own.

Sources and Further Reading

Algeo, J. (Ed.) (2015). *CHEL*, vol. 6, *English in North America*. Cambridge: Cambridge University Press.
BBC News (2014). "The Unstoppable March of the Upward Inflection." 11 August. Available at: https://www.bbc.com/news/magazine-28708526
Buhari, M. (2023). "President Buhari's Farewell Address to the Nation." Available at: https://www.channelstv.com/2023/05/28/full-text-of-president-buharis-farewell-address-to-the-nation

"Defense.gov News Transcript: DoD News Briefing—Secretary Rumsfeld and Gen. Myers, United States Department of Defense (defense.gov)." February 12, 2002. Available at: https://archive.ph/20180320091111/http://archive.defense.gov/Transcripts/Transcript.aspx?TranscriptID=2636

Goldberg, E. (2020). "The New Words for Our New Misery." *New York Times*, December 24. Available at: https://www.nytimes.com/2020/12/24/opinion/coronavirus-language-words.html.

Guardian Staff (2013). "Selfie is the Oxford Dictionaries' Word of the Year." *The Guardian*, 19 November. Available at: https://www.theguardian.com/books/2013/nov/19/selfie-word-of-the-year-oed-olinguito-twerk.

Karr, M. (2015). *The Art of Memoir*. New York: HarperCollins.

Lighter, J. (2001). "Slang." In J. Algeo (Ed.), *CHEL*, vol. 6, *English in North America*. Cambridge: Cambridge University Press, pp. 219–52.

McCulloch, G. (2019). *Because Internet: Understanding How Language Is Changing*. London: Harvill Secker.

McWhorter, J. (2016). "The Evolution of 'Like'." *The Atlantic*. November 25. Available at: https://www.theatlantic.com/entertainment/archive/2016/11/the-evolution-of-like/507614/

Mead, R. (2022). "The Common Tongue of Twenty-first-Century London." *The New Yorker*. February 6. Available at: https://www.newyorker.com/culture/personal-history/the-common-tongue-of-twenty-first-century-london

Orwell, G. (1946). "Politics and the English Language." Available at: https://www.orwellfoundation.com/the-orwell-foundation/orwell/essays-and-other-works/politics-and-the-english-language/

Roberts, J. (1999). "Going Younger to Do Difference: The Role of Children in Language Change." *University of Pennsylvania Working Papers in Linguistics*. Available at: https://repository.upenn.edu/cgi/viewcontent.cgi?article=1659&context=pwpl

Romano, A. (2020). "A History of 'Wokeness'." *Vox*, October 9. Available at: https://www.vox.com/culture/21437879/stay-woke-wokeness-history-origin-evolution-controversy

Wills, G. (1992). *Lincoln at Gettysburg*. New York: Simon & Schuster.

Index

Note: Page numbers in italics refer to figures.

Nostratic language 25
nouns: cases 34, 77, 130; classification
77–8; genders 35, 77; Middle
English (ME) 98–9; Old
English (OE) 77–8; shifts in
function 193
n-word 12, 233

oaths 12
Obama, Barack 230, 231, 233, 238
obscenity 12, 22, 109–10
OE *see* Old English
Ogborn, Miles 225
Old English (OE) 56–60, 62–85;
adjectives 78–9; adverbs 78–9;
building new words 65–6; corpus
linguistics 16; dialects 81–2;
dictionary 16; and Germanic
languages 50–1; grammar and
morphology 73–80; and Middle
English (ME) 90–5; and Modern
English 70–1; nouns 77–8; poetry
83–5; pronouns 78–9; sounds 13,
17, 63, 71–3; syntax and word
order 80; verbs 73–7; vocabulary
64–71, 88–9
Old English Grammar 13
Old Norse 52, 56–60, 68, 70, 101–2
On Early English Pronunciation 183
onomatopoeia 25
open syllables 17, 95–6
Orgel, Stephen 150
Orientalism 249
orthoepists 126, 127, 132, 161
Orthographie 127, 132
Orwell, George 268

Pakistan 243, 255
palatal sounds 7
Paradise Lost 170
parole 2–3
passive voice 187–8, 269
Paston, Agnes 108–9
Paston family 108, 113, 126–7
Paston, John 10, 113
Paston, Margaret 113–14
Pastoral Care 80, 106
performance 3
personal expression 89–90
personification 262

Peterborough Chronicle 90–3
PGmc *see* Proto-Germanic
phatic discourse 12
Phillips, Edward 138–40
phonemes xiii–xv, 3, 9, 164
phonemic inventory 4
phonemic transcription 9, 145
phonetic transcription 9, 132, 145
phonology 15
Pickwick Papers, The 198
pidgins 236
PIE *see* Proto-Indo-European language
Piers Plowman 88
*Plan of a Dictionary of the English
Language* 168–70
poetics: Germanic languages 55–60; Indo-
European 36–9; Old English (OE)
83–5
political lexicography 252–3
politics 267–9
Polychronicon 114
polygenesis 226
polysemy 20, 139–40, 149
popular culture 204, 225, 237, 238, 260
Portuguese 137
postvocalic r 146
power 267–9
Praise of Folly 158
prefixes 24, 50, 73, 95; in making
new words 65–7, 134–5, 192;
morphemes as 4
prepositions 34, 77, 90, 95, 98, 123,
175, 187
prescriptivism 174–5
prestige language 10–11
Priestley, Joseph 176–8
professional terms 191–2
pronouns: and gender identity 270–1;
dual form 78; Middle English
(ME) 100–1; Old English (OE)
78–9; personal 78–9, 100–1;
Shakespeare English 153–4
pronunciation 164, 166; American
English 205–6, 209–10, 214–16;
Australian English 251; British
English 182–6, 198–9, 201;
changes in 123–9, 132–3; early
Modern English 206; and spelling
167; *see also* dialects; Received
Pronunciation (RP); sounds

Printed in the United States
by Baker & Taylor Publisher Services